Praise for

The Newcomers

"A delicate and heartbreaking mystery story . . . Thorpe's book is a reminder that in an era of nativism, some Americans are still breaking down walls and nurturing newcomers, the seeds of the great American experiment."

—*The New York Times Book Review*

"Extraordinary . . . *The Newcomers* puts a human face on the refugee question. The book is a journalistic triumph. Thorpe . . . pens a masterful book that lets readers see the humanity instead of the facts and figures and politics of the immigration debate."

—*The Denver Post*

"Thorpe's fascinating chronicle of a year in an English-acquisition class at a Denver high school provides a timely and much-needed perspective on the global refugee crisis. . . . [She] once again demonstrates her talent for immersive reporting and compassionate narrative as she depicts her youthful subjects doing the hard, and occasionally exhilarating, work of adapting to life in America."

—*The National Book Review*

"This book is not only an intimate look at lives immigrant teens live, but it is a primer on the art and science of new-language acquisition and a portrait of ongoing and emerging global horrors and the human fallout that arrives on our shores. . . . The teens we meet have endured things none of us can imagine. . . . But we learn a great deal, and that's never been more crucial than at this moment."

—*USA Today*

"Thorpe's fascinating chronicle of a year in an English-acquisition class at a Denver high school provides a timely and much-needed perspective on the global refugee crisis."

—*Los Angeles Times*

"Highly recommended for readers hoping to learn more about the refugee experience in the United States. A heartfelt examination of student and family life that speaks to the human experience."

—*Library Journal*

"Thorpe provides a layered portrait of the students and explains the daunting refugee crisis in America and elsewhere . . . [and] puts an agonizing human face on a vast global problem."

—*Publishers Weekly* (starred review)

"An extensive, riveting account that presents the manifold challenges of the refugee crisis through the microcosm of one classroom."

—*Booklist*

"Thorpe writes with great compassion. . . . Her story will entertain and enlighten readers, creating a wider, more sympathetic view of the world and its inhabitants—certainly something we need right now."

—*Kirkus Reviews*

"Few books could be more vital, in this particular moment or in any moment, than this book. Helen Thorpe writes expansively about one school, one classroom, one teacher, one group of students—students who hail from the most severe places in the world and come together at South High. Confused, troubled, bright, magnificent: they converge, ostensibly to learn English, learning so much more than a language— learning about us and about themselves, all the bad and all the good. You need to meet these young people. Once you do, everything you read or hear or say will be illuminated and changed."

—Jeff Hobbs, author of *The Short and Tragic Life of Robert Peace*

"Helen Thorpe didn't miss a detail during the year she spent watching twenty-two young refugees begin to learn how to speak English (difficult) and how to be American (even more difficult). No one with a pulse could fail to be moved by this beautifully reported book."

—Anne Fadiman, author of *The Wine Lover's Daughter: A Memoir* and *The Spirit Catches You and You Fall Down*

"In this time of great anxiety, this splendid, humane, beautifully crafted book is a reminder of America's proud, historic role as a beacon of hope to the world. And it is a terrific story."

—Doris Kearns Goodwin, author of *No Ordinary Time*, *Team of Rivals*, and *The Bully Pulpit*

"I loved this book. It brims with teenage life, with a sense of America being reborn, of new Americans being made. Cultures converge in a high school classroom where teenagers—with all the energy, earnestness, and embarrassment we expect, but also with trauma—learn English with the help of a teacher who appreciates all the ways it's not easy. *The Newcomers* teaches us about parts of the world we can barely imagine and also takes us into their new American homes. Helen Thorpe, herself the child of immigrants, is a terrific writer and a steadfast character witness to these people so many of us fear."

—Ted Conover, author of *Coyotes*, *Newjack*, and *Immersion*

"Helen Thorpe has taken policy and turned it into literature."

—Malcolm Gladwell

"Meticulously researched, thoughtful, and timely, *The Newcomers* provides a vital and joyous window into the lives of teenagers searching for a new home in the U.S., and asks important questions about Americans' willingness to welcome the stranger."

—*Shelf Awareness*

Also by Helen Thorpe

Soldier Girls:
The Battles of Three Women at Home and at War

Just Like Us:
The True Story of Four Mexican Girls Coming of Age in America

The
Newcomers

Finding Refuge,
Friendship, and Hope
in America

Helen Thorpe

SCRIBNER

New York   London   Toronto   Sydney   New Delhi

Scribner
An Imprint of Simon & Schuster, Inc.
1230 Avenue of the Americas
New York, NY 10020

First Scribner trade paperback edition September 2018

SCRIBNER and design are registered trademarks of The Gale Group, Inc., used under license by Simon & Schuster, Inc., the publisher of this work.

For information about special discounts for bulk purchases, please contact Simon & Schuster Special Sales at 1-866-506-1949 or business@simonandschuster.com.

The Simon & Schuster Speakers Bureau can bring authors to your live event. For more information or to book an event, contact the Simon & Schuster Speakers Bureau at 1-866-248-3049 or visit our website at www.simonspeakers.com.

Interior design by Jill Putorti

10 9 8 7 6 5 4 3 2 1

Library of Congress Cataloging-in-Publication Data is available.

ISBN 978-1-5011-5910-7 (pbk)
ISBN 978-1-5011-5911-4 (ebook)

To my parents, Marie and Larry,
with thanks for showing me the world

From time to time, deep in the thickets of my inner wilderness, I could sense the presence of something that knew how to stay alive even when the rest of me wanted to die. That something was my tough and tenacious soul.

Yet despite its toughness, the soul is also shy. Just like a wild animal, it seeks safety in the dense underbrush, especially when other people are around. If we want to see a wild animal, we know that the last thing we should do is go crashing through the woods yelling for it to come out. But if we will walk quietly into the woods, sit patiently at the base of a tree, breathe with the earth, and fade into our surroundings, the wild creature we seek might put in an appearance. We may see it only briefly and only out of the corner of an eye—but the sight is a gift we will always treasure as an end in itself.

—Parker Palmer, "A Circle of Trust"

Contents

Contents

Part IV: Summer

Part V: Fall

The Newcomer
Those Who Welcomed Them

Room 142 Staff
Eddie Williams, teacher
Ed DeRose, teacher's aide
Pauline Ng, therapist, Jewish Family Service
Ruthann Kallenberg, volunteer, Goodwill Industries

Room 142 Students, in order of arrival
Stephanie (Mexico)
Nadia (Mozambique)
Grace (Mozambique)
Hsar Htoo (Burma, Thailand)
Saúl (El Salvador)
Uyen (Vietnam)
Amaniel (Eritrea)
Solomon (Democratic Republic of Congo)
Methusella (Democratic Republic of Congo)
Jakleen (Iraq, Syria)
Mariam (Iraq, Syria)
Dilli (Eritrea)
Ksanet (Eritrea)
Yonatan (Eritrea)
Lisbeth (El Salvador)
Kaee Reh (Burma, Thailand)
Abigail (Mexico)
Plamedi (Democratic Republic of Congo)

The Newcomers and Those Who Welcomed Them

Bachan (Bhutan)
Shani (Tajikistan)
Mohamed (Mauritania)

South High Faculty, elsewhere in the building
Kristin Waters, outgoing principal
Jen Hanson, incoming principal
Karen Duell, family and community liaison
Carolyn Chafe Howard, PTA president
Ben Speicher, math teacher and wrestling coach
Jason Brookes, Student Senate faculty adviser
John Walsh, math teacher and long-distance coach
Steve Bonansinga, math teacher and organizer of Culture Fest
Rachel Aldrich, science teacher
Jenan Hijazi, upper-level ELA teacher
Noelia Hopkin, upper-level ELA teacher

Author's Note

This is a work of nonfiction. To report this book, I spent a year and a half inside South High School and hired fourteen different translators to interview subjects in their home languages. I changed the names of four individuals, but otherwise, to the best of my knowledge, everything that follows is true.

PART I

Fall

1

Nice to Meet You

On the first day of school—it was going to be a ninety-degree scorcher and you could already feel the air starting to shimmer—Eddie Williams jogged up the four stone steps at the main entrance to South High School half an hour before the first bell rang, eager to meet his new students. THE LIVES OF MEN, THE CUSTOMS OF PEOPLES, AND THE PAGEANTRY OF NATIONS CHART THE COURSE OF TOMORROW proclaimed a large mural by the front door. The teacher was a tall man, six foot four inches in his socks, with an athletic body (when there were no kids in the building, he sometimes used the many staircases in the school for exercise), short black hair, and a clean-shaven, angular face. He was thirty-eight years old, but could have passed for twenty-eight. Earnest, ardent, industrious, kind, and highly sensitive were traits that came to mind when I thought about the parts of himself this teacher brought into his classroom, week in, week out, all year long. He almost always dressed conservatively, in long-sleeved dress shirts and chinos, and his wardrobe often made me think of leafing through an L.L.Bean catalog, but that day he was wearing a short-sleeved purple South High polo shirt. All the teachers had put on purple shirts, that being the school color, so that the students could easily see whom they should turn to if they had a question about how to find a particular classroom, how to read the confusing schedules they carried, or where they could find the school's elusive cafeteria, way up on the fourth floor. Mr. Williams usually avoided short-sleeved shirts, even in August, because they revealed the dark blue tattoo that circled one of his biceps, and he feared his students might misinterpret the inked designs as macabre, given their

3

backgrounds. He worked diligently to communicate in all sorts of ways that he was a person they could trust.

Mr. Williams had inherited his Anglo father's rangy height and propensity to freckle, along with his Latina mother's dark eyes and hair. Fluent in both Spanish and English, he was the sort of teacher who devoted an enormous portion of his warmth, vitality, and intellect to his students. South was a century-old castlelike structure that stood on the edge of a rolling, green, 160-acre park in central Denver, Colorado. The rectangular park boasted meadows, manicured flower gardens, two lakes, a lily pond, meandering carriageways chock-a-block with Lycra-clad joggers, ten much-in-demand public tennis courts, and the busiest recreation center in the city. The grand old homes that ringed the park were selling for upward of $1 million, while modestly sized homes nearby that did not look directly onto the park might sell for half that amount. The neighborhood public high school was a popular choice, even for families who possessed significant wealth. Most of the classrooms were crowded with noisy, chattering teenagers. That morning, however, as he looked around his room, Mr. Williams saw many empty chairs and only seven students. The teenagers assigned to him wore shut-door expressions on their faces. Nobody in the room was talking, not even to one another. The teacher had expected this, for his room always got off to a quiet start.

"Welcome to newcomer class!" he said, in a deliberately warm tone of voice. "My name is Mr. Williams. What is your name? Where are you from?"

The seven teenagers who had reported to Room 142 made no reply. Just the act of showing up by 7:45 in the morning had required enormous fortitude. It was August 24, 2015, and the students had spent on average more than an hour negotiating the local public transit system to get to the school. They lived crammed with other relatives into small houses or one- or two-bedroom apartments located in far-flung neighborhoods nowhere near this upscale zip code, in parts of the city where a dollar could be stretched. Rents had jumped dramatically in central Denver in recent years, and affordable housing could be found only on the city's periphery, if at all. Getting from the patchwork zones of cheap housing located on the farthest edges of the city to South via the public transit system took dogged commitment, but that was a quality that Mr. Williams's students typically possessed in abundance. What they did not possess, for the most part, was the ability to understand what he was saying.

"Welcome to newcomer class!" the teacher repeated, taking care to enunciate each word deliberately. "My name is Mr. Williams. What is your name? Where are you from?"

Mr. Williams often said things twice. It gave his lessons a singsong quality. The students continued to stare back at the teacher without speaking. The technical description for what was happening is "preproduction," which in the academic literature about language acquisition is also known as "the silent period." The vast majority of second-language learners begin in a quiet receptive phase, able to produce hardly any English themselves, even as their brains furiously absorb everything being said by their teacher.

That year, about sixteen hundred teenagers attended South High School, and roughly one-third had been born in another country. South served as a regular neighborhood school that drew many English-speaking students as well as one of the designated destinations in the Denver Public Schools system for students who spoke foreign languages other than Spanish and whose education had been interrupted. For many years South had handled the bulk of the city's teenage refugees, for it was primarily children in those families who had significant gaps in their education. War—that was what generally caused children to be unable to attend school for long periods of time.

About three hundred students at South were presently enrolled in English Language Acquisition classes, and hundreds more had taken those classes in years past. Among them were students who had seen every kind of catastrophe on the planet. The other two-thirds of the student body had always lived in the United States and had been speaking English since birth. Across the United States, students from non-English-speaking backgrounds had become one of the fastest-growing segments of the K–12 population. Such students now made up 42 percent of the students served by Denver Public Schools. What was remarkable about South was how well it had been integrating students displaced by extreme forms of upheaval with their American-born peers. The school cultivated a mind-set, widely shared by faculty and students, that everybody under its roof was an asset. Native-born kids helped new arrivals learn English, even as foreign-born students helped their American peers become more global-minded. But first, the newcomers had to adjust. Of all the students jammed into the vast five-story building, the seven souls in Mr. Williams's room had been evaluated as knowing the least English. If any teacher in the building wound up working with a child who had just arrived in the United States as a refugee and did not yet know anything about life on this side of the globe—how to ask a bus driver where to get off, what exactly the Broncos were, and whether to eat "spicy chicken" (the cafeteria served that a lot)—it was Mr. Williams.

Some people viewed ELA students as occupying a place on the low end of the scale, socially. Eddie Williams disagreed; he saw the chance to work with these teenagers as an extraordinary, life-changing experience, one that lit up his own days with meaning. What took place inside his room always struck him as being as close to a bona-fide miracle as he was likely to experience. If these students showed up every day, he believed, they would evolve and heal and adapt and flourish. Their progress might be achingly slow at first, but after a while they would accumulate small victories with rapidity—he had seen it happen before. The closed faces of the students before him would unlock.

Not right away. They were still getting acclimated to so many things: the weird sound of American-accented English, the frighteningly large new urban high school, their strange-looking teacher, and the idea of students changing classrooms throughout the day (in many parts of the world, teachers changed rooms). They were still learning the unfamiliar transit routes to and from South and still getting used to homes made of building materials radically different from any structure they had ever lived in before. Even the weather wasn't like the weather they had known previously. But one by one, the students would get over the enormous shock of it all and start speaking back to him, he knew, and ultimately the whole room would be transformed.

He also knew that these seven students were only the first to materialize. Over the coming year, the strife-ridden parts of the planet would dispatch many more students to Mr. Williams, he was sure. They turned up that way every year—higgledy-piggledy, not when the calendar advised. Some of them would arrive looking alarmingly thin. They could be anywhere from fourteen to nineteen, and a few would not know exactly how old they were. They came from nations convulsed by drought or famine or war, countries that were barely countries anymore. Many came directly from refugee camps. Every so often, he got a student who arrived in the United States alone, having left or lost every other member of his or her family. The students walked into his room dazed at the abruptness of the transition, looking profoundly lost. And then they started over—started to figure out where they were, started to wonder who he was, started to ask whether to call this place home.

Mr. Williams knew the additional students would come because they always had, and because for several months the front pages of newspapers like the *Denver Post*, the *New York Times*, and the *Wall Street Journal* had been filled with photographs of homeless multitudes. Over the summer, the news cycles had been consumed by reports of Middle Eastern asylum seekers arriving by the boatload in Greece and then walking to Germany. Millions of Syrians had been forced from their homes by the civil war gutting that country; in neighboring Iraq, millions more had been uprooted by a decade of fighting; additional millions had fled escalating violence in Afghanistan. The massive movement of people around the Middle East had thrown the whole region into turmoil. Meanwhile, wars of even longer duration in Asia and Africa had inundated camps in those regions with refugees, too. A total of fifty-nine million people around the world had been displaced from their homes as of that year, according to the United Nations—more than at any point since World War II.

Because it provided services that drew such families, South High School's population mirrored the state of the world. Twenty years earlier, when the school first put its expanded English Language Acquisition program into place, many of the foreign-born students who walked into the front office had been from Bosnia. Generally, they had been well educated, although perhaps they had missed one or two years of schooling, and they typically lacked English; getting them up to speed had been, in hindsight, relatively straightforward. After the school began its second decade of work with students from other parts of the globe, the front office staff had started greeting an increased number of students from the Middle East, especially Iraq and Afghanistan. Throughout the same period, the school had received large numbers of students from Southeast Asia, primarily Burma, home to the longest-running civil war in the world, a conflict that had raged across its river deltas and its mountain passes for more than sixty years. The school had also welcomed many students from the war-torn parts of Africa—at first from Sudan and Somalia, and later from Eritrea, Ethiopia, and the Democratic Republic of Congo. South did not yet have a large number of Syrians, but they were coming. If war erupted halfway around the globe, Mr. Williams knew in a few years he would see children from that place.

So he did not brood about having too few students; more were on their way. Nor was he anxious when the newcomers did not answer, because when they first arrived, they were almost always speechless. Several years might elapse before certain students would come back to tell him in unbroken sentences who they really were. He was consistently staggered by how much his former students had to tell him, once they got hold of enough English. That was his job, to help them find the words. First he had to get them settled, and that was the biggest challenge. Loss of all kinds had robbed these teenagers of certitude, and his main job at the start of the school year was to show them that they were in a room where they would come to no further harm. It was hard, convincing them it was safe to hope.

Mr. Williams taught in a capacious room with a navy blue carpet, white walls, and a high ceiling. A large clock hung directly over the door. The opposite wall featured ten-foot-tall windows with dusty blinds he had closed to keep the room cool, although the sun was peeking through the chinks. Mr. Williams stood with his back to the half-darkened, half-glowing blinds. Because most of the students appeared confused by his greeting, Mr. Williams turned to his aide, Ed DeRose.

"Welcome to newcomer class!" the teacher said again, enunciating each word even more slowly. "My name is Mr. Williams. I am from the United States. I speak English. What is your name? Where are you from? What language do you speak?"

"My name is Mr. DeRose," his aide replied. "I am from the United States. I speak English."

"Nice to meet you," said Mr. Williams.

"Nice to meet you," responded Mr. DeRose.

The two men shook hands and grinned with genuine amusement, as they had worked together for several years. "Nice to Meet You" happened to be the title of the first chapter in the English Language Acquisition textbook that Mr. Williams employed—the book was titled *Inside the U.S.A.*, and the unit began with the most common greetings used by Americans. Mr. Williams walked over to one of his students, extended his hand, smiled warmly, and repeated his questions.

"What is your name? Where are you from? What language do you speak?"

"I am Stephanie," the girl responded. "I am from Mexico. I speak Spanish."

Mr. Williams nodded at her while she spoke, to indicate that she was doing a good job. Stephanie had a heart-shaped face, straight bangs that fell over her forehead, and a shy smile. She had good pronunciation, and she had answered with confidence; clearly, she had some basic English. The teacher gathered that she had just arrived from Mexico but wondered if she had lived in the United States at some previous point.

He walked over to another student and greeted her in the same emphatically friendly manner, smiling widely, giving her all his attention.

"I am Nadia," she said. "I am from Mozambique. I speak Portuguese."

"I am Grace," said the next student. "I am from Mozambique. I speak Portuguese."

That was odd: Mozambique had endured a lengthy civil war from

1977 to 1992, but it had not been producing large numbers of refugees in recent years. How had two girls from that country arrived in his room at the same time?

"Are you sisters?" asked Mr. Williams, with an even wider smile.

"Yes," said Grace and Nadia at the same time.

Mr. Williams thought for a beat. According to his roster, the two girls did not have the same last name. Their facial structure was also quite different. Were they biological sisters? Possibly. But a few of his prior students had arrived with makeshift families, after cobbling together sibling-like relationships somewhere along the road. Those were some of the hardest stories he had heard. On the other hand, African naming habits were quite different from American ones, and the whole matter of what constituted a last name varied around the world. Mr. Williams did not ask the girls any more questions. If they declared they were sisters, that was good enough for him. Maybe someday they would tell him the whole story.

He knew from experience that most of his students had lived through harrowing ordeals. Every year, trauma had been represented in his cohort. This year, for the first time, a trained therapist from Jewish Family Service would visit his classroom each week, and she would ask the students if they wanted to talk about what had happened before they made it to South. It was not his job to get his students to tell him about earlier chapters in their lives. Some would say nothing about an agonizing subject all year, then visit him later and supply the whole narrative; others might never disclose certain parts of their stories. Mr. Williams knew that he was surrounded by young people who had witnessed more disturbing events than he had ever been subjected to himself, yet at this moment they could not explain what had happened, not in any language he could understand. This was humbling. It made him listen to his students with extraordinary care. He didn't want to miss anything.

Mr. Williams moved toward the next student, smiling kindly again, his right hand extended. Each student received the same unswerving gaze and firm handshake and friendly grin, body language that stated, *I consider you worthwhile.*

"My nay, Hsar Htoo," the student said haltingly. "Froh Thailand. Spee Karen."

Mr. Williams was aware that students who spoke the Sino-Tibetan languages often had trouble saying English words. Words in Karen generally do not end with hard consonants, so it was difficult for Hsar Htoo to make the final sound in English terms. As people grow, their bodies as well as their brains become less plastic; by the age of eleven or so, the muscles in the face solidify around the ability to produce commonly used sounds. After that, it is much harder to learn foreign languages that require different muscle formations. Hsar Htoo might always struggle to produce some of the sounds that English speakers make effortlessly. But Mr. Williams also noted that Hsar Htoo seemed alert and focused. And he had offered the teacher a huge, incandescent smile, giving Mr. Williams a glimpse of a sunny disposition. The majority of the Karen people came from the mountains or the river deltas of Burma, but they had been subjected to such extreme forms of persecution by the Burmese military—bombs, land mines, rapes, beheadings, indiscriminate butchering, the burning of entire villages down to the ground—that they had vanished in huge numbers over the mountain peaks and down into neighboring Thailand. That country treated them like illegal immigrants and held them inside enclosures that functioned like prison camps. Many Karen families had lived in the camps for so long that their children or grandchildren had been born in them. Mr. Williams wondered whether that might be true for Hsar Htoo, given the way he had introduced himself as being from Thailand. If so, everything here would be new—running water, appliances, grocery stores, snow, freedom.

As Mr. Williams went around the room, he decided that a student named Saúl seemed to understand the least English of anybody. He was fifteen years old and had just arrived from El Salvador. He wore track pants and a T-shirt, and his hair was mussed as if he had just rolled out of bed. Communicating with Saúl was not difficult, however, because Mr. Williams spoke Spanish. All of the academic literature about second-language acquisition suggests that using a student's first language to aid in comprehension can be tremendously helpful;

Mr. Williams and Mr. DeRose both used Spanish a lot. If they had spoken other languages, they would have used those as well, but Spanish was all they had. When Saúl did not respond to Mr. Williams's query, he switched to Spanish and explained the greeting, then practiced it in English until Saúl could say, "My name is Saúl. I am from El Salvador. I speak Spanish."

The final two students, Rahim and Ghasem, were both from Afghanistan. Everybody could see they were close friends. Later that year, Rahim and Ghasem would describe their shared odyssey to their classmates—the two families had followed the same route to Eastern Europe and spent many months together in the same refugee camp before resettling in the United States. For the moment, what registered with Mr. Williams was that their English was surprisingly good. After several days, he would determine that Rahim and Ghasem knew so much English that he could move the two boys upstairs, into language acquisition classes that were more advanced.

After his students practiced writing their introductions, Mr. Williams asked them to stand up and form two lines facing each other. He organized the students into pairs and told them to take turns reading out loud to their partners the sentences they had just written. Stephanie said, "Hello! My name is Stephanie. I am from Mexico." Grace said, "Hello! My name is Grace. I am from Mozambique." And so on. By that point, the students had listened to their teacher say those phrases, read the phrases on the Smart Board, written the phrases, and spoken them out loud. Mr. Williams went through these four steps—listening, reading, writing, and speaking—with every big concept that he wanted to convey.

Following the exercise, Mr. Williams pointed out artwork by previous students that hung on the walls. "Saúl, here we have the flag of El Salvador," he said slowly and carefully. "Right? Is this the flag of El Salvador? Is this the flag of El Salvador?"

Saúl nodded.

"We have had other students from El Salvador in this room," Mr. Williams told him. "*Otros estudiantes de El Salvador en esta clase.*"

Then Mr. Williams turned to Stephanie.

"Stephanie, do you recognize this? What is this?"

"The flag of Mexico," Stephanie replied right away.

Mr. Williams saw that with her he could speak more quickly. He handed out sheets of paper, distributed markers and crayons, and asked the students to draw the flags of their home countries. Stephanie drew two flags—the flag of Colorado and the flag of Mexico. She wrote: "I am from Denver. I am from United States. I am from Mexico."

"You're originally from Colorado?" asked Mr. Williams.

Stephanie nodded.

"And you've also lived in Mexico?"

She nodded again. There it was, the bare bones of a life journey—a few important plot points disclosed, all the details still hidden. He'd heard a lot of stories about parents moving back and forth between the United States and Mexico, usually due to the availability of jobs.

"Which do you consider home, Colorado or Mexico?" Mr. Williams asked.

"Colorado," Stephanie responded confidently.

High comprehension, the teacher thought. He suspected she had once known a lot of English and that it would return to her quickly. At the end of that week, when he would assess her reading and writing abilities, Mr. Williams would decide that Stephanie was not yet ready to move upstairs, but he thought she might transfer to a more advanced room before the end of the year.

On his drawing, Hsar Htoo wrote: "My namee Hsar Htoo." Mr. Williams recognized that for what it was: an accurate phonetic representation of what those unfamiliar English words sounded like to a newly arrived Karen-speaking person. For someone in the preproduction phase of English-language acquisition, who had arrived speaking a Sino-Tibetan language after never having lived outside a refugee camp, it was good work. Some years, Mr. Williams got kids who could not produce the Latin alphabet, or who were illiterate even in their own language. Hsar Htoo drew the flag of Thailand and the flag of the United States, though he had never lived here before. He seemed eager to embrace his new homeland.

Grace also drew two different flags, both of which had been used to represent Mozambique. The second flag she drew, a correct rendition of the flag used by that country today, featured an open book, a hoe, and an AK-47. Her sister Nadia drew two flags as well—one was Mozambique's and the other Burundi's. The history of Burundi bears parallels to that of Rwanda, its immediate neighbor to the north, including waves of mass killings between members of the Hutu and Tutsi tribes. Grace and Nadia were not alive during those phases of Burundi's history, but it was possible that older members of their family might have sought refuge in Mozambique after one of the catastrophic waves of violence in Burundi.

Near his desk, Mr. Williams had displayed an essay written by a former student. It read:

> Life was difficult. I was living in the middle of a civil war. 2002 was when the Ethiopians came. They were firing at everyone. . . . All the kids were running. I was holding onto the back of a truck. . . . After that I lost my eye. Then we went to Ethiopia and lived in a refugee camp. We went from Addis Ababa to Amsterdam, then to Chicago, and then to Denver. It took 2-3 days. Our apartment here smelled bad like marijuana. My life here is really good now. Compared to my life in Mogadishu it is much better here.

Mr. Williams did not point out that essay to the new students, because they would not be able to read it. He kept it on the wall for himself—as a reminder of what stark environments his students had left behind, and evidence of how much English he could teach them in a single school year.

Meanwhile, Saúl drew the flag of his country and wrote underneath, "I am from: El Sarvador." The fact that Saúl had misspelled the name of his own country touched Mr. Williams and suggested that perhaps Saúl had not attended school for quite a while. Only when Mr. Williams brought up parent-teacher conferences a few weeks later would Saúl mention that neither of his parents lived in the United States. He did not explain why he was here, at age fifteen, parentless; he just asked if his older sister could come to the conference. That would be fine, Mr. Williams told him. He was curious to know more, but to quiz Saúl on the whereabouts of his parents would have worked counter to his main priority, which was to build rapport. He couldn't teach the students English if they did not trust him.

Mr. Williams affixed his students' crayoned pictures of flags to a bulletin board that hung beside the door to his room. The hand-colored flags appeared simple, but they raised complex questions. The world was riven by ethnic conflict, gang violence, armed rebel groups, terrorist organizations, oppressive regimes, full-blown civil wars, and wars between countries. When families lost their homes, children often struggled to find a foothold in a foreign place. What obligation, if any, did the rest of the world have to make things whole again for those children? The flags spoke to the subject of nationality, and around the world, the global refugee crisis was bringing up intense sectarian political forces, centered on this idea of individual nations, and the matter of what obligation one nation might or might not owe to the citizens of another. As the 2015–2016 school year began, Germans were filling train stations to wave homemade signs of welcome at arriving Syrians and to offer them blankets and hot drinks. The increasing numbers of displaced people coursing through Europe were simultaneously unnerving citizens of other countries, however, and in Hungary officials had started building a fence along the border to keep out the refugees who were seeking to escape the devastation of the Middle East.

In the United States, controversial bills to block the entry of refugees had recently been introduced in the House of Representatives, and opponents of resettlement were using terms like "jihadi pipeline" to describe the flow of Arabic-speaking people streaming out of Syria and Iraq. Meanwhile, Donald Trump had held a press conference at Trump Tower in New York City to announce that he was running for president on the slogan "Make America Great Again!" It seemed likely that the huddled masses walking across Europe would become a centerpiece of the coming presidential election, which would unfold throughout the first year these students spent in the United States. In other words, at the very moment when Mr. Williams was welcoming the latest newcomers into his big, mostly empty classroom, and resettlement agency staff were working closely with their parents to find employers willing to hire people who arrived with little or no ability to speak English, some political leaders around the United States had started asking whether such people ought to be welcomed here at all.

Once, the United States had been the most generous of the world's wealthy countries in terms of its resettlement policy. Historically, the United States had taken more refugees than any other country. The federal government had pledged to take seventy thousand refugees during fiscal year 2015, and President Obama wanted to admit more the following year, but candidates like Donald Trump were calling for the number to be reduced. Should the United States continue to shelter large numbers of refugees seeking an end to hardship? Should a school-age child who arrived unaccompanied by an adult from a violence-plagued country such as El Salvador be given asylum? How many foreign people with strange customs could one country absorb and still retain its identity? What about immigrants who frequented mosques? Was it possible that the violence taking place in other regions might be imported along with refugees to host countries, making them less secure?

Those were the sorts of questions preoccupying people who were running for political office. They were not the questions that beset Mr. Williams. His concerns were much more basic: Could his students understand his sentences? Had he sufficiently challenged those who had more English yet kept things simple enough for the rest? Did the kids feel safe in his room? Could they open their lockers? Were they going to be able to find their next class? And did they have enough to eat?

Probably not, he suspected. Before the bell rang for their next class, Mr. Williams beckoned to his seven teens and asked them to follow him into a large walk-in closet on the far side of the room. Inside, neatly arranged on wire shelving, the students beheld pasta, rice, lentils, beans, cans of vegetables, boxes of cereal, and individually wrapped protein bars. The food bank had been started one year earlier, by one of South's English-speaking families. Although their own daughter had graduated the previous spring, Jaclyn Yelich and Greg Thielen had nonetheless spent the past several days stocking these shelves with everything they could imagine a newly arrived family might want for dinner.

"This is the food bank," Mr. Williams announced. "You can come here on Friday afternoon and take home bags of food."

The students stared at all the boxes and all the cans and said nothing. Did they understand that the food was there for the taking?

"On Friday, if you want, you can take food," Mr. Williams repeated, more slowly.

Silence.

"Are you hungry now?" he asked.

Silence. They were probably hungry. Mr. Williams handed out protein bars, two per student.

"*Gracias*," said Saúl.

"Thank you!" said Stephanie.

Grace and Nadia whispered their thanks. Hsar Htoo said nothing at all, but gave Mr. Williams another immense smile. At the end of that week, when the last bell rang on Friday, boisterous teenagers of all shapes, sizes, and skin colors—some wearing hijabs and others in Rockies gear or shirts with Nike swooshes—poured out of the vast high school. Several of Mr. Williams's students returned to his ground-floor classroom from elsewhere in the building. As he prepared to go home himself, the teacher saw his students line up and wait their turn to be given food. They walked out of his room carrying recycled plastic bags bulging with beans, lentils, rice, all the staples. Yes, they had been hungry.

2

The Chair Is Short

W hat does this picture look like?" Mr. Williams asked his class in the middle of September.

Three weeks had elapsed since the beginning of school. The hot days of August had slid into the cooler-in-the-morning-but-still-hot-in-the-afternoon days of early fall. Mr. Williams wore khakis and another dress shirt—light blue today, with the sleeves rolled halfway up his forearms. He projected a picture of a room filled with desks onto a large screen.

"Classroom," answered Nadia, one of the sisters from Mozambique. She was holding her chin in both of her hands.

"Yes," confirmed Mr. Williams. He pointed to something in the picture. "And what does this look like?"

"Pencil sharpener," said Stephanie, the girl who had moved back and forth between Mexico and the United States. Her faded blue jeans were decorated with two sequined peace signs, one on each side of her behind.

Mr. Williams asked the students to name a few more objects—a desk, a chair, a map, and a clock. Then he asked them to copy down partial sentences about the classroom and fill in the missing words. The teacher had moved on to the second unit in the curriculum, called "My School." The intent was to use the students' immediate surroundings to expand their vocabulary. The dialogue remained basic, but the lessons were progressing. Various students were acquiring new words at varying rates—even as the class roster kept changing. By this point, Mr. Williams had sent the two young men from Afghanistan upstairs and had welcomed one additional charge to his room: Uyen, a willowy eighteen-year-old girl from Vietnam. Meanwhile, I was gaining a better appreciation of the individual students in the classroom, what their home languages were like, and what factors promoted or inhibited their learning. Mr. Williams read out loud from the textbook, *Inside the U.S.A.*: "'This is my classroom. There is a large map on the wall.' Okay, Hsar Htoo? Is it a small map or a large map?"

"Large," said Hsar Htoo in a tiny voice.

Mr. Williams had called on Hsar Htoo because the boy so rarely spoke; if the teacher didn't ask him to talk, Hsar Htoo would happily have said nothing all day.

"All right, Uyen, can you say more? What else can we say? Uyen, what else? About our own class?"

"It is big," said Uyen.

"Our classroom is big," replied Mr. Williams.

"Um, the whiteboard," said Uyen.

"Is it big?"

"It is large."

"The whiteboard is large," echoed Mr. Williams. "Okay."

He turned to the other sister from Mozambique.

"Grace, let me hear more about our classroom."

"The chair is short," replied Grace.

"Okay," said Mr. Williams.

A native speaker probably wouldn't have said the chair was short, but Mr. Williams let that slide. He was cautious about correcting the newcomers—too much criticism and they fell silent, ashamed of how badly they spoke English. Generally, he tried to think of a better phrase, and then, without actually telling the teenagers that they were wrong, offer it as a potential alternative: "Or, you could say, the chair is small."

Naming tangible objects was one way to make his students feel a little less lost. Mr. Williams walked around the room and pointed out additional things for them to name.

"Table," the students called out.

Mr. Williams pointed at Mr. DeRose.

"Teacher," they chorused.

Then Mr. Williams pointed toward a locked cabinet on the far side of the room.

"What other things do we have in our classroom?" he asked. "Guys, what are those back there?"

"Computers," Nadia said softly.

Mr. Williams clapped at her success. Nadia and Grace had gone to school in the nearby suburb of Aurora for part of the previous school year. They also had the advantage of speaking Portuguese, a Romance language with many parallels to English. Mr. Williams believed they might know more words than anybody else in the room, although it was hard to tell during the preproduction phase, when all of the students were busy doing so much listening.

"Is there another word?" he asked, seeking to challenge his more advanced pupils. "How about if we say laptop computers? Or just laptops?"

Silence. A few of the students wrote down the new word, "laptops."

"What else?"

"Blinds," said Nadia.

"Okay, we have blinds," said Mr. Williams, noting that Nadia's vocabulary was impressive. "Windows and blinds." He pointed to the windows, so that the other students could grasp what he was talking about. "And what's this right here?"

"Fan," said Stephanie.

"We have a fan," confirmed Mr. Williams.

The temperature was going to climb to eighty-one degrees later that day and the classroom caught the full brunt of the morning sun. The teacher had the fan running at top speed, making a noisy hum. Mr. Williams asked his students to write sentences using the words they had generated, and then he walked around coaxing them along.

"Good!" he said over and over again. "Good!"

Constant encouragement—that was how he shepherded the foreign speakers toward the second phase of language acquisition, which was called "early production." He sprinkled praise in the direction he wanted the students to go, as if he were putting down breadcrumbs to mark the path forward. To keep the kids talking, he told them over and over what they were doing right (never what they were doing wrong). After the lesson about classroom objects, Mr. Williams imparted the names of several states located near Colorado, and then worked on giving and following commands, something they had to understand throughout the rest of the school day. When they were not in Room 142, the students took classes in math, science, physical education, and the arts. They took math and science in special sections designated for ELA students, while they took gym and the arts with everybody else in the school. But they spent roughly half of each day with Mr. Williams, staying with him for multiple periods; in total, they spent twelve hours a week in his room. Studying English so intensively was grueling, and Mr. Williams tried to give them some kind of relief each day, such as standing up to speak, or playing games, or drawing—anything that would get them out of their purple plastic chairs and break up the monotony.

English contains roughly a quarter of a million words, and most native speakers of the language deploy about ten thousand of them. During the preproduction phase of language acquisition, which could last for three to six months, ELA students might acquire perhaps five hundred words. The students would be able to understand that many words in English, even though they might not be able to retrieve them and use them in a sentence properly. When they reached the second stage, early production, they might have a working vocabulary of about one thousand words. In both the preproduction and early production phases, second-language learners tend to be better at memorizing and repetition, but they struggle with producing original phrasing.

Mr. Williams had a few students who were already capable of early production, but many kids in his room remained stuck in preproduction. During this time frame, it was often hard for them to show Mr. Williams what they were learning, because they stayed so quiet. He knew to expect this, but to an outsider like me this period was baffling. I found it difficult to get a sense of students' personalities when we could not talk to each other. It was even hard for me to hold on to the names of some of them because their names sounded radically different from what my ears were used to (for a while, I was writing Hsar Htoo's name in my notebook as Sartu). What drew me to Room 142 was this very conundrum: I wanted to learn more about where these teenagers had come from and I wanted to puzzle out what their collective presence in this room said about the world. Which parts of the planet were producing the most refugees, and what were those people fleeing? In a deeper sense, being in this classroom allowed me to ponder what it meant to be fellow human beings who shared one globe, some with privileged lives, and some with lives that were much, much harder. Needless to say, Room 142 also turned out to be a fascinating vantage point from which to observe the presidential election.

The room spoke to me for personal reasons. My Irish-born parents immigrated to this country, and being with foreign-born kids and their families reminded me of experiences with my foreign-born cousins, aunts, and uncles. In the end, though, I found Room 142 most meaningful not because of what it reminded me of in my own past but for all it taught me about places I had never been—in some cases, places I had never even heard of before. Because I was learning as much as I could about the different countries represented in Room 142, trying to absorb as much as I could about each of the kids on a personal level when we didn't share a language, and simultaneously trying to discern what it was the ELA teacher was doing, it took months for me to sort everything out; I might as well have been in preproduction myself at the start of the school year. There was a lot of flux in the room, with kids coming and going, and a few kids turned up who spoke languages I did not even know existed. Ultimately, I had to make a chart of the languages they spoke to keep it all straight. As the weeks and months flew by, however, the kids and I did learn essential things about one another. Imperfectly, for sure, but better than I imagined would be possible during August and September, when the kids were so quiet and Mr. Williams was talking so much but saying only such basic things.

I saw right away that I was lucky to be in the presence of this teacher, who thought about the well-being of his students from the first bell until the last. He wondered, for example, what effect I might have on his students. Sometimes, Mr. Williams and I stepped upstairs to the second-floor copy room, where teachers and paraprofessionals went to make photocopies or to eat their packed lunches, and we talked about my role in his classroom. "I think it helps them, to tell their stories, don't you?" he mused one day. And I could hear, behind the simple-sounding melody of his assertion, the harmony of a real question in his voice. "Maybe—it depends," I answered. "Some of them might have lived through traumatic things, and they might not want to tell their stories. That's fine. I would never push them to say more than they want. They have to feel empowered by the act of telling their stories."

With this in mind, we came up with some ground rules. I would wait until the students had settled into school before trying to interview them; generally, I gave the kids several months to acclimatize. I also hired interpreters so that I could speak to each student in his or her home language. The interpreters and I met with individual students during their lunch period to explain my interest in their teacher and their classroom. If they expressed the desire to talk further, I asked about their backgrounds in a short interview, conducted in their home language. The students were free to say as much or as little as they desired. If it seemed that they had witnessed armed conflict, I did not ask them for details. Instead, I said I would like to meet their parents. I kept the interviews with students to half an hour at most—unless they invited me home—and I tried to have a light footprint, emotionally. After a while, I got to know three refugee families at a much deeper level. One family was from the Middle East, one was from Africa, and one was from Southeast Asia—the three regions producing the largest numbers of refugees. Understanding these families better enhanced my understanding of everything I saw transpire in the classroom.

Once I had explained my presence to the majority of the kids, Mr. Williams began asking me to help out a little bit, reading with the kids or playing some of the instructional games that he had invented. But I went to great lengths to communicate clearly with every student that I was not a member of the South High faculty, that I was a journalist visiting the classroom so that I could write a book, and that it was their choice whether or not to be included. In the end, twenty-one of the twenty-two students who spent large parts of the school year in Room 142 said they wanted to be part of the project. On the whole, my sense was that they felt a strong desire to tell the world what it was like to arrive in the United States from somewhere else, so that more people would understand how hard it was to negotiate such a transition. And they very much wished for people who lived in developed countries to know what was happening in places that were less fortunate.

Because teenagers are teenagers all the world over, the kids in Mr. Williams's class were keen to interact with one another (far more so than they were to interact with me or their teacher), although they generally could not communicate by talking. I found it touching to watch their earliest attempts at friendship. In September, Stephanie started spending a lot of her free time with Nadia and Grace, the two sisters from Mozambique; they did not share a common language, but Spanish and Portuguese were similar enough that they could pretty much understand one another.

One day, upstairs in the bright, airy fourth-floor cafeteria—a cathedral-sized room with great banks of windows—Stephanie saw Uyen sitting at a table all by herself and asked the new girl from Vietnam if she would like to join the others. Uyen could not decipher either Spanish or Portuguese, but she and Stephanie figured out how to communicate, using the Google Translate application on their cell phones. Stephanie typed a text message in Spanish, used Google Translate to swap her words into Vietnamese, and asked Uyen what kind of movies she preferred. Uyen wrote back in Vietnamese, used Google Translate to convert the text into Spanish, and said that she loved horror movies. "So do I!" wrote Stephanie. One of Stephanie's favorite movies was *The Conjuring*. Uyen said that was one of her favorites, too. Also, they both loved shoes. They agreed via Google Translate that the coolest shoes in the world were Converse High Tops, which they both wore to school every day. Stephanie and Uyen began holding hands in the hallways and eating lunch together all the time. Once Mr. Williams walked into the classroom to behold Stephanie sitting in Uyen's lap, as Uyen stroked Stephanie's hair and called her "my baby."

Over lunch in the school's cafeteria, Stephanie told me that she had been born in Denver and had attended school in the United States until the age of seven. When her parents separated, her mother had returned to Mexico, taking along her three daughters. Stephanie repeated third grade in Mexico and continued her schooling there through ninth grade. Then her mother began dating a new boyfriend, and the family went through a period of strife. Ultimately, her mother decided that she could no longer manage her teenage daughters, who were ignoring her commands. She sent all three girls back to Denver to live with their father. Stephanie was glad, because she had not liked her mother's new boyfriend; also, she found her father less histrionic than her mother. Stephanie seemed highly pleased to have returned to the United States.

Uyen and I spoke much later, after her English had improved radically. She said she preferred to talk without an interpreter. We were sitting in the bleachers in the school's enormous, echoing gymnasium, watching other students play dodgeball. Uyen's parents were also divorced, and, like Stephanie, she had moved to the United States to live with her father. For Uyen, however, the change had been painful; she had never lived outside of Vietnam, and she was intensely homesick. Her eyes filled with tears when she mentioned FaceTiming her mother every day, but she believed her father's invitation to live with him in the United States gave her a chance at a better future. When she arrived in Mr. Williams's class that fall, Uyen was still adjusting to living with her father, a stepmother, and two half siblings for the first time, even as she was making the epic adjustment to a new country. I could see why a friendship had sprung up so quickly between her and Stephanie. Neither was a refugee, but both were dealing with the consequences of broken families, which was another form of hardship.

While Stephanie had forgotten most of her English during the years she had spent in Mexico, lost words began reappearing in her mind within a few weeks. Uyen had studied English in Vietnam, and she seemed determined to keep up with her new best friend. Nadia and Grace also called out answers frequently. Of all the factors that affect how easy or hard it is for a given student to learn English, what linguists call "language proximity" generally has the greatest effect. Portuguese and Spanish both evolved from Latin, and sentences in those languages are basically structured in the same way as English sentences (a subject, followed by a verb, then an object). English and the Romance languages also share a vast number of cognates. While English is a Germanic language, it includes so many words of Latin origin that more than 30 percent of its vocabulary is either the same or highly similar in Spanish. The two languages include thousands of perfect cognates (altar is translated as *altar*) and thousands of near-perfect cognates (furious is translated as *furioso*). Because of the great similarities between English and Spanish or Portuguese, Stephanie, Nadia, and Grace were having an easier time than the other students acquiring their new language. Saúl would progress rapidly as well once he recognized how much Spanish had in common with English, but he had not yet spent as much time in the United States as Stephanie, Nadia, or Grace.

English is much harder to learn for speakers of Asian languages. Most Asian languages are tonal, employ characters, and structure sentences differently. Because of the dominating presence of Portuguese missionaries starting in the seventeenth century, Vietnamese is written using the Latin script, and this facilitated Uyen's ability to write in English. Hsar Htoo did not have the same advantage, however, for all three of the languages that he knew fluently—Karen, Burmese, and Thai—used other kinds of lettering. And Hsar Htoo could not rely on finding cognates between Karen and English or Burmese and English. The languages he spoke and the language he was trying to learn shared no common ancestry and did not even employ the same sounds. For Hsar Htoo, acquiring English would be more difficult than for anybody else in the room. When Mr. Williams posed questions to the class, the four girls frequently volunteered responses. It was the two boys—Saúl and Hsar Htoo—that the teacher had to prod into talking.

Even as Mr. Williams was trying to manage his original students, he kept having to incorporate additional kids into Room 142. At the end of September, the newcomer class doubled in size when six new students arrived over the course of four days. The fall months typically generated a rush at South, for the city's refugee resettlement agencies were hustling to assist all the new arrivals sent to them at the close of the fiscal year, when international aid groups tried to meet year-end quotas. Amaniel, the next student to arrive, was fourteen years old. He was originally from Eritrea, a country with an authoritarian government and a long history of conflict with its neighbor, Ethiopia. Amaniel had transferred from another school, and had already lived in the United States for long enough to adopt the habit of wearing his pants down low. He had to hold on to his belt buckle to keep his jeans on his body when he strode around the classroom. Amaniel also wore multiple gold necklaces and had a star cut into his hair. He spoke Kunama, a language spoken by one of Eritrea's ethnic minorities.

Solomon and Methusella arrived the following day. The two boys, obviously brothers, were both shy, quiet, and handsome. They had high cheekbones and wide-set eyes, which lit up when they smiled. In the weeks that followed, I noticed them wearing the same articles of clothing over and over—sports-oriented T-shirts and tracksuit jackets in carefully matched colors—but their clothes were always spotless. Methusella's favorite shirt was a yellow-and-red-striped Barcelona soccer jersey, while Solomon's was a medium-blue long-sleeved New York Giants shirt. Methusella was fifteen years old, and Solomon was seventeen. They were from the Democratic Republic of Congo, and they spoke Swahili. The DRC had been the site of the largest conflict anywhere on the African continent, and certain provinces in the DRC continued to experience serious violence even after the official ceasefire. If any of his students had witnessed bloodshed firsthand, Mr. Williams understood, it was likely to be these two striking, well-dressed boys.

Shortly after the brothers from the Congo arrived, Mr. Williams noticed Nadia and Grace chatting with them.

"Do you know Swahili?" he asked the girls from Mozambique.

"Yes," Nadia said with shy pride.

That was news to Mr. Williams. The two sisters had never mentioned knowing Swahili. Mr. Williams thought it also helped explain their rapid learning curve, for in his experience, multilingual students often progressed more quickly than those who were monolingual. At this point, Mr. Williams mistakenly believed that Nadia and Grace spoke three languages—Portuguese, Swahili, and a little bit of English. Later in the year, however, Nadia would confide that she could speak seven languages—the three that Mr. Williams knew about, plus four languages indigenous to Africa.

Throughout the school year, the sisters from Mozambique would remain enigmatic to me. We ate lunch together several times, both with and without an interpreter, but they never wanted to say much. Grace preferred not to be questioned at all, although she listened with rapt attention to my vain attempt to interview her sister. Nadia simply said, in response to almost every question I asked, "I don't know, Miss." At one point, she added, "I don't remember—I don't remember anything." I learned more about Nadia from a single picture that she drew, which Mr. Williams hung up on the bulletin board. Using colored pencils and fine-tipped markers, she created a detailed rendering of eighteen different people. Across the top, she wrote "My Family," and then she labeled each person by name and by type of relation, using Portuguese terms. The picture included brothers, sisters, aunts, uncles, a bespectacled grandmother, and even a tiny cousin in a finely drawn baby carrier. I assured Nadia that it was okay if she didn't want to say more—some students wanted to share their stories, and others did not. I respected Nadia's choice to be guarded.

Regardless, I grew to like both girls because of their quiet propensity to help out. When Mr. Williams missed a day, it was Nadia who told the substitute where she could find a particular stack of handouts. If Mr. Williams couldn't remember where they had left off reading *Inside the U.S.A.*, Nadia or Grace would remind him. Mr. Williams was glad to see the sisters welcoming the brothers from the Congo. Students found it confusing to arrive partway through the year, and it helped to talk to someone who had been in the room from the start.

Two days after Solomon and Methusella arrived, a pair of girls named Jakleen and Mariam walked into the classroom. They stood close together and murmured to each other in Arabic. Both were remarkably pretty, with oval faces, olive skin, and long black hair, and both favored heavy eyeliner painted like cat's eyes. Sisters, clearly. Mariam wore tortoiseshell glasses and had done her hair in a hip-length braid, which from time to time she flung back around her shoulder so that the braid inscribed a wide arc in the air. Jakleen did not wear the navy blue glasses that she kept inside her backpack, and her black hair was loose, hanging down to her rib cage. Mr. Williams told the class that Jakleen and Mariam were from Iraq.

Mariam's face wore a soft, tentative expression, while Jakleen studied everybody in the room with fierce curiosity. Mariam was sixteen years old, and Jakleen was fifteen. They had arrived in the United States at the end of August, but for several weeks they had lived with a friend in a suburb that fell outside the city limits. Only after their mother found an apartment they could afford on the outskirts of Denver did they become eligible to attend South. When Jakleen and Mariam walked into their new high school on October 1, 2015, the sisters had missed almost two months of school, and they had lost just about everything they had once called their own, including their father. They had left Baghdad in 2006, at the height of the Iraq War—nine years earlier—and they had been looking for a safe haven ever since. The two girls would tell me later that they entered Mr. Williams's classroom believing that the hard times were over. Mariam and Jakleen imagined that by coming to America, they had put any kind of trouble behind them. This idea was untested, however, because they had been in the United States for only a few weeks, and did not yet know what kind of reception awaited them here.

Mr. Williams watched all of the new students closely. He knew that the brothers from the Congo had lived in a country that had been riven by conflict for two decades, and that they had not been able to attend school continuously. The same was true of the sisters from Iraq, who had fled an active war zone. Mr. Williams wanted to gauge the ability of his newest students to understand English. He also wanted to find out if they had arrived with school supplies and whether their families could afford food. Solomon and Methusella impressed him right away by demonstrating an instant readiness to learn—anytime Mr. Williams checked on the boys, they were hard at work.

Mariam and Jakleen seemed more distracted. They did not appear to be in immediate distress, for their clothes were clean and they had taken the time to fix their hair and put on makeup. The girls appeared alert, and had shown up with pencils and notebooks. They also demonstrated the kind of basic learning skills found in students who had been able to attend school regularly. When Mr. Williams wrote something on the whiteboard, they copied his words down in their notebooks. Soon there were indications that the girls might be experiencing inner turmoil, however; while both had come to school with their heads uncovered, within a short time Jakleen began wearing a hijab, while Mariam did not. Mr. Williams did not know what to make of this divergence in behavior, but he imagined the two sisters might be struggling with questions of identity and belonging.

On the Friday after Jakleen and Mariam's arrival, volunteers from Goodwill appeared in the classroom. They had been visiting every week and were surprised to see twice as many students as the week before. Mr. Williams pointed out all the recent additions—Amaniel, with the gold chains, from Eritrea; Methusella and Solomon, the neatly dressed brothers from the Congo; Jakleen and Mariam, the cat-eyed sisters from Iraq—and asked the volunteers to practice verbal introductions. Half of the class had done introductions on the first day of school, but that had been six weeks ago, and it would be helpful for the longtime students to review the material; meanwhile, the recent arrivals could get acclimated. The volunteers fanned out across the room and repeated what the teacher had said. Mr. Williams assigned Nadia and Grace to different groups, then did the same with Solomon and Methusella as well as Jakleen and Mariam—he separated siblings, to make sure they didn't lapse into speaking to each other. Jakleen sat down with Uyen and Methusella, two students she did not know at all, and a Goodwill volunteer joined the group. Mystified, Jakleen stared at the volunteer. She had eloquent eyes, and without using words nonetheless managed to say she had no idea what was happening; her eyes had a little bit of laughter in them, too, as if this were funny.

The volunteer pointed to the whiteboard, where Mr. Williams was writing the scripted dialogue. Jakleen seemed unclear how to proceed. The volunteer pantomimed the act of writing, and then Jakleen turned to her notebook.

"Hi, I'm Jakleen," she wrote in English. "I'm from Iraq, and I speak Arabic."

I noticed that she had no trouble writing from left to right in Latin script, even though Arabic employs different letters and is written in the reverse direction. She must have studied English before. When Jakleen finished, I asked her a question.

"Jakleen, you're from Iraq. Did you come in an airplane?"

"Airplane, yes. No Iraq, Turkey."

"Oh, you lived in Turkey first?"

"Yes. One year, Turkey."

Then Mr. Williams interrupted, drawing the room back together again. He asked the class to read a handout about a fictional TV game show called *Name That City.* The banter between the host and the contestants mentioned several major U.S. cities—Philadelphia, Los Angeles, Santa Fe, and Baton Rouge. Mr. Williams walked around the room listening carefully as the students read the dialogue aloud to their respective volunteers. Jakleen could read English haltingly and stumbled only over bigger words such as "contestants" and "congratulations." For her second day at school, she was doing very well. Uyen could read all the words, although her pronunciation was harder to make out. Methusella read softly, and even though he could say most of the words, he did not always know their meaning. He asked the Goodwill volunteer for help when he came to the unfamiliar word "river."

"It is water," explained the volunteer. "Like the Nile River." She made a flowing movement with her hands. Methusella nodded in recognition.

Then he asked about the meaning of "hometown." I was impressed that he was asking so many questions—newly arrived students rarely did that.

"It is where your family is from," said the volunteer.

When we chatted about our hometowns, Jakleen named Karrada, a neighborhood in Baghdad known for its diversity, even though her family had left there when she was five years old. Methusella said his hometown was Goma, a large city on the eastern side of the DRC. When I read more about the DRC, I learned that was the part of the country that had experienced the most dire forms of upheaval.

As his class grew, Mr. Williams gave the students weekly assessments to measure their ability to write, read, understand, and speak English. At the same time, he tried to watch over his students' general well-being. He noted who made friends and who didn't. He saw that Hsar Htoo had nobody with whom he could speak Karen, and that Amaniel had nobody with whom he could speak Kunama. Uyen seemed heavily dependent on Stephanie, who was starting to discover other Spanish-speaking students around the building. He worried about the two girls from Iraq, because they were the only students in the room who spoke Arabic, and he did not want them to isolate themselves and withdraw from the group as a whole. At first he held similar concerns about the brothers from the Congo, but then he saw them quickly forge an alliance with Nadia and Grace. They showed up at school every single day, always on time, always nicely dressed, always ready to tackle whatever he wanted them to learn. He was struck to see such motivation. The boys were making the most of every minute they had in his room.

The same was not true for Jakleen and Mariam. For reasons Mr. Williams had yet to discover, their motivation seemed to wax and wane. Hanging over them was a palpable aura of sadness. Often Jakleen stared vacantly out the classroom's large windows instead of doing classwork. One day Mariam left the room to see the school counselor because she was too upset to stay in class. Why did their level of participation in school fluctuate? After Jakleen began wearing a hijab every day, she encountered vocal prejudice on the city buses that she used to commute to and from school. Even within the school building itself, one student called her a "terrorist." I wondered if the prejudice she encountered served as a drag on her spirit. Jakleen and Mariam also appeared profoundly weary. Sometimes, they failed to come to school, and after one of their absences, when I asked where they had been, they said, "Sleep."

This became a kind of joke after a while. "Jakleen, what do you want to do after you graduate from high school?" I asked her one day. "No work," she said. "Eat, sleep." Then I noticed that her eyes were laughing. Eventually she admitted that she wanted to pursue a career in fashion design. But she would have to finish high school to do that type of work, and meanwhile she and Mariam were accruing more absences than anybody else in the room. Mr. Williams worried about keeping the sisters engaged. He also wondered about their sadness, which they wore to school every day like a down jacket, as if it offered them some sort of protection. They did not have enough English to explain that to him, however; they did not have the words, and maybe what they had lived through was too big to describe easily in any language.

Eddie Williams felt a sense of kinship with these students who struggled to determine their place in American society. He had been born in a tiny border town in Southern California. His mother had grown up nearby, in a Spanish-speaking household. Her parents had emigrated from Mexico, and when she was a child, Mr. Williams's mother had learned English in ELA classes. For her, the experience had been searing. As an adult, she had not taught her own children Spanish, for fear they would encounter the sort of virulent prejudice she had experienced in school. When her children were small, she did not even share with them the complete story of her own background, because of the degree of prejudice toward those of Mexican descent. She had married an American, and when her children were small, they believed they were Anglo. One day, while we were standing on the front steps of South, chatting about his background, Eddie Williams recalled that when his mother had finally revealed her Mexican identity, his sister had cried. In her mind, to be Mexican was to be dirty or unlovable. It was not something she wanted to be. Although he did not say so, I thought perhaps he, too, might have struggled to embrace fully the part of himself that had been treated as inferior by white society. I could see why teaching at South might make him feel more whole.

Given his mother's experience, Mr. Williams was careful to treat his students with the utmost respect. He never wanted a student like Jakleen to feel he disapproved of her heritage—the way his mother had felt. At the same time, the students presented him with huge challenges. They arrived all throughout the school year, from all over the world, speaking every kind of language imaginable, and they learned at vastly different speeds. Some of them showed up in bad shape and needed time to heal; some grew frustrated with the pace of their own learning, and he had to cajole them to keep trying; others learned so fast he could barely keep pace. The more students he got, the harder he had to work to stretch those who were learning quickly without leaving anyone else behind.

With the addition of the latest students, the class size grew to eleven. So far, Mr. Williams had collected students from the Democratic Republic of Congo, El Salvador, Eritrea, Iraq, Mexico, Mozambique (or Burundi), Thailand (or Burma), and Vietnam. Two students spoke Spanish, while the other nine spoke languages that Mr. Williams did not know. Eight had learned to write using the Latin script, and three using other kinds of lettering. Already, the room included students from some of the countries in the world that were producing the largest numbers of refugees: Burma, the Democratic Republic of Congo, Eritrea, and Iraq.

Most people fleeing the continuing violence in El Salvador did not arrive in the United States with refugee status; typically, they entered without legal permission and then sought asylum. Saúl, for example, had left his home country in the company of an eighteen-year-old sister, crammed into the back of a panel truck along with more than seventy other travelers. So many bodies were squeezed into the truck that several passengers fainted. Saúl found it difficult to breathe. He was apprehended by immigration officials on the U.S. side of the border in McAllen, Texas, and was released into the custody of a twenty-six-year-old sister who lived in Denver. Given the conditions he had fled, Saúl was hoping the federal court system might grant him permission to remain in the United States.

Meanwhile, it was only October, and more kids were almost certainly on their way. Mr. Williams expected the class to double in size again before year's end. His goal by that point was both straightforward and daunting: to ensure that as many students as possible could answer basic verbal questions in English in both the present and past tenses. He hoped the majority of students could also justify their answers, giving him either a rationale or an opinion. If they could produce original phrasing, they would enter the third phase of language acquisition, known as "speech emergence," and they would be ready to move upstairs. If not, they would stay with him for another semester. He thought that was fine—some kids simply needed more time to adjust.

When the teacher was not in his classroom, I generally found him glued to his laptop in the copy room, worrying about how to help the growing number of students he had acquired to evolve simultaneously. What he brought into the classroom every day was a passion to help the newcomers thrive. He was like a gardener, excited by seedlings. Where others might see students with limitations, or students who were lagging behind their peers, Mr. Williams saw a room filled with kids who had lived through titanic experiences, teenagers who could do anything at all, once they accepted whatever sort of history they had brought with them and grasped the full extent of the opportunity lying ahead. He often told me that he felt lucky to work in a room like this one—a room that spoke of just how big the world was, and how mysterious.

Meanwhile, I started visiting some of his students at home, and that was when I began to appreciate more fully how illuminating Room 142 was going to be, for the room quickly began to serve as an almost perfect microcosm of the global refugee crisis as a whole. Once I began meeting with particular families, I started hearing about every kind of journey a refugee family could survive. The stories that intersected in this one classroom brought to life the global crisis in a way that I never saw represented in the daily papers. The kids were at South to learn English, but in the process they were sharing with me and with the school's staff and with their American-born peers all kinds of lessons—about fortitude, about resilience, about holding on to one's humanity through experiences nobody should have to witness. About starting over, and about transformation.

3

Smile

My early conversations with Jakleen and Mariam took place at their school. The girls agreed to have lunch one day with me and an Arabic-speaking interpreter named Nabiha, a stylish woman in her midfifties who was also from Iraq. At our initial meeting, my only goal was to explain to the girls who I was and what I was doing at South in a language they could understand. As Nabiha and I walked to the classroom, she mentioned that she was a former refugee herself. When the bell rang for lunch, we climbed up four flights of stairs with Jakleen and Mariam to the crowded cafeteria and chatted with the girls while they stood in line for food. With Nabiha's help, I told Jakleen and Mariam that Nabiha's daughters had lived through something like what they were going through right now.

"Her children had to learn English here," I said. "And they would come home crying! They would say, 'We are so smart, and the classes are so basic.'"

"Yeah, it's true," Mariam said, through Nabiha. "That is what it is like."

The girls carried their trays of food back downstairs to Room 142, where they customarily ate lunch. We sat down with them and I explained with Nabiha's help that I wanted to tell them why I was visiting their classroom. Earlier, I had tried to convey with hand signs that I was a writer, but I had no idea what if anything had come across. "Mr. Williams has agreed I can write a book about him and his class," I said to the girls. "I hope to write about some of the students who volunteer to tell their stories. Some of the students have said, 'Yes, I want to talk to you.' Some have said, 'No, thank you.'"

"It's okay to talk," said Mariam.

I gave the girls a letter for their mother, written in Arabic, and said we would speak further if she agreed it was okay.

"I'm sure my mom, she will say okay," Mariam assured me.

It was interesting to see that once I had an interpreter in the room, Mariam tended to speak for both girls. Previously I had mistaken her for having a softer personality, and had imagined that Jakleen would be more outspoken.

When we met again, during another lunch period, the girls explained that although they were from Iraq originally, most of their schooling had taken place in Syria. In essence, they were double refugees—first they had been displaced by the Iraq War, and then they were displaced again by the civil war in Syria. It was while they were living in Syria that their father had gone missing.

"My dad got lost," Mariam told me. "When we were in Syria, it was very expensive, we didn't have any money."

"Everything got expensive—like oil, we couldn't buy oil for heat, for the winter," Jakleen added. "We didn't have any way to heat the apartment, we just had to cover ourselves with a blanket. And the food also, it was very expensive. We had to eat just a potato or just an eggplant. And nothing else. And the rent on the apartment got expensive."

"So my dad said, 'I'm going to go back to Iraq to work,'" Mariam elaborated. "After that, he was gone. We didn't see him again. We don't know where he went."

I asked what they remembered about their early years in Iraq, before their father had gone missing. The girls had been only five and six years old when the family had left Baghdad, however, and their understanding of events from that time was jumbled, vague.

"They threatened my dad," Jakleen said.

"Who threatened him?" I asked.

"We don't know," she said. "The terrorists."

"We remember just a tiny bit about Iraq," Mariam added. "Not a lot."

"He was working with the Americans," Jakleen said.

*　*　*

We agreed that I should hear the rest of their story after I met with their mother. Jakleen and Mariam lived in Pine Creek Apartments, a low-rent housing complex in far southeast Denver. On my first visit, I strayed off course among the dozen or so identical buildings, and wandered around in the dark for a long time. All of the utilitarian structures appeared indistinguishable, one white stucco building after another; eventually I saw that the buildings were individually numbered, but the girls had given me only a street address. Nabiha had come to the meeting, too, but she was lost in a different part of the apartment complex. I kept calling her, she kept calling me, and we both kept calling the family; the phone calls only led to greater confusion and we spent more than thirty minutes trying to sort things out. If we had all been able to speak the same language, it would have been a five-minute complication, but the language barrier magnified every blip in communication. I could see that this was simply what it was going to be like, trying to get to know individuals from a culture so different than mine. There would be a lot of fumbling around in the dark before any potential illumination.

We found one another only after Jakleen and her mother, Ebtisam, came outside to search for me. I recognized Jakleen across one of the complex's large open areas by the familiar silhouette of her hijab, which she wore in the traditional Iraqi manner. She pinned up her long hair, pulled on a cotton headband along her hairline, and then wrapped a large wool scarf around her face. Ebtisam did not wear a hijab. She was a pretty woman with short brown hair, a heart-shaped face, mauve lipstick, and eyebrows carefully stenciled into arches. Her attire was Western, a close-fitting orange T-shirt and tight blue jeans. When we found each other at last, Ebtisam hugged me. We had never met before, but she was a demonstrative woman, and we had been looking for each other for a while.

I was carrying a box of Middle Eastern pastries from a restaurant called Jerusalem because I wanted to share something that would taste like home. I was nervous about the meeting, given the increasingly hostile atmosphere toward Muslims in the United States, and I wanted the girls' mother to feel comfortable sharing her version of the family's story. Ebtisam and Jakleen showed me the way to their apartment, on the ground floor of Building #1. We walked down an endless hallway illuminated with fluorescent lights. The textured walls were painted a shiny bright white and indoor-outdoor carpeting gave the place an institutional feel. Mariam opened the door to the family's home. The apartment had two bedrooms, a galley kitchen, and a generous-sized living room, filled with the characterless furniture of a doctor's office: an oak coffee table, two oversized green sofas, beige carpeting. They had not chosen the furniture; it had been donated by their resettlement agency. The walls were bare, but Ebtisam had tried to add a splash of life by arranging orange and yellow artificial lilies in a white china vase.

Mariam was wearing chunky headphones, the kind that covered her ears entirely. I put my hands over my own ears to mimic them. "Is it good music?" I asked. "No! No music," she said. She had been watching an Arabic-language TV program on her cell phone. Mariam was especially fond of an Egyptian talk show called *Al Hokm* (*The Verdict*) hosted by Wafaa Al Kilani, the Barbara Walters of the Middle East. The girls also watched a lot of Arabic-language news reports on YouTube about Iraqi and Syrian refugees, avidly devouring news clips about people who shared their circumstances.

In anticipation of our visit, Ebtisam and her daughters had spent the afternoon baking cookies filled with dates and walnuts. They had also arranged apple slices and orange segments in fan shapes on a large plate. Between what I had brought and what they had made, we had quite a spread. The girls carried trays of food to the low coffee table and we all sat down in the living room. Mariam ducked into the small kitchen to make coffee, as Jakleen sat down on a sofa with her legs tucked under her. She had on skinny-legged blue jeans and a T-shirt. When she unwound her gray scarf, I was surprised to see that her hair was now auburn.

"I like the color of your hair," I said, as Nabiha translated for me. "Is it new?"

"Yes," Jakleen said.

"I didn't know, because I haven't seen your hair for weeks," I told her.

Jakleen smiled politely—a stay-off-my-turf kind of smile. I did not ask why she wore the hijab when her sister and her mother left their hair uncovered because I could see it would be a sensitive subject. I didn't want to make her uncomfortable on my first visit to her home.

Mariam came into the room bearing tiny red cups of thick, spiced coffee. As she handed us the little cups, I said thank you and Nabiha said *shukraan*.

"Oh! Arabic coffee!" said Nabiha in English.

"It's actually Turkish coffee," Mariam corrected in Arabic.

Entire essays have been written on the distinction between Arabic coffee and Turkish coffee; the coffee Mariam served us was extra-strong and velvety, and in it I tasted cardamom. Nabiha and I ate the oranges and the apples and the cookies while Ebtisam and her daughters ate the baklava. They exclaimed over the familiar treats I had brought. We had been welcomed warmly and I believed we were ready to start talking, so I was dismayed when Nabiha announced she had to leave shortly. She explained first in English and then in Arabic that she had allotted only one hour for our conversation, and we had used up more than half the time trying to find one another outside in the dark. I had hoped this evening might yield answers to questions about what this family had lived through while their country had been at war with mine, and about what it was like to be Muslim and arrive in the United States at this juncture, when political candidates were debating the wisdom of accepting refugees, sometimes in inflammatory terms. I had also been wondering what had happened to Jakleen and Mariam's father. My questions were going to have to wait, however, because Nabiha could stay for only twenty more minutes. Trying to bridge two cultures would be slow, awkward, and convoluted, at least at the beginning, apparently. I squelched my frustration, telling myself that I had to learn to manage a relationship with an interpreter even as I was forging a connection with Ebtisam.

In the same moment, I decided that I liked Nabiha a lot, and it seemed as though Ebtisam did, too. Nabiha's face relaxed into a look of total absorption whenever she listened to someone speak, and she was highly responsive when anybody said something moving. Her manner was kind and unreserved, and she put all of us at ease.

As we were drinking Mariam's spiced coffee, Nabiha explained to Ebtisam that she had arrived in the United States as a refugee herself in 1997, from a part of Kurdistan that fell in northern Iraq.

"My daughters told me, 'Mom, you have ruined our lives!'" Nabiha recounted in English and then in Arabic. "They hated it here at first. They said, 'We don't understand English, this place is terrible, we want to go home!'"

Her daughters were saying the same sort of things, Ebtisam told us. Nabiha assured her that this was only a phase. It would pass.

"Now, one of my daughters, she is a pediatric dentist, and another daughter, she is studying medicine, to become a psychiatrist," Nabiha said proudly. "And my son, he is an engineer."

Nabiha showed us pictures of her children on her cell phone.

Nabiha had spoken Kurdish at home and had studied Arabic at school. She learned English only after arriving in the United States, by taking classes at a local technical college. Throughout the conversation, there were times when she had to pause and search for the right word in English, and sometimes her English sentences were not completely grammatical. I wondered how much would be lost in translation. As I listened to her comfort Ebtisam, however, I saw how quickly the interpreter was able to build kinship. Ebtisam seemed starved for reassurance about the choices she had made, and it mattered a lot that Nabiha had shared a similar journey.

As we spoke, Mariam and Jakleen half listened and half played with their phones. They were writing messages on Facebook to friends in Iraq, Syria, Turkey, and Germany, and were simultaneously listening to Arabic-language songs or watching Arabic-language videos. Their phones transported them back to the familiar world of the Middle East, allowing them to escape the strange English-speaking environment that surrounded them here. Jakleen and Mariam were sitting on the sofa with their legs intertwined, and it was clear they were especially close. When their little sister Lulu emerged from one of the bedrooms and joined us, she seemed left out, but she handled this with goofy aplomb, clowning around with her mother. Where did the girls go when they were not at school? I asked at one point. They were here, they said. They just stayed in the apartment. I could imagine that huddling on the sofa together felt a lot safer than braving the bus system, where Jakleen's hijab drew taunts and stares.

Ebtisam bought the phones for her daughters after they had gotten lost a few times. Once Jakleen and Mariam had tried to go home from school by a different route than usual, catching a bus that stopped right beside the main parking lot at South, but instead of transferring to a second bus correctly, they rode the first bus all the way to the end of the line. There were hardly any people in the vast echoing bus terminus where they disembarked. They tried speaking to one young man who looked to be roughly their own age, but after Mariam pantomimed making a phone call, he seemed to think that she wanted his phone number, which he happily provided, to Mariam's mortification. Then they found a kindhearted older woman, and this time while Mariam pantomimed holding a phone to her ear, she also said, "Mum Mum!" The woman let them use her phone and even stayed with them until Ebtisam figured out how to find them.

Their initial experiences in the United States had made the girls nostalgic for Turkey. They had learned Turkish quickly and had done well in school there, they said. By contrast, they felt confounded by English, and the difficulties they were having understanding their teachers at South made them feel stupid.

"I think you are very bright and you will learn English quickly," I told them.

"I don't think so!" Jakleen replied in Arabic. "We are not acquiring a lot of English yet."

"It must be hard to be enrolled in Mr. Williams's class, where the sentences that you are making are so basic," I said.

"Yes, I was laughing at myself," Jakleen replied. "I was saying, 'This is for kids.'"

At that point, Nabiha had to leave, but we arranged to meet again. While we were looking at our calendars, Ebtisam grew anxious; she had been forgetting appointments, she confessed. Recently, she had lost her cell phone while she was riding on a bus, which meant she had lost her calendar, her contacts, and all of the photographs she had possessed. The loss of the phone nagged at her. Ebtisam fretted when Nabiha gave her a business card—everybody wanted to give her their cards, and she kept losing those, too. What did American people do with all the cards they collected? I could see that Ebtisam might be fragile. She had mustered all of the determination she possessed to transport her family here, but since then she had been under enormous stress. She was finding English hard to acquire, and she was struggling to figure out how to support the entire family by herself in a place that was more expensive than anywhere else she had ever lived. Due to her lack of English, she had difficulty making friends. There were some Arabic-speaking men who lived at Pine Creek, but they leered at her daughters and spoke disrespectfully to Ebtisam. As a single parent, she had no partner with whom to discuss all of the challenges she faced. Ebtisam had welcomed us into her home with aplomb, but obviously she was going through an enormous struggle, and I sensed that she was lonely. Ebtisam looked as disappointed as I felt when Nabiha said that we had to cut our conversation short.

As we were leaving, I asked how to spell Ebtisam's name. Nabiha wasn't sure how to do that in the Latin script, and Ebtisam helped us figure this out.

"Smile," Ebtisam said to me in English.

"Your name means 'smile'?" I asked, to clarify.

"Yes, that's right," she confirmed through Nabiha.

When she was little, I imagined that Ebtisam's name must have felt like a blessing. Now it seemed more like an exhortation: Smile, for the sake of your children. Smile, even when you might rather weep. Which she had done, I thought, that very evening. I was impressed by Ebtisam; she had a lot of grit. Rapprochement was taking place at a much slower pace than I was accustomed to, however, due to our need to use an interpreter. The obstacles between us were bigger than any I'd surmounted previously, and I had no idea whether I was going to succeed in actually getting to know this woman. But I wanted to, because I could sense the scale of what Ebtisam had lived through, and I liked her style. I left feeling stymied at the brevity of our first conversation but optimistic about the chance of more meaningful encounters because of the warm manner in which we had been received and because of the extent to which Nabiha and Ebtisam had bonded.

4

Do You Want a Pencil?

The third major unit in the newcomer curriculum was called "My School Day," and it consisted of descriptions of time. Mr. Williams's students had trouble remembering the English names for the days of the week, so he wrote a song about that subject. He knew the song was juvenile, but he figured the kids might be entertained to hear him sing it anyway.

Which he did—to the tune of the French nursery rhyme "Frère Jacques."

Monday, Tuesday,
Wednesday, Thursday,
Fri-i-day, Fri-i-day.
These are all school days.
We have school on these days.
Yes we do. Yes we do.
Saturday, Sunday.
Here is the weekend!
I can rest. I can play!
I can't wait for Monday.
It's the most fun day!
Back to school, school is cool!

The performance broke up the monotony, anyway. As the days sped by, almost as fast as in the song, the mornings started off with a bite in the air, then all of the trees in the city started turning bright yellow.

Closer to sea level, fall shows off its glory in bloodred and blazing orange, but Colorado has an abundance of aspens and cottonwoods, and fall manifests as buttery gold.

In the middle of October, a few weeks after the big clump of new students showed up at South, a therapist from Jewish Family Service named Pauline Ng walked into Room 142. "Miss Pauline," as the students called her, was an Asian-American woman with a calm demeanor and short black hair. She wore a black T-shirt, a knee-length brown skirt, and black clogs. Since many of the students had lived through traumatic experiences, Mr. Williams and his team at South believed they might benefit from participating in group therapy, which Jewish Family Service was providing at no cost to the school district. Miss Pauline typically took half of the newcomers away for what she called "group," then brought those students back and borrowed the other half.

Sometimes, if the students did an art therapy project, they would line up at the front of the room afterward to show their classmates what they had made. (The school also employed a full-time social worker, Stephanie Onan, who routinely saw students from all sorts of backgrounds to discuss serious issues including child abuse, suicidal ideation, pregnancy, drug use, and various experiences common among the refugee population, such as rape, parent loss, and exposure to extreme levels of mass violence.) Miss Pauline always separated siblings, as Mr. Williams did when he broke the class into smaller groups. That morning, she beckoned to Jakleen for the first group. She and Mariam conferred hastily in Arabic; they seemed anxious at being separated. Mariam remained seated, her long hair pulled back into its habitual braid, as Jakleen, in her hijab, sullenly stuffed a pair of white earbuds in her ears and left the room with Miss Pauline. "I hate group," Jakleen told me later. I thought it was probably good for her.

Mr. Williams worked with the students who remained. After covering greetings, the school environment, and descriptions of time, Mr. Williams moved on to the kind of language that students might expect to hear on a visit to a store. Their textbook included various lessons on American culture, and this one had to do with different work environments. Mr. Williams put photographs on the Smart Board, showing types of jobs a person might have in America: a food server working at McDonald's, a store clerk selling items at Walmart, a firefighter wearing all of his gear. The students discussed the images for a while. Then Mr. Williams walked over to the whiteboard and wrote examples of the sort of language that they were going to practice that morning.

Worker:
How may I help you?
What size do you need?
What color . . . ?
Can I show you . . . ?

Customer:
I'm looking for some/a _____ [green shoes].
Yes, that would be great!

Mr. Williams asked the students to stand up so that they could behave as if they were customers trying to buy something. He told them to pretend that they had just walked into Walmart and needed school supplies.

"Hi! How may I help you?" Mr. DeRose said to Mariam.

Mariam looked bewildered. She had none of her younger sister's ferocity, and her face radiated soft vulnerability mixed with a hint of panic.

"Hi! How may I help you?" Mr. DeRose asked again.

"Backpack," Mariam said eventually, in an uncertain voice.

"Okay, that will be three hundred dollars!" said Mr. DeRose. Stephanie burst out laughing at the absurd price, which threw Mariam into a state of embarrassed confusion. A rosy blush crept over her face. Had she made a gaffe? Mr. DeRose attempted to reassure Mariam that she had done nothing wrong, yet she seemed too chagrined to listen. The students practiced asking for various items they might need at school for another ten minutes, and then did a written exercise along the same lines. At the end of the lesson, Miss Pauline returned with the rest of the students. When the bell rang for lunch, Jakleen took Mariam's hand and pulled her along on their way to the cafeteria in search of food.

Like many of the other newcomers, Jakleen and Mariam had adopted the habit of pushing their way through the school's jammed hallways and scaling four flights of stairs to the cafeteria, then turning around and walking back downstairs carrying disposable cardboard lunch trays to eat in Room 142. It was more peaceful there, compared with the chaotic cafeteria. Mr. Williams's room represented an oasis of safety in an otherwise jumbled environment where everybody was unintelligible. As a result, the newcomers formed their own separate community, a little apart from the rest of the school. They stayed on the periphery of things. As I watched the girls go, I saw that Jakleen carried a pink backpack, while Mariam's was lavender with white polka dots. Neither had cost close to $300, and the girls knew their price—Mariam's skill at listening to spoken English simply was not good enough yet to hear that Mr. DeRose had said the words "three hundred."

Over the course of the school year, learning would take place in Room 142 at varying rates, depending upon an interplay of factors. In addition to language proximity, exposure to trauma also influenced the rate at which students acquire knowledge. Miss Pauline had explained to Mr. Williams that students still coping with traumatic events were likely to have increased activity in the amygdala. At the same time, there was typically decreased activity in those parts of the frontal lobe where learning takes place. Mr. Williams could go over and over a given lesson, but if a student was in a triggered state, he or she might not learn readily, no matter how good the teacher was.

By the middle of October, most of the students who had been with Mr. Williams since the beginning of the school year were starting to move into early production. Stephanie, from Mexico, and Uyen, from Vietnam, had raced ahead of other students and were producing full sentences already. Nadia and Grace, from Mozambique, showed high comprehension and were able to respond appropriately, albeit in sometimes muddled ways, which was typical of the early phase of production. The Iraqi sisters Mariam and Jakleen, on the other hand, seemed to ping-pong between high comprehension and no comprehension, and I wondered if traumatic memories might be interrupting their learning, but I didn't know enough about their backgrounds to judge. Saúl, the unaccompanied minor from El Salvador, was starting to appreciate how many cognates English had with Spanish. Hsar Htoo, whose family was originally from Burma, appeared to be easing his way gingerly into early production; he was getting better at reading and listening, although speaking remained difficult. And Solomon and Methusella, from the Democratic Republic of Congo, were astonishing Mr. Williams with the rate at which they were rocketing from preproduction straight into production.

Even as all this was happening, new students continued to show up throughout the fall, at the rate of roughly one per week. The next to arrive was Dilli. Impossibly tall, sixteen-year-old Dilli had a body like a reed, and her head was covered in wild skinny braids that pointed in all directions. She came from Eritrea and spoke Kunama—the same language as Amaniel, although Dilli seemed too shy to speak to anybody. She watched everything that happened in total silence, keeping her face impassive. I did not know anything about Dilli's background for a long time, because it was hard to locate an interpreter who spoke Kunama, but eventually I learned that she and her parents had come to the United States directly from a refugee camp in Ethiopia. Her older sister had been left behind (she was married with children of her own), although Dilli's family was hoping she might join them in the United States at some point in the future.

Two more students from Dilli's home country arrived in quick succession. Ksanet, an ambitious young woman who dressed in tailored blazers, appeared in the classroom in the middle of October. A few weeks later, Ksanet's younger brother, Yonatan, joined her. At nineteen, Ksanet became the oldest student in the room; Yonatan was seventeen. They spoke Tigrinya, the primary language of more than half Eritrea's population. Even though they shared a home country, Ksanet and Yonatan could not communicate with Dilli or Amaniel—the Kunama people constitute a small minority and their language is closer in origin to Luo, Dinka, and Maasai, whereas Tigrinya is a Semitic language that is more closely related to Arabic.

Mr. Williams had taught many students from Eritrea before, and he was not surprised to receive four young people from that country in the space of one month. Shortly after Yonatan and Ksanet joined the class, some of Mr. Williams's former students who spoke Tigrinya began haunting Room 142. A young woman named Luwam attached herself closely to Ksanet and began appearing in the classroom so regularly that one day Mr. Williams joked about Luwam being his newest student, before he shooed her out of the room.

From his previous students, Mr. Williams knew that Eritrea shares a contested border with Ethiopia, and the two countries have warred frequently over that territory. Military service is compulsory in Eritrea and can last indefinitely; the army keeps young people for as long as they need bodies. The oppressive regime has caused a large-scale exodus. Months later, Yonatan and Ksanet would reveal to Mr. DeRose that they had been thrown into prison when their family had attempted to leave. After they were released, they slipped over the border into Ethiopia, where they lived in a refugee camp before resettling in the United States.

Lisbeth showed up in Room 142 toward the end of October, around the same time as Ksanet and Yonatan. She had hair that grew in long corkscrew curls, big brown eyes, a mobile face, and a personality as animated as an arcade game. Her wardrobe appeared better suited to a dance hall than a classroom, and she flirted with her teachers as well as her peers. Unlike the other students, she was almost never quiet. She presented a variety of behavioral challenges, but at the same time she acted like a catalyst. Her splashy, boisterous personality added an element of vivacity that had been otherwise missing from the classroom, and her intense desire to communicate with everyone transformed the social interactions taking place there. Basically, Lisbeth got everybody talking.

Because I speak some Spanish, Lisbeth was able to explain to me that she had grown up in the same part of El Salvador as Saúl, an area known as Chalatenango. Stephanie, from Mexico, instantly befriended her. Within days of Lisbeth's arrival, Stephanie was spending a lot of time pulling the new girl's curls out to their full length, then letting them go and watching them spring back into place. In her first weeks, Lisbeth felt dazed by the scale of South, which was three times the size of the school she had attended in El Salvador. The building was vast and confusing—in one area, you could take half a staircase up to a level that was located strangely in between the second and third floors, and elsewhere there was an almost unreachable fifth floor, hidden inside the clock tower. All of the hallways in the enormous building looked exactly alike, each featuring shiny tan linoleum floors lit by long panels of fluorescent lights, and rows and rows of tan metal lockers. But Stephanie kindly walked Lisbeth upstairs to the cafeteria, showed her where her classrooms were located, and introduced her to Spanish-speaking friends. The two girls jabbered constantly in Spanish. This drew Stephanie away from Uyen (and distracted Lisbeth from paying attention to Mr. Williams), but soon Lisbeth adopted Stephanie's habit of texting Uyen via Google Translate. Lisbeth also discovered that she could communicate fairly well with Nadia and Grace, who always understood her Spanish even if she could not entirely follow their Portuguese.

Lisbeth was so chatty that Mr. Williams found he could not place her at the same table as Stephanie, Uyen, Nadia, or Grace. If he did, she would take over and nobody else would be able to work. After a while, Mr. Williams assigned Methusella to sit at the same table as Lisbeth; he hoped that Lisbeth's effervescent personality would add some joy to Methusella's life, and he hoped that Methusella would anchor flighty Lisbeth. Methusella was proving to be the most diligent student in the room, and Mr. Williams imagined that he would be able to concentrate despite the distraction. Instead, Lisbeth started coaching Methusella on popular phrases in Spanish, and pretty soon Methusella was greeting Lisbeth each day by saying "*Cómo estás?*"

When Lisbeth arrived, most of the students were still remaining silent unless Mr. Williams called on them to speak—the room had continued to be preternaturally quiet. Everything began to change with Lisbeth's arrival, however, as if the constant dialogue she was always trying to have jump-started the very idea of talking in general. Early attempts at conversation were terribly stilted. At one point, Methusella walked over to Yonatan, and said simply, "Tigrinya?" Yonatan nodded. That was the whole conversation: one word. But it represented one of the early attempts by a student (other than Lisbeth) to interact socially with somebody from a different country. They were trying, and the attempts began in earnest only after Lisbeth entered the room.

If she wasn't whispering to Methusella, or walking over to interrupt Stephanie, Lisbeth slid her smartphone out of her backpack and pretended to use it for translation purposes, which Mr. Williams allowed, but instead pulled up Facebook, where she had 4,990 friends, most of whom she had never met. Of all the newcomers in Room 142, Lisbeth was the queen of selfies. Throughout the school day, she took dozens of photographs of herself—alone, with another newcomer, or with one of the other Spanish-speaking students scattered throughout the building—which she posted to Facebook relentlessly. Lisbeth thought it was important to alert adults in the room about any content on social media that struck her as risqué. "Miss! Miss!" Lisbeth called out to me one day. "*Mira!*" She held up her phone to show me a Facebook post of a young woman wearing extremely short shorts and bending over to find something in a school locker. Lisbeth made a shocked expression, lifting her eyebrows skyward—she was aghast and bewitched and in love with the drama of it all. "*Muy interesante,*" I told her, and then asked about the assignment she was supposed to be doing.

Mr. Williams vigilantly policed the use of electronic devices. After warning Lisbeth that she could use her phone only for translation, he confiscated the device for the rest of the day when he caught her using it for other purposes. She was not the only offender—Jakleen and Mariam also had a hard time putting down their phones, which they used frequently as a form of escape from the English-speaking environment. Jakleen surreptitiously texted friends in the Middle East using WhatsApp, while Mariam spent large portions of the school day whispering in Arabic to her boyfriend, using earbuds and a microphone hidden underneath her long hair. Abdullah was twenty-nine years old and lived in Iraq. They were engaged, she said. I expressed surprise that her fiancé was twice her age, but she said this was considered normal in Middle Eastern societies. When he caught the Iraqi sisters socializing, Mr. Williams confiscated their phones, too—but Mariam got away with the whispered calls for ages, because few teachers realized what she was doing.

While all this was going on around them, Solomon and Methusella invariably remained absorbed in their schoolwork. Solomon wrote while sitting bent over at the waist, with his nose four inches from his notebook. This doubled-over posture exemplified for me his desire to focus scrupulously on his studies. If he was copying something that Mr. Williams had written on the whiteboard, then he rocked back and forth, bending over his table to write, and then leaning way back to look at the whiteboard with his forehead wrinkled in absorption. Methusella was just as diligent but twice as fast as his older brother at completing his lessons. The interruption of schooling was another major factor that interfered with the ability to acquire English, and Mr. Williams believed the reason that Solomon lagged behind his younger brother was largely related to this issue. From speaking with the boys, he had learned that Solomon had been taken out of school for several years, whereas Methusella had remained in school almost continuously.

After I had been coming to the room every day for a while, Methusella began getting up out of his chair when he finished his work, coming over, and wordlessly putting his notebook down in front of me. He had figured out that I would happily correct his work if he did this. Other students soon began to follow his lead, but Methusella was the first to realize that I was an underutilized resource in Room 142. I admired his initiative, and once he began walking over to show me his work, I could see that his writing was more advanced than that of any other student in the room.

The bigger the class grew, the harder it was for Mr. Williams to control the increasingly complex behavioral dynamics while at the same time juggling his academic goals for the newcomers, all of whom were learning at varying rates. Some teachers are extroverted and shine at the front of a classroom with many eyes upon them. They are entertainers, essentially. Mr. Williams, on the other hand, was best at one-on-one interactions. As much as possible, he structured the school day so that he could work individually with students, pushing each of them along as he carefully monitored their progress. In this way, he came to know his students better than some teachers ever did, and under his thoughtful attention, they blossomed.

On Yonatan's first day at South, I watched Mr. Williams work with him for about half an hour, as was his habit with each new arrival, so that he could assess the student's reading and writing abilities. Yonatan had shown up wearing jeans, a charcoal-gray dress shirt, a large crucifix, and a stony expression. Mr. Williams broke the class up into small groups—Jakleen and Mariam were absent that day, but everybody else had turned up—and the Goodwill volunteers dispersed themselves around the classroom, sitting down at various tables. This freed Mr. Williams to focus on Yonatan, whom he asked to sit down beside him.

They were reading a book called *Using Rocks*, which Mr. Williams had chosen deliberately because the subject matter allowed him to illustrate the meaning of unfamiliar words through pictures. Mr. Williams began by leafing through the book, pointing to the photographs, and saying the names of various structures made of rocks. The teacher wore a white dress shirt that day, with black trousers, and looked especially fastidious.

"We have mountains," said Mr. Williams. He turned a page. "What do you see in these pictures?"

Silence.

"This is a wall," said Mr. Williams, answering his own question. "It is made from rocks. Look at that giant wall. This is wall, yes. W-A-L-L. But also rocks."

He turned to Yonatan. "Do you know what this is called?"

Silence.

"Bridge," prompted Mr. Williams. "Bridge. Can you say that word?"

"Bridge," Yonatan echoed carefully.

"What do you see here?" Mr. Williams pointed to a stone building with what looked like a steeple.

"Church," Yonatan said immediately.

"Church, yes, that is a church. Is it made from rocks?"

Yonatan looked baffled.

"Rocks—this material. Is it made from rocks?"

"Yes."

"It *is* made from rocks, yes."

Mr. Williams turned back to the beginning of the book and read it aloud, enunciating each word carefully. ("These are rocks. Rocks are found everywhere. This is a path. It is made from rocks. This path is made from rocks, too. This is a wall. It is made from rocks.") Then he had Yonatan read out loud with him, and after that he asked the student to read out loud by himself. The large crucifix that Yonatan wore swung forward when he leaned over the book. He looked frustrated, as if it was hard to tackle material so basic, when he was seventeen and in a hurry to start his new life. Yonatan stumbled over the unfamiliar words and mispronounced a few of them, but Mr. Williams never told him that he was saying things the wrong way; instead he simply repeated what Yonatan had just said, showing him the correct pronunciation. Then Yonatan would try again, and his English would be a little better. Finally, Mr. Williams leafed through the book, asking questions to gauge Yonatan's comprehension. Mr. Williams asked what material had been used to make a path.

"Rocks," answered Yonatan.

"Can you write that?"

The question perplexed Yonatan. Mr. Williams pantomimed the act of writing, as he asked again, "Can you write that?"

Yonatan did not appear to have anything with which he could write.

"Do you want a pencil?"

Yonatan did not seem to know what that was.

"I have some pencils right here." Mr. Williams got up to fetch one, and when he returned, he made sure to repeat the word again, asking, "Would you like this pencil?"

Mr. Williams was curious to see if Yonatan could shape the letters of the Latin alphabet. Tigrinya is a Semitic language, and uses the Ge'ez script, which is an abugida, or a type of writing in which each symbol represents both a consonant and a vowel. Yonatan took the pencil, scribbled the word "rocks," and handed what he had written to Mr. Williams, who nodded vigorously. Yonatan had produced the Latin alphabet easily.

By this point, the hard expression on his face had begun to soften. Mr. Williams asked if he had any questions. There was one word Yonatan did not understand, and he reached across to point at it. The problematic word was "this."

Usually, Mr. Williams tried to illustrate the meaning of unknown words by pantomime or by a picture, but those tools were useless for an abstract concept such as "this." Instead the teacher said "this" over and over while pointing to various objects—"this is a book, this is a chair, this is a table"—until Yonatan got the idea.

Mr. Williams asked Yonatan to complete a handout with questions about the reading, and left to check on the other reading groups. Then he returned to look over Yonatan's answers.

"Good job, Yonatan!" Mr. Williams said. "Nice work today."

Yonatan tried to hand the pencil back, but Mr. Williams held up his hands.

"You can have that pencil. You can have it."

Yonatan started to walk away, then turned around.

"Thank you," he said.

As I observed Mr. Williams read with Yonatan, I remembered that while listening to the radio in my car that morning, I had caught part of a news story about Donald Trump's candidacy for president. "We *need* to *build* a *wall*," Trump had said, in his iambic cadences. As Mr. Williams worked with Yonatan, I found myself thinking about how much I admired this teacher who lived to build bridges between people, even when the chasms dividing them were especially large. This was a fraught moment to arrive as a refugee in the United States, and I thought the political climate itself also affected what was taking place in the classroom. Xenophobia was not listed formally as a factor that inhibited learning among ELA students, but as the weeks slipped by and the cacophony of the presidential election ratcheted up, elevating all kinds of sentiments in the voting populace, including a virulent dislike of people from other countries, I came to think of the fear some people in my own country felt toward foreigners as an issue that itself inhibited the newcomers' learning. They were acutely sensitive and could detect when they were misunderstood.

Slowly, over time, I learned how much I did not know about them and how much they did not know about life in America. At the end of October, for example, shortly after the arrival of Ksanet, Yonatan, and Lisbeth, Mr. Williams had the students rearrange their seats by language groups. Then he asked them to take out their textbooks to begin going over a lesson about holidays celebrated in the United States. Halloween was four days away. The basic idea of Halloween was familiar to Lisbeth, Saúl, and Stephanie—who were sitting together at the table assigned to Spanish speakers—because Mexico and El Salvador have similar traditions. The holiday was largely unknown to the students from Africa, Asia, and the Middle East, however; a Muslim parent later told me that people at his mosque found Halloween especially befuddling, as they feared a holiday that celebrated black magic might constitute devil worship. Why would Americans worship spiders, skeletons, and ghouls?

Mr. Williams asked his students to complete the following sentence:

Halloween is a _____ that is _____ on October _____.

Then he listed the words they could use to fill in the blanks:

if
the
celebrated
holiday
31
Friday

This looked like a rudimentary exercise, but the newcomers had only just learned the English words for the days of the week and the months of the year, and it took them a little while to complete. After everybody had finished the sentence, the class went over other vocabulary words related to Halloween. Mr. Williams asked about "ghost" and "jack-o'-lantern." Did they know other terms related to Halloween?

"*Una bruja!*" Lisbeth called out happily.

"A witch," translated Mr. Williams. "Lisbeth, do they have haunted houses in El Salvador?"

"*Sí!*"

She had arrived less than a week ago, yet she was already answering questions. Mr. Williams could see that Lisbeth was going to light up his classroom. He didn't mind that she had answered in Spanish—she had answered correctly, which meant that she had understood his query.

"Mariam, do they have haunted houses in Iraq?"

"No!" Mariam said, shaking her head. She looked slightly alarmed at the idea. Her braid was rumpled that day, as if she had slept on it.

"Have you ever worn a costume for Halloween?"

"No," Mariam said wistfully.

"Stand up if you have eaten a pumpkin," suggested Mr. Williams.

Grace stood up. She said that she had eaten pumpkin soup and pumpkin cake. Most of the room looked mystified about what exactly a pumpkin might be, so Mr. Williams paused to explain. Pumpkins grew in a garden; they were big, round, and orange; you could bake them in a pie. Mr. Williams showed the class a picture of a pumpkin.

"Stand up if you have been to a haunted house," said his aide, Mr. DeRose.

Stephanie stood up immediately.

"*Casa de terror,*" Saúl gallantly translated for Lisbeth.

The three Spanish-speaking students understood the concept of a haunted house, but students who spoke Karen, Tigrinya, Kunama, Swahili, and Arabic seemed bewildered. Why would anybody want to make a house appear terrifying?

Inside the U.S.A. focused on American culture, but Mr. Williams knew that for foreign-born students to grasp the meaning of the conversation, it would be helpful to discuss concepts with which they were already familiar, so he broadened the topic. Could the students name other holidays they had celebrated in their home countries?

"I like to celebrate *Navidad,*" said Saúl.

"Okay," said Mr. Williams. "And in English, that's Christmas."

"Thanksgiving," Stephanie said in English.

"Great."

Mr. Williams turned to Mariam. "What are some of the holidays you celebrated in Iraq?"

Mariam said nothing. It was not clear whether or not she followed his meaning.

"Ramadan?" prompted Mr. DeRose.

Silence.

"Is that the most important holiday in Iraq?" asked Mr. Williams.

Silence.

Mariam knew it was her turn to speak, but she seemed uncertain what to say. Was this because it was hard for her to produce spoken English, or was the subject of religious holidays in Iraq more complicated than her teachers realized? It seemed as though there was a lot that Mariam wanted to share, although she could not verbalize any of it in English. Meanwhile, the teachers wanted an answer to what they saw as a simple query: Was Ramadan the most important holiday in Iraq?

"Yes?" ventured Mariam, her tone making a question out of the answer.

And it was true—most people living in Iraq would consider Ramadan a significant holiday. Mariam's family had lost their place in Iraqi society after Muslim fanatics had turned on them, however, and during their time in exile, questions about how the girls would classify themselves and which religious holidays to mark had grown only more complex. In terms of understanding Mariam's predicament, I was as blind as her teachers: I saw her sister's hijab, and I thought, Muslim. But nothing was so simple, and my assumptions were causing me to misunderstand the girls entirely.

5
Have You Seen War?

At about nine o'clock one Saturday morning, I knocked on the door of the rented house on Wabash Street where I believed that Solomon and Methusella were living with their family. Nobody answered. The house had a weathered clapboard exterior painted tan, but not recently. The yard was filled with dried brown leaves flung over bare dirt, surrounded by a chain-link fence. The homes in the neighborhood were modest, and it had a significantly higher rate of crime than surrounding locations. I lived less than ten minutes away, but on the other side of Colfax Avenue, an economic dividing line in this part of the city.

I knocked again, but it seemed nobody was home. I knocked a third time, more loudly, and suddenly the front door swung open. A small child stood before me, wearing a green silk party dress with sequins and a large bow. The dress was a little grubby.

"Hello there," I said to the girl. "Is this the house where Solomon and Methusella live?"

"No!" the girl in the party dress said emphatically.

The boys had written down the address for me in my notebook. I double-checked the number of the house. It was correct.

"Solomon doesn't live here?" I ventured again.

"No!" said the child again. She spoke with confidence.

"Okay, I'm sorry, maybe I am at the wrong house. Do you have a brother named Solomon?"

"Solomon?" she said, brightening. "Oh, yes—Solomon is right here!"

She pronounced her brother's name with a British accent, so that it sounded quite different from the way I had been saying it. The girl's

59

name was Sifa ("praise" in Swahili), and she was Solomon's sister. Soon a bevy of small children flocked around my knees. Two girls with bright yellow hair ribbons took me by the hand; one of them had on a sparkly purple tutu, while the other was naked. One of these girls was Solomon and Methusella's sister Zawadi (Swahili for "gift") while the other was their niece. A small boy ran around us in circles, wearing blue shorts and clutching a green T-shirt in his hands. This was their brother Ombeni ("prayer"). We passed by a bedroom. I glanced inside and saw two twin mattresses covered in plastic wrap, even though the mattresses were clearly being used, as comforters lay strewn about. The children forgot about me and swept into the living room, where they began dancing exuberantly to African gospel music videos playing at top volume on a large TV.

In the kitchen, I found Solomon's mother, busy at the stove. Beya was forty-five years old and had a beautiful face that she held completely still while I spoke in English. Her feet were bare and she wore an outfit that spoke of life in the African countryside: a floor-length skirt of multicolored cotton, a red T-shirt, and a green wool beanie perched on top of her head. Her hat said MARVEL AVENGERS on it and appeared to have been borrowed from one of the children.

"*Jambo*," I said in Swahili.

At the sound of the familiar greeting, a quick flash of a lightning-swift smile lit up Beya's features. She answered warmly, but I could not understand what she said. I gave her a pineapple and coffee cake that I had brought for the family. Solomon came down a flight of stairs and helped me explain the gifts. I thanked his mother for welcoming me to their home, and she said *asante sana* (thank you) for coming. Solomon and his mother conferred, and then Solomon told me that his mother was inviting me to sit down. When I sat at the kitchen table, one of the girls with yellow ribbons climbed into my lap, where she amused herself by gathering my hair into a ponytail over and over again. Ombeni pulled the green T-shirt over his head but did not put his arms through the sleeves. Solomon explained that his oldest brother, Gideon, was married and had three children of his own; Gideon and his family did not live in this house, but Beya was watching her grandchildren that day.

Solomon and I were still sorting through the question of which children were his siblings and which were his nieces and nephews when Solomon's father, Tchiza, entered the kitchen. He was a dignified man of fifty-two, wearing a navy collared shirt and navy trousers. He studied my face intently as he said hello. I felt as though I were looking at a much older Solomon—both their faces were dominated by the same high cheekbones, although Tchiza's black hair included strands of gray, his face was lined, and his brown eyes were rimmed with pale blue.

Almost immediately the doorbell rang, and we were joined by the interpreter I had hired. Julius was from Sudan, but he recognized Solomon's father, because he had translated for the family at a recent visit to a medical clinic. The two men greeted each other warmly in Swahili. All of us sat down at the kitchen table, and Solomon's mother brought over a tall plastic pitcher, which held some type of reddish-purple semiliquid substance. Julius exclaimed in happy recognition, and then explained to me that this was a Congolese version of porridge, made out of millet. Beya poured the porridge into coffee mugs and handed one to each of us; apparently, Congolese people drank their cereal. The porridge was hot and delicious, sweetened with sugar. It reminded me of oatmeal, although the consistency was more grainy.

"Do you have this every day?" I asked Solomon.

"Not every day!" he exclaimed in surprise. I understood this to mean his mother had made something special, because they had a visitor.

When his mother handed a mug of porridge to his father, Tchiza said *asante* and gave his wife a look of loving regard. As she smiled back at him, I was struck by the couple's obvious warmth.

I told Tchiza that he should be proud of his sons. Solomon and Methusella were very good students. "They are learning very quickly," I said.

Tchiza asked Julius a question in Swahili.

The interpreter told me that Tchiza wondered if I were their teacher.

The misunderstanding surprised me. I had sent home a letter written in Swahili, and believed I had described myself plainly, but apparently that was not the case. I put aside my list of typed questions and instead tried to explain slowly and clearly who I was.

"I am a visitor to the classroom," I said. "I am a journalist, and I've been working on a book about their teacher and their classroom."

I explained that I was hoping to write about several families who had children at South in more detail, which was why I was here. I told Tchiza that the classroom served as a mirror of the global crisis, and that by telling the stories of various students, it would be possible to illustrate the crisis as a whole. I thought he could help me understand what was happening in the Congo, for example.

Tchiza had some questions for me.

"Are you writing this book because you are still in school? Is this something you are doing so that you can graduate?" he asked. "Or this is your hobby?"

For me, writing was more than a hobby, I replied. I had been a professional journalist for more than twenty-five years and had written two other books. I gave Tchiza a copy of my first book that I had brought with me and explained that it was about undocumented students whose families had emigrated from Mexico. We talked about that subject for a while. I also told Tchiza a little bit about my own background and how that had sparked my interest in these subjects. My parents had been born in another country, and so had I—we had moved to the United States when I was one year old.

"So are you telling me you were not born here?" Tchiza asked in Swahili.

"I was not born here," I confirmed.

"Where were you born?" Tchiza asked.

"My mother grew up on a farm in Ireland—" I began.

"Ireland," said Julius. "England. London."

I restrained myself from pointing out that Ireland and England are not at all the same thing.

"Europe?" Tchiza asked.

"Yes, Europe," I said. "My mother and father both grew up in Ireland. They came here in 1965, and I was one year old. I have been living in this country for fifty years."

Julius translated all of this.

"So it's like you were born in this country, pretty much, because

62

when you came here you were so little you didn't understand anything else," Tchiza said in Swahili.

"Exactly," I confirmed.

Beya sat down at the table with us. I asked her if it was hard to find the ingredients to make Congolese food. Was it problematic for her to find familiar items, like the porridge we were eating?

Beya rolled her eyes dramatically and slumped against Tchiza to indicate just how difficult it was. Julius didn't have to translate at all—I understood her perfectly. The impassive manner Beya had worn when I first arrived seemed to be a mask, put on before a stranger. It fell away once she felt safe, and underneath she was a highly expressive woman. I liked her theatrical eye rolling.

Tchiza said his sons had struggled tremendously during their first weeks in Room 142. "It was very difficult for them at the beginning, because when the teacher would say something, they could not understand. But at the same time, the other students could not explain to them, even if they knew, because they had no way to communicate. Pretty much, the one sitting next to them, they did not speak the same language. They could not talk to one another. So they could not say, This is what the teacher wants. It was really, really frustrating. When they came home, they were so frustrated, because they could not understand anything. But as time passed, they began to understand more and more."

We talked about what life was like for Tchiza in the United States. He worked as a dishwasher in a cafeteria at a corporate headquarters. I had washed dishes for several years when I was in college, and we commiserated about the nature of the work. I remembered leaving my dishwashing job feeling greasy, and Tchiza used his hands to indicate how he got dirty water all over his body. My job had been part-time and temporary, however, whereas Tchiza had no idea when or if he might find another kind of work. In the Congo, Tchiza had completed tenth grade, which was an unusually high level of education for a man living in a rural part of that country. He had worked as a farmer, but he had also consulted with other farmers in his region, seeking to help them produce more food. People had come to view him as a leader, and at one point he had even run for public office. Now he washed dishes for a living—a job that was dull and wearying. He commuted by bus, and it took him almost two hours each way. Tchiza spoke four languages fluently—Swahili, French, Kinyarwanda, and a tribal language. During a subsequent visit, I would find him seated in a chair, teaching himself English by reading a creased English-French pocket dictionary, which he had found at Goodwill for $1. He understood a lot of what I said, but his ability to speak English remained poor, which limited his work opportunities. He was grateful to have any job, however, and he never complained about washing dishes being beneath him.

What Tchiza found most difficult about life in the United States was something more intangible: the way people in this country seemed to prejudge him. If they discovered his intelligence, they reacted with surprise. "When you are black, people don't look at you as if you can even do the thing you are doing," he offered. "When you are black, pretty much you are nothing. That's the assumption. But at the same time, I know more than maybe people think. People wonder, You are black—how do you know it?"

I told him I understood that here black people were constantly underestimated by white people. I had visited Africa once, many years ago, when my college roommate was teaching English in a rural school in western Kenya. I had glimpsed how different the matter of identity seemed to be there. I could feel the difference between the two places in this regard, I said.

"It's a good thing you have been there," Tchiza told me. "That's what the human being is supposed to be like. Judge me by my character. Not because of my color, not because of how I look."

In the living room, the small children had switched to watching cartoons, and the clamor of their shows threaded through our conversation as we turned to the subject of war. I asked Tchiza if he could help me understand what his family had endured. From conversations with Solomon and Methusella, I knew that the family had lived on the eastern side of the Democratic Republic of Congo, not far from the city of Goma. And from reading about the Congo, I knew that this area had experienced more violence than any other part of the DRC. One day during their lunch hour, the boys had told me that their family had escaped from the DRC in 2008, and had spent seven years living in a refugee settlement in Uganda. The boys had done the first half of their schooling in the Congo and the second half in Uganda. Solomon had stopped going to school because he was needed to help with the chores and watch the younger children, as well as guard the home against intruders. Originally, Solomon had been ahead of Methusella in school, but by this point he had fallen behind. Both boys had seemed to find this reversal funny, Methusella in a way that suggested it made him feel proud, and Solomon in a way that suggested he felt embarrassed.

The boys had told me the names of their closest friends at the refugee settlement—Methusella had been particularly close to a boy named Stivin—and in their voices I could hear how awfully they missed the friends they had left behind. They had not yet made any friends in America, the boys said. But they were happy to be in the United States nonetheless, even if they were lonely, because in ten hundred ways, life in America was easier.

When I asked the boys why their family had left the Congo, Solomon said, "The problem was, soldiers fighting."

Methusella added, "Maybe at night, maybe when you are sleeping, soldiers fight, and so you run away from the house and you have to hide yourself."

"Where would you hide?" I asked.

"In the bush," Methusella replied.

They could not remember an extended period of peace; all the years they spent in the Congo were marked by warfare. Solomon and Methusella seemed to have a sense of mission about educating people in the developed world about what was happening in the DRC. At the same time, I was conscious of the fact that the boys were young and had only just arrived in the United States. They were very close to my own son in age, and we were speaking over lunch, while they were in the middle of their school day. I would not have wanted a journalist grilling my son about things that were bound to be upsetting while he was at school, so I did not press for details about what horrors they might have witnessed. Instead I had asked if it would be possible to meet their parents. Yes, the boys had said. But not during the week, because their father worked long hours. It would be better to visit on the weekend.

I explained to Tchiza that the boys had told me a little bit about their time in the Congo, but I was hoping to hear from him the full story of the family's journey. Tchiza agreed that consulting him would be better than interviewing his sons. He waved his hand at Solomon. "Even my children," he said, "they don't know. The elders, you know how it is—you know how to go from here to here, when you are walking. You know what the trip is going to be like, you know how difficult it will be. With the kids, they don't know. They just follow you."

The only problem was that Tchiza worried I wouldn't understand what he and his family had lived through. Some things are simply untranslatable.

"People here, most of them don't know what a war means, actually," he observed. "They don't know."

I acknowledged this was true. The wars my country had fought while I was alive had all taken place on foreign soil.

"You've been living here for fifty years," he continued. "Have you seen war?"

"Never," I conceded.

"Here there are gangs, and gang shootings, but that is nothing," Tchiza said dismissively, brushing the air away with one hand.

Julius spoke up at this point to tell us his story. He was from southern Sudan (he left that area before it became the separate country of South Sudan). Once upon a time, he had been a child soldier, or *askari watoto*. Speaking first in Swahili and then in English, Julius explained that he had come to the United States at age sixteen, without any family members. He would have been the same age as Methusella, I thought to myself. Earlier, Methusella had come over to say hello but then he retired to another part of the house; Solomon remained at the kitchen table and was listening intently to our conversation. Julius pulled open his warm-up jacket to show us that he was wearing his King Soopers work uniform, because he needed to go from here directly to the grocery store where he was employed. He pointed out his name tag, which said JULIUS. ONE OF THE LOST BOYS.

"So *you* understand," Tchiza said to Julius in Swahili. "You know what war is."

The two men looked at each other, and then they turned to me. There was a lull in the conversation. In their eyes I saw a question: What are we supposed to do about the terrible innocence of Americans? My life had always been safe and secure, even as conflict raged across other parts of the globe. How could I tell the story of a family from the Democratic Republic of Congo? Even if Tchiza had wanted to explain, where would he begin?

Tchiza mused, "If I see a dent in a wall here, that triggers memories of home. Because back home, everywhere you go, the walls are filled with holes. And you know, when you look at them, what made each one of those holes."

The walls of my country were not riddled with bullet holes. I told Tchiza that I could understand what his family had lived through only with his help—but perhaps the rest of the story should wait for another day, as Julius needed to get to his job at the grocery store. If we talked any longer, we were going to make him late. Besides, we had already taken up most of Tchiza's morning, and he probably wanted to enjoy some time with his family. Tchiza agreed that it would be better to resume the conversation at another time.

"The problem with life in America is, you cannot see your kids," Tchiza said regretfully. "They leave for school at six o'clock in the morning. And then it's time for me to go to work. When I come back in the evening, the kids are in bed already, the small ones. And the older boys, they are busy doing their homework. It's just so difficult. Sitting like this—it's not possible, most days of the week. There is no time to sit around the table together. Only on the weekend is there time to be with your family."

Like so many things about America, this sort of schedule was entirely new to him.

Before we left, Solomon asked a question about the parent-teacher conferences that Mr. Williams had mentioned recently. His father would be at work. Could one of his brothers come in his place? I told him I believed that would be fine. We could double-check with Mr. Williams by email.

"Oh!" said Solomon. "You can talk to him by email?"

"Yes, we can talk to him by email," I assured him.

Using my phone, I sent an email to both Mr. Williams and Solomon's older brother Gideon, who spoke English, so that they could communicate about the parent-teacher conference. Then Julius asked Solomon if he knew much about ROTC. On a day when Julius had visited the boys' classroom to help me speak with them in Swahili, a student from Kenya had dropped by, wearing a blue Air Force uniform. As we sat at the kitchen table, Julius urged Solomon to speak with the Kenyan student about the advantages of the military recruitment program. "ROTC, it's a very good program," the interpreter advised. "Very good. You should ask her about it."

"Did you do ROTC?" I asked Julius.

"Yes, I did, but I was also running. So I got a scholarship for running. But it's a very good program."

"You end up in the military afterward," I pointed out.

"You only have to serve for four years," countered Julius. "Then you can opt out. It's a good program, I've been here twenty years, I know. I've got friends who are generals now in the army because of that. They don't even see bullets fired. They sit at a table like this, doing the planning."

"So I agree with you, it's a very good program in terms of the economic benefits," I said. "But I'm wondering—Solomon and Methusella, after they've seen war, would they really want to become soldiers?"

Solomon burst out laughing when I said this. It seemed to me that he was laughing in relief because somebody had mentioned out loud that it might be possible to have such a hesitation.

"I don't think that would be a problem," Julius insisted.

"I think I can do that program when I am good with English," Solomon said diplomatically.

"It will not take you that long to learn," Julius reassured him. "By the time you are ready for college, you will be fine. You don't have to wait. Look, you can start now."

Then Julius really did have to go. I left with him, feeling some consternation that after I had brought him to this house, he had tried to sell Solomon on ROTC. I wasn't sure that I agreed with Julius that the program would be good for the boys.

As we walked to the door, the small children shouted enthusiastically, "Bye-bye!" Then they started giggling, as if this were the funniest thing in the world.

I thanked the boys' mother once more. Both parents walked out of the house and accompanied us to the gate in the chain-link fence.

"This is how we did things in Africa," Tchiza explained. It was customary to walk someone outside, as a sign of respect. We said *asante* several times. I waved goodbye, and Tchiza waved back with both hands.

Later, I found myself turning over in my mind the depth of intention Tchiza put into everything. I could see that he did nothing casually, not even waving. Visiting the family's home, I had stepped into an alternate universe, culturally. We had different ideas about how to say hello, how to say goodbye, what kinds of hats to wear, how to eat porridge. On the subject of war, apparently, my own perspective was rather blinkered. How much more did I not know about life in the Democratic Republic of Congo?

6

Bonita

"Guys, what month are we in now?" Mr. Williams asked one Tuesday morning as Thanksgiving approached.

"November," Stephanie said promptly.

"Is tomorrow Thursday?" he asked.

"No," said Stephanie, Nadia, Grace, and Uyen in unison.

"Is tomorrow Friday?"

"No!" cried the girls.

"Is tomorrow Wednesday?"

"Yes!"

It was Tuesday. There had been no school the day before, and Mr. Williams asked the students how they had spent their free time. Saúl reported that he had been bored. As always, Saúl was dressed in track pants and a T-shirt, with his hair messy from sleep. Lately he had begun calling me *tía* and crooning the lyrics of Spanish-language love songs to all the female Spanish speakers in the room. I believed it had become something of a game for Saúl to see what he could get away with singing without my realizing what he was saying. My Spanish slang was non-existent, and I was fairly certain he was getting away with quite a lot. *Adorable*, as they say in Spanish (another perfect cognate).

"Methusella, how about you?" asked Mr. Williams. "Were you happy? Bored? Sad?"

"So-so," he said.

This was becoming one of Methusella's favorite expressions. He seemed to like the way the word sounded, and perhaps he also liked the fact that it allowed him to answer personal questions without revealing much. He and Solomon moved through the classroom tentatively, alert—poised on the verge of flight. I thought I had never seen human beings so fully present yet so ready to bolt.

It snowed on eight separate days that November. Mr. Williams worried when he saw some of the newcomers arrive at school wearing thin jackets instead of proper coats. For many, it was their first experience of winter. He sent an email about this to the school's community liaison, who reached out to a network of parents and outside organizations. She provided donated winter clothing, which Mr. Williams distributed privately.

No matter how bad the weather got, most of the newcomers materialized faithfully—but not the sisters from Iraq. One day, Jakleen and Mariam woke up to a furious blizzard but gamely trudged three-quarters of a mile to the bus stop in their tennis shoes and then took the bus all the way to the school, only to discover that the doors were locked. They waited outside the school for half an hour, banging on various doors, standing on one leg and then the other, trying to wiggle their wet, frozen toes, before someone conveyed to them successfully that it was a snow day, which was a new concept for them. By then the snow had soaked the bottom half of their jeans, and they could no longer feel their legs below the knees. Jakleen was crying from the cold, which stung her cheeks. She wound her hijab over her face, but the thin scarf was ineffective. They rode the bus back home, slogged from the bus stop all the way back to the apartment, and clambered back into their beds to get warm. The experience of being stuck outside in that storm seemed to frighten Jakleen and Mariam, and afterward the two girls skipped school anytime the weather was bad.

Mr. Williams worried about whether the sisters would progress in their learning, because of the number of absences they were accumulating. If they missed too much school, they might even have to repeat newcomer class. He dreaded the idea of *that* conversation. Mr. Williams decided to arrange a buddy system, if he could track down peer mentors who spoke the right home language for every student in Room 142. South had many students who spoke Arabic, and finding the right mentors for Jakleen and Mariam would be easy, but it would be challenging to find a mentor for Dilli, who spoke Kunama, or for Hsar Htoo, who spoke Karen.

A guidance counselor knew exactly whom to assign to Jakleen and Mariam: Sama and Sana. They were high-achieving twins from Iraq who spoke fluent English and were outperforming many native-born students in the high school's Advanced Placement classes. Nobody on the staff could keep their names straight until Sama started going by "Sam." Their older sister, Oula, a senior at South, had just spent the summer months enrolled in a program at Harvard; the summer before that, she had gone to a camp at Stanford. Like her, Sam and Sana were also getting straight A's. If anybody could help Jakleen and Mariam perform better at school, the counselor thought, it would be the well-adjusted Iraqi twins. Mr. Williams hoped the other two sisters could have a positive influence on Jakleen and Mariam's attendance.

At the same time that Mr. Williams was worrying about clothing his students properly for inclement weather, keeping them inside his classroom, evaluating their progress accurately, and assimilating all of the additional newcomers who kept arriving every month, he also spent a fair amount of time trying to think up novel ways to impart meaning to the intimidated teenagers that the war-torn parts of the world kept sending his way. One lesson, on a blustery day in the middle of November, had to do with the meaning of basic verbs. To make the lesson more fun, Mr. Williams decided to play a glorified version of Simon Says. He asked the entire class to stand and act out the meaning of various verbs, which he wrote on the Smart Board: listen, show, point, read, talk, walk, run, see, poke, scare, think, throw, write, learn, fly, jump, make, and cook.

Mr. Williams demonstrated for the students how they should flap their arms when he said "fly" and jog in place when he said "run" and pull their arm back when he said "throw." The technical term for what Mr. Williams was doing is "total physical response," a teaching method highly popular among ELA instructors. His colleague Ben Speicher was employing the same approach with the newcomer students when he taught them math upstairs. So far, the students could act out addition, subtraction, multiplication, and division. If Mr. Speicher said the word "addition," they crossed their arms vertically and horizontally to make a plus sign; if he said "multiplication," they crossed their arms diagonally to make an X. Acting things out was entertaining, but coordinating physical movement with intellectual concepts also helped foreign-speaking students understand and remember English terms by using various parts of the brain at once to reinforce learning.

Downstairs in Room 142, the students were clearly amused when Mr. Williams acted out each verb on his list. After he got them all to practice the basic moves, he demonstrated how to play Simon Says, a game that appeared new to almost everyone in the room. Then Mr. DeRose led the class in a vigorous competition as Mr. Williams determined who remained standing and who had to sit down.

"Simon says walk!" said Mr. DeRose.

Everybody began walking in place, dragging their shoes over the navy carpet.

"Simon says write," said Mr. DeRose.

Everybody scribbled in the air.

"Simon says stop."

Everybody held up one hand in the universal sign for halt.

"All right, poke. Oh, Hsar Htoo!"

Hsar Htoo looked confused as to why he should not have pantomimed poking, when Mr. DeRose had clearly told him to poke, but he obediently sat down.

"Simon says scare!"

Everybody put their hands next to their faces and spread their fingers in alarm.

"You guys are good," said Mr. DeRose.

"Simon says fly! Mariam, have a seat."

Mariam had forgotten to fly. She sat down, her long hair held back from her face by a leather headband, an abashed look on her face. Jakleen was eliminated soon after her sister. So were Solomon, Yonatan, and Amaniel.

"Learn! Saúl, *siéntate, amigo.*"

"Read your book. Oh, Methusella, sorry!"

Only Grace, Stephanie, Ksanet, and Lisbeth remained standing. The girls pantomimed think, listen, run, talk, point, and jump. Then Grace and Stephanie were eliminated, leaving only Ksanet and Lisbeth in the contest.

"Cook," said Mr. DeRose. "Oh, sorry, Ksanet. Lisbeth is the winner!"

Lisbeth had been in the classroom for only two weeks, yet she had integrated herself more completely than some of the students who had been there since the beginning of the year. I thought this was partly a result of her outgoing personality, partly due to the fact that both of her teachers could speak her mother tongue, and partly because of the extensive similarities between English and Spanish. Almost every day, Lisbeth discovered another word in English that she essentially knew already. She also possessed perhaps the most positive attitude of any kid in the room, as I learned when she shared more about her journey to the United States one day over lunch.

I was taken aback to hear that immediately before she joined Mr. Williams's class, Lisbeth had been locked up in a federal detention facility, after entering this country as an unaccompanied minor. The grim story was hard to reconcile with her happy-go-lucky demeanor, but she provided court documents to back up what she said. At the same time that she was managing the transition into South, Lisbeth was also juggling what would become a lengthy legal odyssey over her status in the United States. The same was true for Saúl. Both of them had been apprehended by immigration officials while attempting to cross the border illegally, both had been minors at the time, and both had entered the country without a legal guardian. Throughout the school year, these two students from El Salvador were required to show up for hearings at the federal courthouse for what were known in official parlance as "removal proceedings." The scary terminology was written across the top of the summons that Lisbeth showed me, which had been mailed to her home.

News reports of children fleeing violence in Central America and traveling to the United States by themselves had been appearing in newspapers and on television almost simultaneously with word of the global refugee crisis—the main differences between the two trends being the manner in which the individuals entered this country and the precarious legal position of the unaccompanied minors after they arrived. Refugees enter the United States with the legal blessing of the federal government and carry visas that are good for one year; after that, they must apply for green cards and legal residency. Essentially, refugees are fortunate because they arrive with a path to citizenship. Lisbeth and Saúl, by contrast, had arrived without entrance documents and hoped to rectify their illegal status through the courts.

When Lisbeth was little, her mother had worked as a police officer in El Salvador, she told me. She had admired her mother's crisp navy uniform and shiny silver shield. On two occasions, her mother had moved to the United States to find other jobs, mostly janitorial work that was not as glamorous to Lisbeth. During those extended absences, she had left Lisbeth and her younger brother behind in the care of their maternal grandmother. Lisbeth did not describe her frightening emotions she grappled with when her mother vanished, but only the warm bond she forged with her grandmother. She described her grandmother's adobe house as a rural idyll, surrounded by trees that bore mangoes, papayas, and oranges.

Recently, Lisbeth's mother had been forced to leave El Salvador again, after she had arrested several members of a violent gang and received death threats. Then the gang members had come after Lisbeth. "It used to be true that the gangs were mostly concentrated in the cities, but then they spread all over the place, and we saw the change in Santa Rita, a little bit at a time," she told me in Spanish, speaking through an interpreter. "At first it was just that some kids were smoking pot. Then all of the boys started speaking really bad words and giving gang signs to everybody. And then we heard a lot about stolen cattle and people getting killed." The gang members began their pursuit of Lisbeth by sending text messages asking for her mother's location. When Lisbeth refused to reply, the gang members proposed a trip to a city called Apopa, which they described as a fun outing. After she refused to go, the gang members threatened to kill her.

Lisbeth told her grandmother, who called her mother in the United

States, who phoned an uncle in El Salvador. Within forty-eight hours, the uncle made arrangements with a man from Mexico, whom he paid to escort fifteen-year-old Lisbeth and her twelve-year-old brother as they made an illegal crossing into the United States. Her uncle put Lisbeth and her brother on a bus that was headed to the U.S.-Mexico border. Fearful of what might happen on the journey, Lisbeth made sure to keep her brother close; the only mishap that occurred was that some other children stole her brother's sweater. Lisbeth gave her own sweater to her brother, to make sure he stayed warm. She stared out the bus windows at the captivating scenery. The lengthy ride was one of the most exciting things that had ever happened to her, Lisbeth said. Later that year, when Mr. Williams would ask everybody in Room 142 to choose one word that would exemplify their journey to the United States, Lisbeth would choose *bonita*. It had been beautiful.

That was Lisbeth: She bubbled with enthusiasm and saw the good in everything.

Lisbeth and her brother had been apprehended by immigration authorities while they wandered around a dusty Texas border town in the company of other children who had crossed with the same coyote. They were held for one day in a place that was like an ice box, then transported to a holding facility for unaccompanied minors in Chicago ("The furniture there was really nice!"). Because they had been found without a legal guardian, they qualified for hearings to determine if they were eligible for asylum. Asylum seekers can change their status while remaining on U.S. soil—the law treats them differently from undocumented immigrants—if they can prove that being sent home would put their lives at risk. The risk cannot consist of general violence, but must represent a specific threat aimed at the individual in particular. After federal officials determined that Lisbeth and her brother had a legal guardian living in the United States, they put the children on a flight to Denver ("I came here in a plane! It was my first time ever! We took off and we flew and I got really scared because the plane was shaking—there was some turbulence—and then I looked out the window, and I said, Wow! It was extraordinary! I loved it!"), where they were released into the care of their mother. Lisbeth's mother worked two jobs: She cleaned a local McDonald's and she cleaned residential houses. Because her mother worked long hours, they were unable to spend a great deal of time together, and Lisbeth missed her grandmother terribly, as well as the beauty of rural El Salvador. At the same time, she was joyful to be reunited with her mother, and she found city life compelling ("I know how to get to Walmart!"). At South, she had been nervous because of the size of the school, but Stephanie had been kind and she had made friends with other Spanish-speaking students. The ongoing removal proceedings upset her, but she hoped in the long run to be granted asylum.

While Mr. Williams was doing his best to teach all the students that the world kept sending him, I was doing my best to be a helpful presence in his room, and one way I did this was by sharing the stories of students I got to know. Mr. Williams knew nothing about Lisbeth's odyssey until I told him what she had recounted. Nor did he know about Saúl's harrowing journey in the packed truck, nor that Jakleen and Mariam had lived through the civil war in Syria. He and Miss Pauline knew that Solomon and Methusella came from the DRC, but not that they had lived in a particularly violence-prone province. Whenever I learned details about a student's background, I passed them along to both the teacher and the therapist. The students volunteered minimal personal information in the classroom, and I assume they were fairly reticent in group therapy, too, due to their lack of English and the inhibitions they must have felt about disclosing anything revealing in front of their peers. Neither Mr. Williams nor Miss Pauline had a budget that allowed them to use interpreters at will—the school district had a translation hotline, and there were paraprofessionals in the building who spoke a variety of languages, but I was the only person in the room who hired interpreters simply to understand the students better. Mr. Williams told me he had not previously been able to get to know his students so well.

When I told Miss Pauline what I knew about Lisbeth's background, she suggested that perhaps Lisbeth's over-the-top extroversion might be a coping strategy; I could imagine that the legal proceedings probably left her feeling precarious about where she belonged and anxious about the possibility that her new life could be upended. It made sense that she might be using constant social interactions to distract herself from her worries about being "removed." Mr. Williams found the background information helpful, too, as it made him feel more forgiving toward the student who was the most disruptive force in his classroom. For my part, I was relieved that I was able to let someone like Miss Pauline or Mr. Williams know when students had shared particularly difficult experiences, as some of them needed a kind of assistance that I could not provide.

After learning that Solomon and Methusella might have witnessed violent events in the Congo, Miss Pauline brought in a male colleague who pulled the two brothers out of the classroom for individual therapy. After hearing that Jakleen and Mariam had lived through the civil war in Syria as well as the Iraq War, Miss Pauline provided the two sisters with individual therapy herself. I have no idea what they discussed, but when I looked at the screening questions that Miss Pauline used to determine which students should qualify for the additional therapy (which was also subsidized entirely by Jewish Family Service), I saw a few things that might have applied to Solomon, Methusella, Jakleen, and Mariam. To screen for students who had seen high levels of trauma, Miss Pauline asked if they had been assaulted, if they had witnessed violence, if they had lost a family member, or if they had seen dead bodies. I assume that the brothers from the Congo and the sisters from Iraq must have said yes to several of those questions, but I did not ask them such things myself, out of a concern that doing so could be retraumatizing. In terms of our respective professions—teacher, therapist, journalist—I think being in Room 142 left all three of us wondering, Will we be worthy? Once we got beyond our own propensities to misconstrue or underestimate or overlook, and caught sight of who the students really were, we could see that they were splendid kids who had lived through things that were quite simply beyond us. They left us asking ourselves, Can we rise to meet the challenges presented by such a room?

When I told Mr. Williams about my interactions with Hsar Htoo, I mentioned a request that the student had made. He had asked through an interpreter that I please not pose any questions about the death of his father, because that topic remained too sensitive for him to discuss. It was the only time during my career when a person I wanted to interview had known ahead of time what subject would be too upsetting and had forthrightly warned me away from that part of the story. The main things I learned during my short interview with Hsar Htoo were that he had spent his entire life inside a refugee camp called Mae La, which sits just inside Thailand, close to the border with Burma, and that his name meant "Golden Star." Hsar Htoo had two older sisters and one older brother who had resettled in the United States before he arrived, which had eased the transition somewhat for the rest of the family. Hsar Htoo had come to the United States at the start of the previous summer, with his mother and two other brothers. For him, the highlight of the summer had come in August, when his family drove to Nebraska to visit close friends from Mae La who had resettled in that state. The reunion comforted Hsar Htoo—it was reassuring to see another family he knew so well also making the surreal jump from the reality of Mae La to life in America.

The only family members who had enrolled in school in Colorado were Hsar Htoo and his younger brother; everybody else took jobs to support the family. One of his sisters worked at a laundry facility washing sheets and towels for hotels in the Denver area, and his other siblings worked at a meatpacking plant in Greeley. They commuted to the work site on a daily basis, even though it was a one-hour drive each way. Many Karen-speaking people worked in the meat-processing industry, because the jobs paid well and employers in that sector were willing to hire workers who spoke no English, had no formal work history, and were often illiterate.

As requested, I asked nothing about Hsar Htoo's father's death, but I thought about it a lot in the months that followed. I admired Hsar Htoo's straightforward dignity around his father's loss; he rose in my estimation because of how he handled my curiosity. I believed I could see a special bond forming between Hsar Htoo and Mr. Williams, and imagined that it was good for Hsar Htoo to have a male teacher—an alternative father figure to show him the way forward during the unsettling first months in America.

It was hard to find an interpreter who spoke Karen. In the end, I worked with a young woman named Christina, who had been recommended by the Goodwill volunteer coordinator who visited Mr. Williams's classroom every week. Miss Ruthann had known Christina for a long time and had a soft spot for her. After we met, so did I. While the purpose of our encounter was to speak with Hsar Htoo, in the end it was Christina who wanted to share the most. She had arrived in this country as a refugee herself during her middle school years and had subsequently attended South High School. When we met, she was enrolled at a local community college.

Like Hsar Htoo, Christina had lived in a refugee camp in Thailand, though she had been born in a Burmese village that her family had left in haste amid an attack by the Burmese military. During her first year in the United States, while she was still getting used to everything—one day she wore flip-flops to school during a snowstorm because she had never worn regular shoes before—Christina's grandmother had given her away as a child bride to a man who was more than ten years older than she. Christina was in eighth grade at the time. As we sat in one of the purple booths in South's bustling lunchroom, she told me about one encounter with her supposed "fiancé." He had shown up at the door of her apartment and demanded that Christina perform sex acts. She refused and threatened to call the police. I assumed this represented the full extent of their interactions, as Christina said no more about him. I told Christina that I thought she was incredibly plucky to have known at such a young age that she did not have to "marry" the man to whom her grandmother had wanted to give her away.

"I was *thirteen*!" protested Christina. "You don't even know what love is at that age! I'm twenty-one now, and I still don't know what love is. *Jesus Christ!*"

It was one of those stories that stayed with me. I remained in touch with Christina, and she invited me to her home to meet her adoptive family. Christina taught me many things about Karen culture, sharing books and photographs, showing me traditional Karen clothing, cooking Karen meals for me. Often, I learned as much from the interpreters I was working with as I did from the students themselves; many of the interpreters had arrived when they were school-age, and visiting the newcomer room seemed to transport them emotionally back to that earlier moment in their lives, when it had all been such a struggle. They identified strongly with the students because they remembered how hard it had been learning English and getting accustomed to life in a strange country, wondering if they would ever blend in. The interpreters had processed their own experiences, whereas for most newcomer students it was too soon for them to put words to what they were enduring. Hurled into the developed world at high velocity, they had not yet caught up with themselves.

One of the books that Christina and her adoptive mother suggested I read was *For Us Surrender Is Out of the Question*, a piece of gonzo journalism by Mac McClelland, which includes a scene in which McClelland temporarily moves in with some Karen activists who are living on the border of Burma, just inside Thailand. Upon her arrival, McClelland is shown around the house, where she sees a concrete trough filled with cold water. A Karen man pantomimes pouring cold water over himself, using a small bucket. McClelland then engages her housemates in a prolonged conversation about showering, in which she eventually realizes that nobody else in the house, at any point in their lives, has ever taken a hot shower. They are skeptical that such a thing exists. Even when she attempts to convince them that bathing with hot water is pleasurable, the Karen activists are dubious. One of them insists stubbornly that cold water is better. McClelland uses the story to illustrate the naivete of an American such as herself about her degree of privilege: Americans just take their hot showers for granted.

Hsar Htoo had made the same journey in reverse, traveling from the Karen refugee community to a place where people took hot showers all the time without giving any thought to the money spent on their physical comfort. The change was too big, it was too much for him to describe, even with the help of an interpreter who had made the same journey. When I asked him what the transition had been like, he just said "hard."

Toward the middle of November, a new student named Kaee Reh arrived. He was from Thailand and spoke Karenni, a related but separate language from Karen. Later, Kaee Reh would tell me through an interpreter that, like Hsar Htoo, he had been born in a refugee camp in Thailand, after his family had escaped persecution in Burma. While the news media focused almost exclusively on the refugees who were at present fleeing from turmoil in the Middle East, both Africa and Southeast Asia had been generating large numbers of refugees for such an extended period of time that newspapers had long ago ceased to cover those stories. The popular term for this among humanitarian workers is "protracted refugee situations." In the case of Burma, the stunningly brutal civil war had been grinding on for more than half a century. Just as Kaee Reh showed up, there were signs of democratization in Burma—an election was due to be held that fall for the first time in twenty-five years—but renewed fighting kept breaking out.

Hsar Htoo was compact and burly, while Kaee Reh was tall and slender, but both boys arrived at school with their hair short on the sides and longer on top, with the longer hair gathered into a ponytail. They had similar experiences and were from the same part of the world, but they could not understand one another. Each of the students from Asia—Hsar Htoo, Kaee Reh, and Uyen—had nobody else in the room who spoke their given language. While Uyen had managed nonetheless to become friends with Stephanie, thanks to Google Translate and a common love of Converse High Tops, both Hsar Htoo and Kaee Reh were far more isolated. At least Hsar Htoo was familiar with the other students already, but Kaee Reh seemed especially cut off. One day, he brought his lunch to Room 142, sat down by himself, put on a large pair of headphones, and began singing. He wasn't humming; he was singing with his full voice. It was a beautiful tenor. It was impossible for anybody else to discern the meaning of his song, but the room filled with his keening. To me, it sounded like a song about loneliness.

* * *

After Kaee Reh's arrival, there was a pause in the growth of Mr. Williams's class. No new students arrived in Room 142 during the entire month of December. Mr. Williams now had sixteen students, who hailed from eight countries and spoke nine languages. Eight of the students were from Africa, three from Central America, three from Southeast Asia, and two from the Middle East. Coincidentally, the makeup of nationalities mirrored national trends.

In fiscal year 2015, the United States had accepted 70,000 refugees. Of that total, 27,000 had come from the Middle East, with almost half of those coming from Iraq. The United States had taken another 20,000 refugees from Africa, with Somalia and the Democratic Republic of Congo sending by far the largest numbers, followed by Eritrea and Sudan. And the United States had welcomed another 18,000 from Southeast Asia, almost entirely from Burma. Mr. Williams had students representing all those countries, with the exception of Somalia and Sudan. He used to see a lot of students from those countries, but after rents in Denver had escalated, Somali and Sudanese families had begun settling instead in other parts of the state such as Fort Morgan and Greeley. Rents were cheaper there, and the nearby meatpacking plants were hiring large numbers of foreign-born workers.

More students would arrive in January, but by this point Mr. Williams had amassed the bulk of his class. After Kaee Reh joined the group—during the lull that extended through December—Mr. Williams made certain to spend one-on-one time with each of his students. He gave reading assessments and listening quizzes and tested writing and speaking abilities. He found that Nadia and Grace almost always understood his instructions and often knew the right answers. Uyen and Stephanie could do the same and had surged ahead of others in their ability to read and write. Also, the two boys from the Congo were absorbing English at an astonishing rate. "Isn't it incredible to see what's happening with Solomon and Methusella?" Mr. Williams said one day while we were upstairs in the copy room.

Conversely, Hsar Htoo was struggling more than any other student.

Mr. Williams feared Kaee Reh might experience similar challenges, but it was too early to tell. He thought Hsar Htoo's difficulty was due largely to the fact that the Sino-Tibetan languages are about as far as you can get from English. Like most Asian languages, Karen and Karenni are tonal, which meant that Hsar Htoo and Kaee Reh were accustomed to deciphering the meaning and significance of words based on whether their sounds rise or fall. To further complicate matters, in the Sino-Tibetan languages, verbs do not change their endings. Tense, person, and number are expressed by adding other words, or are left to be inferred. Instead of conjugating a verb in Karen or Karenni, you simply add a word like "tomorrow" or "yesterday." Thus Hsar Htoo and Kaee Reh had a steeper learning curve than anybody else in the room, because they were learning how to change tenses for the first time in their lives.

Another factor that shaped the rate at which students could learn English was the level of education of their parents, and Hsar Htoo had told me that his mother was illiterate. When I visited Kaee Reh's parents at home later in the year, his father would mention that he could not read or write. Both Hsar Htoo and Kaee Reh operated at a disadvantage, because books and literacy were absent in their home environments. Solomon and Methusella's father, by contrast, knew how to read and write in several languages, giving his sons an edge over Hsar Htoo and Kaee Reh, because an important adult in their life had modeled the act of reading.

Like Hsar Htoo, Jakleen and Mariam were slow in acquiring English. The girls seemed highly intelligent, but English appeared to leave them flummoxed. This was due in part to the extensive differences between English and Arabic, Mr. Williams understood. The girls had learned to read and write using an entirely different script, which was written from right to left. They had also grown up structuring sentences in an alternative order: Arabic sentences typically begin with the verb (for example, "Struggle Jakleen and Mariam with English"). But they knew how to conjugate verbs, and they were recognizing some words in English that were familiar.

The words that Arabic and English have in common are not cognates, technically. The terms are borrowed, as opposed to derived from a common origin, and are more properly called loanwords. A loanword moves from one unrelated language into another because of social interactions. Most African languages contain a high number of loanwords from Arabic, due to the extent to which Arab people served as merchants across that continent. English doesn't have many loanwords that came directly from Arabic, but it does have a significant number that arrived through Spanish. Some of the many words that are identical or similar in all three languages are alcohol, elixir, giraffe, lemon, safari, and talisman. One day, as I was talking with Mariam and Jakleen about Arabic loanwords that passed into English through Spanish, an upper-level ELA instructor who was originally from Puerto Rico heard me rattle off my meager list. She called out enthusiastically, "*Pantalones! Blusa!* The Moors were in Spain for five hundred years!"

Mr. Williams suspected there might be more to the difficulties that the girls were experiencing than just the lack of similarity between English and Arabic, however. He knew they had lived in places consumed by violent events, and he understood they might have lost a parent, because their father's absence had become common knowledge after the girls had mentioned it to several staff members. Mr. Williams thought that whatever the sisters had endured while living in a war zone might also be inhibiting their progress. He worried, too, that the increasingly polarized political climate in the United States might be causing them to experience a particularly chilly reception.

As it happened, Kaee Reh's appearance in Room 142 coincided with a major shift in sentiments toward refugees throughout the developed world. During the same week that Kaee Reh arrived at South, a series of coordinated terrorist attacks broke out across Paris and the nearby suburb of Saint-Denis. The news media spoke incessantly of the suicide bombers who detonated explosives inside a football stadium, the gunmen who assaulted concertgoers at the Bataclan theater, and the mass shootings at a series of nearby cafés. The simultaneous incidents left 130 people dead and 368 injured. After ISIS claimed responsibility for the attacks, France responded by bombing Raqqa (a city in Syria on the banks of the Euphrates that had become the de facto headquarters of ISIS), declaring a state of emergency that allowed police to conduct searches without warrants, and banning public demonstrations.

In Europe, the attacks provoked a deepening backlash against refugees from the Middle East, and the period of relative openness to the Syrian plight came to an end. Some Germans continued to support Chancellor Angela Merkel in her stance that Europe should admit large numbers of refugees to alleviate pressures in the Middle East, but opposition to her position grew apace, creating a much muddier environment in that country. Public opinion elsewhere in Europe tilted against refugees even more dramatically. Pundits predicted that the flow of migrants would diminish, due to the cold of winter and the danger of trying to cross the Aegean Sea during rough weather. In fact, a second wave of Syrians began leaving, because of the much-publicized warnings that access to Europe might become more constricted. Suddenly many people who had not yet left Syria thought they should go right away, before it was too late.

In the United States, sentiments turned hostile, too. The governors of thirty-one states announced that they would refuse to accept Syrian refugees who sought to resettle in their jurisdictions. The attacks also amplified the heated rhetoric in the ongoing presidential campaign. Donald Trump had already made headlines by insisting he would force Mexico to pay for the construction of a wall along the U.S.-Mexico border. After the attacks in Paris, Trump also called for an immediate ban on Muslims entering the United States. He said this was purely a national security precaution, but after he made such remarks, some of his followers who harbored previously unspoken prejudice felt free to express hatred of Muslims. All this was palpable to Mr. Williams's students, and young women in hijabs attracted particular ire. One day, when Jakleen said miserably that she wished she could go back to Turkey, I asked what she missed about life in that country. "Respect," she said. I thought her transition might have been easier if she had felt truly welcomed, but in that regard her life was getting harder by the minute.

7

Does She Know Jesus?

Nabiha and I returned to the Pine Creek Apartments one Saturday afternoon. We located Ebtisam's apartment without difficulty, joking about how simple the door was to find in broad daylight. Inside the apartment we discovered a middle-aged neighbor seated at the round wooden table beside the kitchen, an old tea towel draped over the shoulders of her worn dress. Jakleen, wearing plastic gloves, hovered behind her, watching a timer. An open box of Revlon Luxurious Colorsilk stood on the table, and the woman's hair was steeped in dye. Nabiha and Jakleen chatted for a moment, and Nabiha explained that Jakleen had formerly worked in a beauty salon.

"She knows, she has experience," said Nabiha. "She says, 'Come here, I will do your hair.'"

Ebtisam greeted us in the traditional Middle Eastern fashion, with three kisses on alternate cheeks, and I presented her with some fruit. Refugee families always insisted on feeding me, because their cultures demanded that they show hospitality to guests, so I tried never to arrive empty-handed.

"*Shukraan*," Ebtisam said.

By now, I recognized "thank you" in Arabic.

We sat down in the living room, where the family had just eaten lunch. I saw the remains of kebab, eaten with flatbread. For the next two and a half hours, Ebtisam told us the saga of the family's journey. At first, the pace of the conversation was leisurely, as I asked questions in English, which Nabiha translated into Arabic; Ebtisam answered in Arabic, and then Nabiha translated her answers into English. After a while, however, Ebtisam began speaking more hastily, and eventually I didn't have time to ask questions. The girls' mother had lived through intense experiences and while recounting them she became caught up in the drama again emotionally.

Ebtisam had grown up in Suq al-Shuyukh, a small town in southern Iraq in the marshy lowlands of the Tigris and Euphrates river delta, the same region that was once called Mesopotamia. Like the majority of people living in the delta area, Ebtisam and her family were Shia Muslims. Although reviled abroad, Saddam Hussein had successfully held Iraq together as a country, despite the fact that Iraqi society was divided between Shia and Sunni, between Muslims and people of other faiths, between Arabs and Kurds, and between supporters and nonsupporters of the Ba'ath Party (the governing political party in Iraq at that time, which was secular in orientation).

During the 1990s—after Iraq invaded Kuwait, precipitating the first Persian Gulf War—the United Nations imposed severe economic sanctions on Iraq. Many Iraqis left their home country as a result. Most of Ebtisam's siblings immigrated to Germany during this period; although her parents remained in Iraq, they moved to Karbala, a holy city to Shia Muslims. Meanwhile, Ebtisam herself moved to Baghdad, drawn by the cosmopolitan environment. One day a friend invited her to a birthday party, where she met Fadi, an Iraqi Christian of Armenian descent. He and Ebtisam began dating, which caused a breach between Ebtisam and her parents. Her father disavowed her right away; when Ebtisam and Fadi married in 1999, her mother attended the ceremony, but subsequently decreed that her daughter should never contact her again.

Children arrived quickly: Mariam was born in 2000, Jakleen in 2001. While Ebtisam and her siblings had been given Arabic names, she and Fadi chose Christian names for their children—Mariam was named for Mary, the mother of Jesus, and Jakleen for a saint. Ebtisam told me that in her mind, Islam and Christianity held equal merit, but she had embraced Christianity because it had been important to her husband. Ebtisam told her daughters that they were free to attend either a mosque or a church when they became adults.

*   *   *

At present, Ebtisam and her daughters were attending Arabic-language services held on Sunday afternoons at New Life Community Church in Aurora. This evangelical Christian church had reached out to the fast-growing immigrant and refugee community moving into the low-rent housing available in that suburb. On my first visit to New Life, I mistakenly sat through part of a Christian service held in Oromo (a language spoken by millions of people in Ethiopia and Kenya) before I found the second-floor room where the Arabic-language service was held.

Shortly after Ebtisam and her daughters arrived in the United States, a devout parishioner from New Life named Mark started volunteering with the family. He had been introduced to them by their resettlement agency, Lutheran Family Services. Mark ferried them back and forth to church, fixed anything that broke in their household, and accompanied them on errands that required translation. He had grown up in a rural part of Texas, but he and his wife had lived in Lebanon, and he spoke Arabic fluently.

Because Jakleen wore a hijab, and because the family was Arabic-speaking, I had assumed they were practicing Muslims; it had not occurred to me that they might attend Christian services. Mark was about the last person I expected to meet through Ebtisam. I am a registered Democrat, and I'm pretty sure he was a registered Republican, and our views on everything from politics to proselytizing appeared divergent. In many respects, however, Mark was representative of the typical volunteer who worked with refugee resettlement agencies—he was motivated by his faith. Many of the major resettlement agencies were originally faith-based organizations with ties to specific religions, and the aid groups still relied upon local congregations to send them volunteers.

When I met Mark, one of the first questions he asked me was, "Where do you go to church?"

I told him I attended Quaker Meeting, which seemed to satisfy him—I was Christian.

Then he asked me about the interpreter I was using. "Does she know Jesus?"

I had never quizzed Nabiha about her faith, but I knew that she observed Muslim holidays.

"She is Kurdish—are most Kurdish people Christian?" I wondered.

"No, most Kurds are Muslims," Mark acknowledged.

"Yeah, I think she might be Muslim," I conceded.

I sensed that Mark was troubled by my answer. He and I did not see things the same way on a variety of subjects, but his basic goodness to Ebtisam and her family impressed me. When I looked at literature about New Life, I saw that Mark was living out loud what the church urged its members to do: "step out of our white, Anglo comfort zone and take intentional steps to become a multi-ethnic church that reflects the ethnic and socio-economic diversity of our city." Mark's service rendered Ebtisam less alone than she would have been otherwise. She could call Mark at any time of day, and he would patiently explain all the things she did not understand about the United States.

For some time, I remained confused by Jakleen's choice to wear a hijab. She later explained that she considered herself a Muslim, even though her mother preferred to attend Christian services. Only after spending a lot more time with Ebtisam and her daughters did I come to understand that in the Middle East, it was common for women of different religious persuasions to wear veils of various types, and in fact, it had been a Christian priest in Syria who had first urged Ebtisam's daughters to adopt the hijab. When I attended services at New Life with Ebtisam, I saw several women wearing scarves over their hair. That Sunday, a particularly fervent parishioner spoke at length about his profound joy in converting a Kurdish friend who had been a practicing Muslim. The gist of the conversion story was that the man had been "saved" from an afterlife in hell by adopting Christianity. Ebtisam did not spend her free time trying to convert those of other faiths, and the evangelical nature of the church ran counter to her idea of respecting both Christianity and Islam.

At the same time, New Life provided her with Arabic-speaking adults with whom she could socialize, as well as material support in the form of donated household goods. The services also lifted her up spiritually. That day, the congregation did a close reading of Psalm 84—Mark turned around and shared with me an English-language psalm book that he carried everywhere (it was cup-shaped from living in his back pocket) so that I could follow along, because all the Bibles in that particular room were in Arabic. I could feel Ebtisam's body relax in the pew beside me as the speaker went over the psalm. The preacher said that a person may undergo an especially difficult journey, and travel through a vale of hard times, but ahead there lies a safe dwelling place: "Even the sparrow finds a home, and the swallow a nest for herself."

In 2003, when the Iraq War began, Ebtisam and Fadi were living in Karrada, an area of Baghdad where Muslims and Christians lived peacefully side by side. The couple hoped to raise their children in a way that would demonstrate that the two faiths could coexist. Fadi worked as a painter and an electrician. He sided with the United States when it invaded Iraq, and after American troops captured Baghdad, he signed up to work with the U.S. military, according to Ebtisam. He was sent to Kuwait for three months of training. After he learned how to become a bodyguard, he began a new job protecting important members of the Coalition Provisional Authority, the interim government of Iraq established by the United States and its allies.

At the outset of the war, the Bush administration assumed the conflict would end quickly. After establishing control of Baghdad in the spring of 2003, the U.S. military and allied forces rapidly took a series of other major cities, including Kirkuk and Tikrit. When Ebtisam's youngest daughter, Lulu, was born in 2004, it seemed as though most of the major skirmishes might be over. As the United States attempted to turn power over to the newly installed leaders of the provisional government, however, conditions in Iraq rapidly deteriorated. Rifts opened up between Sunni and Shia Muslims, between Arabic speakers and Kurdish speakers, and between supporters and opponents of the United States. Even as the Bush administration attempted to throw its weight behind a series of newly installed leaders, Iraqi society fractured along sectarian lines. Civil war followed.

The Coalition Provisional Authority worked to hold democratic elections at the parliamentary level and then at the general level, culminating in the establishment of a new government in 2006. At the same time, however, violence escalated dramatically. During 2004 and

2005, the two years following the invasion, twenty-five thousand Iraqi civilians were killed; half of those deaths occurred in Baghdad. Another twenty-six thousand civilians died in 2006. Lists of the dead (such as the meticulous database compiled by Iraq Body Count) cite air strikes, improvised explosive devices, suicide bombings, and assassination-style gun executions.

Amid this escalating violence, civil servants at all levels of the government required bodyguards to ensure their personal security. Fadi worked as a bodyguard for a judge in the Iraqi court system, Mahdi Abu Maali, who presided over tribunals that tried to reimpose order on the rapidly worsening state of Iraqi society. The idea was to combat lawlessness by providing accountability, but the judge himself quickly became a target. Over a period of two months, several bodyguards who worked for the judge were assassinated, and then a failed attempt was made on the judge's own life. Fadi received a written threat that he might be killed next.

On May 15, 2005, the judge and his son, Hani, were driving outside the predominantly Sunni town of Latifiya, one of the most dangerous places for the U.S. forces and their allies. Both were assassinated. Secretary of State Condoleezza Rice had paid a surprise visit to Iraq on that very day, seeking to assure the new leaders that U.S. troops would remain in place until the government could, in her words, "defend itself." During the twenty-four hours that Rice remained in Iraq, two dozen bodies were discovered, and a car bomb almost killed a provincial governor. Despite Rice's attempt to deliver the opposite message, the single day's grim headlines confirmed what everyone there already knew: The Bush team's attempt to establish a stable regime was failing badly.

Fadi started chain-smoking and drinking heavily. He kept a gun accessible at all times and constantly watched for cars that might be shadowing him. One evening when the family was at home eating dinner, there was a series of rapid knocks on the front door. Instantly alarmed, Fadi asked if Ebtisam was expecting anyone. She said no. Fadi ran for his gun and told Ebtisam to take the children and go.

The apartment had a back door that opened onto a flight of stairs leading down to an alley—that was where Ebtisam usually shook out the rugs. Wearing only bedroom slippers on her feet, she picked up Lulu, almost two years old, and hustled the older children, five and six, out the back door. Jakleen gingerly descended the stairs, and Ebtisam, afraid of what lay behind them, urged her to move more quickly. Jakleen let go of the railing and tried to run but lost her balance and tumbled to the bottom, breaking one of her legs so badly that the thigh bone protruded.

Ebtisam picked up Jakleen and ran down the street carrying two children. She could hear gunfire and feared her husband was being murdered. With tears streaming down her face, and the children crying, too, Ebtisam looked for an Iraqi police officer who sometimes patrolled the area, but he was nowhere to be seen. A taxi drove past, and Ebtisam herded her daughters into the cab. When she reached this point in her story, Ebtisam began beating her chest and rocking back and forth, and wailing loudly, to show us what she had been doing in the vehicle that day, ten years earlier—lamenting the possibility of her husband's death. Alarmed, the taxi driver dropped the girls and their mother off at the hospital and sped away.

Ebtisam called her brother-in-law, who arrived at the hospital to find Jakleen screaming, her lips blue from pain, while Mariam was crying and saying repeatedly, "My dad! My dad!" Ebtisam tried to explain, but she was shaking and semihysterical. Doctors fixed the bone that was protruding, but said that Jakleen would have to return later so that an orthopedic surgeon could insert a titanium rod. Afraid to retreat to their own apartment, Ebtisam and the girls slept at her brother-in-law's home that night.

Fadi found them there at two o'clock in the morning. He had exchanged fire with his assailants, barricaded the front door, and ran out the back himself. He zigzagged down the darkened streets, then caught a taxi to a part of town where nobody would expect to find him. He took shelter in a cafeteria, where he drank countless cups of tea. Once he believed it was so late that nobody would see him arrive, he set out for his brother's house.

After the attack, Fadi spoke with friends who worked for the U.S.

military, and all of them told him the same thing: U.S. troops could not give the family round-the-clock protection. Baghdad was probably no longer a safe place for them to live. If they fled to another country, however, they could apply for refugee status.

Before the Syrian refugee crisis began, there was a much less publicized Iraqi refugee crisis, which was the origin of the region's destabilization. The United Nations defines a refugee as a person who is living outside his or her country of nationality, "owing to well-founded fear of being persecuted." The official list of reasons a person can fear persecution (according to Article 1 of the 1951 UN Convention as modified by the 1967 Protocol) include belonging to a tyrannized race, religion, or nationality, being a member of an ostracized social group, or holding undesirable political opinions. After the U.S.-led military invasion of Iraq resulted in "an eruption of criminality and sectarian violence," in the words of a report by the United Nations High Commissioner for Refugees, "one of the principal manifestations of Iraq's protracted crisis has been the exodus of its citizens, primarily to neighbouring and nearby countries, but also to more distant parts of the world."

The scale of the exodus from Iraq swelled in 2006, after the bombing of the al-Askari mosque in Samarra, one of the holiest sites in Shia Islam, which unleashed a particularly severe response. As it happened, that incident coincided roughly with Fadi and Ebtisam's departure from Baghdad. The events that caused them to leave were the same as those of many Iraqi refugees. In a survey funded by the UNHCR, based on interviews of 3,553 people who fled from Iraq to other Middle Eastern countries, 57 percent had received a direct threat, such as the evening visit by armed assailants to Fadi and Ebtisam's apartment.

Most Iraqi refugees sought safety as close as possible to their homeland. As of April 2007, more than 1.2 million Iraqi refugees had moved to Syria, with another 750,000 moving to Jordan, and 500,000 scattered across other parts of the Middle East, including Lebanon, Egypt, and Turkey. Dealing with refugees from Iraq presented the United Nations with a novel set of issues. All of the organization's prior experience had been with displaced people who were willing to settle in camps. In this case, however, almost all the Iraqi refugees had left large urban centers and they generally preferred to relocate to other cities in the region, intermingling with regular citizens in Aleppo, Damascus, Amann, and Beirut. They generally lacked legal status, however, meaning they were asylum seekers who had not been welcomed officially by their host countries. Many legal residents viewed the new arrivals as intruders. Refugee experts at the UN were frankly bewildered about how to contain the situation. They admitted, "[T]he organization had not planned for this scenario and was unfamiliar with the challenge. . . . The situation remains a fragile one."

For the first time, the UNHCR found itself dealing with a largely middle-class refugee population, displaced into middle-income countries. The refugees themselves had higher expectations for their standard of living and they were living in cities where rents were pricier and food more expensive than anything the organization had dealt with previously. Reflecting the scale of the catastrophe, the UNHCR's budget for refugees from Iraq would balloon from $40 million in 2005 to $271 million by 2008. When the Iraqi influx was at its peak, the UNHCR was registering three thousand people per day.

At the same time, the economy of the Middle East began to contract, as economic migrants were returning home in large numbers from the Gulf States, depriving their home countries of remittances and flooding local job markets. In Syria, Lebanon, and Jordan, many people blamed the incoming refugees for their own economic hardship and were "hostile to their presence," in the words of the UNHCR report. The Iraqi refugee crisis had turned into a full-blown disaster—one that would help spark the subsequent Syrian refugee crisis—even though the majority of the world's developed countries were not yet paying a great deal of attention. The Iraqi refugee crisis alone looked unresolvable to the UNHCR. "The majority of Iraqis do not have any immediate prospect of finding a solution to their plight," wrote the authors of the report. "Most of them consider that the current conditions in Iraq prevent them from repatriating. . . . Only a limited number of the refugees can expect to be accepted for resettlement, and yet those who remain in the three countries of asylum have almost no prospect of local integration or gaining secure residency rights, both of which have been effectively ruled out by the authorities."

The biggest problem for the Iraqis seeking asylum in neighboring countries was their inability to find legitimate jobs, due to lack of documents. As the UNHCR report said, "The vast majority of Iraqi refugees do not have access to the formal labor market . . . yet they find themselves living in the capital cities of middle-income countries, where they are obliged to rent accommodation and meet the cost of other essential items, such as food, clothing, and transport." By registering with the UNHCR, the displaced Iraqis were hoping to resolve this dilemma, acquiring legal status through the act of resettlement.

To qualify for refugee status with the United Nations, a person must have left his or her original country under duress and relocated elsewhere. Ebtisam and Fadi could not submit an application from within Iraq; maybe they should go to Jordan or Egypt, Fadi's friends advised. Because Fadi had been employed by the U.S. military, and because his life had been threatened, he would have a good case—he might even be granted permission to live in the United States. The family could not leave Iraq right away, however, because Jakleen's leg required several operations, everybody in the family had to get passports, and they had to sell their apartment. It took months to prepare for their departure.

Then came an extended period of wandering around the Middle East. In Amman, Jordan, the family did not even make it out of the airport. Although Fadi and Ebtisam had paid for five airplane tickets and were carrying heavy suitcases bulging with all of their belongings, immigration officials turned them away. Jordan had already taken in more than half a million Iraqi refugees—a huge influx given that the country's total population numbered six million—and feelings toward Iraqis had soured after Iraqi suicide bombers attacked three hotels in Amman.

Next they flew to Cairo, where they were able to obtain a renewable residence permit with a duration of six months. They found a decent place to live in a suburb of Cairo called Nasr City, but then they foundered economically. Egypt was fast becoming a more popular destination for Iraqi refugees, and the numbers of displaced Iraqis living there had ballooned from about 1,000 to 150,000 in the three years since the Iraq War had begun. Fadi and Ebtisam registered as refugees with the United Nations, but found work permits impossible to come by and jobs almost as scarce.

Fadi could not obtain a formal position of any kind in Egypt. As he and Ebtisam waited to hear whether another country might accept them for relocation, their savings dwindled. In a desperate move, Fadi invested most of the family's money in a start-up business venture dreamt up by an acquaintance. When it failed (Ebtisam believes they were swindled), they lost everything they had earned from the sale of their apartment in Baghdad. Theirs was a common story, representative of what many displaced Iraqis were encountering as they surged into other parts of the Middle East. In the UNHCR survey, 37 percent of the respondents said their main source of income was their savings, and one-third said they expected their funds to last less than three months.

After they wiped out their financial reserves, the family decided to move to Damascus, Syria. It was December 2006, and Saddam Hussein had recently been captured by the American forces. Maybe the level of violence in Iraq would subside, Ebtisam hoped; perhaps her family could soon return to Baghdad. They just needed somewhere to stay until Iraq grew more stable, or until the United Nations found them a new home. Given that Jordan and Egypt had proved inhospitable, Syria seemed like the best place to seek refuge.

Iraqis had been pouring into Syria, as the two countries shared a border and were strongly aligned culturally. Because Syria had admitted more than one million Iraqi refugees—causing intense domestic turmoil—the United Nations announced that it would open a new office in Damascus, specifically to handle uprooted Iraqis. They would be given a particular certificate, different from non-Iraqi refugees. Maybe they would have better luck if they applied for the certificate available in Syria, Ebtisam and Fadi thought.

That December, the family found a one-bedroom apartment in Jaramana, a suburb of Damascus highly popular with refugees. It had a large population of Christian residents living alongside those of other faiths, and many Iraqi families whose stories were similar to theirs had settled there. In the years that followed, as violence in Iraq worsened, more and more Iraqis would arrive. As the number of roadside bombs, suicide bombers, rocket-propelled grenades, and shootings taking place in Iraq reached new peaks, Fadi and Ebtisam welcomed a continual stream of new arrivals from their homeland, which was falling apart as a country. The neighborhood of Jaramana more than doubled in size, swelling from 100,000 residents to over 250,000.

Among the new arrivals was Fadi's brother, who moved in along with his wife and their children. Then Fadi's brother's wife's sister and her children joined the household. At one point, fourteen people crowded into the one-bedroom apartment. As the economy shrank and refugees glutted the job market, competition for work grew ferocious. Fadi found black market employment installing satellite dishes and earned just enough to cover the rent, along with help from his brother. There was nothing extra for luxuries. Meanwhile, food and fuel prices increased, tightening the economic vise.

Ebtisam assumed that Jaramana would be a way station, but her family remained there for six years. During that time, they grew close to many of their neighbors. Jakleen and Mariam became especially fond of two girls named Haifa and Noor—sisters their ages who had also escaped from war-torn Iraq. The Arabic spoken in Syria was slightly different from the Arabic spoken in Iraq, but it was not hard for the girls to adapt, and they thrived at school, completing all of their elementary education in Jaramana. The older girls started middle school there, too. All around them, however, many Iraqi students were dropping out of school. One-third of the children living in Iraqi refugee households quit school before graduation, due to the price of tuition, overcrowding in the schools, or pressure to work in the informal labor market to supplement their family's income.

Fadi and Ebtisam kept hoping for a phone call from the United Nations. They heard that Australia, Canada, Sweden, and the United States were accepting refugees from Iraq, but years slipped by, and nobody contacted them. Fadi checked regularly with the UN to make sure their case remained active, and each time he was told to wait. Rumors circulated in the expatriate community that refugees could pay bribes to speed up the process of getting chosen by the local branch office of the United

Nations—supposedly it was controlled by relatives of President Bashar al-Assad—but Fadi was not well connected, and even if he had been, he could not have afforded a bribe of any significance.

Then Fadi and his brother fell afoul of the Assad regime. Ebtisam recounted a long story about her husband's lending $400 to a Syrian, then getting crosswise with the other man after he sought repayment; supposedly the man said he didn't owe Fadi any money and then insinuated that he could make the refugee's life difficult. Ebtisam believes the Syrian man made a false report about her husband to the secret police, claiming that Fadi and his brother opposed the Assad regime. Actually, like most residents of Jaramana, well known as a stronghold of support for Assad, Fadi preferred him to the alternative, especially as ISIS grew in power. Whatever the origins of their disfavor, in 2010 both Fadi and his brother were arrested by Assad's security forces.

Their woe was not unique. The Assad regime reportedly jailed hundreds of thousands of alleged dissidents, and it is popularly believed that inmates were tortured. Ebtisam sold her last few remaining pieces of gold jewelry to bribe jail officials, but even after she turned over the money, she did not manage to secure Fadi's freedom. She tried many times to visit her husband, yet was never able to see him. Seven months elapsed. When Fadi finally returned home, Ebtisam found him thin and anxious but otherwise himself; his brother, however, was missing several teeth and exhibited signs of mental illness, she said. The brothers reported that they had been kept in underground cells and beaten.

Upon his release, Fadi was instructed to leave Syria. He told Ebtisam that she should remain in Damascus, to await the outcome of their case with the United Nations, while he traveled back to Iraq. He thought it would be easier to find work in a country where he had friends and relatives. Because several years had passed since the assailants had visited their apartment, he hoped that returning home might be safe. Ebtisam did not want to stay in Syria without Fadi, but her husband said that any day she might get the phone call that would change the rest of their lives. So Ebtisam remained in Damascus, and Fadi departed for Baghdad.

Fadi grew a beard, put on a hat and dark glasses, and returned to the city where the two of them had first met. Ten days after he arrived in

Baghdad, he vanished. Ebtisam's brother-in-law mounted a vigorous search, but even after visiting every morgue and hospital, he could find no trace of his missing brother. Ebtisam believed her husband had been killed. She did not often say this out loud, however, because her daughters wanted so badly to imagine that their father was whole and well.

By the winter of 2010, Ebtisam was living as a single mother on the edge of Damascus with three children and no steady income. One-third of the Iraqi refugee households were structured similarly—women and children, scraping by. She cobbled together a living by cutting hair, giving manicures, cleaning houses, and watching other people's children. It was hard to earn enough to pay for both rent and food. The family's diet became restricted to whatever Ebtisam could afford. That same winter, in Tunisia, a fruit vendor set himself on fire, sparking protests that flared into a full-blown revolution. The following year, the revolt fanned widespread protests around the region, known collectively as the Arab Spring.

Across the Middle East, governments started to wobble. Dissidents waved signs and gave speeches; armies dispatched tanks. Huge crowds assembled to demand change in Damascus, but when Bashar al-Assad tried to quell the insurrection, the conflict erupted into a full-blown civil war. For the second time in her life, Ebtisam found herself living in a war zone; conditions in Jaramana had been onerous already, but soon the situation became unbearable. Life expectancy in Syria dropped from seventy-six years old to fifty-five. The country's economy spiraled off course, reaching an 80 percent poverty rate and a 58 percent unemployment rate. More than 60 percent of school-age children stopped attending school, including Jakleen and Mariam.

In other words, the girls' relatively casual attitude toward attendance and their failure to show up regularly in Room 142 was in fact a product of the refugee crisis in the Middle East. As the UNHCR report stated, the Iraq War had resulted in a regionwide tragedy:

There is considerable cause for concern in relation to the education of Iraqi children. Many of the refugee parents, both fathers and mothers, have completed secondary and tertiary education themselves and have high ambitions for their offspring. But the destruction of the

Iraq education system . . . coupled with the difficulties they are now encountering keeping their children in school, has created a risk that those young people will grow up without an education . . . Many refugees refer to the fact that the future of an entire generation has been squandered.

Jakleen and Mariam first described what had happened while they lived in Jaramana during one of our early conversations at South High School. We spoke about this over lunch one day in Room 142—before I met their mother. Nabiha was there to serve as our interpreter. As we sat in their classroom, I shared with Jakleen and Mariam how my interviews with their classmates conveyed so much about what was taking place around the world. The way their classroom led outward to all these other countries and every kind of turmoil on the globe fascinated me, and I tried to convey this phenomenon to Jakleen and Mariam. Whose story could I share? There was Lisbeth, sitting nearby, wearing earbuds and nodding in time to the Spanish-language music playing on her cell phone. I waved at Lisbeth to get her attention and she pulled out one earbud. I told her in Spanish that I had an Arabic-speaking translator, and asked if we could recount her story to Jakleen and Mariam. Lisbeth gave us a thumbs-up.

"Lisbeth is from El Salvador, and her mother worked as a police officer there," I said in English. Nabiha repeated everything in Arabic to Jakleen and Mariam, as I turned back to Lisbeth to let her know what I was saying in Spanish. I told Jakleen and Mariam about the extraordinary level of violence in El Salvador, and how Lisbeth's mother had arrested several gang members. "The gangs threatened to kill her mother, so her mother left and came here—and then they threatened to kill Lisbeth, too. So Lisbeth's uncle put her and her little brother on a bus and sent them to America. And immigration authorities picked up Lisbeth and put her in prison."

"Oh! She has been through all this!" cried Mariam, instantly sympathetic.

"She is very strong," observed Jakleen.

From their suddenly more alert expressions, I could see that Jakleen and Mariam thirsted for stories about their classmates. They looked at Lisbeth with new regard. The newcomers had not been able to communicate directly, even though they had been learning alongside one another for many weeks, and they were keenly interested in having these sorts of interactions—but they needed both me and Nabiha to facilitate communication across the language barriers that separated them from one another. I translated what the Iraqi girls had said about her into Spanish for Lisbeth.

"*Piensan que tú eres muy fuerte!*" I told her.

A tangible bond formed among the girls, because Lisbeth had been willing to describe her journey.

"We thought only Iraqi people went through these kinds of things," marveled Jakleen. "Our story is like this. It is also a big story. Big, big story. Maybe even bigger than hers!"

Jakleen and Mariam conferred about something and then turned to Nabiha. The translator said, "They say, 'Can you tell Mr. Williams that we understand everything when he explains, we understand when he is teaching? But we cannot make sentences to answer him.'"

"I will tell him," I said. "Also, I can see that. I know that already. And because you understand so much—that's why the speaking is going to come very fast. Pretty soon this class might even be too easy for you."

"*In sha' Allah,*" Mariam said.

"We hope so," Nabiha translated.

I knew that *in sha' Allah* (sometimes spelled *inshallah*) meant literally, "if God wills." It was interesting to me that Nabiha had chosen to translate the phrase into a more secular form. The girls spoke several varieties of Arabic; their mother and father had spoken two different dialects, and they had learned a third version while living in Syria. Throughout our conversation, Nabiha checked and rechecked things the girls were saying to make sure that her understanding was accurate. She was highly conscientious, and if she said that *in sha' Allah* meant "we hope so," then I believed she was conveying her best sense of what the girls had meant. And yet I wasn't getting a literal translation. Never in my life had I had to work so hard to understand the people I was trying to write about.

In almost every interview, I caught moments like this—small issues that highlighted the difference between my culture (highly secular) and another's (habitually religious).

I asked the girls what they remembered about Syria.

"They tried to kidnap her while we were in Syria," Mariam replied, pointing to Jakleen.

I asked what had happened, and Jakleen spoke at length in Arabic. Her voice was more fierce, more propulsive, than Mariam's, and it had a slightly deeper pitch. Nabiha gave a little groan of sympathy at something Jakleen said.

"I was walking to the grocery store to buy some stuff for my mom," Nabiha said to me, speaking as Jakleen. "It was dark, there was no electricity. A car started following me. The car was dark, the windows were dark, I couldn't see inside. Then they called out to me. And one of them got out and grabbed my hand and started to pull me over to the car. And I hit his hand and I pulled my hand back and then I ran away."

"Right around that same time, they kidnapped two girls in our neighborhood," Mariam added.

"What happened to the girls who were kidnapped?" I asked.

"We don't know," Jakleen said. "They never came back."

"They raped them," Mariam supposed.

"All right," I said. "So the country was getting more dangerous."

"A lot more dangerous," agreed Jakleen.

"We were at home, and there was a big explosion," said Mariam. "It was a bombing, close to us. And the school . . . going to school was dangerous, because my friend, she got killed by the bombing. They bombed the schools."

Later, when I read news articles about the bombings that had happened while Jakleen and Mariam were living in Jaramana, I learned that during the month of November 2012, eight different car bombs had been detonated in that neighborhood, killing more than one hundred people. Home to many Christians, Druze, and Sunni Muslims, the neighborhood was being held by the government's forces, and it was considered a loyalist stronghold, a place supportive of Bashar al-Assad. The lethal car bombings were among the bloodiest attacks to take place anywhere in Damascus since the start of the civil war. Although no group formally declared credit, they were thought to have been orchestrated by a group linked with Al Qaeda known as al-Nusra Front.

Four of the eight bombs went off on November 28, 2012, the day Mariam had remembered. The first blast—a Mercedes, packed with about twenty pounds of explosive material—ripped through a crowded central square, close to a gas station, at 6:15 A.M., during the morning rush hour, when it would hurt the greatest number of people. The second bomb was deliberately timed to hit the crowd of would-be rescuers who rushed to the scene of the first catastrophe. It blew up only a few minutes later, at a nearby roundabout, more than doubling the number of casualties. Soot covered the walls of nearby buildings, and the force of the two blasts sent buildings crumbling down onto the cars below. Blood lay spattered over the dusty vehicles, and body parts were strewn everywhere. Two more bombs went off an hour later, at the gates of nearby schools, timed to coincide with the start of the school day.

Mariam and Jakleen lived close to the square where the first bomb detonated, so they did not go to school that morning. The explosion they had heard from their apartment was the first one.

"It was near to our house," Mariam said. "We saw all the bodies."

"Was anybody that you knew hurt?" I asked.

"We knew all of them," Mariam responded. "Jaramana was a small city. We knew each single person who died."

I didn't ask them any more questions. They were fifteen and sixteen years old, and it was the middle of their school day; what they had seen had to have been deeply disturbing. Afterward, I told Mr. Williams and Miss Pauline what the girls had said. In the wake of the disasters, their mother kept the girls at home, as did many parents in Jaramana (half of Iraqi refugees living in Syria had personal experience of bombings). It had become too dangerous to attend classes. The girls stopped going to school before they completed the seventh and eighth grades. For them, the period from the fall of 2012 to the fall of 2013 was a lost year, spent mostly hiding inside the apartment.

They resumed their education when they arrived in Turkey, where they were placed into the ninth and tenth grades, skipping over the time they had missed. They learned Turkish quickly and stayed in school for two full years, completing the tenth and eleventh grades. Then they dropped out of school for a second time, so that they could work. Mariam washed dishes at a restaurant and Jakleen worked at a hair salon. I asked if the girls had hoped to go to college in Turkey. They said no, that was not possible—college cost too much money. Mariam, Jakleen, and Ebtisam had been able to find only informal work in Turkey, nothing that would have enabled the girls to afford higher education.

The sisters resumed their schooling upon arriving in the United States, but they were dismayed to be ranked as freshmen at South because of their lack of English. This was galling to Mariam in particular, who thought she should have been a senior. Also, their education wasn't proceeding at the pace to which they were accustomed. In Syria and in Turkey, they had progressed swiftly. Here, the kinds of sentences Mr. Williams asked them to form seemed infantile, and the girls laughed to hear themselves say such childish things as "I can walk" or "I can sing." Yet it was all they could manage. And knowing it was all they could manage made the task of mastering English seem insurmountable. They had so far to go before they would reach competency, and their pace of learning was slow. "We relaxed more in Turkey," Mariam said. "It was easier for us." The United States was, by comparison, profoundly discouraging. "We thought we were going to learn fast, we thought it would be easy for us, but it is the opposite," Jakleen said. "We are depressed right now."

PART II

Winter

1

Delicious Stick of Butter

Language proximity, education level of family members, whether schooling had been interrupted, degree of trauma—all these matters shaped how fast a newcomer could learn. There was another critical factor that drove the speed with which students in Room 142 gathered English words: motivation. Closely related to self-worth—or hope—this quality colored all of their goals and shaped their own beliefs about how far they could go. Over time, as I became a more frequent visitor to the classroom, I became increasingly aware of each student's level of motivation—who believed in herself the most, who was failing to live up to his potential because he did not believe in himself enough. And I learned a lot about how far the newcomers might go after they left Room 142 by visiting other classes at South.

One afternoon early in December 2015, just as Europe was becoming less hospitable to refugees and the United States was debating whether to do the same, I walked over to another wing of the high school to observe the Student Senate, where students were practicing public speaking. An Iraqi-born senior named Oula had come up with the idea of holding an impromptu speak-off in which contestants would debate whether Coke was a better drink than Pepsi, whether students believed one AP instructor at the school was better than another, and whether or not the United States should elect Donald Trump as its next president.

Especially during the early part of the campaign, students at South High School did not take seriously the candidacy of a person like Trump, who represented the opposite of their hypertolerant school culture. Political divisions within American culture had grown so extreme that the country functioned like two separate nations, and students who attended South had little or no contact with voters who supported Trump. Newcomers never discussed the ongoing campaign or any aspect of national politics in my hearing; it was hard for them to follow, especially while they were busy trying not to get lost on the bus system, trying to figure out the right kind of clothing to wear in America, and trying to understand what Mr. Williams was saying. At several junctures, Ebtisam asked me distractedly when the election was being held—for her the whole concept of having a primary season and then a general election proved to be highly confusing—and she wondered out loud about what would happen to Muslim refugees living in the United States if Trump were elected. Would they be deported? Otherwise, none of the students in Room 142 or their parents brought up the election. Trump's campaign came up often elsewhere in the building, however, and the main tool South students employed to deal with Trump was generally scorn, as I learned from visiting the Student Senate.

Oula, who was presiding over the student debate, was the older sister of Sam and Sana, the twins who had been asked to mentor Jakleen and Mariam. Oula, Sam, and Sana had arrived in the United States back in 2008, before they were old enough for high school. Their parents were doctors, but it had been hard for them to find American institutions willing to hire medical personnel who had trained elsewhere. To earn qualifications that would allow them to work, they had to repeat parts of their education. Oula's father secured a residency in Corpus Christi, Texas, while her mother was admitted to a medical technician postgraduate program at Denver Health. The couple was not able to find jobs in the same state, but both were able to continue their careers. Meanwhile, their three daughters excelled at school.

After going through an English Language Acquisition program in middle school, Oula had arrived at South ready to take Advanced Placement classes. She quickly emerged as one of the school's leaders. At the moment, she was working closely with the two American-born students who served as the school's head boy and head girl, helping to run the Student Senate. I was delighted to see Oula in action because I had been hearing about her for months; the school's community liaison had mentioned her, the parents who ran the food bank had talked about her, and the head of the PTA had sung her praises. The entire school took pride in Oula's accomplishments because they thought she exemplified what was possible at South: You could arrive here from halfway around the world without any English, and the school would help you realize your dreams.

That day, Oula was wearing a purple South High T-shirt and had braided her dark hair into a thick rope. She was sitting behind a desk at the front of the room with her bottom on the back of a chair and her feet on its seat, which made her seem taller than anybody else. Spread out on the desk before her were a red backpack, a notebook opened to a page of notes about the public-speaking exercise, and a bottle of Diet Coke. She spoke with authority as she explained the rules of the contest: Speakers could use only positive statements in favor of their position. They were not allowed to say anything negative. The speeches would be timed and the contestants would speak without preparation. Oula would announce who was speaking and then the contest would begin.

"All right, our first topic is Donald Trump," she declared. "Emma will be pro, and Kate will be con."

Emma was an American-born, white student—the Senate skewed more native-born than the school's hallways. Emma was tall and she had pulled her brown hair into a messy bun. She seemed to relish the chance to argue in favor of Trump. "All right, so a lot of people want to know, why Donald Trump, what's up with this guy?" Emma began. "So I want to tell you first off, he looks like a delicious stick of butter."

That line got so much laughter that Emma decided to riff on it.

"Or like mayonnaise. Or like pudding." More laughter. "So there's that."

"Second off, he hasn't offended the gays yet."

Emma observed that Trump owned a lot of real estate, and perhaps it could be put to good use.

"Like, he owns four hotels, maybe more. You know, we could put people in those hotels. We could put homeless people in those hotels, or we could put not-homeless people in those hotels. There are a lot of options, just with the hotels. And, he has a really hot wife. He has a *really* hot wife. A lot of people are, like, Michelle Obama, her arms are too ripped, she's too buff, we don't like it. His wife—nobody says that about her. That's why you should vote for Donald Trump, guys."

Emma's close friend Kate, also white and American-born, argued against Trump. She was petite and earnest.

"I would just like to point out that while he hasn't offended gays yet, he's offended a lot of other people," said Kate. "He's a pretty offensive guy. And while he may look like a stick of butter, I don't want anybody to be in power that doesn't have real hair. His hair is just not good."

Kate suggested that Trump did not seem to understand that Hawaii, while admittedly far away, was actually a state, based on statements he had made about the birthplace of President Barack Obama.

"I mean, if you want someone blatantly racist and sexist as your president, like, be my guest," she concluded.

Emma won—the stick of butter line had been irresistible to her peers. I was old enough to be saddened by the level to which American political discourse had sunk, but the candidates themselves were not modeling behavior that was any better.

Oula said, "Next: Coke or Pepsi?"

As the students in the room grew raucous, my gaze drifted to a poster taped to the wall beside where Oula was sitting. On an oversized piece of paper, members of the Student Senate had compiled a lengthy list of the qualities they thought leaders at the school should possess:

ebullient	no profanity	communicative
respectful	can laugh at yourself	solve problems
spirited	culturally sensitive	humility
focus	good listening skills	speak in turn
prepared	empathy/sympathy	unafraid
punctual	open-minded	responsible
creative	take initiative	speak up
honest	NO CELL PHONES	

It could have been a description of Oula herself. The busy juniors and seniors who ran the Senate, no matter where they had been born, possessed a self-assurance that made a striking contrast with the uncertainty of the newcomers. After the lack of exchanges that took place in Room 142, the abundance of humor and the way everything happened at a faster clip was refreshing. But I had learned enough to know that the dampened level of interchange that took place among Mr. Williams's students was not a reflection of their potential; it was a reflection of their struggle. One could take any of the well-rounded, assured students who served on the Senate and put them into a similar predicament—bomb their home city until it became unlivable, separate some of them from their parents, force them to witness atrocities, starve them for a while, transport them to a foreign country where they understood nothing, give them a teacher who spoke a language they could not comprehend—and most of them, too, would have fallen quiet.

Would any of the newcomers that Eddie Williams was teaching make it all the way to the Student Senate before they left South? I was not sure it would be possible to travel that far. At first, I thought Oula might serve as an example of what some of the newcomer students could become in a few years, but then I reflected on the advantages she possessed. Her parents were highly educated; she had walked into South ready for AP classes. I wondered if it would really be possible for any of the newcomers to join an elite body like the Senate, or to go to college. Then I met more of the kids who were serving in the Student Senate alongside Oula.

On the day of the debate about Trump, the head boy and head girl observed that there were many visitors in the room. About a dozen eighth graders were "shadowing," or visiting to see if they might choose South as their high school. A greater number of private school students were shadowing this year; when South first began focusing on ELA students, the high school had earned a bad reputation in the surrounding neighborhood, particularly in wealthier, white households, where overachieving parents feared their children would be held back by going to school with students of color who did not speak English as their first language. "'Okay, it's great that you're helping these people who are in need with all this emotional and physical support, but my kid who knows English could get lost in the shuffle,'" was how the school's community liaison, Karen Duell, summarized the sentiment. "That was the idea." By this point, however, things had shifted to the point that parents who could send their children to private schools sometimes opted for South. Among them was Carolyn Chafe Howard, the head of the PTA. She had sent her children to Graland Country Day through eighth grade but saw the neighborhood high school as a place where her children could step outside of the almost all-white scene they had been part of and learn more about everybody else on the planet.

Ethan, the head boy, sat at the front of the room on a gray metal stool, wearing a purple South hoodie and jeans. He had curly blond hair and a hipster's cool demeanor. The head girl sat beside him on another stool. The rest of the Student Senate was distributed across a series of round tables, and scattered among them were the scared-looking eighth graders. Ethan described the Student Senate to the visitors by saying that its members organized major events at the school, such as the recent homecoming dance, and did fund-raising to pay for them. The Senate also tried to introduce its members to leadership skills that would serve them well later in life, such as public speaking.

Then Ethan asked a student named Keegan to take over. Keegan was a junior who would serve as head boy the following year and, coincidentally, looked almost exactly like Ethan—another good-looking, athletic white guy with a mop of blond curls. Ethan and Keegan looked so much alike and were together so often that I had a hard time telling them apart, and when I apologized about this one day, in a crowd by the front door, Ethan or Keegan (I honestly don't know which one it was) told me not to worry—everybody at the school had the same problem.

Keegan asked the eighth graders to introduce themselves and give the name of their school. Then he called on various members of the Student Senate to ask each visitor one question. The questions were "Dodgeball or kickball?" (Eighth grader: "Kickball.") "Thin Mints or Samoas?" (Eighth grader: "Thin Mints.") "Favorite cereal?" (Eighth grader: "Froot Loops.") "Do you have a joke?" (Eighth grader: "What do you call a bee that comes back to life?" Keegan: "A zombie!") "Favorite football team?" (Eighth grader: "Broncos.") "Favorite breakfast food?" (Eighth grader: "Pancakes." Keegan, with kind admonishment: "You could also answer bacon. Maybe next time.") "Favorite Will Ferrell movie?" (Eighth grader: "*Elf*." Keegan: "*Elf* is, like, timeless. I literally watch that movie, like, three times a season.")

Then a few students from South introduced themselves and explained why they had chosen that high school. Oula's younger sister, Sama, volunteered to go first.

"Hi, my name is Sam, and I'm a sophomore here," she began. "I came to South—well, I have an older sister who goes here, and whenever I came to events here, the size of South was just perfect. You can have a lot of friends and there are a lot of different kinds of activities and all of the programs here mesh well together, like, you can have a sport and still be an honors student."

The next student to speak was a slight, boyish Asian American wearing a blue hoodie. He was originally from Cambodia.

"Hi, I'm Kimleng, and I'm a senior," he said. "I like the environment here at South. I think the teachers here—they're really nice, and I'm thankful to them for helping with my transition, coming from another country, and learning a new language. Yeah, you guys should come here—you will like South."

While Sam and Oula had immigrated before their high school years, Kimleng had entered the United States at age seventeen. Three years prior, when he first enrolled at South, he had been ranked as a freshman and placed in Mr. Williams's newcomer classroom. Like Hsar Htoo, he had struggled tremendously with the pronunciation of English words at first. Kimleng had learned fast, however, and after spending one full year as a newcomer, he had placed out of the next level of English Language Acquisition classes, and as a sophomore he had gone straight into ELA level 2. By his junior year, Kimleng was taking mainstream classes. Now he was a senior, enrolled in two honors courses, and had applied to six colleges. He was an example of what some of the students in Mr. Williams's class might prove capable of achieving—if they had ambition.

The next student to speak was the son of PTA president Carolyn

Howard. George had unruly brown hair and a surfer dude's bumbling cool. The other kids loved to rib him.

"I came to, uh—" George began.

"You're at *South High School*, George!" advised Keegan.

"And I'm a senior," said George, without missing a beat. "What I really like about South is there are just a lot of people who do a lot of different things. Like, I have friends who like to skateboard and friends who like to go to football games—I know a lot of different people, and I'm friends with different groups of people. I think it's really nice that you can do that, that you can be friends with people from all different areas of the school. I don't feel that I have to hang out with certain people all of the time."

George was dating a young woman whose family had immigrated to the United States from West Africa. Like Oula, she spoke English perfectly and took mainstream classes, but she also celebrated her family's West African culture, and later that year she would give George a green dashiki, which he proudly wore on Senior Ditch Day. Their union represented the type of cross-cultural romance that was possible at South. Friendships and romances between foreign-born and native-born students were common, and immigrants were included in all types of activities at the school. They did not remain stuck in outer orbit, socially. That fall, the school had selected as its Homecoming Queen a Vietnamese-American student named Teresa, the daughter of refugees. Teresa had been born in California, but both of her parents had arrived in this country during the refugee crisis that followed the Vietnam War.

After the eighth-grade shadows left to take a tour of the building, Keegan asked me to introduce myself to the remaining students. I mentioned that I was a writer who lived in Denver and had written several other books, including one called *Just Like Us*, which was set in a different high school and told the story of four girls who emigrated from Mexico, two with documents and two without. I explained why I was now at South and asked if the students had questions for me.

"Would you rather be an egg roll or a spring roll?" Keegan asked.

"Oh!" I said. "A spring roll."

"What do you like to do for fun?"

"I like to snowshoe."

"Are you a John Cena fan?"

"I have to confess I have no idea who that is, but I'm excited that I'm about to learn."

"*George!*" bellowed Keegan.

George dug his cell phone out of his pants pocket and obligingly played a song by the professional wrestler and rap star. I think it might have been "The Time Is Now." (I am not a John Cena fan but admit a grudging admiration for certain rhymes, such as, "I got my soul straight, I brush your mouth like Colgate.")

"Do you have a spirit animal?" Keegan asked.

"Yes, I actually went through an official exercise to figure that out, and I discovered it's a red fox," I said.

Keegan wanted to know if other students in the room had questions. This was the most entertaining interview that I'd been on the receiving end of in recent memory, so I didn't mind.

"If you could speak any foreign language you wanted, or you could speak to animals, which would you choose?" asked one girl.

"I was a shy kid growing up, and I was always the one reading a book on the school bus, so I spent many years secretly convinced that I could speak to animals, because I had read the Narnia books so many times."

"I actually read *Just Like Us*," said another student. "And I wanted to know, are you still in contact with those girls? How are they doing?"

"I am still in touch with them. We get together maybe twice a year. Several of them are married now, and they are all about to turn thirty, which is incredible to me. All of them have some form of legal status or ability to work—in one case, through President Obama's executive order known as DACA. So their lives have really evolved. They are all doing professional work now, the kind that requires a college degree."

"Why did you decide to write a book about newcomers?" another student asked.

"I get a lot of my ideas by paying attention to the news, and I've been watching stories about the refugee crisis for many months. I was wondering how that international story intersected with my hometown, and when I talked to people who work with refugees, they told me that South had expertise in welcoming people from around the world, and that there was a critical mass of foreign-born people here, which made this such an interesting environment. I think what's happening with refugees is one of the biggest and most important stories in the world right now, and I think that story about people having to find a new home takes place every day here at South in ways that are really fascinating."

A girl with masses of dark curly hair, sitting at the back of the room next to Kimleng, raised her hand. This was Sara.

"I was a newcomer, like, three years ago," Sara said. "And if there's anything you want to know, you can ask me. I would be more than happy to talk to you."

Sara was originally from Morocco, and she spoke both Arabic and French. She and Kimleng had been newcomers with Mr. Williams at the same time. Many of their peers had moved more slowly through the additional levels of English Language Acquisition instruction, but like Kimleng, Sara had learned English at such a quick pace that she was able to skip ahead and enter mainstream classes before other newcomers from her year. There were additional students in the room who had been born elsewhere—including a star member of the school's basketball team—but Kimleng and Sara were the only two newcomers from their cohort who had made it all the way into this room, arguably the social epicenter of the school.

I asked Kimleng how he had gotten involved in the Student Senate.

"Actually, she talked me into it." Kimleng pointed at Sara.

"I was just walking down the hallway and I saw a flyer about it," Sara said. "I talked to one of my teachers, Ms. Hijazi"—one of the school's upper-level ELA instructors—"and she was like, 'It's a great thing, you're going to do great,' so she kind of encouraged me to do it. We just applied and got accepted."

"I can't believe I'm sitting here right now," Kimleng said. "Three years ago I would not have thought this would be possible for me."

Kimleng and Sara remembered exactly how hard it was to be a newcomer. "Not being able to express their feelings, or being afraid to talk, because they are afraid other people will judge them because of their accent," Sara said. "They are afraid that other people will make fun of them. They are afraid that other people will think their accent is funny or their culture is funny."

Kimleng added, "And they are afraid to ask their teacher for help. They don't know who is going to help them."

I said that Mr. Williams's current newcomer students seemed to think their English was terrible, even though I could see how fast some of them were learning.

"I still think my English is terrible," Sara confessed.

"Yeah, my English is terrible," agreed Kimleng. "That's why, even now, in the Student Senate, I still feel like I don't fit in. I don't feel comfortable speaking. I'm still shy."

Sara had simply decided to get over those kinds of feelings. "You have to develop confidence," she said. "Me, I decided one day, I don't give a damn what I'm saying, if it's wrong or if it's right, I am just going to express what I'm thinking. Like, I don't care if people laugh. At South, we don't have that problem of people making fun of you so much—they understand. Some of them laugh, yeah, but not that many."

"That's why I love South High School," said Kimleng.

While South's students were debating whether to drink Coke or Pepsi and the matter of who should lead the country, parents were trying to figure out who should run the school.

PTA president Carolyn Howard was consumed by the looming transition in leadership. The longtime principal, Kristin Waters, had announced over the previous summer that she was leaving. Dr. Waters was a petite woman with blond hair, a cheerleader's bubbly disposition, and acute political skills; she walked the halls of South every day, hugging kids from all kinds of backgrounds. She had a penchant for bright purple dresses and had acquired that gift which the best principals attain, of radiating a firm yet warm parental kind of authority to all within her purview. In other words, the kids knew that she cared, and it gave them a certain kind of assurance.

As principal, Dr. Waters had presided over the transformation of South into a place that excelled at both English Language Acquisition and Advanced Placement. Thanks to her leadership, the school could support equally well a student who had arrived from a strife-ridden foreign country and a student who had previously gone to Graland Country Day. "It is with mixed emotions that I am writing to inform you of my decision to end my tenure as Denver South's principal in December 2015, at the end of the first semester," Dr. Waters stated in a letter sent to parents. "I will be joining my husband in Atlanta, Georgia, where he has accepted a new position." Waters had remained at South for the first half of the school year, but she was leaving at the end of the month. The district had yet to name her successor. Dr. Waters was beloved by students, faculty, and parents, and her imminent departure made the entire school community anxious.

Throughout the fall, the PTA had organized a series of town meetings designed to capture the full span of families served by South High. One meeting took place in a location convenient for the wealthy parents who owned spacious old houses in the nearby, affluent neighborhood of Washington Park; a second meeting took place downtown; a third took place in the common room of a building that offered affordable housing to recently arrived refugees. At each meeting, parents said there was one thing Dr. Waters had championed that they wanted to remain a priority: South's diversity. Both the wealthier families and the newly arrived refugee families cherished the experience of walking through the hallways filled with hijabs, niqabs, dreadlocks, head scarves, tracksuits, baseball hats, purple cheerleader uniforms, and a cacophony of languages. Their own children had benefited from the mix. They had all grown. "There are human beings who have seen atrocities and lost everything, and here they stand, ready to start over—which is just astounding," Howard said.

South was looking for a new principal who would celebrate what was happening in Mr. Williams's classroom, just as Dr. Waters had done. After spending four months as a regular visitor to the school, I could feel why that might be true. Just the daily experience of walking down the halls proved liberating. Young women from Africa came to school wearing floor-length skirts in bright orange or hot pink, with contrasting head scarves in electric blue. Their counterparts from Southeast Asia showed up wearing hijabs adorned with sequins. Young men from Southeast Asia sometimes wore stripes of yellow paint on their cheeks as a form of blessing. Female students from the Middle East did their hair in elaborate updos and then draped wool scarves over their big coiffures, but wore jeans and American T-shirts. One day, I saw an Iraqi student wearing a black head scarf and a gray T-shirt that said I KNOW THAT GUAC IS EXTRA. You could be anything at all and register as gorgeous—you knew this, if you walked the hallways of this school. It was a place that eroded prejudices and expanded ideas of beauty. Parents and faculty feared that without Dr. Waters, this splendor might vanish. Rising rents were pushing new arrivals farther and farther away. What if South became more and more white? That was the main concern of the school community—a funny reversal from the days when parents had worried that South focused too much on ELA students.

Perhaps the main way that the Student Senate and the PTA connected with Mr. Williams's students was through their support of the food bank in Room 142. The kids in the Senate held a fund-raising drive, which raised $1,000 for the cause, and the PTA matched their gift. I often spoke with Jaclyn Yelich and Greg Thielen as they restocked the food bank shelves, which they generally did during the lunch hour. One day that winter, Jaclyn proudly reported that on the previous Friday they had given grocery bags bulging with food to sixty students. They had started off the school year by serving only twenty students—the number of families being served had tripled, and it was only December. Greg used a clicker to track the number of families they served, and the total kept growing. At the start of the next calendar year, they would be serving more than eighty families each week.

In addition to all the canned vegetables and dried goods, Jaclyn showed me new items, including fresh produce and toiletries that had been provided by the Student Senate. Carolyn Howard's son, George, had led a "personal care drive" for shampoo and body wash and toothpaste. The toiletry items had proved wildly popular with the refugee students, whose families often could not afford such things, which they considered luxuries. Certain items had been so popular, they had run out. Jaclyn held up two plastic shopping bags filled with the goods she had needed to replenish.

"I just went shopping," she said. "I bought laundry detergent, body wash, and maxi pads."

She opened up a plastic bag filled with maxi pads to show me.

"I gave some of these away to girls last week—you would have thought I was handing out a brick of gold. This stuff is expensive."

For the rest of the year, tampons and maxi pads were the most coveted items that Jaclyn distributed to the school's impoverished female students. Their families could not afford to buy disposable pads, and if the girls did not get them from Jaclyn, they had to use cloth pads instead, which were messy and leaked. Generally, boys did not select toiletries for themselves. Instead they took food their families needed, or asked Jaclyn shyly what toiletries she thought their mothers might like. Body lotion, she suggested, and that became the most popular nonfood item with the male students. Generally, though, they wanted to play the role of provider, bringing home the items their mothers most desired—usually rice or beans. The canned vegetables were harder to give away, because newly arrived families were not as familiar with them.

Many of South's student leaders had been born in the United States, but clearly there was room at the top of the school's social hierarchy for the young people Mr. Williams was teaching, if they learned fast and moved quickly into mainstream classes. Kimleng and Sara had succeeded in going all the way from Room 142 to the Student Senate, and both of them were planning to go to college. After meeting them, I began to wonder who among the current newcomers would rise as fast. I thought that ambition was key—they had to have high hopes for themselves and be able to sustain their hopes even during difficult times. Because the newcomers' personalities remained highly cloaked, it was hard for me to discern exactly which of them possessed that kind of drive. After I started riding public transit with the students, however, I could see how their level of motivation played out in that arena. It was interesting to correlate their behavior on the buses and trains with what I saw in the classroom.

Lisbeth, for example, arrived at school early every day of the week. She was never late and she was never absent, unless she had a court appearance. When I drove over to her apartment complex one morning at 6:00—like most of the city's affordable housing, it consisted of a vast series of similar-looking buildings, but the exteriors had been painted in cheerful colors including deep red and olive green—Lisbeth emerged from her apartment with her corkscrew curls still wet from the shower. She explained that when she had first arrived in Denver, her mother had taken a day off from work to show her how to navigate the city's bus system, which she quickly learned to manage adroitly on her own. Lisbeth waved to other students as they boarded the same bus. Then she showed me some selfies she had taken with a Spanish-speaking boy whom she liked. After that she pointed with excitement at a squirrel that sat upright to eat something, saying, "*Mira!*"

At a certain point, we got off the bus, and Lisbeth confidently showed me where to catch a light rail train for the second leg of our journey. Whereas the bus had been filled primarily with people of color who were dressed in jeans or sweats, the train included more white commuters in suits. The bus and train rides together took about an hour and fifteen minutes, and Lisbeth delivered her usual optimistic patter in Spanish for the entire time. It was 7:16 when we arrived at South, and she had a full half hour to relax upstairs in the cafeteria over breakfast before the bell rang for the day's first class. I saw Nadia, Grace, Hsar Htoo, Kaee Reh, Ksanet, Yonatan, Solomon, and Methusella elsewhere in the cafeteria. Lisbeth took another selfie, scrutinized the image, and turned to me.

"Miss," she said. "*Soy bonita?*"

Was she pretty? It was quintessential Lisbeth, to have that question on her mind at 7:30 A.M., and to ask it out loud. She was living through a year when she wasn't sure if she was getting "removed," wasn't sure if she could keep living with her mother, and wasn't sure where she stood in the affections of a boy with whom she had spent one afternoon in a park. But she was never late, and she knew how to ask for assurance.

"Yes, Lisbeth," I told her. "You are beautiful."

Solomon and Methusella had other priorities. One afternoon, I asked the boys if I could ride home with them. Methusella looked faintly horrified at the prospect of being accompanied by a middle-aged American woman (I knew from having a son that my presence might represent a form of social death), while Solomon gravely accepted this trial without betraying any sign of alarm. Even though the shortest route home consisted of simply catching two different city buses, one of which they could board close to school, the boys preferred to take a longer but more scenic route. Along with a steady stream of other students from South, I walked with them for about three-quarters of a mile to a nearby light rail station. At the station, we eschewed the stairs, which would have been dull, and rode down in an elevator, because it was cool and shiny and we could.

On the train platform, Methusella spotted a friend of Yonatan's from Eritrea sitting on a nearby bench and walked over to sit beside that young man—even though they did not share a common language, at least Methusella was able to align himself with a fellow African. Solomon appeared to feel that his job was to serve as my chaperone, and remained at my side. When we all boarded a train, Solomon and Methusella sat down on a bench seat, but a young African-American man abruptly grabbed the two seats facing them (one seat for his rear end and one seat for his backpack) before I could claim that space. I sat by myself in another part of the train, and the seats around me quickly filled up with students. As soon as a few passengers disembarked, however, Solomon moved over to join me, because that was the polite thing to do. We barely spoke, because he preferred to look out the windows.

At first, the train hugged I-25, the main north–south thoroughfare that bisects Denver. Wealthier commuters moved alongside us in their private cars, two forms of transit shuffling people of different income levels along in tandem. Eventually, the train curved along with the highway toward the glass-and-steel skyscrapers of downtown. Watching the high-rise buildings slip into view, I could see why the boys liked this route: It took them through the heart of the city.

We exited the train at a busy intersection in the middle of downtown and walked to a bus stop where we waited for the number 15 bus. It was windy and cold and the boys had no jackets; they insisted they were not freezing, but I saw them shiver when they sat down on the cold metal bench. Finally a warm bus pulled up and we found seats about halfway down its length. The boys stared out the scratched plexiglass windows as the driver made several stops, navigating the lumbering bus past the limestone bulk of city hall and the gold-domed statehouse. Then we headed east down Colfax Avenue toward the seedier parts of the city, where we saw more dive bars and tattoo parlors. Partway along Colfax, the driver stopped the bus and, without saying a word, got up and climbed off the vehicle, leaving us all sitting there, stranded.

"What the fuck he doin'?" asked an African-American kid whose jeans were down below his behind, in a theatrically loud voice.

"I always wanted to sit in that chair!" exclaimed a white kid with dyed scarlet hair, eyeing the driver's seat.

Conversation broke out among the American-born passengers. Why had our bus driver abandoned us? Was he hungry? Did he have to take a piss? Had he always wanted to walk off the job like this, leaving behind a bus full of passengers voicing questions about his whereabouts? Solomon and Methusella silently took in the hullabaloo. The expressions on their faces remained accepting, alert, and watchful. The only question on their minds appeared to be whether they faced danger. Their response to the situation differed from that of the nonimmigrant passengers, who had gone straight to anger and defiance, because they felt entitled.

The bus driver climbed back on board without a word of explanation and we continued down Colfax Avenue. A little while later, Solomon turned to me and pointed out a redbrick building near the intersection of Colfax and Quebec, on the eastern side of Denver. His father went to church there, Solomon said, his voice barely audible over the rattle of the old bus, which was how I learned that a Swahili-language church service took place within walking distance of my own house. The boys got off the bus an hour and fifteen minutes after they had left school. If they had taken the shorter route, the trip would have taken only forty-five minutes. To them, however, it was worth the extra half hour, riding on the light rail train, checking out the city's dramatic skyline, wandering around the granite-and-glass canyons of downtown, and staring at the statehouse through the bus's scratched windows. Technically it was a detour, but they were absorbing all kinds of extracurricular lessons about where influence was concentrated, and how one got from here to there.

Jakleen and Mariam, on the other hand, cared more about sleep. Often they did not manage to catch the early bus that would get them to school on time and instead caught a later bus that let them snooze, which meant that they regularly walked into Mr. Speicher's first period math class shortly after the bell had rung. Typically, they were accompanied by Ghasem, the young man from Afghanistan who had spent only a few days in the newcomer class. Ghasem was devoting himself to Jakleen, walking her around the school and meeting her for lunch. He made clear he was fond of Jakleen, though she remained coy about whether his feelings were reciprocated.

Jakleen and Mariam walked for almost one mile each morning to catch a bus that would take them all the way to the school without requiring transfers. It was the fastest route, and their total commute took about forty-five minutes, which allowed them to maximize their rest. On the way home, when they were invariably more tired, they opted for a longer commute that eliminated the long walk. They caught a bus that stopped right beside South, then transferred to a second bus that let them off close to their apartment. Going to school for seven hours a day in English exhausted the girls, and by midafternoon they were looking for the least strenuous way home.

One day, I bumped into Oula's sister, Sam, after a Student Senate meeting, and asked how it was going, in terms of mentoring Jakleen and Mariam. When I wondered which sister she was mentoring and which sister was being mentored by her twin, Sam told me, "We just kind of share them." Mr. Williams had arranged for Sam and Sana to join Jakleen and Mariam in his room one day over lunch. The four girls had spoken to one another animatedly in Arabic.

Jakleen and Mariam already understood everything that Mr. Williams said, they told Sam and Sana. They wanted to move into a more challenging class. Sam and Sana tried to act as go-betweens, and conveyed to Mr. Williams that the newcomer class felt too basic to Jakleen and Mariam. He pointed out that the sisters could not yet answer even simple questions with full sentences. He acknowledged that their comprehension was high, but they were not able to speak or write with proficiency. He gave his students constant assessments, and the girls would have to demonstrate much greater language control (using English words properly) before he would move them upstairs.

Jakleen and Mariam also expressed to Sam and Sana that they were upset at being classified as freshmen, when they believed they belonged in the upper grades. They wanted to graduate in a year or two, which they felt was justified by their age—but they were being told it would be four years, or possibly longer. Why couldn't anybody see how old they were and how intelligent? Newcomer class was beneath them! Sara, the former newcomer in the Student Senate, had mentioned having the same feeling of lagging behind her peers. "The age—you think you're not going anywhere," she said. "You know you're going to be like twenty or twenty-one by the time you graduate. Usually at twenty-one years old, you're like a junior at college. And instead, you're a senior in high school. That's, like, a humongous difference."

Sam and Sana tried to cheer up Jakleen and Mariam by explaining that if they worked harder, they could move up more quickly. They reported to Jakleen and Mariam the many successes of other students from Iraq. The twins mentioned that Oula had spent summers at Harvard and Stanford. News of Oula's triumphs lifted Jakleen and Mariam's spirits temporarily—they dared to imagine that maybe someday they could attend a prestigious college—but when they spoke with Oula, she explained that she had arrived in the United States at a younger age and had begun South ready for AP classes. Disheartened, Jakleen and Mariam's spirits fell even lower. They could never do what Oula had accomplished, they decided. It was hopeless, so why even try?

The twins mentoring them grew perplexed about how to be of assistance. They offered encouragement, only for Jakleen and Mariam to counter that they hadn't faced the same obstacles. The twins watched with mounting concern as Jakleen and Mariam continued to skip school, uncertain how to intervene. Sam told me that she worried about the girls getting low grades, having to repeat newcomer class, and getting so frustrated that they might even drop out of school. "I don't know how to tell them, you are going to fail at life if you don't come to school," Sam said miserably. "I feel like I should say that, but I don't know how to do it."

Jakleen and Mariam were not without aspirations, but their drive seemed to come and go. I also thought they might be enterprising in ways that were simply different from Oula or the twins. Those girls often appeared at school without any makeup, wearing baggy sweatshirts, looking relatively androgynous. By contrast, Jakleen and Mariam took great care with their appearance. Jakleen, in particular, watched her diet carefully, made sure her eyebrows were always sculpted, and coordinated her clothing with her lipstick. If she wore a hot-pink sweater, then she wore hot-pink lipstick, and she might even paint her nails a frosted version of the same hue. In a way that looked effortless but was actually the product of a fair amount of effort, she exerted power over boys. In certain regards, Jakleen seemed as competitive as her mentors—just not as school oriented.

During the winter, Jakleen and Mariam missed more days due to weather, and when they did show up, they sat around lethargically and announced that they did not like school. One day a Goodwill volunteer asked Jakleen to take a turn reading from a book, and instead Jakleen typed into her cell phone in Arabic, used Google Translate to change the words into English, and then held up the phone so that we could see the message: "I don't want to read." Sadness hung over the two girls like a bank of fog. Even while they were physically in Room 142, they spent an unusual amount of time on their phones. They perfected the art of holding the devices low in their laps, hidden under the tables, and texting while Mr. Williams was busy with another student. Sometimes he caught them and confiscated their phones, but often they got away with what I imagined to be silly socializing. I was perplexed by Jakleen and Mariam's frequent absences, refusal to participate, and obsession with texting until I visited them at home again, and the girls explained that they were distracted because their close friends Haifa and Noor had just departed from Damascus, even though it was the dead of winter.

Despite the freezing weather and the harsh reception awaiting them in Europe, the other two sisters had just started the risky trek to Germany. They had traveled by bus from Damascus to a border town in Turkey, and from there they had continued west across the length of Turkey to a coastal city filled with Syrians crammed into tents and hostels. They were about to attempt a boat crossing over the Aegean Sea. Criminal gangs were charging tens of thousands of dollars per crossing, often in rubber dinghies filled beyond capacity. Haifa and Noor were hoping to land on one of the islands off the coast of Greece, such as Kos or Lesbos, and from there to find safe passage to the mainland. After that, they planned to walk to Germany.

Complicating matters enormously, Haifa was eight months pregnant. Several years earlier, at age sixteen, she had married a young man whom she had met in Syria, also a refugee from Iraq. Unable to earn a living in Syria, he had returned to Iraq in search of work. Their relationship had foundered, even though Haifa was carrying their child. Mariam showed me a picture of Haifa and her husband. He wore dark jeans cuffed at the ankles with a white T-shirt, and looked like he could have been an extra in the movie *Grease*. Haifa and Noor's father had left Syria earlier, due to his inability to earn a living. The girls' parents had subsequently divorced. Now Haifa, Noor, and their mother were attempting the trip to Germany on their own because Damascus had become unlivable.

Jakleen and Mariam knew that thousands of people had died attempting to cross the Aegean. But they also remembered how frightened they had been by the violence in Jaramana and could imagine what several more years of war had wrought. If Haifa and Noor were attempting the dangerous crossing at a time of year when storms were especially fierce, while one of them was eight months pregnant, then the situation in their old neighborhood had to have grown appalling. Jakleen and Mariam could not focus on what Mr. Williams was saying because their hearts were not in Room 142; emotionally, the girls might as well have been en route to Germany themselves.

Jakleen and Mariam texted their friends constantly. The exchanges were not particularly interesting. They would write, "How are you?" And Haifa or Noor would write back, "We are tired." Every once in a while, Haifa or Noor would send a picture—like the image Mariam showed me of one of the girls wearing a quilted pink ski jacket and a black fleece hat, while carrying a black backpack and a plastic bottle filled with water, standing beside the blue-gray expanse of the Aegean. The photographs never included a full view of the girls' faces, because in the Middle Eastern way, they would avert their gaze or hold their hair across the lower half of their faces like a veil. Jakleen and Mariam did the same thing whenever Lisbeth tried to photograph them. They had all kinds of rules about modesty that diverged from American norms—they wouldn't use their real names on Facebook, for example.

Jakleen and Mariam wanted to accompany their friends every step of the way, as much as they could, so they replied instantly when Haifa or Noor texted. They told the other girls they would make it, everything would be all right. People who had lived through those car bombings in Jaramana were bonded in a way that transcended all else. When the successive cars had exploded, killing so many neighbors, the blasts had welded Haifa and Noor like family to Jakleen and Mariam. The girls might squabble or go without speaking for a period, but they always reunited. Right now, what was happening in Haifa and Noor's lives—the uncertainty over whether they would succeed in making the winter passage across that choppy, gray body of water—seemed more important to Jakleen and Mariam than anything taking place in Mr. Williams's classroom. For them, the only story that mattered was what was happening over in Syria, Turkey, and Greece. Would their friends find a boat pilot who knew the best route? Would the craft they boarded stay right side up, or would it capsize? If they landed safely in Greece, would they make it to Germany? And what kind of reception would they find there?

The Realist

I n the second week of December 2015, three days after Donald Trump called for a ban on all Muslim immigrants coming into the United States, putting the subject of refugee resettlement squarely at the center of the election discourse, Troy Cox drove over to the tan clapboard house where Solomon and Methusella had been living for the previous three months. It was time for him to do a ninety-day home visit with the family from the Democratic Republic of Congo. The visit marked the moment when the family was expected to attain self-sufficiency. Troy was a case worker with the African Community Center, a local nonprofit that was part of a national refugee resettlement agency known as the Ethiopian Community Development Council—one of the nine agencies that partners with the federal government to resettle refugees in the United States. Troy had worked closely with the family since they had arrived, because he had been assigned to help Tchiza and Beya and most of their children find their place in America.

From the get-go, Troy had found this particular assignment more perplexing than most because the family was large and were processed as three separate cases. The oldest child, Gideon, had arrived in the United States on May 20, 2015. Timoté, the next oldest, arrived four months later along with his parents and his other siblings, but he had been considered a separate case because he was over the age of twenty-one. While the family had been living in the Kyangwali refugee settlement in Uganda, Gideon and Timoté had "aged out" of the original application, and could no longer be included in the same file as everybody else.

Troy had met the bulk of the family when they landed in Colorado on September 10, at Denver International Airport. Their pending arrival had been announced on a rectangular slip of white paper pinned to the bulletin board in the common area at the African Community Center, alongside two dozen similar slips of paper describing other families slated to appear that week. The Arrivals Notifications listed the name of the primary applicant, the number of people in their party, the various languages spoken by the family (many slips of paper listed multiple languages), and the exact date, time, and flight number. Solomon and Methusella's plane landed at 11:58 P.M. Troy went to the airport with a colleague, Bizimana, who was originally from the Congo and spoke Swahili. Troy and Bizi got credentials that let them go through security to meet the family at the gate. They always did this on a pickup—otherwise, refugees tended to wander around the airport for hours before connecting with their case workers.

Almost invariably, the refugees were the very last people to disembark. That night was no exception. Dozens of passengers emerged from the walkway before Troy spotted a large group of ten people who looked disoriented from too much travel and starry-eyed at the glass-and-chrome surroundings, all wearing white IOM badges. The International Organization for Migration is an intergovernmental body with 166 member countries that coordinates the movement of refugees between nations. The IOM badges were what Troy looked for when he wanted to find a given family, but this clan would have been hard to miss. They had that glazed look that refugees wore. "There was too much going on, and they had been on airplanes for three days," Troy said later. "They were pretty quiet."

Right away, Troy handed Beya, Tchiza, and their two adult sons, Timoté and Elia (he had recently turned eighteen), each a $20 bill. This was pocket money, to use as they liked. It came out of the funds that the federal government gave to newly arrived refugees, who typically arrived penniless. With Bizi's help, Troy explained that they could use the money to buy a pack of gum or a bottle of juice or whatever they and the children might need. The money was theirs legally, to spend as they desired; Troy was just going to give it to them in small increments, until they could see the big picture. The following day, Troy would visit the family to check on them (he always did a twenty-four-hour visit, to make sure that refugees knew how to find food in America), and then he would hand every adult another $100 in cash. If he gave them that much money at this moment, when they were exhausted and disoriented, who knew how it might be spent. Tomorrow, after they had rested, Troy would go over the household budget and explain why they should save that $100 for necessities.

Troy already knew that this family's resettlement would be one of the most complicated matters he would work on that year. To begin with, he had been handed two separate case files for the ten individuals he was meeting, which in itself was unusual. Beya and Tchiza and their seven youngest children comprised one case, with nine individuals listed in that paperwork; their second-oldest son, Timoté, who was twenty-four, had a case number of his own. Then Troy had dug up Gideon's file as well.

Also, the family was especially large, which complicated everything. Each refugee was permitted to bring two checked bags, for example, and most families brought all the suitcases they were allowed. Troy and Bizi had debated how many vehicles they would need. Ten people would require ten seat belts and room for twenty suitcases. The family and their bags were not going to fit into the ACC's passenger van, which sat fifteen but had limited luggage space, so Bizi brought a second vehicle, and they had a third driver on standby. Troy had loaded ten winter coats of approximately the right sizes into the van, because the nights were getting cold, but as the family disembarked, he saw that some other aid worker must already have given them coats—nobody living in an African refugee camp possessed garments like those—so he would use the coats he'd brought for other families he would meet that fall.

August, September, and October were Troy's busy months. The flow of refugees typically swelled at that time because the UNHCR and the IOM moved as many refugees as possible into host countries right before the end of their fiscal years, which concluded on September 30. During the fall, Troy sprinted through his days, without time to eat proper meals. Each night he went to bed feeling as though there was more he should have done, and each morning he woke thinking of all the things he had forgotten to do the day before. He worked at a flat run, every day, from August to November. Whenever I spoke to him, in his small third-floor office at the ACC, he would look at me with a slightly surprised expression on his face, as if to say, *You want me to sit still and talk to you without worrying about somebody else's well-being?* Speaking with the aid worker vastly increased my understanding of what Tchiza and Beya were living through while I was observing their sons' classroom.

Most of Troy's cases were simpler. Other families he was shepherding through the process were smaller, the children were closer in age, and they had only one file, not three. Tchiza and Beya's youngest child was about to start elementary school, while their oldest already had children of his own. The welter of benefits that each individual in this particular family did or did not qualify for was proving bewildering for Troy himself. Trying to explain to the family members the various means by which the ten individuals could receive aid while they adjusted to living in the United States and attained self-sufficiency was going to occupy a lot of his time.

Troy liked to describe himself as "the realist." Refugee resettlement work attracted idealists who wanted to make the world a better place, but the job of a case manager was to be unabashedly pragmatic, as Troy saw it. You had to make a refugee's dreams conform to the day-to-day reality of living in the United States, at the bottommost rung of the socioeconomic ladder. Prospective employers might be reluctant to hire people who spoke foreign languages, and the skills that refugees arrived with sometimes had no utility in the developed world. The streets of America were paved, but just with tarmac. You had to break it to the refugees gently, but they had to get the point, fast: They must surrender the vain illusion that from this point forward everything would be easy. Not at all. Everything was going to be brutally hard. It would be tough to find a decent place to live that they could afford; it would be difficult to find any kind of job, let alone one they might enjoy; learning English would be mind-bogglingly frustrating. Plus, nobody in this country would understand their story. They would feel so unrecognized, they might as well have become ghosts.

Then there was the matter of finances. Refugees were given a one-time cash grant from the federal government upon arrival of slightly more than $1,000 per person, administered by the resettlement agency on their behalf. They could also qualify for any assistance program open to a legal resident of the United States, depending on their income level. But they were expected to become self-sufficient within a short time. Moneywise, the main challenge would be grasping that costs were going to be sky-high, and that their cash was going to vanish rapidly. The one-time stipends given to each member of this family would last perhaps three months, Troy had calculated. In other words, they had ninety days.

Troy felt optimistic about this family's chances, however, because he had already met Gideon. Whenever Troy or one of his colleagues at ACC mentioned Gideon's name, they broke into wide grins; Gideon was working full-time, his salary was high enough that he no longer qualified for public subsidies, and he had acquired a working command of English. Plus, he possessed an ever resourceful, unflaggingly cheerful attitude, which the resettlement workers admired. He represented everything that the ACC staffers hoped for, in terms of a successful outcome. At the moment, Gideon was waiting for everybody else to arrive back at the tan clapboard house, where he and his wife were cooking the rest of the family a welcome meal.

By the time a refugee family walked into their new home, a case worker had to have secured appropriate housing, arranged for bedding and furniture, provided basic cooking utensils, cleaning supplies, and groceries, and prepared a warm meal of food that the family would find familiar. Much of Troy's time over the previous two weeks had been spent finding and furnishing the house, which had three bedrooms, plus a full basement. Simply finding a suitable property large enough for this family had taken longer than usual. Even though the family might have preferred a property that was smaller and less expensive, the federal government stipulated how many bedrooms there had to be per number of individuals. In the end, Troy had been able to secure the tan clapboard house only after agreeing to an odd clause in the rental agreement. The case worker always had to cajole property managers into renting to individuals with no rental history, no job, and no Social Security numbers—it took a few weeks for refugees to obtain those. In this case, the manager had been especially reluctant, but he had agreed to rent the property to Troy after charging a higher price for the first half of the year: $2,250 per month. Then the rent would drop to $1,400 if the property was well maintained. "It was such a weird clause and it was so hard to go over it with them," Troy would say later. "I had to convince them this was basically the only option we could provide."

The money Troy had used to secure the house is often called "welcome money," although it is officially known as "reception and placement funds." The cash can be used in almost any way that a resettlement agency deems wise. It is not given directly to refugees in case they fall prey to the barrage of advertising they encounter as they enter the developed world. They might use the money to buy material goods like cell phones and television sets, only to discover they had nothing left for housing. Almost every refugee I spoke with told me they feared their case worker had stolen some of their welcome money, although the case workers were able to provide a thorough description of exactly how the money had been spent down to the last penny. In the case of Solomon and Methusella's family, the African Community Center received cash stipends of $1,025 per individual, meaning that the organization received $1,025 for Timoté and another $9,225 for Beya, Tchiza, and their seven youngest children. The ACC could legally hold on to the money for a period of three months, after which time they had to disburse the remaining funds to the family.

There was virtually never anything left to disburse. Even before the family's plane had touched down in Denver, Troy had spent $2,500 on a security deposit to secure the property on Wabash Street. He had also paid $1,400 in prorated rent for the month of September and $1,802 on furniture. Usually, he didn't spend that much—Troy was good at furnishing a house with used items that cost next to nothing—but by law all the mattresses had to be new, and he was required to buy enough mattresses to sleep ten people. He also used another $362.77 for groceries, cooking utensils, and cleaning supplies. And he purchased a $100 gift card at King Soopers, the local supermarket chain, so that the family could buy more groceries. Troy had tried to create a home with which the family would be pleased, and to that end he had spent a total of $6,224.77. In other words, before the family had even left the airport, more than half their cash was gone—and Troy had been doing this for years and was good at managing money.

It was close to 2 A.M. by the time Troy and Bizi got everybody to Wabash Street. "The reunion with Gideon was pretty emotional," Troy recalled. "Beya was superexcited and teary-eyed." Watching a family reunite always elated Troy and remained the single most rewarding aspect of his job. It was part of the reason why he worked so hard for these people, even though they were angry with him half the time, because he had to tell them things they did not want to hear. Troy wanted to let the family get reacquainted, but before he could leave, he needed to walk through the house with Tchiza and Beya and explain a few things. The housing orientation was perhaps the most critical thing Troy would do that day.

Hot water exists in America, Troy told the family. They had to be careful with the faucet handle on the left side, especially when bathing small children. Troy asked Gideon to go over the hot-water heater with Tchiza later in more detail. Electricity was another thing Troy wanted to describe. As a general rule, refugees from the Middle East understood matters like electricity and hot water, but refugees from Southeast Asia or Africa did not. This family was familiar with solar power but had never received an electricity bill. Troy showed them how to turn the lights on and off, and mentioned that as long as the lights were burning, it was costing them money. Here is what a smoke alarm sounds like, Troy said—and then he set one off. He wanted every person in the family to know what that earsplitting noise meant, in case it woke them up while they were sleeping.

He spent most of his time talking about the stove. Neither Beya nor Tchiza had ever owned one before. This was almost always the case for families coming straight from a refugee camp in Africa. In the Congo, and at the refugee settlement in Uganda, Beya had cooked the family's meals over an open fire, using wood scavenged from the surrounding area. Troy went over how to operate the stove. It was imperative that the entire family understand the appliance was for cooking. You did not use a stove to heat your house, Troy admonished. "It's never happened to me, but I've heard some terrible stories about people leaving the gas stove on all night long," he told me later. "Especially with September arrivals, it's important to go over that stuff, because it's cold."

The following day, Troy returned for his twenty-four-hour visit and handed out $100 each to Beya, Tchiza, Elia, and Timoté. This was all the cash they would get. The remainder of the welcome money would be applied toward their rent. By November, they would have exhausted the one-time stipend, but Troy hoped that at that stage, all of the adults might be working. Troy didn't get into the minutiae of the household budget he had drawn up yet, because it would be too overwhelming when the family had been in the United States for only one day. At this visit, the main thing he tried to convey was that he was available as needed; they could call him anytime. Usually, Troy would take a family grocery shopping, but in this case, Gideon brought his family to the supermarket. Their first trip could last for hours; faced with such an array of goods, refugee families frequently could not decide what to put in their carts.

Troy saved "the talk" for a few days later, when the entire family came to visit him at the ACC offices. This was called, in official resettlement parlance, "arrival and orientation." The meeting had to happen within seven days. Troy needed only the adults, but Beya and Tchiza brought everyone—ten people plus himself. Troy ushered them all into the staff room, where the family sat down at a large conference table ringed by fancy chairs, with the little children constantly swiveling in their seats. Bizi translated as Troy explained things. The theme of "the talk" was that life in America is hard. They had to become self-sufficient as quickly as possible. Troy urged them to take any job that was offered, no matter how menial. The faster the adults started working, the better off the whole family would be; even a job that paid minimum wage was better than welfare. And they had to work as a team. Elia and Timoté had to contribute to the family's well-being—they had to help pay the bills that were about to start coming in the mail—or else Troy could not make the math work.

Next, Troy went over the documents. They had all received I-94s, a special visa given to refugees. "Do not lose this," Troy told them. The visa allowed them to work, and it also enabled the adults to acquire another document that would serve as their main form of identification, something called an employment authorization card. After one year, the visa would expire, and then they would need to apply for legal residency and obtain green cards.

After that, Troy went over their rights and responsibilities. They had to pay taxes, and they had to obey the laws of the United States. Cars were expensive and required insurance; if they started driving, they would need to know traffic regulations. He recommended using the bus system. Also, in the United States, it was illegal for an adult to have sex with a minor. If the older boys wanted to date, they had to make certain the girls they developed a fondness for were at least seventeen. Most critically for a family of ten with no income at present, they qualified for all of the state and federal subsidies available to people living below the poverty line.

Next, Troy went over those benefits, always the most confusing topic. Different programs had varying age cutoffs, which meant that various family members would be eligible for a unique set of subsidies. Basically, one or more members of the family would qualify for each of the following programs, available to every American living below a certain income: TANF (Temporary Assistance for Needy Families), food stamps, and Medicaid. Plus, a few family members would qualify for CARES, the refugee cash assistance program that provides a brief safety net to refugees who do not qualify for TANF. Typically, families qualify for either TANF or CARES, and it was unusual for one family to participate in both programs.

The main income subsidy that most of the family would depend upon until the adults found work was TANF. Gideon, Elia, and Timoté had to be subtracted from the TANF equation, however, because they were over eighteen. The rest of the family—Tchiza, Beya, and the six younger children—qualified. A family with two parents and six dependents that had no income qualified for the maximum subsidy allowable, $895 per month. As soon as Tchiza started working, the allotment would go down, but he could continue to receive some assistance as long as his income remained below a certain level. Because he was going to expedite the benefit, Troy told them they could expect to start receiving TANF money within seven days.

Meanwhile, Elia and Timoté qualified for CARES, a program that supports refugees who do not qualify for TANF (single adults over the age of eighteen, or couples without children). Both Elia and Timoté would receive $335 per month from CARES. At the moment, Solomon was seventeen, so he remained part of the family unit that qualified for TANF, but on January 1, 2016, when he turned eighteen, he would go off TANF and on CARES. CARES would be available to Elia, Timoté, and Solomon for only eight months, starting from the moment they arrived in the United States. Troy doubted that they would use it for that long. As soon as any of them started working and earned more than $335—which Troy expected would happen quickly—they would stop receiving the subsidy. Most of his clients did not use CARES or TANF for lengthy periods. The resettlement agency stressed the need to become self-sufficient, and the refugees themselves disliked handouts. They could earn more by working.

Confusingly, the rules for food stamps were different. Dependents are eligible until the age of twenty-two. Therefore, Elia was included in the family's food stamps benefit, although Timoté was not; for the purposes of this subsidy, the family would consist of two caretakers and seven children. The family's food stamps allotment was $1,315 per month, as long as they had zero income. As soon as anybody started working, this subsidy would drop. Also, Elia and Timoté had to report the income they were getting from CARES, which affected the amount the family got in food stamps; TANF income did not affect their food stamps allotment.

"It was very hard to explain all this to them," Troy said.

I had no doubt that was true. It was hard for him to explain all of this to me, and I had been speaking English my whole life. We were sitting in his office at the ACC as we spoke. Troy was a fervent young man in his early thirties with a full beard and tortoiseshell glasses that made him look like an academic, although he spent his days buried in the nitty-gritty of how to get by in America on very little money, rather than books. Behind him, on the wall, he had hung three black-and-white photographs of small children from Sudan. He had moved there directly after finishing college and had rebuilt schools, hospitals, and churches destroyed during one of that country's civil wars. After war broke out again, Troy worked in a refugee camp distributing food rations.

During our time together, Troy fielded a stream of interruptions. Refugees called his cell phone and his office phone; colleagues knocked on his door, or walked in without knocking. Every interruption involved some query related to a family who had recently arrived in the United States. The African Community Center employed only four case workers and handled close to 600 active cases. As we spoke, Troy was juggling more than 150 cases himself. Even though he had to concentrate on a given family for only three to six months, he still carried a crushing workload. I felt a little guilty for distracting him from his job.

Troy said that after "the talk," he imagined that Solomon and Methusella's family would be fine until his next regularly scheduled visit, thirty days after their arrival. Instead he drove over to check on them the following week, because the ACC had been notified that they were running low on food. Most of the children were enrolled in school, so the only people Troy found at the house were Tchiza, Beya, and their daughter Zawadi. He took them to the building that housed the state's food stamps program and secured approval for the benefit that same day. Then he brought them to a grocery store to show them how to use the plastic card they had just received. It functioned exactly like a credit card or a debit card, but Tchiza and Beya had never owned either of those before, so the whole idea of swiping a piece of plastic to buy things was unfamiliar. Troy explained that the food stamps benefit sounded like a lot of money, but was not really enough to feed them all, unless they were thrifty. They could not afford to buy steak, he emphasized—they had to buy the cheap cuts of meat. Also, the food stamps benefit could not be used to obtain prepared food from the deli, or home supplies such as paper towels or Ziploc bags. Once he was satisfied that they understood how to buy food, Troy said he would see them at the thirty-day home visit.

Actually, the thirty-day home visit took place twenty-three days after their arrival, because of Tchiza's confusion around finances. He thought that he understood everything Troy had told him, but many things proved mystifying. For example, Tchiza feared he was not receiving any money from TANF; actually, Troy explained, the TANF money had been attached to the same plastic card that he thought of as being for food stamps. Troy spent three hours with Tchiza and Beya, going over all of the household finances a second time. He drew up a rent calendar, labeling each month and writing down what the ACC would contribute and how much the family would have to pay. While the ACC had been able to cover the October rent, using up another $2,250 of the family's cash, by November all that would be left of the one-time stipend was $678. After Troy applied that to the November bill, the family would have to make up the remainder. And then the cash would be gone. The family would have to pay the entire December rent bill themselves.

Troy thought he had been completely clear and didn't expect to see the family again until the ninety-day visit, scheduled for the middle of December. At the beginning of November, however, their landlord complained that Tchiza had neglected to pay his portion of the rent. Troy drove over and learned that Tchiza had not known how to get the TANF dollars off the little plastic card and into the hands of his landlord—nobody had shown him how to generate a money order. Troy felt terrible that he had neglected to cover this; he usually went over it during the twenty-four-hour visit, but Gideon had managed the first trip to the grocery store, and Troy had forgotten to tell Gideon to instruct his father in how to get a money order. "It was worrisome for me because they were a huge family and I did not want them to end up in a bad place," Troy said later. "Like, close to homelessness. I've had a few clients end up homeless, but they were special cases—mental health issues, huge amounts of trauma."

Troy took Tchiza to King Soopers to show him how to obtain a money order. From that point forward, Tchiza made his rent payments on time. All of the adults in the household scrambled to find jobs, as Troy had advised. When they had visited the ACC for "the talk," Troy had walked the grown-ups over to the area where the employment team worked, and had red-flagged Tchiza and Beya's case. "We need to get as many people in this family working as possible as quickly as we can," Troy had told his colleague Hussen Abdulahi, an employment specialist. "Anybody old enough needs to work." Hussen and the rest of the ACC's employment team scoured the community to find jobs that refugees could do and then played matchmaker between employers and employees. Hotels, local manufacturing sites, and meatpacking plants were the largest employers of refugees in the region. The first thing that Hussen always did with a refugee looking for work was perform an assessment, which he did right away with Tchiza, Beya, Elia, and Timoté. As Hussen spoke with Tchiza about his level of education and his job experience, he sized the man up. To understand a given refugee's state of mind, Hussen asked himself: Is this person stressed? Does he have a happy home life? Is he shy or outgoing? Tchiza had many strengths. He was gregarious, had a supportive family, and possessed humility. He was also in superb physical condition, from a lifetime of farming, which meant that he could handle hard labor. Employers would like this man, Hussen imagined.

Like Tchiza himself, Hussen was originally from Africa—Ethiopia, in his case—and he did not make the mistake of underestimating Tchiza. When Tchiza said he had no work experience that he could list on a résumé, Hussen asked him to describe how he had fed a family of eleven with his bare hands. Then he translated what Tchiza said into résumé-speak. They listed the following skills: sowing crops, preparing crops for market, assisting in the births of live animals, caring for newborn animals, cleaning and disinfecting buildings used to house crops and animals, and preventing the spread of disease among livestock. Hussen also took note of the fact that Tchiza had a tenth-grade education. "In the region that he's from, that's very rare," Hussen said afterward.

Hussen and Tchiza worked to create both a long-term plan and a short-term plan for the family's integration into the United States. The long-term plan was easy. Tchiza wanted to learn how to speak English, become a citizen, and buy his own home. Hussen assured him that was doable, perhaps even within the span of five years, if he worked hard and embraced the concept of borrowing money. The idea of borrowing a huge sum from a bank to buy a house was foreign to Tchiza. "You are here in America now—think like an American," Hussen told him. The short-term plan was more difficult. How to get from here to there? Hussen worked with Tchiza to identify intermediate steps he could take. They agreed Tchiza would attend English as a second language classes, go to job-training seminars, and get a job.

Yet Hussen had a hard time finding work for Tchiza. By the time Troy Cox returned to the tan clapboard house for the ninety-day visit, on December 9, both Elia and Timoté had successfully found work as "housemen," cleaning the public areas of a Hyatt Place hotel. They were earning $10 an hour, more than they had been getting from CARES, and both of them had stopped accepting that subsidy. They had also enrolled in English classes at a local community college. Troy spoke to the two young men firmly about not buying material goods. Sneakers, jeans, watches, cell phones, cars—they lusted for all those things. Troy counseled them to buy gadgets and flashy wardrobes later. Right now, they had to help their family pay the rent. Both Elia and Timoté had to give their parents $300 toward rent every month, Troy urged, or else the family could face eviction.

Tchiza felt he should support the family himself and did not want to rely on his sons for money; Troy replied that in the United States they were going to have to work as a team. Using their TANF money and the incomes that Elia and Timoté were earning, the family paid December's rent without help from ACC. Troy expressed concern, however, that Tchiza had not yet found a job. "Age discrimination," Hussen said, when I asked why securing a job for Tchiza had proved more difficult than for his sons. Employers preferred to hire young men or women rather than older adults, according to the employment specialist. The other factor, Hussen said, was Tchiza's desired schedule. Whereas Elia and Timoté had been willing to work any hours, Tchiza preferred not to work on Saturday or Sunday. He wanted time with his family, and it was important to him to attend church. Hussen was having a hard time finding a family-friendly job with weekends off for a refugee who was fifty-two.

At the ninety-day meeting, Troy impressed upon Tchiza the importance of securing employment: "Any job in America will pay more money than TANF," the case manager advised. Troy also wanted Beya to take a shift at a local day care, but she balked—Beya had never worked outside the home and wanted to devote herself to caring for her own children. Tchiza spent the rest of that month assiduously attending job-training classes at the African Community Center. On December 22, he applied for a position as a dishwasher at a corporate cafeteria, working the day shift Monday through Friday. Early the following month, he was offered the post. He started on January 19, 2016. Once they established the three income streams—Tchiza's new dishwashing job, and Elia and Timoté's two hotel jobs—the family achieved what the ACC considered economic self-sufficiency. Tchiza earned so little and had so many dependents that the family still qualified for food stamps, but at a reduced amount.

Money remained tight because of the whopping rent. Instead of following Troy's advice and asking Beya to work, the family looked for cheaper housing. In January, they found an apartment that cost $1,000 less than what they had been paying. It had only two bedrooms, and the ten family members would be jamming themselves into a smaller space than Troy would have considered feasible, but they deemed the space adequate and planned to move there in February. At that point, their finances would stabilize. In each case, Tchiza, Elia, and Timoté had taken the first job they were offered, as advised. Beya had not yet embraced the idea of working, but by squeezing into a smaller living space, the family found an alternate way to achieve the goal of economic self-sufficiency. Troy received no more phone calls about financial emergencies. In four months' time, the family had transitioned successfully from living in a refugee settlement in Uganda to living in a large urban center in the middle of the United States.

"It was pretty spectacular," Troy said.

Meanwhile, a few of the students in Solomon and Methusella's classroom were exhibiting growth that could be called pretty spectacular, too. And during the second half of the school year, after they had settled into their new lives a little bit, the newcomers began revealing far more of their true personalities.

3

What Five Times
(or, "I Work My Ass Off")

When school resumed after the holidays, in January 2016, Mr. Williams opened the new semester by asking all of his students to tell him what they had done over winter break.

"Guys, what do we mean by this word, 'break'? B-R-E-A-K, break?"

"Vacation," Uyen said promptly.

Uyen had put on her pink Converse High Tops that morning. She was about to leave the newcomer classroom for good, as was Stephanie. The two friends—one from Vietnam, the other from Mexico—had progressed so rapidly that they were being moved into a more advanced ELA class. They would switch rooms in a couple of days.

Mr. Williams asked Hsar Htoo and Nadia to stand at the front of the room and discuss what they had done over the holiday. As the students acquired more facility with English, he wanted to push them to get over their fear of speaking in public. Hsar Htoo said that he had watched two movies, slept a lot, and played soccer.

Mr. Williams asked if he had been happy or sad.

"Happy."

Then Mr. Williams asked Nadia how her break had been.

"Sad," said Nadia.

"On my vacation, I felt sad?" Mr. Williams asked. (He was suggesting that she should say it in a full sentence.) Nadia nodded.

Mr. Williams wrote on the whiteboard that Nadia felt sad, but Hsar Htoo felt happy. Then he wrote a lot more sentences like that—sentences involving comparisons, using the word "but" in the middle. The teacher wanted the students to practice using conjunctions to connect clauses.

He was also showing them how to use the past tense at the same time. Over his break, Mr. Williams had spent a lot of his free time riding his mountain bike in parks with his son, Owen. By this point I knew him well enough to recognize him as a fellow introvert. That was how he tested on the Meyers-Briggs personality rubric, he confirmed. He had been teaching for fourteen years, however, and the time he had spent in the classroom had caused a shift in his personality—he was now more extroverted than he had been at the start of his career. He still needed to watch his energy level, though, because the hours he spent in the classroom were depleting. Escaping from the demands of his students for a while had allowed him to return filled with new energy.

Mr. Williams asked his students to gather in pairs and discuss their vacations with each other. Jakleen and Mariam were absent, but everybody else had made it to school. Amaniel, from Eritrea, could not stop smiling as he announced that his family had thrown a party and he had danced all night. Ksanet and Yonatan said that for them, the holiday of Natale (their name for the commemoration of the birth of Jesus Christ) fell on January 7. I asked what they were going to do to celebrate, and they looked at me in surprise.

"Go to church," Ksanet said, as if the answer were obvious.

"For how long?" I asked.

"All day!" said Ksanet, like, *of course*.

Saúl said he had spent his break shoveling snow. I thought it must be hard for him to allow his older sisters to pay the rent, and perhaps shoveling sidewalks assuaged the guilt he carried for letting his sisters support him when he was an able-bodied young man.

Later, Mr. Williams distributed a handout with a story about a soccer game, written in the past tense. Titled "An Upset," the story concerned a contest in which an underdog team triumphs. Mr. Williams asked if anybody could name a really lousy soccer team, and Methusella said, "QPR!" The Queens Park Rangers were a second-tier British soccer club out of London. Mr. Williams asked Methusella to come up to the front of the room.

"We're going to act this out, okay?" he said.

Methusella and Mr. DeRose faced each other as Mr. Williams read the story aloud. Mr. DeRose feinted and spun and grimaced and cheered, while Methusella stood still, staring at the teacher's aide. Perhaps he had never seen a grown teacher behave like this before. Instinctively, though, Methusella dodged when Mr. DeRose approached him. Then he sponta- neously faked a goal, and an unbidden smile broke through his reserve.

Nicole arrived in Room 142 the following day. Like Solomon and Methusella, she was originally from the Democratic Republic of Congo, and like the two brothers, she was from the eastern side of that coun- try, the side that had slid into armed conflict countless times over the past several decades. The boys were from North Kivu, and she was from South Kivu; the two adjacent provinces were separated by Lake Kivu. When Nicole first showed up, I had no idea where to find either of the Kivus, or the lake of the same name. American news coverage could be spotty when it came to world affairs, and I had formerly prioritized domestic news over international news in my own reading. As a result, Solomon and Methusella had grown up in circumstances that were unknown to me, even though I was an educated person who considered myself well informed.

Nicole did not join the other students as a peer. She was a senior at South, and she came to the classroom as a volunteer. Mr. Williams thought she could help him manage the room and she could show the other students that you could arrive in the United States from a difficult place and you could heal, grow, adapt. Every day of the week, while liv- ing in an apartment that she shared with many other people, without either of her parents to watch over her, Nicole assembled the kind of outfit that one might see on a fashion runway. One day, for example, she arrived in leopard print tights, with a patterned minidress, a short jacket, and electric-blue extensions in her hair; another day she wore paisley leggings with combat boots and purple braids. She had a tough story, but her outfits announced that she wanted to be defined instead by her colorful aspirations.

On her first day in Room 142, Mr. Williams asked Nicole to intro- duce herself to everyone. Could she say a few words? Nicole told the room that when she had arrived in the United States, she hadn't known any English, either. "I didn't know how to say 'Hi,' or anything, when I first came," she said. "Don't be shy. Keep trying. You should always talk to people, and you should ask a lot of questions."

When the newcomers did not understand something, Nicole advised, they had to ask. She quantified: "You have to say, 'What?' like, five times."

Nicole spoke Swahili, French, Lingala, Kirundi, and English. Over the days that followed, she moved around the classroom, murmuring to Nadia, Grace, Solomon, and Methusella, the four students who spoke Swahili; later, when others arrived who spoke French, Nicole whispered with them, too. She shared a running side commentary about the day's lessons with the students from Africa, just as Mr. De-Rose did with those from Central America, making the room more comprehensible.

Nicole stitched together disparate parts of the room. She helped me understand the boys from the Congo better, and she helped various kids from Africa make sense of Mr. Williams's instructions. A feeling of community was starting to form in Room 142, and Nicole accelerated that process. One day, when we had some spare time, I mentioned to Nicole what I had learned about Solomon and Methusella's background. I wondered if she was familiar with the city of Goma, where they had said they were from. She was. She had lived in Bukavu, she told me, a city that faces Goma from the opposite side of Lake Kivu.

Goma and Bukavu had turned into battlegrounds at various points in the DRC's history. The Rwandan genocide of 1994 had sparked mass killings throughout the eastern Congo, a place that is similarly divided between Hutu and Tutsi. After spilling over into the Congo, the situation had grown multifarious, and many different tribes had gotten snared in the widening conflict. "You see blood everywhere and people are running around and mostly people are crying and trying to find a way to go somewhere else," Nicole said, describing her memories of combat in her home city. "Sometimes the soldiers come to your house and ask you for money, and if you don't have money they might take your husband or cut you. Some people, they get raped. And they kill some people. Most people were just waiting to die. That's how it is. Just waiting to die."

Nicole's mother and father came from different tribes that began slaughtering one another. One night, some of her mother's relatives broke into their home and murdered her father. She was awakened by an older brother, who hustled her out of the house, saying they had to run away. Nicole was eight at the time, and she escaped with a jumbled sense that maybe her mother's relatives had wanted to kill the children, too. Nicole and her brothers wound up walking for several months, until they reached the safety of Tanzania. One of her brothers died along the way, though Nicole did not know why; maybe he had died of starvation, maybe it was dysentery, maybe it was something else. She was too young to make sense of what befell him. In Tanzania, Nicole and her siblings sought shelter in a refugee camp, where an older woman adopted them. Later, this woman told the children that she was their grandmother. Was she truly a blood relative? I was hazy on this—parts of Nicole's story were hard to verify.

The refugee crisis had been building over many decades, and Nicole's story represented an earlier chapter in the global narrative. Her flight from the DRC occurred before the civil war in Syria, back when the refugee crisis had been fueled primarily by upheavals in Africa and Southeast Asia. Nicole was part of the hidden side of the crisis, before Middle Eastern refugees started walking to Germany and wound up on the front pages of newspapers in the United States and Europe. The major conflicts in Africa (in Somalia, Ethiopia, Eritrea, Sudan, and the Democratic Republic of Congo, among other places) had produced so many refugees that Africa now contained the world's biggest camps. Ben Rawlence, a former researcher for Human Rights Watch, did a masterful job depicting Dadaab, the largest refugee camp anywhere on the globe, in his book *City of Thorns*. It was hard for me to reconcile an eight-year-old version of Nicole with the kinds of scenes depicted in *City of Thorns*, but I knew that was the kind of life Nicole had led for six years.

In 2012, when Nicole was fourteen, she and her brothers were accepted for resettlement in the United States. Shortly before Nicole began volunteering in Room 142, a Congolese woman who had recently arrived in the United States shared some photographs with her, and Nicole recognized her mother in one of the images. For the previous decade, Nicole had feared that her mother had been killed, but she was actually living in a refugee camp in Uganda. Nicole had just resumed contact with her mother, and they were now speaking regularly by phone, even though they had not seen each other in ten years.

As we sat at a table in Mr. Williams's room, Nicole said that she had only just started telling people her story. "Like before, I really didn't want to talk about it," she added. When she said this, I realized that Nicole was offering her story to illustrate why I should not ask the newcomers too many questions. Tread lightly in this room, she seemed to be saying. These kids have only just arrived, and you have no idea what they've lived through.

In the second week of January, Mr. Williams spent a lot of time going over the words who, what, when, where, and why, using them in the interrogative form. Known as the Five W's, the words are understood by journalists as the key questions that must be answered to collect a complete story. As I looked around the room, I realized that I had gathered answers to many of these key questions: I knew who was in the room, when they had arrived, and where they were from. In most cases, however, I did not know why certain students had left their homelands, or what had forced them to do so. I had learned a lot about Jakleen and Mariam's departure from the Middle East, but I understood much less about Solomon and Methusella's reasons for leaving their home in Africa. And I knew next to nothing about any of the families from Southeast Asia. Because of the discussion I'd just had with Nicole, however, I decided that it was fine to proceed at an unusually slow pace, by journalistic standards. In time, maybe I would discover more.

The interrogative words were hard for Mr. Williams to explain. Previously, he had smiled in an exaggerated way as he said "happy," and he had frowned and put his fists on his hips as he said "angry." At another point, Mr. Williams had used dry-erase markers to show the students words for shapes and colors; he had drawn a red circle, a blue square, and a green triangle on the whiteboard, and written words for those colors and shapes. But it was hard to act out the meaning of "who" or to draw the meaning of "what." Instead he used those words in sentences, employing familiar people or routines from South. Then he asked Methusella to stand in front of the class and pretend to be the teacher and ask someone else a question.

"When does school end?" Methusella asked Lisbeth.

Lisbeth lifted her shoulders and her eyebrows toward the ceiling and looked imploringly at Mr. Williams.

In the past, Mr. Williams might have translated the question into Spanish, but at this stage he thought it was time for Lisbeth to find her voice in English.

"You could say, 'Can you repeat that?'" Mr. Williams suggested.

"Can . . . you . . . ," Lisbeth said to Methusella. Then she turned to Mr. Williams. "Ree-peet?"

"Repeat," he assured her.

"Can . . . you . . . reepeet . . . that?" Lisbeth said haltingly.

"When does school end?" Methusella asked again, more slowly.

"Ah! School ends at three o'clock," Lisbeth answered perfectly.

Mr. Williams gave her a high five. Then he asked other students to raise their hands if they could think of a question that began with the word "who."

"Who is the math teacher?" asked Solomon.

"Mr. Speicher!" called out his classmates.

"Who is the nurse?" asked Yonatan.

"Ms. Kelly!"

"Who is the janitor of South High School?" asked Saúl.

Nobody knew.

Saúl's hair was going in nine different directions. He did not have a mother in this country to help him to find a comb, and he'd spent his break shoveling snow. I thought he was deliberately pointing out that there were people in the building we could not name.

One table away, Mr. DeRose crouched down beside Jakleen.

"Who is Mrs. Small?" he asked.

Jakleen chose each word with exquisite caution, as if she were picking up glassware and did not want to drop anything.

"Mrs. Small. Is the teacher. For. Dance class," answered Jakleen.

"Yes!" said Mr. DeRose.

On the far side of the room, Mr. Williams was leaning on a purple plastic chair, balanced on two legs, as he asked questions of Dilli. She wore a yellow T-shirt, purple jeans, and pink-and-black-checked sneakers, her loud clothing at odds with her quiet demeanor. Then Mr. Williams put his head down to catch Dilli's exceedingly soft answer—inaudible to me, on my side of the room. Nadia and her sister Grace watched their exchange with broad smiles, as if they were proud of Dilli for producing actual sound.

Following the lesson about the interrogative words, Mr. Williams introduced a new book called *Alexei's Week*. It told the story of a Russian student named Alexei who moved to the United States. On the night before his first day of school, Alexei couldn't sleep, because he was worried about how things would go. At school, Alexei felt confused and lonely, and could not find his way around the new building. At lunch, he sat by himself, friendless. Things improved later, when he met another student from Russia.

After they read the book out loud together, Mr. Williams asked the class if they knew the meaning of the word "worried," and everybody competed to see who could make the best worried face. Mr. DeRose won by doing Macaulay Culkin in *Home Alone*, hands slapped against his cheeks, mouth in a big O.

We broke up into small groups to talk about when each of us had felt worried. Methusella said he had felt worried while watching a scary movie. Yonatan announced that, like Alexei, he had not been able to sleep the night before, but in his case that was because he had been on Facebook. A general conversation ensued about Facebook, which led us far afield from worriedness. I was worried about Jakleen and Mariam, who had made it to school every day this week but had just run into difficulty again. It was their father's birthday, and halfway through the school day, the girls wound up crying in the school social worker's office.

Meanwhile, Mr. Williams was worried about navigating a fundamental shift in his lessons. At this point in the year, the teacher was pivoting from conversational English to more academic skills. Summarizing was an essential skill that the students had yet to master—they could repeat things by rote, but they ran into difficulty if he asked them to recount a story in their own words. It was hard for them to come up with original phrasing. This ability grew with speech emergence, the third phase of language acquisition, after preproduction and early production.

That afternoon, Mr. Williams asked if I would help him. Mr. DeRose was going to coach the students as they acted out passages from *Alexei's Week*. Would I sit at a table and ask questions that would prompt a series of students into retelling the story? I got nothing from the students when I said, "What is the main idea of this book?" Or when I asked, "What happened to Alexei in this story?" But the students started talking when I asked, "Why was Alexei sitting alone at lunch?" Alexei's solitary status was something they all wanted to explain. One student said, "He's new!" Another said sadly, "He doesn't have friends."

This was the condition of the three new students who arrived in Room 142 on a single day the following week, in the middle of January. All three looked completely bewildered, as Mr. Williams went around smiling and shaking hands. He had the most luck connecting with Abigail, a girl with deep dimples in her cheeks and straight black hair plaited into two braids. She was from Mexico and spoke Spanish. Mr. Williams made certain to introduce her to Lisbeth, who became instantly maternal. "Do you have free and reduced lunch?" I heard Lisbeth asking Abigail in Spanish later that day, as she escorted her new friend upstairs to the cafeteria.

Mr. Williams also shook hands with a tall boy named Plamedi, who wore a polo shirt buttoned all the way up, a brown sweater, and a gray parka that he kept on all day, even though the school building was exceedingly well heated. Plamedi was from the Democratic Republic of Congo. Mr. Williams tried introducing him to Solomon, but the two boys could not speak to each other. Plamedi was from the capital city of Kinshasa, and he spoke only French, the dominant language on the western side of the DRC, which Solomon didn't know. Solomon wore a grave expression as he greeted Plamedi formally in English, holding Plamedi's hand for the entirety of the exchange, in the traditional African manner. Because Nicole spoke French, she helped the new student from her home country get settled.

Nobody could talk to Bachan. During a period of ethnic cleansing, many Nepali-speaking people were forced out of their homeland of Bhutan, located in the Himalayas. Later that year I would learn that Bachan's family was among the dispossessed. On his first day at South, Bachan wore a flannel shirt, faded blue jeans, and an I'm-stuck-in-another-world expression. Finding himself marooned in a place where nobody shared his language, Bachan's response was to tune out everything that happened. He stayed in a dreamy place of his own, not paying attention to anything Mr. Williams said. He drew pictures in his notebook or put his head down and slumbered. From time to time, Mr. Williams tried to bring him back to Room 142 by calling out his name—usually in a singsong, "Bacha-a-a-an, Bacha-a-a-an"—which invariably caused the Bhutanese boy to jerk in surprise. He looked around perplexedly, as if he had no idea what to make of all this tomfoolery.

Mr. Williams now had seventeen students. (He would have had nineteen, but Uyen and Stephanie had advanced upstairs.) Nadia and Grace immediately started coaching the latest arrivals. The two sisters from Mozambique opened up the other students' textbooks to the right pages and showed them where Mr. Williams kept the extra pencils. Other students soon followed their lead and displayed an extraordinary level of kindness to the new kids. Mr. Williams jumped right back into a lesson on relative pronouns—they were now using who, what, where, when, and how in the middle of sentences—trusting that the most recent arrivals would eventually make sense of what he was saying. "Room 142 is where we have newcomer class," Mr. Williams said. "The fourth floor is where we eat lunch." The teacher wrote these sentences on the whiteboard. He was supplying examples of how to use relative pronouns, and also providing guideposts to orient the new students. He asked everyone to complete an exercise in their textbook involving relative pronouns.

Saúl—wearing a gray T-shirt that said PARIS, with a picture of the Eiffel Tower on it—got up and walked over to Abigail.

"*Quieres ayuda?*" he asked the new girl from Mexico.

She did want help. Saúl proceeded to dictate all of the correct answers to her. I did not think it was the best teaching technique, but I liked his impulse to be generous.

* * *

A few days after the new students arrived, Room 142 filled with hubbub as Mr. Williams drew a picture of a hedgehog on the whiteboard. The students who had been with him for several months were opening up and talking more freely, mostly in English.

"Mister! Is it like a big rat?" asked Grace.

"It's cute," said Saúl.

"Short," said Grace. "Fat."

"Small nose," said Yonatan.

"*Qué bonita!*" sang Lisbeth.

Both Jakleen and Mariam were present, even though it was snowing. Meanwhile, Dilli had acquired magenta extensions and looked like an entirely different person. Mr. Williams told the class to open their notebooks to a fresh piece of paper.

"A new page?" asked Grace, seeking to clarify.

"Yeah."

Mr. Williams showed the class an animated video of a hedgehog enjoying various winter sports. The animal had a series of misadventures while snowboarding, ice-skating, and sledding.

"How many people have been sledding?" Mr. Williams asked.

Nobody in the room had gone sledding.

Mr. Williams asked the students to come up with a group summary of the video as he pantomimed whatever the students said, to their delight. The teacher was using the video as a segue to get the students to produce more original language. The ability to retell a story—summarizing— remained the key skill that he wanted them to practice. Today he was employing a video that made the kids laugh, but in the weeks to come, he would coach them to retell stories they had read as well. He and Mr. DeRose also took turns pausing to integrate the newest students into the room. Plamedi's family had arrived in the United States after winning a green card lottery, and he had never lived in a refugee camp. Because he spoke French, a Romance language, he found English relatively easy to absorb. Abigail spoke another Romance language, but she was much more introverted, and her inhibitions slowed her down. At first she was too shy to say a single word in English, but soon she began to discover all the vocabulary it had in common with her native Spanish. Bachan remained in his own dreamland, stubbornly out of reach. When Mr. Williams tried summoning him with another lullaby—"Bacha-a-a-an, Bacha-a-a-an!"—the student glared at the teacher, with a haughty expression on his face, as if to say, *You call that blather a language?* Accepting a second language involved letting go of the idea that meaning could be found unswervingly in one place, and apparently Bachan was having none of it. I was impressed by his dreamy refusal, his I'm-elsewhere resistance, even though it meant he didn't get very far academically.

As the students who had been present for many months grew linguistically, they branched out socially, too. At lunch, half the room brought trays of food back down to Room 142. Ksanet talked to a friend in Tigrinya on her cell phone, as Dilli sat quietly beside her, gaudy magenta ringlets at odds with her reticence. Kaee Reh began singing to himself in Karenni again, as Grace and Nadia chatted in Portuguese. Then Jakleen arrived holding a Starbucks Frappuccino, sat down at the same table as Ksanet and Dilli, and slid a stick of gum across to each of those girls. The kids were beginning to interact.

After lunch, the newcomers resumed writing the narration about the hedgehog. Mr. Williams walked around the room, checking to see how each student was faring.

"Skates?" Ksanet said to him. A one-word question.

Mr. Williams drew a picture of ice skates, then pantomimed putting those objects onto his feet and skating across the room's navy carpet. Ksanet nodded in recognition: *Oh,* that's *what skates are.*

On to the next student.

"Mariam, do you have any questions?" he asked.

Mariam looked at him blankly.

"*Ella no entiende,*" Lisbeth told Mr. Williams in Spanish.

"Okay, Abigail, *hay palabras que no conoces?*"

"*Todos!*" said Saúl, joking.

Were there any words that Abigail did not know? All of them!

Saúl may have been right. Mr. Williams asked the room to tell him, on a scale of one to five, how hard they found the material. Abigail said one, very hard. Yonatan, same. However, Jakleen, Grace, Methusella, Solomon, Hsar Htoo, and Plamedi all said five, very easy. The other nine students in the room fell somewhere in the middle. At the midway point in the school year, this had become Mr. Williams's central challenge: teaching English to one classroom filled with seventeen students who spoke ten different home languages and exhibited vastly differing abilities to comprehend his lessons.

Mr. Williams took out a green dry-erase marker and underlined every verb in the narration. He showed the students how to pantomime each verb, illustrating their meaning with body language, and then he persuaded the entire class to act out the story. Jakleen acted woodenly; Lisbeth, dramatically. When it was her turn, Abigail's dimples reached new levels of deepness, she was so embarrassed at being asked to perform in front of the class. I noticed Hsar Htoo take out a yellow highlighter and Solomon a blue one. Both of them mimicked Mr. Williams, diligently highlighting all of the verbs themselves. Bachan stared out the window, courting oblivion. How could one instructor push a prodigy like Methusella, salvage a child as lost as Bachan, and keep up with his other students, all at the same time?

Plus another: At the end of January, one more new student walked through Mr. Williams's door. She would be one of the last pupils to arrive, meaning that the formation of his class was almost complete. Her name was Shahnozakhon, which was virtually unpronounceable, so everybody called her Shani. Shani was from Tajikistan, and nobody in the school knew how to speak Tajik. Mr. Williams had absolutely no means of communicating with Shani. She had coal-black hair and pale white skin and she wore tiny gold earrings with ruby stones. Despite being impossible to communicate with verbally, she had an affectionate, puppy-like personality. Also, she had the endearing habit of winding up by accident in remote parts of the building. A few days after she arrived, one of the school's uniformed security guards walked into Room 142, five minutes after the bell, with a dazed-looking Shani. "Shani got lost," the guard announced. "So . . ." He shrugged, as if to say, *I had to rescue her.*

After a few days, Mr. Williams wondered if Shani might speak other languages. He mentioned various countries close to Tajikistan. "Iran!" Shani exclaimed excitedly at one point. "Farsi?" asked Mr. Williams. Shani nodded happily. "Farsi!" she repeated. Mr. Williams dispatched someone to summon Rahim, one of the young men from Afghanistan who had reported to Room 142 at the beginning of the year. Tall and elegant, Rahim towered over Shani. He said something in Farsi.

"No Farsi!" Shani cried in English, objecting to this. "No Farsi! *Tajik!*"

At least the girl was communicative, even if she did not know Farsi. Mr. Williams would try Russian, next—but not today. He had other students to worry about.

By this point, many of the newcomers had picked up enough English to have genuine interchanges during their lessons, the kind that carried some sort of emotional charge. One of those took place a few days later, as Mr. Williams coached the students on making sentences that began with "I am" and "You are." This was a review for his longtime pupils, and new material for the rest. He wrote on the whiteboard:

I am in math class.
Are you in my gym class?

Then he asked the students to pose questions of their own. Saúl announced that he had a question for me.

"Are you married?" he asked.

"No, I am divorced," I replied.

Nobody in the room seemed to understand my state, so I pantomimed wearing a wedding ring and taking it off. Oh, yes—they'd heard about that American custom. Where they came from, for the most part, ending a marriage was frowned upon.

"Are you married?" Nadia asked Mr. Williams.

"No."

"Are you divorced?" she pressed.

"No."

The students were riveted—and confused. They knew that Mr. Williams had a son, Owen, because he often spoke of his child. How could this be, if the teacher was neither married nor divorced? In many of their home cultures, a single parent would be shunned.

"Don't you have a baby?" asked Nadia, suddenly speaking in a higher register.

"Yes, I have a son," said Mr. Williams. "But I was never married."

"Does he have a mother?" Nadia asked, trying to figure this out.

"Everybody has a mother!" said Mr. Williams.

Enough about his personal life. Mr. Williams swiftly changed the subject, asking the students to stand in two lines, facing one another. He said they should practice asking and answering questions using "Are you" and "I am." I stood facing Yonatan.

"Are you twenty-seven?" Yonatan asked me.

"No, I am fifty-one," I said.

"Are you sure?" he blurted, with obvious surprise.

"I *love* that you just said that," I told him. "But yes, I am positive. I had a birthday this week. I am definitely fifty-one."

"Happy birthday!" Yonatan said warmly.

Only later did it occur to me that perhaps older women in Eritrea did not look as young as I did because of how hard life was in that country. Age turned out to be a sensitive subject for Yonatan's sister, Ksanet, as I discovered later that month. At nineteen, she was the oldest student in the room. When Ksanet turned twenty-one, she would age out of a free public high school education, before she could graduate from South. To complete her degree, she would have to go to a local technical college. Ksanet had noticed that Stephanie and Uyen had moved up to a higher-level ELA class, and I heard her ask Mr. DeRose if she could do the same. She was hoping that if she could move through the ELA curriculum more quickly, it might allow her to complete her high school education at South. Mr. DeRose told her that she didn't have enough English to move up. From the young woman's stormy expression, I could tell it was not what she wanted to hear. Ksanet's struggle was a common one—every year, Mr. Williams got one or two older students who shared her plight. It was hard for the teachers to deliver this sort of news and then maintain the student's morale. In the months to come I would watch Ksanet battle with despair over this question of where she would be allowed to complete her education.

Even though the newcomers were starting to talk more—and were interacting with each other—they had not yet integrated themselves into the regular activities that constituted high school social life for most of South's student body. I witnessed this during Spirit Week, which fell at the very end of January. It was basketball season and South had a tall, fast team, including three players born in Africa. Hand-lettered signs taped to the walls of the school described what the students were supposed to wear (Twin Day, Wacky Tacky, Crazy Purple and White) to support the winter sports teams. Nicole dyed her hair purple for the Friday pep rally, and Nadia and Grace wore South T-shirts. Nobody else in Room 142 appeared to be aware that it was Spirit Week.

The Goodwill volunteers returned to read with the students. Mr. Williams placed Ksanet and Methusella in a higher-level reading group, where they tackled a book called *Amazing Sea Lizards*. Their volunteer paused to explain the meaning of the words "tentacle," "float," and "swallow." Over at another table, Jakleen sat with Nadia and Grace, reading a book called *Mighty Mountains*. Their volunteer struggled to explain the word "melt." She talked about sun shining on snow, snow turning to water, and then pantomimed drinking. "In Denver, when you turn the tap on to get a glass of water, it comes from the mountains," she said. "It is snow that has melted."

"Really?" said Jakleen, incredulous. *That* didn't happen in Iraq.

The students worked on a handout about the language of comparison, which had been used a lot in that book. Nadia asked if I would read over her work.

"Nadia! You are the smartest!" I told her.

She laughed—she got the joke.

"Who is the oldest?" I asked, looking at Nadia and Grace.

"She is," Nadia said, pointing to her sister.

"Words of comparison end in E-S-T. Okay? So coldest is the most

162

cold of all. High, higher, highest. What about this? Can you make this tall, taller . . ."

"Tallest," said Nadia.

"Yes, good. That's right. So, hot, hotter . . ."

She wrote H-O-T-E-S-T.

"English is funny—so it has two *t*s," I told her. "H-O-T-T-E-S-T."

She fixed the mistake.

"Yes, good."

Then Jakleen had a question. Mr. Williams had explained that there was a change in the schedule. What was this thing, a pep rally?

"In the United States we love sports," I told her. "And people root for their teams. They wave pom-poms and they sing songs. So the last period of the day is now going to be a pep rally for the basketball team. I think it will be very, very loud. All the students will be yelling, 'South High School! Yay!'"

"*Every day?*" Jakleen asked, in complete dismay.

I started laughing. "No, no, no, just one day," I assured her. "The schedule is changed only for one day. Just today."

"How about if we are not interested to go?" said Jakleen. "Do we have to stay for this?"

"I don't know," I told her. "It's a good question."

I pulled up some pictures of pep rallies on my phone and tried to convey that it might be fun. At the end of the day, I followed a river of students toward the gym. When I stopped in the girls' bathroom, I discovered cheerleaders changing into their uniforms. The skirts were so short that the cheerleading squad was almost exclusively American born, with one exception—Rodica, an especially outgoing young woman who was originally from the West African country of Benin. The cheerleading coach had tried recruiting other foreign-born students, but their parents deemed the uniforms too risqué. Most foreign-born parents wanted their daughters to go to church and get married; they did not want them attracting unwanted male attention by exposing their legs.

As I walked into the gym, the cavernous space echoed with the sound of "Time of Our Lives," by Pitbull and Ne-Yo. A throng of American-born kids danced below bleachers filled with their peers. "I knew my rent was gon' be late about a week ago," Ne-Yo sang. "I worked my ass off, but I still can't pay it, though."

Milling about under the bright fluorescent lights I saw a girl in a purple tutu, a girl in a purple tiara, and a couple of girls sporting purple short shorts. I spotted one foreign-born student wearing a floor-length purple dress with a purple hijab—fusion attire. Then came a boy in a purple Superman cape, a boy with a purple mohawk, and another carrying a clear purple life-sized plastic blow-up doll. More kids started dancing as Pitbull took over. He sang about dirty talk, her saying yes, him getting blessed.

All the kids from the Student Senate were there, in their full South regalia. The DJ played songs by Outkast, Unk, and Pitbull again ("It's going down, I'm yelling timber / You better move, you better dance"). An ensemble performed a routine to the song "Bang It to the Curb" ("Oh word, we absurd / Got that fire, we can burn"), cheerleaders cheered, and the drum line played every kind of drum. The head boy and the head girl announced the school's sports teams to wild applause.

I looked around for the newcomers. The pep rally seemed like a rare chance for them to mix with the rest of the school; surely anybody could figure out this was a party. Finally, I spotted Mr. Williams's students, sitting in the last two rows of the bleachers closest to the exit, as high up as they could go. Half of them had their backs pressed against the white cinder-block wall; the rest were clumped together one row below. The loud fuss in the gym ran at odds with what was deemed appropriate in many of the places they came from, and the frenetic scene was also a long way away from the safety of Room 142, such a chaste place by comparison. The kids who had made it to the pep rally looked frozen, silent, appalled. Becoming American was going to take some time, apparently. Jakleen and Mariam were nowhere in sight.

4

Our Souls at Night

The next time Nabiha and I visited Ebtisam, we found her prone on one of the big green sofas in her living room, with kitchen items spread all over the place. Dishes, dry goods, and silverware were piled on the nearby coffee table and on the round table where the family ate meals. Elsewhere in the building, exterminators were going up and down the hallways, knocking on doors. Ebtisam had been told to take everything out of her cupboards to get ready for the team to spray for bugs. Consumed by that task, and by a variety of other concerns—she was in the middle of looking for a job, and she was in the middle of fighting with her daughters—she had forgotten about our appointment. We caught her in a down moment.

At school that day, Jakleen and Mariam had been absent. Before I could ask why, Ebtisam brought up the subject, which was the origin of the fight.

"Jakleen has made me so angry," said Ebtisam. "She didn't go to school today, for no reason at all. My heart is hurting me right now, because I am so angry!"

Though I had not seen Mariam at South, either, Ebtisam said only Jakleen had stayed home; apparently Mariam had gone to school but had cut Mr. Williams's class. After all the sacrifices Ebtisam had made—how hard she had worked to get her daughters out of harm's way, how desperately she was struggling to make it in America—having them defy her in this manner left her distraught. Her smile was gone, her face, weary.

Meanwhile, Jakleen had locked herself in her bedroom and was yelling intermittently at her mother. Eventually she strolled out to greet us, wearing an impudent look.

"We missed you at school today," I told her.

"I don't like school," she said in a surly voice.

"How come?"

"I don't like waking up early," she said in Arabic, through Nabiha. "I need to sleep for at least eight or ten hours."

"I think Mr. Williams is worried about you."

"Why?"

"He thinks that you're really smart, but he's afraid if you don't come to school more often, you might have to repeat the class, and he doesn't want that to happen."

"I don't care. I have decided next year I will stay in the same class."

"So you're okay if you're in newcomer class again next year?"

"Yes," snapped Nabiha-as-Jakleen. "No problem."

"Okay, but here's what happens," I said. "To graduate, you have to take newcomer class first, then you have to take English Language Acquisition 1, then you have to take English Language Acquisition 2. And then there are two more required English classes that you must take. So, at a minimum, it's five years before you can get a high school diploma. If you repeat newcomer class, then it will take you six years."

Jakleen was taken aback. "If I decide not to go to school, it's going to be six years?"

"Yes. Although you could also skip ahead—if you learn English quickly. I think if you showed up every day, and did all the work, you would learn twice as fast."

"No, we do not learn the language quickly," she said. "It will take a while."

"For you, it is harder, because English and Arabic are not close," I agreed. "But there are a lot of different things that affect how fast a student learns, and one of them is motivation. I think you have lost your motivation, lost your hope. So you are not learning as fast as you could."

"I'm supposed to be in twelfth grade!" Jakleen burst out. "And they moved me to grade nine!"

"I know you feel that you are behind, and maybe it will take you longer to get a high school degree—but it's still worth getting the degree. You will have a better life if you can accept that it might take five years to graduate, but that's okay—you can get the high school degree, go to college, and have a much better life."

"I know about all of that," Jakleen said scornfully. "I know that—but this eight hours, it is too long for us. We are too tired when we get home."

"If I could wave a magic wand, I would make your school day four or five hours long. But this is just the hardest year. Next year will be better."

"Yeah, maybe, if we have friends, communication with American people, it might be better," conceded Jakleen. "If we were happy in the United States, it would be easy, everything, for us. But we are not happy in the United States."

"Not yet," I said.

"Not now and not ever!"

"You've decided to be unhappy in the future?"

"Yes!" she retorted.

But even Jakleen smiled as she said this. I started laughing out loud.

"I hope you change your mind," I told her.

"There is no life here," Jakleen said, in a more serious tone. "We used to be with a lot of people around us, a community. People who had the same experiences. Here there is no community. We are all by ourselves."

I reminded her that Mr. Williams was trying to facilitate a relationship with other Iraqi students.

"Sana wants to meet with you, to encourage you, to make you feel less lonely," I said.

"We would like to talk with her," Jakleen said.

"Maybe soon."

"*In sha' Allah.*"

She retreated to her bedroom.

"It's hard," I said to Ebtisam. "They are being teenagers."

"Yeah, and in a new country," added Nabiha. "It's not easy."

"Mmmm," said Ebtisam.

We fell silent.

"I am tired," Ebtisam told us after a while. "I am looking for a job every day. I'm tired. The kids, and then the rent, and looking for the job."

There was a knock on the door. A volunteer from Jewish Family Service had come to give Ebtisam a lift to a therapy appointment.

"Are you ready to go?" he asked.

"No."

"You will not come?"

She shook her head. She was too weary.

"Okay, cancel," said the man, and he left.

Ebtisam told us that warring with her daughters had exhausted her. "I think I will take a nap, because I am so tired. I have a pain, here. I am stressed, and when I get angry, right here, starts the pain." She pointed to her chest.

There was another knock on the door. It was the bug-spraying team, with all of their equipment.

"Ready?" said a worker for the extermination company, in a mock-cheery voice.

Ebtisam and Jakleen had to leave the apartment for two hours. The longed-for nap would not happen—not now, anyway. Jakleen wound a gray scarf tightly over her hair, then rustled around in the closet for a pair of red sneakers. She flashed us a triumphant smile, as we said goodbye, clearly pleased with herself for having defeated her mother. In contrast, Ebtisam looked downtrodden. I left thinking about how demoralizing it had to be, getting passed over for menial jobs and then coming home to face her beautiful middle daughter's merciless intransigence. Afterward, I told Mr. Williams and Miss Pauline what I had witnessed. Later, I also described Ebtisam's condition to Whitney Haruf, a licensed clinical social worker employed by Lutheran Family Services, the resettlement agency that handled Ebtisam's case. The social worker helped me understand what I had seen in the larger context of all the refugees with whom she worked.

Whitney Haruf had been concerned about Ebtisam's state of mind from the beginning. They had met for the first time when Ebtisam had come to Lutheran Family Services for her initial meeting with staff at the resettlement agency, seventy-two hours after she and her daughters had arrived in the United States. Ebtisam had come to see her case worker, Yasir Abdulah, and during their conversation he grew worried about

Ebtisam's mental state. She appeared traumatized by the disastrous turns in fortune she had experienced over the previous decade. Yasir understood exactly what she had survived, for he was an Iraqi refugee himself.

Ebtisam liked Yasir a lot. She told me this one day when we happened to go to Lutheran together. As we sat in the lobby, I faced a large banner that bore a quote from the Bible: I WAS A STRANGER, AND YOU WELCOMED ME IN, Matthew 25:35. By that stage, Ebtisam had spent many hours at Lutheran, and various staff members kept waving and saying, "Hi, Ebtisam!" Eventually, Ebtisam turned to me with an expression of sheepish pride on her face and said ruefully, "I am famous."

As we waited, Ebtisam caught a glimpse of Yasir, and then tapped her temple several times.

"Yasir, very good, here," she said.

"Oh, Yasir is very smart?" I asked. "He's very intelligent?"

"Yes!" said Ebtisam.

Yasir had lived in the United States for only two years and his command of English was imperfect, but his commitment to his fellow refugees was steadfast. He was stretched, like every case worker I met; anytime I saw him, he apologized for how long he took to respond to my emails or my requests to meet. Just like Troy Cox over at the African Community Center, Yasir worked at a run, every day, all the time, because of the exploding refugee crisis.

Yasir had met Ebtisam and her daughters at the airport at the end of August, along with a friend of theirs—a Kurdish man named Anker, who was letting them stay at his apartment until they found a place of their own. When he first greeted Ebtisam and her daughters, Yasir recalled, "She was happy, but she don't know—what would happen, what are the rules here." Three days later, on September 1, 2015, when Ebtisam came to Lutheran for the intake meeting, Yasir tried to go over everything (welcome money, TANF, Medicaid, food stamps), but as he did so Ebtisam lost her nerve. Faced with the harsh reality of life in the United States on a poverty-level budget, she lapsed into gloomy fear. "She understood but she was worried," Yasir remembered. "She said, 'That's a really small amount, how can I survive? And the rents here are really high.'"

Noticing Ebtisam's dejection, Yasir went to find his colleague, Whitney Haruf, who served as the director of the Family Stabilization Unit at Lutheran, a group that tried to prevent refugee families from spinning into crisis upon entering the developed world. Previously, Whitney had worked in Mae Sot, Thailand, along the border of Burma, for an organization called Burma Border Projects, meaning that she had seen just about everything that could go wrong in this world.

Whitney provided extra support to individuals with refugee status who required services beyond what a case manager could offer. Refugees experiencing domestic violence, refugees with mental illness, and child refugees abused or neglected at home comprised the majority of her caseload. Whitney has strawberry blond hair, thousands of freckles, sky-blue eyes, and a face as wide-open as the prairie. Her father was the novelist Kent Haruf, the author of *Plainsong*, *Benediction*, and *Our Souls at Night*, among other books. His early work breaks your heart talking about teen pregnancy, while his late work is the most beautiful writing about old age that I have read; throughout he captures the rhythm of life in small-town America. I came to think of Whitney as one of those people who straddle worlds (rural and urban, artistic and practical, literary and therapeutic) and are therefore simply bigger human beings than most.

"They definitely seemed shell-shocked or something," Whitney recalled of Ebtisam and her family. "It seemed like their systems were overwhelmed, kind of in shut-down mode. Like they had made it here, and that was as far as they could go. They just looked exhausted. And they were not really able to engage too much." Whitney shared some almonds and dried fruit with the family. She told them that things were going to be all right. "I just tried to be a welcome presence and to give them a sense of safety or comfort or security," she said. "It seemed like they needed time to decompress. And I think things did improve from there—but then, they've had all these different issues that came up."

Whitney made clear that the level of difficulty Ebtisam experienced during her resettlement placed her in the minority, in terms of Lutheran's overall clients. The agency had roughly one thousand active cases, and only a fraction of those had been referred to the Family Stabilization Unit. Ebtisam was referred to the program because of mental health problems, Whitney said. When Ebtisam shared her IOM packet with me, I saw that somebody else had noted issues in that arena, too ("depression, seen by psych in Syria, once given a medication that she did not take as it was making her sleepy . . . started exercising and felt better . . . has insomnia and cries and is worried about her future but also has plans and hopes . . . may benefit from counseling"), probably brought on by trauma and chronic stress.

The day after her intake meeting, Ebtisam called Yasir and said she was thinking of moving to another state where rents were cheaper. Yasir told her to decide soon, because she needed to sign up for benefits right away, or she would run out of money. The following day, Yasir called to ask if she would stay or go. She had not decided. Yasir wanted to fill out all those forms, so he could find this woman some money. He called again a day later and pushed her to make a choice. Ebtisam said she would stay in Colorado.

Yasir immediately signed Ebtisam up for food stamps, Medicaid, and TANF. As a single parent with three dependents, the monthly assistance she got from food stamps was $649, and her income from TANF was $561. This was a problem; it was virtually impossible to find shelter in the Denver area for so small a sum. Yasir and Whitney spoke about Ebtisam's situation to their colleague Eh Klo, a refugee from Burma who was Lutheran's housing expert. She solved real estate riddles cheerfully, digging into each situation with relish as if the low-income-meets-no-affordable-housing equations were Sudoku puzzles. Within a few weeks, Eh Klo obtained for Ebtisam a lease on the two-bedroom apartment at Pine Creek, which was going to cost $825 per month, *and* she found a rare, hard-to-secure housing voucher from a nonprofit that ran an affordable housing program. The voucher would cover 70 percent of Ebtisam's rent for two years. This would buy Ebtisam a critical window of time. She would earn more money after she landed a job, but in the meantime she could get by with TANF, thanks to the voucher. Collectively, the family's "welcome money," the cash stipend she and her daughters received from the federal government, amounted to $4,200. Yasir used most of that to cover their rent for September, October, and November. He also spent $110 on food, $50 on kitchen supplies, and $70 on furnishing the apartment, and the surplus was given to Ebtisam.

The employment specialists at Lutheran felt that Ebtisam should start working as soon as possible. Not only did her family need the income, but having a routine would also help combat her depression. Refugees entered the fast-paced American economy at the low end and worked their way up; the sooner Ebtisam started working, the higher her earnings would climb by the time the voucher expired, Yasir told her.

At times, as she attempted to look for a job and tried to learn English, and felt unsuccessful at both, Ebtisam grew disheartened. Once, she called Yasir and told him maybe coming to the United States had been a mistake. Maybe she should move back to Turkey. "Of course, your situation is really hard," Yasir told her. "I'm not blaming you. To see you like this, it's really hard for me, as a man. But here you can change your life, step by step. You have the most important thing, which is housing. You have time right now to learn English, and to watch your daughters. In the future, you can find a job and you can save money. We already pay the rent for you for two years—that's really good." Yasir talked with Ebtisam until she agreed that resettling in the United States was beneficial for her daughters, because she wanted them to obtain an education.

Yasir made several home visits, to ensure Ebtisam got established. And she did. It was just that things kept happening over and over again that proved unsettling, and then she decomposed emotionally. It was almost tidal, the way the flat beach of Ebtisam's interior got scoured by fear, frightening memories from the past surfacing and getting strewn all over the smooth sand of her mind, anytime the waves got rough. That was the condition in which I found her on that day when Jakleen would not listen and the exterminators were saying she had to leave the house so that they could spray the cupboards.

When Nabiha and I returned one week later, we found Ebtisam back on her feet, standing at the stove in the small galley kitchen, cooking fresh spinach. I noticed that Ebtisam had taken a wooden hutch out of her bedroom and positioned it opposite the front door, and carefully arranged on the shelves a set of old rose-colored glasses, given to her by someone at her church. We told her the hutch looked nice there. I had brought her some potatoes, and we laughed about that, because it was a peculiar thing to bring. It turned out that "potatoes" is one of the words that Arabic, Spanish, and English have in common. In Arabic, potatoes is *albtatis*, but the way Ebtisam said it, she dropped the *al*, and it was just *btatis*, which sounds exactly like the (related) Spanish word, *patatas*. One day, when I was trying to explain Ireland to Ebtisam, I said in Spanish, "*Patatas, patatas, patatas, patatas.*" Potatoes, potatoes, potatoes, potatoes. We ate them at every meal whenever I visited the farmhouse where my mother grew up; feeding a large Irish family plus all the farm-workers always involved a big pile of potatoes.

That day, Ebtisam was wearing pink leggings and a black hoodie. She said that she had to wash the spinach well because it was organic and there was a lot of sand. Then she told us with pride that she had just moved up to a higher level in her English classes at a local technical college. Once she got all of the leafy greens into the saucepan, Ebtisam came over and said in English, "Last, next—I very tired." Then she turned to Nabiha for the right words and apologized in Arabic for her dark mood on our previous visit. In a cheerful tone, she invited us to stay, saying she was making a traditional Iraqi meal, spinach soup with beef. I wanted to try the soup, so I accepted on the condition that some other evening she allow me to take her out for a meal. Nabiha and I crowded in at the round table, along with Ebtisam, Mariam, Jakleen, and Lulu. Then Anker, their Kurdish friend, turned up, and Ebtisam fed him as well.

"I'm glad to be having dinner with you," I told Mariam. It was about 5 P.M.

"This is lunch!" Mariam said.

She explained that to them, dinner meant an even later meal, one they would have at 8 or 9 P.M. I remembered that we had done the same thing in Ireland, two evening meals, although we called the second one "tea."

I tried asking Jakleen about why she wore the hijab, but she didn't want to say. Then I asked the girls about religion. I knew that Ebtisam attended Christian services, and Jakleen had described herself to me as a Muslim. But I didn't know what Mariam considered her faith to be.

"I like Mary, I like Jesus," Mariam said.

"Are you Muslim or Christian?"

"Just normal," Mariam replied. "I am okay, no matter what religion."

Ebtisam handed us each a bowl of soup. She put out a tray of flatbread, which was a lot like pita, except triangular in shape. In the soup, I could taste the lighter flavors of lemon and cilantro, mixed with the hearty taste of beef. I said I loved the soup and Ebtisam wanted to know was I just saying that? I said no, I really loved it. Ebtisam told us this soup was one of the healthiest dishes we could eat; it was filled with iron and minerals. I could see she had been strengthened by the act of cooking. The tide had come back in and smoothed out the beach.

Previously, Ebtisam had recounted the family's journey from Iraq to Syria. That evening, as we enjoyed the soup, she told us about their life in Turkey and their journey from that country to the United States. Anker had made the same pilgrimage. He was originally from the area around Kirkuk, a city in northern Iraq that is home to large numbers of Kurds; as it turned out, Anker knew one of Nabiha's cousins. Because he had worked with the U.S. Army, he had received threats and had fled to Turkey. Ebtisam and Anker reminisced about the years they had spent in that country, as part of the vast community of Iraqi expatriates who sought shelter there. First Iraqis had crowded into Turkey, then millions of Syrians had followed. Of all the countries in the world, Turkey was hosting the largest number of refugees from Syria—more than 2.7 million.

Turkey had felt much safer than Syria, Ebtisam told us. But it had been a hard transition, because Turkey was more expensive. Ebtisam had paid only $150 in rent in Jaramana; in Kırşehir, the Turkish city where she and the girls relocated, her rent jumped to $300. Like most refugees in Turkey, Ebtisam found herself stuck in the underground economy. Unable to work legally, she found informal jobs as a waitress and a cosmetician, which she explained by rubbing her hands in circles over various parts of her face, so that we could see what she meant (facials). Illegitimacy was costly: Anker estimated that Ebtisam earned perhaps half what a Turkish person with documents would make.

While Ebtisam struggled to master Turkish, her daughters conquered that language adeptly. Jakleen and Mariam spoke of the time they spent in Turkey as a golden period; whenever they had a hard day in America, they said they wanted to go back to Turkey. Later, when we drove around town in my car, Jakleen would play Turkish music from her cell phone on my car stereo, and at other times, if Mariam started singing in her fluting soprano while she was cleaning the apartment, and I asked her what she was singing about, her answer was as often a Turkish ballad about loneliness as it was an Iraqi ballad about love.

In Kırşehir, the girls said, they were surrounded by people who respected them. Their neighbors understood why they were half-Muslim girls with Christian first names and Arabic surnames, who sometimes wore hijabs and sometimes did not. Why they loved Iraq but hated what had happened to their country, and loved Syria but hated what had happened there, too. Why their father had sided with the Americans, and what that sacrifice had meant. In Kırşehir, there had always been fun things to do—they heard live music, they frequented art galleries, and they saw movies that they could actually understand. After a while, however, both Jakleen and Mariam dropped out of school to work. Because college was out of reach, many school-age refugees saw no reason to continue their education. Like Ebtisam, however, neither Jakleen nor Mariam could work legally in Turkey. They had been consigned to the kind of life that an illegal immigrant lived in the United States.

Ebtisam aspired to live in a country where she could work legally, and where her children could go to college. When she had first arrived in Turkey, she had gone to an office in Istanbul to register with the United Nations as a refugee; she still carried the ID card that she and Fadi had been given in Syria, and the UN officials made note of the fact that she was now living in Kırşehir. In Syria, their case had languished, but once she arrived in Turkey, Ebtisam began receiving a series of emails and phone calls that suggested her case was moving through the system.

The United States was conducting an extra layer of vetting of refugees from the Middle East. Over the following year and a half, Ebtisam made multiple trips to Ankara and Istanbul to keep appointments with UN officials and with officials from various branches of the American government. Each trip required a lengthy bus ride with all of her girls. It took three hours by bus to reach Ankara; the trip to Istanbul took ten hours.

After a series of background checks, conducted by employees of the Department of Homeland Security, Ebtisam and her daughters traveled to Istanbul again for a three-day-long, comprehensive medical screening. In May 2015, nine years after the family's departure from Baghdad, Ebtisam received a phone call with the news that she had been accepted for resettlement by the United States.

"We had to jump up and down because we were so excited, me and my kids!" she told us, as we sat at her table eating spinach soup.

"I was very excited, but it was all mixed up—happiness, sadness—it was all mixed," said Ebtisam. "Because I was leaving behind good people, nice friends. And I had a beautiful place to live. That was the sadness.

"And the happiness was, I saw a good future for my kids. I just decided to come here, to see our future. And I had to be strong. Because it was stressful, the decision. Hard decision, and stress for me. I left everything behind, and I looked forward to the future. The important thing is my three girls. If they are happy, I am happy."

The trip from Turkey to the United States lasted three days. They took another ten-hour bus ride to Istanbul, and spent the night in that city. They flew from Istanbul to Chicago and slept there. Finally they boarded the plane that delivered them to Denver. The all-female group arrived in Denver with eight suitcases filled with shoes and clothing—their most prized possessions. Not one thing in those suitcases had come with them all the way from Iraq; most of their belongings had been acquired in Turkey. The airfare for four had cost $3,700, and Ebtisam was paying off the loan from the IOM in tiny installments, $35 each month. (This was standard, and Tchiza was doing the same.)

Anker wanted to make sure I knew how hard it was to resettle in the United States. He said that after moving here alone, with no family, he had cried every day for five months. He spoke Arabic, Kurdish, Russian, and Turkish, but the task of learning English had crushed him. It was just so different from the other languages he knew. Nabiha commiserated, saying that when she first arrived in the United States, she had been consigned to pushing passengers around Denver International Airport in wheelchairs, because it was the only kind of work she could do with the minimal English she possessed.

The girls finished eating and retreated to the living room, half glued to their cell phones, half listening to us talk. Jakleen and Mariam sat intertwined; Lulu sat by herself. One of the girls started playing songs on her phone. "Hello from the other s-i-i-i-de," sang Adele. The grown-ups stayed at the table: three refugees, commiserating, and me, their witness. Sharing soup with Nabiha and Anker seemed to provide Ebtisam with a potent antidote to her sense of isolation. That evening, she created a warm, convivial atmosphere in her apartment, and I could see why her daughters did not want to leave that haven. Long ago, staying inside had become their primary way of battling feelings of insecurity, as well as actual threats.

Over the months that followed, most days that I visited I found Ebtisam capable and cooking and smiling; occasionally, I found her overwhelmed and unsmiling. If it were a bad day, she would list her problems, taking inventory of her trouble. A woman at a bus station punched her in the face one day for no reason; men at the apartment complex behaved in a threatening manner; she bought a used car for very little money, and it broke down. Each of these setbacks sent her into a tailspin. She counted her problems, lining them up for inspection. On the bad days, Ebtisam would cast about for an explanation, a grand theory to explain such a daunting list of calamities. "I am very unlucky woman," she told me once. "Very unlucky!" On another occasion, she floated the theory that the apartment might be haunted; the source of her problems might be supernatural. I could see that the fluctuations in her moods disturbed her daughters. Once Mariam interrupted Ebtisam during a recital of disasters. "Mum, Mum!" Mariam said. "Stop!" Then I would return and find Ebtisam buoyant again. She would cook kebabs or I would take her and the girls out for shawarma or Nabiha would bring over dolmas, and we would enjoy one another's company. I would leave feeling reassured.

Trying to comprehend Ebtisam's struggles, I mentioned to Whitney Haruf that I had seen what looked like minor setbacks cause Ebtisam to slide into full despair. Things that seemed small to me could elicit a dispro-portionate response. Whitney said this was typical, in her experience, of a person who had witnessed armed conflict and lived through several major displacements. "I think that fits with the level of trauma," she said, as we sat in her office. "Where she still responds that way, kind of going from zero to ten. Anything that triggers the sense of things not being okay or not being safe—it just causes a person to go to the extreme, to come into this hyperaroused state, and then you can't really modulate your response."

What I had imagined to be Ebtisam's baseline personality, Whitney saw as an imprint of the Iraq War and the Syrian civil war upon her original persona. I was witnessing what war did to a person. In terms of her struggles with mental health, Ebtisam was representative of the Iraqi refugee population as a whole. Among Iraqi refugees who participated in the UNHCR survey, 89 percent reported depression, and 82 percent reported anxiety. "Every survey respondent reported experiencing at least one traumatic event," wrote the authors of the survey. "And the prevalence of post-traumatic stress disorder was extremely high (67%)."

Whitney and Eh Klo stepped in at key junctures, seeking to stabilize Ebtisam, so that the disasters didn't compound. After Yasir told Whitney that Ebtisam mentioned seeing demons in the apartment, and using a sofa to barricade the front door to make sure nobody could attack the girls while they were sleeping, Whitney paid Ebtisam a visit. She found Ebtisam in a good frame of mind that day, and no furniture blockaded the front door. Ebtisam denied believing that her home was haunted, although she admitted that she did feel unsafe at the apartment complex, because there were men who made inappropriate remarks.

In particular, one of the Arabic-speaking security guards left them feeling hunted. Ebtisam described this man, who was originally from Iraq, as argumentative and bullying. He looked at her daughters in ways that made them uncomfortable; he made suggestive remarks. In Middle Eastern culture, single women were looked down upon and often became the targets of aggressive come-ons. Whitney discussed safety measures Ebtisam could put into place. Ebtisam confessed that she was afraid the security guard had keys to her apartment and might sneak in and assault them. Whitney went with Ebtisam to visit the front office to determine if this could be true. No, a woman there assured them, the security guards did not have access to keys. Ebtisam seemed greatly relieved.

Other dilemmas were not so easily resolved. Whitney, Yasir, and Eh Klo all feared that Ebtisam might be undone by the pressure to become economically self-sufficient despite the high cost of living in the United States. After Eh Klo had unearthed the hard-to-find housing voucher, they thought they had bought her some time. Then Eh Klo heard the awful news that the program was being defunded. Every person whom Eh Klo had stabilized with one of those vouchers now had to be told that the rent supplement had vanished. Most clients lost the rent money immediately, but Eh Klo managed to get Ebtisam an extension. In her case, the voucher would expire in December 2016. She needed to find a job right away, Yasir told Ebtisam. Once she lost the housing voucher, the household budget he had devised for her would fall apart. Her TANF money would no longer cover the rent payments. This made it critical that she secure a position that enabled her to swing the entire monthly rent bill as soon as possible.

Other staff at Lutheran had been trying to help Ebtisam find employment for several months. She had a high school degree and had previously worked as a beautician. Her long-term goal was to work in a hair salon or some kind of cosmetology position; her short-term goal was to find any kind of occupation. Yet Ebtisam had turned down a housekeeping job that would have required her to work at night, saying she was not comfortable leaving the girls on their own. Then she tried working as a home health care aide but quit after one day. Ebtisam could afford to reject jobs while she still had the housing voucher, but now she could no longer be so choosy. The big question facing Ebtisam, in Whitney Haruf's mind, was how Ebtisam would cope with the transition to working full-time, most likely at a low-wage, menial position. Would she manage to summon the gritty strength that had gotten her all this way? Or, put under that much pressure, would she crumble?

PART III

Spring

1

Well-Taped Boxes

The month of February—a gloomy period weatherwise, when snow had been blanketing the city for months, and everybody was tired of shoveling sidewalks and hungry for the sight of crocuses—marked the beginning of a new phase in Room 142, a time I thought of as increasingly convivial. Coincidentally, the Broncos were headed to the Super Bowl. On a designated day, just about the entire high school donned their Broncos gear. Mr. DeRose wore his Peyton Manning jersey, and Miss Ruthann from Goodwill appeared in a jersey emblazoned with the name and number of cornerback Champ Bailey. None of the newcomers wore football regalia, however, and Room 142 appeared as an island of drab gray and brown in a sea of bright orange. The newcomers were oblivious to the vagaries of the NFL season, a sign of how culturally out of step they were in general with the rest of America. But they were evolving, little by little.

One day during lunch, I watched Jakleen walk around the room wearing a black hijab, wordlessly holding out a Tupperware container of peanut M&M's. Later I saw Grace and Dilli cross the room with their arms twined around one another's waists. Another day, Grace stood behind Lisbeth and ran her fingers through Lisbeth's corkscrew curls, and then petted the girl from El Salvador on the top of her head. Shortly after that, Lisbeth walked over to Mariam and picked up big handfuls of her hip-length hair, lifting it up and letting it fall. Friendships were starting to form. It was like seeing leaf buds on tree branches early in the spring; you could not see green yet, but you could tell that leaves would soon unfurl.

Another day that month, Lisbeth found herself facing Abigail, the new girl from Mexico, when Mr. Williams had them stand in two lines to converse, and Lisbeth impulsively reached over to hug the other girl warmly. Then Shani, from Tajikistan, felt inspired to pinch Lisbeth, Abigail dropped her cell phone as she got bumped by Shani in the process, and suddenly all three girls burst into laughter, which startled studious Solomon, who looked over with an expression that said, *What is so funny?* Afterward, Saúl and Yonatan took advantage of a brief pause in the lesson to stage a lengthy push-up competition. When they both proved equally magnificent at ordinary push-ups, Saúl upped the ante by putting both of his feet on the seat of a chair. He cranked out one extra-hard push-up after another, while Yonatan studied his form intently, then proved he could master the same stunt. Even Mr. Williams paused to watch the competition.

The kids were not actually talking to one another a whole lot, but they were engaging. If anybody was trying to talk at this stage, it was Lisbeth. One day, when Uyen showed up to visit her old classroom, Lisbeth cried, "Ayiiieee!" and then stomped over and threw her arms around the Vietnamese girl in a full-body embrace. "Uyen! Back in newcomer class!" Mr. Williams called out. "Hi, Mister," Uyen replied, with shy delight. Uyen was not back in newcomer class—not formally. She was flitting into the room nearly every day, however, trying to regain the sense of security she had once found here. Going upstairs had been hard. When I asked how her new class was going, she gamely said, "Good." Then she shared that the teacher upstairs spoke a lot faster than Mr. Williams, but a girl from Thailand who spoke a little Vietnamese was translating for her when she couldn't follow what the teacher was saying.

That wasn't the real issue, though. The big problem was that she was foundering socially, because she and Stephanie had experienced a falling-out. The way Stephanie explained the rift was that in the higher-level class she had found new Spanish-speaking friends and hadn't wanted to spend so much time with Uyen. After that, Uyen had grown jealous. Uyen's explanation was simply that the two of them were still friends, but were not as close as they once had been. Whatever had transpired, Lisbeth was now Uyen's current favorite person to sit with at lunch. I watched them try to have a conversation in which Lisbeth proposed that they do something in English, in Spanish, and in Vietnamese via

Google Translate, but Uyen seemed unable to grasp the invitation. Lisbeth wound up telling her, in Spanish, "*No me entiendes.*" You don't understand me.

After that, Lisbeth tried to get Mr. Williams to say certain words in Spanish that she thought he might not grasp, such as *nalgas*, which meant ass, but he knew all the slang and told her he was not going to say "*malas palabras*" (bad words). Then Lisbeth turned her attention to Yonatan, and they began having a boisterous conversation, which consisted largely of Lisbeth trying to teach Yonatan various Spanish words while giggling at his accent. I heard Lisbeth saying, "*Perfecto*," to Yonatan over and over, until Yonatan could say the word back to her.

Another day that month, I walked into Room 142 at lunchtime to find three different tables listening to music from three different parts of the world. Jakleen and Mariam were playing a song on Jakleen's phone by a Moroccan musician named Saad Lamjarred. On the other side of the room, Solomon, Methusella, and Plamedi were using Methusella's cell phone to blare African pop music by Eddy Kenzo, a musician from Uganda. I asked Plamedi, using my high school French, if he had ever heard this music before, and he said no, it was his *première fois*, his first time. Nearby, Nadia and Grace were nodding along to music from Rwanda. Grace said her brother had given her the music, and she was not sure who was singing.

Earlier in the year, the kids had listened to music individually, using earbuds or headphones. Now they were sharing what they loved. The room was full of sound, creating a festive atmosphere as the students leaned over their lunch trays. Music was one of the few portable throughlines to before, and perhaps the only familiar thing they could access in the middle of a school day. They didn't yet share a common language, and various groups of kids were listening to different anthems, but the impulse was universal—a song from home comforted each of them. Soon Abigail began playing Latin ballads on her phone, too, which led to a series of lunchtime duets with Saúl. She was from Mexico and he was from El Salvador, but they knew the lyrics to all the same hits.

The following week, when the bell rang marking the end of lunch, most everybody settled down, and then Lisbeth and Abigail burst into the room late, laughing hysterically. Mr. Williams stood at the front of the class, wearing a gray-and-white-checked dress shirt and gray chinos, waiting for the kids to calm down. They had grown a little too rambunctious. He had been lenient for a while, but now it was time to introduce the idea of consequences. He borrowed Saúl's cell phone and also Mariam's, when they failed to put the devices away. He held up the two phones and announced that from this point forward, he was going to turn confiscated phones over to the front office. The students would have to ask a legal guardian to get the phone back.

Next, Mr. Williams announced that he was moving Lisbeth's seat again. At present, Lisbeth was seated in the middle of the room, a location from which she could easily maintain running conversations in Spanish with Saúl, Abigail, Nadia, and Grace. Mr. Williams asked her to move to a table out on the room's periphery, one that, from her perspective, might as well have been the linguistic equivalent of Siberia. He seated her at a table with Kaee Reh and Bachan, two of the quietest students in the room. The languages they spoke (Karenni and Nepali) were about as far from Spanish as one could get.

"I think this is better because you'll be able to concentrate more," Mr. Williams told Lisbeth. "You won't be as distracted."

Then he asked the class to get busy completing the following sentences:

Today is _____.
It is a _____.
We have _____ more days of school this week.
There are _____ days in this month.

He spent only a few minutes on this exercise, because it was a review for most of his students, but it was important to go over so that the recent arrivals could catch up. When Mr. Williams checked on

Bachan, he saw that the Bhutanese student was not writing. "Bachan, do you have a notebook?" he asked. "No notebook? Let me get you one." Mr. Williams brought over a backpack that he kept stocked with school supplies, in case students lacked them. He gave Bachan a notebook and got him started on the assignment.

Then Mr. Williams moved over to work with Abigail. When she failed to answer his questions, he began cupping one hand behind his ear to pantomime that he needed to hear her speak. She really didn't want to. Generally, Abigail understood a lot of English, but she had a crippling shyness about answering back.

"Today is . . . ," prompted Mr. Williams.

A silent stare, no dimples.

"Today is . . . ," he said again.

Mortification. Mr. Williams asked Abigail gently in Spanish if she could please repeat what he said in English, and finally she did, with deep dimples. The teacher worked with Abi until she could say the date in English. After that, Mr. Williams knelt down facing Shani and repeated the whole ear-cupping routine. By the time Mr. Williams went to check on Plamedi, that student had finished the entire warm-up on his own, even though he, too, was new. French has many similarities with English; January and February were recognizable to Plamedi, because in French those months are *janvier* and *février*.

Once Mr. Williams had worked with each of the newest students individually, he returned to the front of the class. The next lesson was about giving commands. Helpfully, some of the longtime students began coaching the newest arrivals. Nadia often played the role of supplemental teacher, but Dilli—the very quiet girl from Eritrea—now began copying her behavior. Four students sat together at one table, with Nadia and Dilli (the longtime students) facing Shani and Abigail (the new arrivals).

Dilli said, with obvious delight: "Say, 'I am from . . .'"

Shani, relieved at getting a question she could answer, replied: "I am from Tajikistan!"

Nadia ordered, in a perfect teacher voice: "Say, 'My name is . . .'"

Shani, gleeful again: "My name is Shani!"

Then Nadia pointed to Abigail and instructed: "Say, 'My name is Shani, but her name is Abigail.'"

And Shani did so, perfectly.

Mr. Williams noticed what was going on. "Thank you!" he said. "Dilli and Nadia, thank you for helping our new students!" Their table remained engaged for the entire period, allowing Mr. Williams to concentrate on the rest of the room; he didn't need to worry about Shani or Abigail, because Dilli and Nadia were tending to them.

Nadia decided to try a linguistic pirouette. "My name is Nadia, but your name is Shani," she announced. "I am from Mozambique, whereas you are from—" but there, she tripped. "What was the name of that country again?" Nadia asked.

"Tajikistan," supplied Abigail.

Nadia tried: "Ta-jiki—, jiki—"

Dilli started tittering, and then the whole table broke up. I brought over an atlas, so that we could all find Tajikistan. There it was, sandwiched between the Middle East and Asia. The tiny country shared a border with Kyrgyzstan to the north, China to the east, Afghanistan to the south, and to the west, Uzbekistan. Shani pointed to Dushanbe, the country's capital, and looked up with pleased expectation in her eyes.

"That's where you're from?" I asked.

"Yes!" she said.

"Big?" I asked.

"Yes, big!" she said, happy with this rudimentary confirmation that I knew at least one thing about her home.

Shani brought out her cell phone and showed us pictures of the city where she had once lived. I saw gray cobblestone streets and high stone walls, interrupted by a door painted bright red. One splash of color in a monochrome landscape. That was her house, Shani said. It was the kind of house that is conjoined with others; I knew that style of building because my father was raised in a town house like that, on the north side of Dublin. As a child, I had been fascinated by the fact that some of the town houses had attics that connected with those of the neighbors.

Shani told us that she was *Muslima*, even though she did not wear a hijab. We all wanted to say who we were to Shani, but she wouldn't understand if we used English. We leafed around in the atlas instead. I found Mexico, and I pointed to Abigail. Then we looked for Eritrea, a skinny country hugging the eastern coast of Africa along the Red Sea, directly across from Saudi Arabia, and I pointed to Dilli. We dropped southward to Mozambique, down beside the Indian Ocean, and I pointed to Nadia. Shani kept saying, "Ah!" She seemed delighted to obtain this information and surprised to learn there were so many places represented at the one table.

Just then, a young woman with short blond hair appeared at the door of the classroom. A senior at South whose family had emigrated from Russia, she had begun in Mr. Williams's newcomer room as a freshman and remembered just how lost she had felt.

Mr. Williams called Shani over.

In Russian, the other girl asked, "Do you speak Russian?"

"*Da!*" Shani cried. "*Da! Ya govoryu po-russki!*"

"Take a moment, please, and welcome her," Mr. Williams instructed the visitor. "Be a buddy, check in, and see: Is there anything she needs from me, or anyone at this school?"

The girls walked over to a far corner of the room to talk, one of them strikingly dark-haired and the other just as fair, babbling together in Russian. Shani had so many questions that the senior made a plan to talk with her at greater length the following day. Before leaving to head back to her own class, the other student reported this to Mr. Williams, who looked pleased—the two girls had hit it off.

Mr. Williams turned his attention back to the rest of the room. Lisbeth was throwing things at another student, and he chastised her sharply. She got red in the face and clutched her hoodie over her mouth to smother the sounds of uncontrollable giggling, but we could hear muffled squeaks emerging anyway. Meanwhile, Abigail handed Dilli a copy of the book the class was reading, and Dilli responded with "*Gracias.*" Abigail's dimples appeared again, hearing this Eritrean girl thank her in Spanish. The students were increasingly engrossed with one another, which forced Mr. Williams to exert more discipline, and at the same time, they were able to comprehend more English, which was how they could interact more. The double effect of all this learning was amusing to observe, because Mr. Williams was succeeding and failing at the same time. He was gaining control of the room academically and losing control socially. Later that month, the kids would even push him to the point of yelling, after he repeatedly asked them to be quiet, the only time I saw him lose his composure all year. We had traveled a long way from August, when the room had been so hushed and watchful.

At the same time that I was tracking the increasingly complex dynamics in Room 142 and trying to get to know each of the students individually, I also was hoping to understand who Mr. Williams was as a human being and to ascertain why he found his fulfillment in this particular room. In terms of his personal life, however, he was highly guarded. All he ever said to me was that he had never been married, and he had a son, to whom he was clearly devoted (Mr. Williams was coaching his son's soccer team, and he referred often to the time he spent with Owen). After his son had been born, his relationship with Owen's mother had not worked out. Period, end of story.

As it happened, Mr. Williams and I lived in the same neighborhood. One evening, I bumped into him and Owen while we were shopping at the local market. Mr. Williams looked slightly abashed to be caught in his role as a parent instead of his role as a teacher. It left me curious to know more, but he did not seem interested in talking about his personal life. When I gave him a few chances to elaborate, and he did not, I figured it was none of my business. Because he allowed me to sit in his classroom for an entire year, shared with me his roomful of kids, and took time out of his own breaks to help me wrestle with this project, I wanted to respect his boundaries.

He was happy to share his thoughts about his charges. Mr. Williams expressed consternation about how much work Jakleen and Mariam were missing, wondered how best to contain Lisbeth, strategized about how to push Methusella, and mentioned that he was keeping an eye on Bachan, who struck him as unusually discombobulated. Over time, Mr. Williams and I discovered that we were getting to know the same students in different ways. Because I tended to know the arc of their journeys, I was gathering information about a side of the kids they did not usually show to their teacher. One day, up in the copy room, when I was telling Mr. Williams about some of the things the students had survived, he grew visibly upset at the level of difficulty some of the families had experienced. "I almost can't know these things," he said. "To teach them, I mean—it's sometimes too much. I almost can't bear it."

Sometimes, because we were getting to know such different aspects of the students, Mr. Williams and I wound up possessing divergent views of the same individuals. Kaee Reh, for example, I knew as one of the loneliest students in the room. He was so quiet about his plight, and I was so busy listening to him be incredibly unassuming (or busy noticing that Kaee Reh had pulled the top of his hair into a small ponytail, and then used a series of rubber bands to make the ponytail stand straight up in a stick-like protrusion, and wondering what *that* was all about, and then noticing that upstairs in the cafeteria all the other Karenni-speaking boys were doing exactly the same thing with their hair), that I missed how vast Kaee Reh's accomplishments in the classroom were until Mr. Williams praised some of his work. The same thing happened with Dilli. Those two students were more confident on paper than they were in class discussions, and until Mr. Williams showed me their written work, I missed their intelligence.

I tended to know the emotional burdens the students were carrying, or the losses they had incurred, whereas Mr. Williams knew how well they read, how strong or how weak their sentences were, whose comprehension did not line up with his or her pronunciation. He knew how they grasped key concepts, whether by listening to him speak, or by seeing something visually, or by acting out. As Mr. Williams said, upstairs in the copy room one day, "I know them as learners."

It says a lot about Mr. Williams that I spent an entire year in his company and he never once mentioned to me (I discovered this fact only during the following school year) that he was a "leader teacher." Even as he was working with all of the newcomers, he was simultaneously coaching five fellow teachers. During first and second period, when he was not with the newcomers, he was either observing one of the other teachers and providing feedback, or he was co-teaching lessons with them, or he was bringing the teachers he was coaching into the rooms of other teachers he wanted them to observe. But he never even alluded to this during our many side conversations. Mr. Williams was, among other things, terribly modest. He was a bit like Kaee Reh and Dilli, in that sense—he was not vocal about his own remarkable strengths, and as a result I was slow to appreciate the full extent of what was doing at South, both in his own classroom and in the rooms of other teachers who also taught ELA students.

By the middle of February, Mr. Williams was feeling both disgruntled with some of the disruptive behavior breaking out in his room and also immensely pleased with the amount his students had been learning. I could see the increased level of comprehension as Mr. Williams questioned the students about a Hmong fable they had been reading. Called *The Eagle and the Moon Gold,* it told the story of a poor boy who was content to be poor, and a rich man greedy for more and more wealth. The poor boy finds an eagle that flies him to the moon, which turns out to be made of gold; they fly home safely with a little gold before the sun comes up. His wealthy neighbor sees the gold and demands to know where he can acquire some, too. When the eagle flies him to the moon, however, the wealthy man refuses to leave. Too busy collecting more and more gold, he is burned alive by the sun.

Mr. Williams assigned each student one vocabulary word from the story. He asked them to write out a definition of their word, use it in a sentence, and make a list of synonyms and antonyms. Jakleen's word was "rich," while Solomon's was "poor." Grace got "content" and Ksanet "greedy." Methusella's word was "moral." Hsar Htoo did not understand his word: "returned." I told him that if he got in an airplane and flew back to Thailand, he would have returned to the country of his birth. Hsar Htoo nodded; he understood.

Several days later, after the students had deciphered the meaning of their assigned words, Mr. Williams quizzed them to see if they had followed the story's plot.

"Where did the eagle take Yao?" he asked.

"The moon," said Nadia.

"Is Yao content or greedy?"

"He's content," said Grace.

"What about Gwa? Is he happy?"

"No," said several students at once.

"Tell me about Gwa, what happens to him?"

"He dies!" Nadia exclaimed.

Mr. Williams started calling on students who were not speaking. He walked over to Shani. "At the end of the fable, Gwa . . ."

"No understand!" objected Shani.

Mr. Williams held up a copy of the book and opened it to the first page. "This is the beginning, okay?" he said.

Shani nodded.

He turned to the last page and said, "This is the end." Then he pointed at a picture of Gwa and looked expectantly at Shani.

"Boy," said Shani.

"Yes," Mr. Williams said. "A boy named Gwa. What happens to Gwa?"

Shani could not answer. Nadia helpfully ran her hand across her throat, a gesture Shani understood.

"Right, he dies," said Mr. Williams. "Because he is greedy."

Just then, I glanced around the room and saw that Lisbeth was not paying attention, as Mr. Williams had hoped, over in her new seat. Instead, she was chatting animatedly with Bachan. He had come to life and was pointing at another student while he spoke to Lisbeth in broken English. She was listening closely and making a series of expressive faces (shock! laughter! horror! vigorous affirmation!) while he talked. I had not thought any non-Nepali speaker could forge a social interaction with Bachan, so withdrawn had been his demeanor, yet somehow she had managed. I knew that Lisbeth was distracting Bachan from the lesson, but I found it striking that she had established a connection with the half-missing boy. Her effort seemed to help bring Bachan further into the room.

*   *   *

Later in February, Mr. Williams told the students to turn to the next unit in their textbook, "Everything We Do." The chapter was about indoor and outdoor activities. He asked the class to make sentences using verbs such as swim and kick and play. Then he asked the students to stand up if they liked certain activities. Who liked to dance? Lisbeth and Nadia stood, and Lisbeth announced, to nobody in particular, "*Quiero bailar mucho!*"

Who liked to draw? Lisbeth, Hsar Htoo, Kaee Reh, Plamedi, Mariam, Nadia, Saúl, Abigail, Ksanet, and Jakleen stood. I knew that about Jakleen—anytime Mr. Williams asked the class to draw, Jakleen came to life. She carried a round metal tin filled with sharp colored pencils, which she kept in her lavender backpack and would bring out for poster-making sessions. I had also seen some of Kaee Reh's artwork, stunningly realistic charcoal drawings. But I hadn't known that the others liked to draw.

Who liked to play the guitar? Kaee Reh, Solomon, Hsar Htoo, Saúl, and Shani stood up. "Shani, you like to play the guitar?" Mr. Williams asked, checking.

"Oh, yeah!" Shani said enthusiastically.

Did she actually know how to play the guitar? It wasn't clear—quite possibly, she only liked the sound of guitars, or appreciated that they were involved in rock-and-roll.

The degree to which Mr. Williams still struggled to impart even basic information to his newest students became apparent to me one day toward the end of February. A winter storm warning was in effect, and students arrived at school shaking snow off their coats. Grace walked in wearing a burnt-orange wool cap and a black T-shirt that said KISS ME FOREVER, while Shani had on a hot-pink headband with a silver bow and a blue down jacket. Solomon and Methusella wore only thin tracksuit jackets, however, and I worried about them freezing later as they walked all the way over to the train station.

Mr. Williams grouped the students into pairs so they could work together to read an important letter.

"Shani, I'm going to read with you," Mr. Williams announced. "Can you try reading?"

Shani looked at him expectantly. Okay! Was he going to read to her?

"No, can *you* read this?" he said. "Can *you* try reading?"

She could not. Mr. Williams suggested they read the letter out loud together, and asked her to repeat every word she did not know, starting with the very first one. ("Greetings," he said. "Greetings," she parroted.) The letter was from Mr. Williams to their parents, and it said that parent-teacher conferences would be held at the end of the month. After he and Shani finished reading, he tested her comprehension.

"So who is coming?" asked Mr. Williams.

"South?" Shani responded uncertainly.

"Parents and families," Mr. Williams said in a kind tone. "When is this taking place?"

"February twenty-ninth," Shani answered. He nodded, that was correct.

"Where is this meeting happening?"

Shani opened up her hands to the sky.

"Okay, not sure," he said. "That's fine."

Mr. Williams thought for a moment and decided to try a new approach. Looking around the room, he saw that Ksanet and Methusella had finished reading. He went over and asked them to dramatize the significance of the letter. Ksanet and Methusella vanished into the hallway. When they returned, Mr. Williams greeted the pair warmly, asking if Ksanet was Methusella's mother, the role he had assigned her to play.

"No, this is my older sister," said Methusella, having a little fun with his teacher.

"Oh! Methusella's older sister!" Mr. Williams said to Ksanet. "Nice to meet you!"

Mr. Williams told Ksanet that her "brother" was earning A's and B's and had acquired a lot of English. Then he asked if she had any questions.

"Methusella is a good student in class, or not good?" asked Ksanet.

"He is a good student," said Mr. Williams. "Sometimes he likes to throw things at other students or pull their ears, but he is a good student."

Methusella laughed out loud to be accused of things he never did. Mr. Williams turned back to the rest of the classroom. He still needed to go over the significance of the letter.

"I'm going to draw some pictures," Mr. Williams announced. On the whiteboard, he drew three stick figures. "This is your family, right, Bachan?"

Bachan heard his name, pulled a face that said what-gibberish-now, and turned to stare at Mr. Williams, awash in puzzlement.

Mr. Williams drew an arrow from the family to an outline of South High School, with its tall clock tower. He faced his class.

"Yonatan, who is invited to South High School?"

"February twenty-ninth!" Yonatan answered confidently.

"That is *when*. First I want to know, *who* is invited?"

"Parents," said Grace.

"Right," said Mr. Williams.

"Mother, father, sister, brother, uncle," suggested Saúl.

"Good," said Mr. Williams. "And what day is this happening?"

"Monday, February twenty-ninth," said Ksanet.

"And Bachan, where is this happening?" asked Mr. Williams.

A glare.

"Solomon, where should families go?"

"South High School."

"Can they see Mr. Speicher?" he asked.

He was referring to the math teacher who used body language to convey math concepts up on the fourth floor.

Solomon said, in an uncertain tone of voice, "Maybe?"

"Yes," said Mr. Williams. "They can. Can they see me?"

"Yes," Solomon answered confidently.

Saúl had a question. "Really?" he asked. "Or is this just an example?"

All this time, Saúl had thought they were just practicing reading a letter about a pretend event.

"Really," Mr. Williams told him.

Saúl wanted to double-check in Spanish. "*Verdad?*"

"*Verdad,*" assured Mr. Williams. Truly.

"Mister, what if they don't have time to come?" Nadia asked in an urgent tone. She splayed her hands out wide to signify just how busy her parents were.

"Good question," said Mr. Williams. "They can come anytime they want. They can call me, we can make an appointment. They can come on a different day, or at a different time. It's also possible to speak by phone."

One day that month, Mr. Williams arrived at school wearing blue jeans and rubber-soled boots because there was more than a foot of snow on the ground. Jakleen and Mariam made it to South anyhow, dressed extra warmly. Mariam was wearing a black cardigan with black leggings and tan suede boots. I had seen Jakleen wearing the same boots just a few days before. (The following week, Jakleen appeared in a white cable-knit cardigan with big wooden buttons, and a few days later Mariam arrived wearing the same sweater, which made me smile because my sister and I used to share clothes when we were in high school.) Given the appalling weather, I was pleasantly surprised to find the two sisters from Iraq in the classroom.

I assumed this was due to an intervention that Mr. Williams had staged. The week before, when the girls had been absent yet again, a somewhat exasperated Mr. Williams had met with their mentors, Sam and Sana (the Iraqi twins), in a corner of Room 142. He had told Sam and Sana that Jakleen and Mariam were at risk of being held back. He wanted Sam and Sana to convey this message in Arabic, so that Jakleen and Mariam would be certain to understand. "Please communicate that it's very important that they come to school," he told them. "Because they have missed a lot of school already."

Sam and Sana had nodded earnestly. The idea of not attending because of bad weather struck them as unfathomable, even though they, too, had struggled to get used to hail and sleet. Whatever they said to Jakleen and Mariam seemed to spur the sisters, for they began showing up much more regularly, participating in class activities with greater enthusiasm, and taking better advantage of the opportunity they had been given. They also started to socialize more.

That same month, Mr. Williams staged an intervention with Bachan as well. He found a Nepali-speaking paraprofessional named Miss Sushantika, a quiet, slim young woman who stood less than five feet tall. She normally worked in another part of the school, but Mr. Williams borrowed her for about one month so that she could help Bachan acclimate. Miss Sushantika began reporting to Room 142 daily, where she sat next to the Bhutanese student and translated everything that Mr. Williams said into Nepali. In Miss Sushantika's hands, Bachan turned into an amiable, chatty boy, eager to please his diminutive new instructor.

All that month, as Mr. Williams focused on pushing his most advanced students forward fast enough ("Grace, Methusella, Ksanet—is there a way to make this more complex? Can you add more description? Can you make compound sentences?") and tugging at the latest arrivals to catch up ("Bach-a-a-a-n!"), side conversations kept breaking out in various parts of the room. One day, Nadia and Jakleen started chatting about footwear, as Mariam began chortling about something Lisbeth whispered to her. It was the first time I had seen the sisters engaging in extended conversations with anybody else in the room; usually, they spoke only to one another. They were branching out.

Mr. Williams had recently separated Lisbeth from Bachan and moved her to a seat beside Mariam. The two of them needed to resort to English to communicate, which boosted Mariam's confidence. The new seating arrangement also triggered the first real friendship Mariam found in the room, as she and Lisbeth grew closer. This vastly increased the amount of spoken English that Mariam produced, but also led to moments when the two girls surreptitiously shared YouTube videos of small furry animals and misbehaving toddlers on their phones. Soon they began chatting so much that Mr. Williams interrupted himself to say sharply, "Lisbeth and Mariam!"

They paid attention to him for a little while, but then resumed snickering.

"Ladies, are we writing?" Mr. Williams said in a stern voice. "Mariam, Lisbeth, are we writing sentences?"

Lisbeth pretended not to know that Mr. Williams had been referring to her. She pointed to Plamedi, seated nearby, and said in a tone of surprise, "Lady?"

Plamedi grimaced at Lisbeth, and she cheerily apologized as if she had just realized her mistake, saying, "Oh! *Lo siento!*"

Despite the genuine distraction that Lisbeth provided, she served a worthy purpose. She exerted a pull on Mariam—and later, Jakleen—that drew the Iraqi sisters further into Room 142 emotionally. Only after the two sisters befriended the ebullient girl from El Salvador did they begin enjoying school. One evening, when the Iraqi family and I were going out to dinner, and we were driving to a Middle Eastern restaurant in my car, Mariam and Jakleen admitted they had begun to like South. When I asked why, Jakleen cried, "Lisbeth!" I believe that Mr. Williams deliberately let Mariam and Jakleen get away with a certain amount of out-of-bounds fun with Lisbeth, even though it meant he had to work extra-hard to manage the whole situation, because he recognized that Lisbeth had become one of the reasons they looked forward to school.

Meanwhile, Mr. Williams and Miss Pauline continued to have side discussions about the psychological well-being of the students. Occasionally, I caught sight of the ways the students revealed themselves to the therapist. One day that month, Miss Pauline took half of the students out of the room, and when they returned, they showed us the rubbings they had made of objects that were patterned. Lisbeth announced that hers was *feo* (ugly) and then told everybody *mira!* (look!) at her drawing. Shani walked over to Mr. Williams and showed him the colored chalk dust that powdered her hands and pantomimed the act of washing. "You want to wash your hands?" Mr. Williams asked. "You can wash your hands." Then Miss Pauline came over to me and chatted about the artwork the students were producing. "They have *a lot* of feelings!" she said. "I don't even know if they *know* they have so many feelings. We made boxes last week and several kids used lots and lots of tape to make sure the boxes were very, very secure— all bound up. How symbolic is that?"

I nodded. I had seen the boxes. One student had wrapped his entire box in the American flag, as though he wanted to embrace his new reality completely and did not even want to acknowledge the past. Another had used miles of tape. When the students showed off their boxes and their rubbings, I was most curious to know what emotions Solomon and Methusella held inside, and what lay behind the self-destructive rebellions that Mariam and Jakleen sometimes staged. I could guess what each of the students might be harboring, but they hadn't revealed themselves to me. I did not think it would be productive to try to prise emotional information out of them; someday, they would tell me, if they felt like it. My job was to stick around and see if that time ever came, and if it did, to listen. To listen hard—because they would never say too much; I would just get a hint of what they kept secreted away inside those well-taped boxes.

At the end of the class, right before the bell rang, Mr. Williams called out to the distracted students, who were packing up their belongings. Somebody had forgotten a cell phone. The device had been left over by the windows, where it was charging.

"That's Ksanet's," said Methusella.

When she walked over to get her phone, Ksanet noticed that a jacket had been left behind on the back of a chair.

"Jakleen! Jakleen!" she cried. "Your jacket!"

In a way, it was nothing remarkable. But in Room 142, it was new, this kind of behavior. They were starting to look out for one another.

Another day that month, I found Mr. Williams getting ready for class, and he asked if had I heard the big news. The district had made its selection: The next principal of South High was going to be Jen Hanson. Mr. Williams was jubilant. Hanson had previously worked as an ELA teacher at South before transferring to a rival high school to become an assistant principal. The entire faculty at South, and especially the ELA team, were thrilled to have Hanson return as their new principal, because they felt confident she would carry forward the legacy they had created together. Hanson's appointment sent a clear signal that South would continue welcoming refugees and immigrants with open arms. Parents were equally ecstatic. "She really had a vision for the school,"

Carolyn Howard, the PTA president, said later. "She was strong enough and charismatic enough to rally all of the stakeholders—the faculty, the parents, and the students."

The other big news at South concerned Carolyn's son, George, who had accidentally done away with the prom. The newcomers did not know this odd word, "prom"—we discussed it in class one day, and Mr. Williams got me to pantomime prom dancing—but during February, it was the only thing that members of South's senior class wanted to discuss, besides the Super Bowl. One day in mid-February, when I swung by the Student Senate, I caught George trying to explain what had happened to other student movers and shakers. Mr. Brookes, the faculty adviser to the Senate, had just asked for an update from each class.

"Seniors?" Mr. Brookes said.

"We canceled prom," the head girl said drily.

"Yes, and after having canceled prom, we decided it's back on," added the head boy.

"Can I just say it wasn't *completely* my idea?" objected George. "They told me to do it!"

"George, explain," suggested Mr. Brookes.

"There's been a lot of tension about which prom theme we should use," George began. "So on Friday we decided maybe, you know, we could try to lighten the subject and get people to chill out. So I figured that maybe people would know I was joking if I said that prom was canceled. And a lot of people didn't know that I was joking. A lot of them did, but some people didn't, which—which was a bit of a problem."

The squabble had begun on social media, primarily the senior class page on Facebook, when one faction of students supported a *Harry Potter* theme, another faction went for *The Great Gatsby*, and a third for *The Secret Garden*. One of the many members of the senior class who had not understood George's dry sense of humor was Rodica, the pom-pom-bearing student from Benin, the school's only foreign-born cheerleader. Rodica and George had exchanged a few testy remarks online.

"So just to be clear, I talked to Rodica and stuff, and we're all cool, we're still friends," reported George, who seemed a little chagrined. "But yeah, I thought I would tell everybody that it's a joke, and prom is still on."

In the end, not enough people had read *The Great Gatsby*, and as many people hated as loved the idea of a prom based on *Harry Potter*. "We decided to go with the one that people were not, like, 'Oh, that sucks,'" concluded George. "We're going with *The Secret Garden*. I think everyone can agree it's a pretty good theme." It was a good theme for South—a book about overcoming obstacles, about rejuvenation, about healing. And then, just as Denver was celebrating the city's Super Bowl victory and Mr. Williams was celebrating the idea of Jen Hanson as his principal and George and Rodica and all the seniors were celebrating the idea that their prom was officially back on, Donald Trump started winning primary after primary.

The kids at South still thought Trump was a joke, but he spoke to other parts of America where good jobs had been vanishing and a sense of security about the future had been lost. The economic pain of small-town, rural America was being largely ignored by media outlets based in large cities, and the press was out of touch with what was happening in the election. As he campaigned, Trump was saying things about refugees that accurately captured the fears of ordinary Americans who lived in conservative places. He asserted, for example, that the United States was letting in refugees "who are definitely in many cases ISIS-aligned." This was supposition. No refugees had been admitted with demonstrated ties to ISIS. Aid workers found the idea of terrorists trying to use the resettlement system to enter a developed country to be implausible, as it was the slowest and most uncertain means of entry. Less than 1 percent of those designated as refugees by the United Nations were given the chance to resettle in a third country, and refugees were vetted more extensively than any other type of entrant to the United States. But these things were not widely understood. Meanwhile, Trump's assertions about refugees resonated with his audiences, and his popularity was growing at a meteoric rate.

2

We Hate Sheep

When I told Solomon and Methusella that I was hoping to visit them at home again, they conferred with their father and told me to come on a particular Sunday. This was shortly before they moved to the two-bedroom apartment, back when they were still living in their first house. The boys did not tell me a specific time. To be polite, I tried texting with their father, Tchiza, to see if 2:30 P.M. would be convenient. I never heard back.

When I arrived at the tan clapboard house with the dirt yard and the chain-link fence, I was welcomed just as before, by the same dancing whorl of children. On this occasion, Julius was not available—his schedule at the grocery store conflicted with the time I had chosen—and I wound up employing a different Swahili-speaking interpreter, a gracious Ethiopian woman named Berhane. She had come straight from church and was wearing a long black skirt and a magenta blazer. Berhane had arrived in this country as a refugee herself, and had learned to speak Swahili while living in a refugee camp in Kenya.

We sat down at the kitchen table. Once again the boys' mother, Beya, busied herself in the kitchen without sitting down herself. This time I could see that her actions were a form of deference. Tchiza belonged at the table, and so did the guests; Beya stayed in the background. I told the boys' father that before we spoke further, I wanted to make sure this was a good time. I had texted to see if this hour was okay, but had not gotten a response. Berhane translated all of this into Swahili.

Tchiza smiled broadly. "Well, we don't have the same concept of time," he explained to me kindly, as if I were his student. Apparently, we were going to study another culture together: Congolese ways. He would instruct me. "We don't pick one hour and ask can we knock on your door then," Tchiza said, as if doing something so formal as *that* were the craziest thing in the world. "We just drop by! If you are home, then it is a good time!"

So, this was a good time.

Beya brought to the table several cans of pineapple Fanta, one bowl of potatoes and beans, and three spoons. There was a spoon for me, a spoon for her husband, and a spoon for our interpreter, but there was no spoon for Beya. I did not sense any resentment on Beya's part about this. She waited on us with an aura of gladness. But to me, it was strange, having her attend to the rest of us and keep herself apart.

"This is a sign of respect," the interpreter told me, pointing at the food Beya had just put on the table. "We will all eat from the same bowl."

Oh, that's nice! I thought. I've been fully welcomed into the family.

"Also, it is a good way not to get poisoned," Tchiza added, with a little glint in his eye. "If you go to someone else's home, and you all eat from the same bowl, then you cannot pour poison into their food, because if you did, then you would eat the poison, too."

He smiled. Our exchange was amusing to him. Me, too. Beya had cooked the potatoes in tomatoes and onions and spices, and served them mixed with red beans that had been simmered until they were melting. The food was hearty and simple and I enjoyed it immensely. I simultaneously felt guilty about eating a meal bought with food stamps, but I was raised by people who consider it an important mark of hospitality to share food. So I found the act of eating with Tchiza to be meaningful. And in Congolese culture, I would eventually learn, when I brought gifts like a pineapple to their home, I was offering them a blessing, and by feeding me, they were offering me a blessing in return.

We spoke about their lives in the Democratic Republic of Congo. I thought maybe I should start with a softball kind of question.

"What kind of work did you do in the Congo?" I asked.

"Actually, in the Congo, people don't do just one job and then come home, no—it's not like this," Tchiza replied.

He had done many different things. He had farmed (beans, cassava, sorghum, corn, peas, and sweet potatoes), advised other farmers, taught, become a leader in his village, and written reports about the movement of goods back and forth across the border for the government in Kinshasa. In his culture, one could not neatly pigeonhole a person by occupation; in my culture, we did so all the time. Time, work—at the most fundamental level, his concept of things differed from mine. Our ways of thinking about all aspects of life appeared a little at odds. And both Tchiza and I enjoyed discovering these discrepancies and turning them over in our minds. It was fun to hear what he had to say to my oh-so-American questions.

After what I considered a decent interval, I turned the conversation to the subject of the ongoing violence in the Congo, which in parts of the country had continued to the present day. What had led the family to flee their home village, walk for months, and spend five grueling years inside a refugee settlement? Why had they left the DRC? Tchiza started talking about Rwanda and the genocide that had swept that country in 1994. Then he spoke of the waves of Hutu and Tutsi escapees who had spilled over into the Democratic Republic of Congo, carrying strife with them. He described how the enmities born in Rwanda had taken root on Congolese soil. And he spoke at length of the various governments of the DRC—Mobutu, Kabila, and Kabila.

Then we got into an alphabet soup of armed groups that had represented the interests of either the Congolese government or its two main rivals, the countries of Rwanda and Uganda. Next came the militia groups that had splintered off the original armed groups. After that, we began talking about the *mai mai*, the villagers who had taken up arms to defend themselves against all of these marauders. I got lost somewhere in the middle, amid the acronyms and the tribal stuff. I could not absorb all the details, but I came away with the notion of a jumble of allegiances and betrayals, mixed with a lot of weaponry. One acronym stood out—CNDP. Tchiza said those letters a lot, always with the French pronunciation ("say, ehn, day, pay"). But who the CNDP was, or what they had against this group or that group, I could not follow.

While Tchiza was describing how their once peaceful village had gotten caught up in an endless cycle of violence, with different rifle-bearing commandos pillaging for food, and I was struggling to understand who was doing the pillaging and why, Beya became obviously distraught. This subject bothered her, a lot. She communicated this wordlessly, by shaking her head back and forth and then waggling both of her hands at Tchiza, as if to say, *Stop, stop, stop.*

Meanwhile, Tchiza spoke only in generalities. What about the particulars? Where did his personal allegiances lie? Whom did he know who had been hurt? Whom had he been trying his utmost to protect? Tchiza mentioned again the underlying Hutu and Tutsi alignments with the various militia groups in North Kivu. More acronyms. I felt as though he kept telling me the story and yet not telling me the story.

"What tribe are you?" I asked.

I had the intuition, as soon as the words were out of my mouth, that this might be a question that only an American would ask.

"Well, people can just look at you and tell," replied Tchiza.

"I can't tell, though," I said. "What tribe are you?"

"You can just tell by looking at someone's face, that's how we know," Tchiza said, demurring.

"I'm sorry, I can't do that. I can't see those differences in people's features. What tribe are you?"

"Hutu," he said finally.

I had gotten an answer, but in the room there was a chill. I sensed that perhaps I had made a mistake. What I would learn eventually is that the tribalism of Africa is subtle, complex, and nearly unfathomable to outsiders. Customs are closely held and generally not written down. Some of the old ways might even go unspoken, or might be passed along from parent to child only at key life moments, a precious gift to be handed over at just the right juncture.

Each tribe has specific habits around what to eat, or which animals to hold in high regard, some of which might sound outlandish in Europe or the United States. A few customs sounded outlandish even to me, but the basic concept underpinning tribalism was highly familiar. The Irish hew to divisions, too; we derive a sense of who we are from similar juxtapositions. We define ourselves by what county our family once farmed, or what side of Dublin the last generation claimed as home, or what type of whiskey we drink. My mother is from County Cavan, which means that her people are known to be closefisted with resources, words, and vital information. If you are from Cavan, most likely your last name will be Brady. Once, I went to a reunion at the small village schoolhouse my mother had attended as a child—I was standing in on her behalf, because she was all the way over in America, and I happened to be in Ireland—and when I went to sign the register recording who had come to the event, I saw that it read: "Brady. Brady. Brady. Brady. Brady." You would not say any more than that, on an official form, if you were from Cavan.

Thus, when Tchiza gave me a one-word answer, said only, "Hutu," I recognized what was happening. This was the truth, but it was given grudgingly, under pressure; consequently, it was only a partial truth. The complete version of the family's story, which I would learn in time, was more whimsical and more particular. Tchiza's family belonged to the Ababanda Ba Bahoma tribe, a subclan within the general grouping known as Hutu. Across Africa, totems and taboos are used by tribes to create a sense of being at home. The Ababanda Ba Bahoma avoided eating certain kinds of meat, for example. "We don't like sheep," Tchiza's brother, Nehemie, would tell me later. "We cannot eat it. We hate sheep."

Or a tribe might hold a certain animal in high regard. If elephants are considered sacred, for example, then the tribe is obligated to protect and defend that totem.

"We respect birds," Nehemie told me. "We respect especially the wagtail bird."

The wagtail bird is so named because of its frequent tail-wagging behavior; it nests on the ground and lays perhaps six speckled eggs at a time. Because it eats insects that devour crops, the wagtail bird protects the food that families grow in that part of the Congo.

Tchiza and his siblings grew up in the village of Buganza, near the town of Rutshuru, in North Kivu. The closest major city is Goma, but Buganza is secreted away in a high and remote area, surrounded by hills. The roads

207

that lead there are unpaved, and the village has running water but no electricity. Although the Congo is a largely Catholic country, Tchiza's father attended a Protestant-based Bible school as a young man (a California-born missionary founded the school). He later started a Baptist church in Buganza, where he served as pastor. He died when Tchiza was still living in the village. When I asked Nehemie what their father had taught them, he said, "To know God. To love God."

The turning point for Tchiza—the moment when he decided it was no longer safe to remain in Buganza—came after he began to play a greater leadership role and thus became a larger target. In July 2006, he ran for public office in the first multiparty elections to take place in the Democratic Republic of Congo in forty-one years. Voters were electing both a president and a new National Assembly, and Tchiza was hoping to join that legislative body. Armed clashes took place during the collection of the results (which were declared inconclusive, leading to a runoff later that year), and during the turmoil, Tchiza heard that his life was in danger. The violence he had tried to curtail had instead come to his door. He would die if he remained in the DRC, that was clear, Tchiza said.

The family left at 2 A.M. Each of them wore four sets of clothing and carried what else they could. They were going to walk to Uganda, and it would take several months. I asked, "How many children were with you at the time?" It seemed a simple question, to me—I just wanted to be able to envision how many of them were walking along those dusty roads wearing so many clothes.

The conversation took a strange turn. There was talk of Beya having three children, when based on the ages of the children I had seen, I thought she must have had six or seven. There was talk about what the word "children" meant. Did it mean tiny ones you had to carry while you were walking yourself? Or were you supposed to include the big ones who could walk on their own? Frustrated with not getting clear numbers, I put my hand on Berhane's arm and tilted my head, a gesture by which I meant, *Hey, why are you guys talking so much in Swahili?* The interpreter looked at me with infinite patience and held up one finger, meaning, *Just wait.* She listened some more and then turned back to me.

Berhane confessed that she was having a little trouble communicating with Beya, because the version of Swahili Beya spoke was different from the version the interpreter had learned in Kenya. As far as she could make out, Beya spoke a version of Swahili mixed with a tribal language, plus a whole lot of French. It was only when I had asked the most elemental of questions that our level of confusion had become apparent: Among the three of us, we did not have an entire set of shared terms. This meant that, at best, I was hearing only an approximation of the story I was seeking. Such was the norm in my encounters with refugees, I had started to accept. There would be a whole lot of talking, we would achieve a muddled exchange, then maybe we might find some clarity about the level of confusion, and perhaps after that we might reach an understanding that was a bit less muddled.

In the end, we required documents to answer my question. Beya got up and returned bearing everybody's Social Security cards. She also retrieved a sheet of paper given to her by the IOM, the agency that handles transit of refugees between countries, which listed everybody's official birth dates, as the aid workers understood them. Using these pieces of paper, eventually we pieced together that Beya had given birth ten times but had nine living children. At the moment when they had left their home village, eight births had taken place, and she had lost one child, so there had been seven living children. Plus, she had been carrying her next child in her womb, for she had been pregnant when they started walking. That child, Ombeni ("prayer"), and the one who followed, Zawadi ("gift"), were born after the family crossed over into Uganda. In 2008, when they had begun their odyssey on foot out of the Democratic Republic of Congo at two in the morning, the children she had already delivered who were still alive were, in order of birth: Gideon, Timoté, Elia, Solomon, Methusella, Innocent, and Sifa ("praise").

Only after I went home and mused about our meeting did I realize that the family had told me nothing about any of the difficult experiences they must have had while living in a village beset by various armed groups. Essentially, Tchiza and Beya had been living in a battleground. But they had not described one incident of violence that they had witnessed personally. Not one attack, when there must have been dozens, or hundreds, over the years. Instead of pushing for more, I decided to honor their habit of not talking about painful subjects. Meanwhile, I would read books about the Congo.

Because the history of the Congo was hard to understand, and because I felt it was my duty to instruct myself instead of relying upon a family in the middle of trying to resettle in the United States to explain their part of the world to me, I read dozens of books about the region from which they had fled. In novels such as *Heart of Darkness* and in nonfiction including *King Leopold's Ghost*, I learned how Belgium had inflicted upon the Congo a particularly brutal colonial regime that resulted in the deaths of millions of Congolese, and how Belgians had gotten rich trafficking in gold and diamonds and rubber taken from the Congo. From old, out-of-print, hard-to-find travel memoirs, such as *Back to the Congo* and *East Along the Equator*—sent to me by an old flame, a former war correspondent—I learned about the iniquities of the Mobutu regime. He was our man in Africa, propped up at critical junctures by various American governments, because he was anticommunist. And he violated his own country just as thoroughly as the Belgians had, stealing billions of dollars from the Congo's rich deposits of gems and ore. Then I read the truly dark books, about the DRC's recent history. They were filled with descriptions of atrocities that I still have trouble putting out of my mind. From *Dancing in the Glory of Monsters* and *Congo: Between Hope and Despair*, I got the full sweep of the two civil wars that Tchiza had referenced, and the story of the involvement of Rwanda and Uganda in the demise of the once viable Congo as a governable place. And then I could see why this family had to leave.

Because North Kivu is positioned on the far eastern side of the Congo, right along the border with Rwanda and Uganda, that province had caught the brunt of it all. In sum, it became clear to me that if any family I was speaking with had witnessed horrific suffering, and must be living with extraordinary levels of grief, it had to be Tchiza, Beya, and their wary, gentle children. Yet they never spoke of these things. They never mentioned one atrocity, they never spoke of a single death, they never alluded to rape, which I knew from those books was epidemic in North Kivu. Our conversations about the DRC had the flavor of a dry history lesson, bled of emotion. Why was this?

* * *

Over a long period during which I visited the family often but did not interview them much—visits in which we shared many merry moments and a lot of fantastic food—I learned that by not talking about the horrible things they had endured, the family managed to maintain an extraordinary level of dignity. I did not want to make the mistake of generalizing too much from my experiences with one family, but I came to believe that there was something essentially Congolese about this manner of preserving dignity—something cultural behind the stoicism. Negative emotions, anyway, seemed to be a private matter. You could share joy with a visitor, but not despair—I thought this might be one of their taboos. It would take dozens of meetings, three interpreters, and much more research before I felt I had anything close to the outlines of their journey, and even then, some of the difficult parts remained untold.

If somebody had died, for example, there was a tendency to not even mention that person by name; it took multiple conversations before I would learn that a deceased person had even existed. I was in the middle of Tracy Kidder's *Strength in What Remains*, a book about a survivor of one of the major genocides in Burundi, when I came across a passage about cultural beliefs in Central Africa around discussing difficulty. "Keep it in the kitchen" was one of the admonitions that Kidder cited. Another could be used against a person who said too much: "You talk like you were raised by a widow." When I read these sayings, I thought of the incredible reserve of Solomon and Methusella's family. I felt that I had a duty to tell their story, but for the time being I relinquished the idea of sitting down at their table and eating their food and saying, *Great! Tell me about your nightmares!*

Instead I would try to follow their ways. I gave up asking Tchiza about what he might have witnessed and simply tried to get to know him better. Largely this involved my being open to discussing subjects that Tchiza wanted to talk about, which were generally practical matters. One day, for example, we spent a lot of time trying to get an old printer to function. This was after the family had moved into the two-bedroom apartment in a housing complex also located close to my home. The complex consisted of about two dozen rectangular buildings arranged around a series of grassy courtyards, and featured a pool, a gym, and a movie room. The apartment walls were painted tan and the countertops and the carpet were neutral shades as well, but Beya had strung garlands of silk flowers along the ceiling and placed bouquets of them in vases all over the living room, making the room blaze with color: purple, gold, maroon, magenta. I wondered how ten members of the family squeezed into the two bedrooms, and Solomon gravely escorted me upstairs to show me the room that he shared with Methusella, Elia, and Timoté, their four twin mattresses taking up the entire space. There were clothes all over the floor. (Messy! Hadn't expected that.) The smaller children shared the second bedroom, while their parents slept in an alcove off the living room. By this point, I had dispensed with interpreters. Either Solomon or Methusella—or their precocious younger brother Innocent, or their hardworking older brothers Elia and Timoté—served as interpreters for their parents as needed.

We were seated at the kitchen table when Tchiza got up and disappeared into the alcove where he and Beya slept, ducking behind the fabric curtain that marked off their sleeping area. He emerged with a dusty black printer. Tchiza asked in Swahili, and Methusella repeated in English: How do you turn it on? It happened that this was not possible. Tchiza had acquired only the printer itself, not the all-important power cord. I asked Methusella where his father had gotten the printer. Goodwill, he said. We went online and looked up the type of power cord that this model required. I wrote down the name of the store where they could buy a power cord: RadioShack. "Where is this place, RadioShack?" Methusella asked on behalf of his father. I said there was a RadioShack on Colfax Avenue, quite nearby.

"He wants to know, can we go there?" Methusella said.

"Can we go there right now? Go together?" I checked.

"Yes," said Methusella.

"Sure!" I declared.

It would be interesting to see what the family would make of

RadioShack, I figured—a quintessential immigrant-in-America moment. Methusella chose to stay at home, while Solomon elected to come with us. By this point, both boys could do a decent job of interpreting—in the classroom, Solomon lagged behind Methusella, and I could tell that this was galling, but the competition meant that Methusella constantly pulled his older brother forward. I thought Solomon was probably learning twice as much as he would have without the spur of his younger brother's astonishing performance to goad him on. When I visited them at home, Methusella sometimes deigned to interpret and sometimes preferred to play games on his phone, but Solomon always hung around, listening closely to what was said. I saw that he showed unflagging kindness to his younger siblings, who took turns gluing themselves to his legs. He also had an endearing habit of smiling very widely and saying, "Oh!" anytime he felt an inkling of surprise or embarrassment, which was often. That's what he had said when I had asked to see the boys' bedroom: "Oh!"

Solomon and Tchiza and I got into my Volkswagen and drove over to RadioShack. Tchiza tsked-tsked about the revealing attire worn by young women walking the streets—halter tops, short shorts, lots of cleavage, lots of leg. I cringed for him, about the general lewdness of America, and also noticed that Solomon, in the backseat, was busy saying nothing. Inside RadioShack we wandered around for a while, admiring gadgets and doodads. Finally we enlisted the help of a thoughtful employee in finding the right power cord. The employee had a question: Did they need a second cord, the one that would connect the printer to their computer? Or did the printer have the capacity to talk to the computer wirelessly? Solomon conferred with Tchiza about this in Swahili for a while, the employee and I conferred about this in English for a while, then Solomon joined our conversation and told us that Tchiza said we should buy this cord. The employee said the connecting cord came in various lengths. Which one did they want? Solomon conferred with Tchiza about this in Swahili for a while, I conferred about this with the employee in English for a while, and then Solomon said his father wanted the shortest cord. The employee wore a big smile as he listened to Solomon laboriously exercise his newfound English.

At the cash register, the employee told Solomon how much they owed in English, and Solomon told his father the amount in Swahili, and Tchiza paid.

Mission accomplished. I was about to take them back to the apartment when Tchiza said something.

"He wants to know, where can you buy paper?" Solomon asked.

"Office Depot. Want to go there?"

They did. First, though, we took a brief detour. We were close to my home, and I offered to show them where I lived. They were curious to see it, so we drove over there and I pointed at the small, two-story, red-brick house that I owned.

"That's where I live," I announced.

"Miss," said Solomon, "I have a question."

"Yes, Solomon."

"You live here?"

"Yes."

"You and your son?"

"Yes."

"Just the two of you?"

"Yes. Just the two of us."

Oh, right. By global standards, I occupied a lot of real estate. This house seemed small to me, because once upon a time I had lived in a much bigger house. I didn't think of my current house as *too* small—to my mind, it was perfect. Cozy. But it wasn't cozy, as far as Solomon was concerned. To him, the house was enormous. We had two whole stories for just two people. I could feel him wondering, in the backseat: What did we even *do* with that much space?

Then Tchiza said, in carefully constructed English, "I want . . . to buy . . . a house."

I remembered Hussen, from the African Community Center, telling me that endorsing the idea of borrowing money was a big adjustment. I explained to Tchiza that I had a mortgage and joked that in reality, the bank owned my house.

Tchiza thought of something else. "I want . . . to buy . . . a car," he said. "A big car! Because I have a big family."

"Yes," I told him. "You will definitely need a really big car. Maybe a minivan."

We headed toward Home Depot. Tchiza's English was improving, I noted.

"Have you ever driven a car?" I asked him.

"No," he said.

"Never?" I asked, surprised.

"No. Not ever."

People in Buganza walked wherever they wanted to go. Or caught a bus.

Other days, we discussed mail. Methusella or Solomon would sit beside me, and their father would hold up one letter after another, and we would decipher the correspondence together. He had gotten a letter from a bank, Tchiza said, it must be very important! I read the letter. No, I explained. He could throw this in the trash. It said that the bank knew he had signed a lease, and might be new in the neighborhood. People who worked at the bank were wondering if he wanted to give them his earnings for safekeeping. They would earn a fee, if he did this. The letter was a piece of advertising.

"Oh!" Solomon said.

What about this letter? Tchiza asked. It was also about money, and seemed extremely significant. It said he might win $1 million!

"This letter is from a place calling themselves Publishers Clearing House sweepstakes," I told him. "They will not pay you $1 million, I don't think—in fact, they might even come up with sneaky ways to get *you* to pay *them* money."

Tchiza protested. The letter said $1 million! If he entered this competition, there was a chance he might win!

"Believe me, we used to get letters like these at my house when I was growing up," I told Tchiza. "I used to fill them out myself, and we never got $1 million."

Sheepishly, Tchiza admitted that he had already mailed back the form, betraying personal information to the company.

"Oh, well," I told him. "That's okay. You're just going to get a lot more junk mail, that's all."

One of Solomon's older brothers had a question about this entity, the one calling itself Publishers Clearing House sweepstakes.

"He is like a sorcerer?" asked Elia.

"Um, yes," I said. "This company is like a sorcerer, pretty much. They are trying to trick you, I think. They are trying to make you believe in something that is not true."

Sometimes, we parsed other American ideas, such as the words written on their clothing. One day I arrived to find Innocent wearing a T-shirt that said STUD. Underneath that word was a picture of a muffin.

"Oh, stud muffin!" I said to Innocent, smiling broadly at his T-shirt. Consternation on his face.

"Is it something bad?" Innocent asked me, innocently.

From his pained tone, I gleaned that perhaps his older brothers had been teasing him about the meaning of his T-shirt. I suspected they had not understood the significance of the muffin.

"No," I assured him. "It is not a bad thing. It's a good thing. It means . . ." How to translate the term "stud muffin" into family-friendly, Congolese-ready terminology? "It means, like, important man."

The tight muscles in his face relaxed. He was not wearing an evil T-shirt.

And other days, I learned things without any discussion. For instance, I learned that the United States was profoundly exhausting on the day when I dropped by to find Tchiza stretched out, shirtless, lengthwise on the long sofa, with one arm thrown over his eyes, blocking out the daylight streaming through the windows.

I said, softly, "Hello . . ."

Then I said, not so softly, "Hello!"

And I said, quite loudly, "HELLO!" But he never stirred.

So I stepped outside and played with the small children and their well-loved toys, which were strewn up and down the outdoor staircase. Probably Goodwill again. We ran dented plastic trucks and little metal cars with chipped paint jobs up and down the staircase, up and down my arms, sideways across my chest, all over my face. Then we each tried on my glasses. Ombeni and Zawadi did most of the truck driving, as Sifa bossed us around in English and Swahili. The children were alternately merry then squabbled and then grew merry again, like a day with clouds scudding across the sky. We had been playing for a while when Beya stumbled out of the apartment wearing a jogging bra and another floor-length cotton skirt. Her belly—it was a glorious, striated testament to childbirth.

My own grandmother had been proficient at birth. My mother's mother had married a bachelor nineteen years older than she and had borne him ten children. Then she had lost one, leaving nine. It was the same math that Beya had lived through. The farmhouse where my mother had grown up was considered big by standards of rural Ireland, because it had two stories; neighbors still lived in one-story thatched cottages. One of my mother's brothers had taken over the farm, and he had five children. When my cousins Geraldine and Caroline were young, Granny had moved into their bedroom. She didn't sleep well, and she didn't like to be awake by herself in the lonely part of the night. She kept a thermos of black tea stashed under the bed, as well as a roll of biscuits, and she would poke Geraldine and Caroline to wake up to join her for some caffeine and sugar at two in the morning. I never saw Granny's tummy, but it must have looked like Beya's—the language of birth scribbled over and over again on the same patch of flesh.

Beya looked sleepily refreshed after her nap. She laughed at the sight of us, playing with toys all over the stairs, and said something that sounded half scolding and half loving, in words I didn't understand. We obediently followed her back inside. Then Sifa taught me how to say, "I do not speak Swahili," in Swahili.

Perhaps the most telling moment I ever spent with Tchiza and Beya would take place several months later, in the parking lot of the apartment complex. It was the middle of the summer, five weeks after Solomon and Methusella had finished their first year at South. Tchiza and Beya were walking me to my car. They liked to do this, strolling along holding hands, with Zawadi and Ombeni tripping at their feet, clutching at Beya's long skirt and using the fabric to play peekaboo. After they escorted me to my vehicle, we were standing by my Volkswagen, enjoying the warm night air, when we heard the rat-a-tat-tat of firecrackers. Soon it would be the Fourth of July.

Beya dropped low enough to touch the pavement. It grew quiet. Slowly, she stood up.

More fireworks. Beya flinched and dropped down low again.

Zawadi laughed and laughed. Why was her mother ducking and cavorting? Silly game! Zawadi laughed so much she covered her mouth with her hands.

I did not think the older boys would have been laughing if they had come outside. Zawadi had been born in Uganda, after the family had left the sound of daily gunfire behind. She had never lived in North Kivu. Almost a decade had passed since Beya and Tchiza and their children had set out from Buganza, wearing all those clothes. But Beya reacted to what sounded like gunshots as sharply as though she had left North Kivu yesterday. The past had shoved through into the present. Solomon and his brothers would have known why their mother was cowering in the perfectly safe parking lot. Strange, how the same stuttering sound meant celebration in my country and death in hers. And that was as much as the family ever said, in an entire year—one wordless statement, when my country caught them off guard—about what they had lived through, back in the Democratic Republic of Congo.

I did wonder, later, how this family, who might have seen more than any other family I had known, how could *this* family be so joyful? And were the two matters related, the not-naming and the joy?

3

Wir schaffen das

O ne day in March, Mr. Williams was writing a list of all the verb tenses he had taught his students on the whiteboard (present, present continuous, simple past, past continuous) as Greg and Jaclyn were restocking the food bank. Class was about to begin. Jakleen and Saúl were wrestling to get hold of each other's cell phones, Lisbeth was preening for another selfie in a revealing gold lace T-shirt, and Hsar Htoo was watching everything while wearing a sunny smile and a black T-shirt that featured white storm troopers from *Star Wars*. Abigail was sitting by herself, lost in thought, shyly gnawing on a gold-plated ring of the Virgin of Guadalupe. The room had not yet opened up all the way, but there were green shoots of affection going in every direction. Mr. Williams wrote on the whiteboard, USING ADVERBS.

"I really want to help you make sentences that are more complex," he announced.

The teacher distributed a list of adverbs printed on blue paper: especially, incredibly, superbly, definitely, masterfully, exquisitely, wonderfully, usefully, strongly, extremely, exceedingly, exceptionally, extraordinarily, tremendously, immensely, remarkably, truly, decidedly, highly, particularly. Mr. Williams wrote a simple sentence on the whiteboard: "It was very hot." He asked how to make that sentence more compelling.

Dilli raised her hand. "Exceedingly," she said.

Mr. Williams agreed that was an improvement. "If we always use 'very,' that kind of makes me go—" He clasped his hands together and laid one cheek against his hands and pretended to fall asleep. "It is boring."

He had most of the class's attention, most of them were listening (studiously), but over on one side of the room, Lisbeth, Mariam, and Shani had fallen into a side conversation about whether Lisbeth had a new boyfriend, and were giggling (boisterously). Shani whispered to me (mischievously) that Lisbeth had a beau. I took this to mean that Lisbeth had a crush on a certain boy. He wrote posts on Facebook about his nuclear family or about soccer—Lisbeth did not appear to be much on his mind.

"Mariam? *Mariam?* Lisbeth?" said Mr. Williams. "Shani, you understand what we are doing?"

The girls looked up. What was Mr. Williams even talking about? They had (absolutely) no idea. Saúl made a blue airplane out of his handout and (daringly) sent it sailing across the room, straight at the girls and their intractable frivolity. Mr. Williams had been talking (dully) about adverbs.

"Mariam, do you understand? You don't understand? No? We'll help you."

Mr. Williams sat down next to Mariam, as Mr. DeRose sat down with Abigail. Abigail (acerbically) wrote a paragraph about how tedious Mr. Williams was today, talking about these stupid things, adverbs. I went over to Lisbeth. She wrote that her summer was "exceptionally" fun because she had gone shopping.

"Good," I told her (encouragingly). "What did you buy?"

She told me, in Spanish, English, and sign language, that she had bought: *zapatos*, shirts, and then she pantomimed painting her fingernails. Nail polish, I deduced.

"What are these?" she asked, tapping on the ends of her fingers.

"Those are your fingernails," I told her. "Or, you can just say 'nails.'"

"Nails?" she asked (incredulously).

"Yup. Nails."

Jakleen wrote a paragraph about eating cake because it had been her sister's birthday, although she thought her sister ate too much. Both girls spoke often of controlling their appetites; while Mariam seemed interested in curtailing primarily her own appetite, Jakleen wanted to police her two sisters' eating habits, too. This would become a theme for the rest of the year, as their personalities emerged, in tandem with their English. Did Mariam and Lulu eat too much, in Jakleen's opinion?

The following day, noticing that the room had gotten rowdy, Mr. Williams made the students change their seats yet again.

Methusella objected. "No good! I can't see!"

He meant that his new chair was too far away from the whiteboard. Methusella adopted the habit of leaving his far-off table near the door and wandering over to stand at Mr. Williams's elbow, as he wrote lessons on the whiteboard. I thought of it as a physical embodiment of how eager Methusella was to learn.

For the rest of that month, Mr. Williams had the students spend a lot of time reading. After they finished the Hmong fable, he brought out a box filled with folktales from around the world and encouraged the students to choose whatever reading material they wanted. Grace picked *Tales of the Shimmering Sky*, stories from a variety of countries about heavenly bodies, the seasons, and the weather. Saúl chose *Blue Moon Valley*, a fable set in China about a girl who leaves her rural home for a big city. Hsar Htoo selected *A Tiger by the Tail*, fairy tales and legends from Korea, and Yonatan chose *Why the Leopard Has Spots*, a retelling of a popular African folktale. The students buried themselves in their books for hours on end throughout the rest of the month. Often, the room was entirely still. All I could hear was the sound of pages turning, or, on a warm day, the hum of the fan. At one point, it got so peaceful and lulling that Shani put her head down and fell asleep. Mr. Williams chanted, "Shah-nee! Shah-nee! Shah-nee!" She surged awake with a jolt, her face crinkled and confused. "You need to be reading and writing right now," he said. "You cannot be sleeping."

Shani had no idea what was going on and tried to engage Nadia for advice. "You should be writing about your own book," Mr. Williams told Shani. "Who are the main characters in *your* book?" That was what they were all supposed to be doing, figuring out their main characters.

In the midst of all this, Abigail leaned way back in her chair, pondering something obscure while staring fixedly at the ceiling. She leaned so far back she assumed a horizontal position and tucked her feet under the table to balance her chair on two legs. Seeing an opportunity to strike, Saúl tiptoed over and tapped Abigail hard on her throat. She was so startled that her chair fell down with a bang and she curled up defensively. Other kids erupted in glee at this spectacle.

Meanwhile, Shani did not understand the term "main characters." I went over to see if I could help. The book she had chosen was *Hippo Befriends Fire*, a fable from Ghana.

We read the whole thing out loud together and then I asked her, "Who is the main character?"

Shani gave me a blank look.

"Okay, Shani, I'm going to tell you a story," I said. "Once upon a time, there was a girl named Shani, who came to the United States from Tajikistan and was put into a class with Methusella and Yonatan. Who is the main character of this story?"

Nothing. The look on her face: soft, vulnerable, lost.

"This is a story about Shani. Shani is the main character."

"Ah!" she said at last, and understanding bloomed on her features.

I tapped her book. "Who is the main character of this story?"

"Hippo!" Shani said delightedly.

And she got busy, writing about that.

"Miss, what's this word?"

It was Methusella, at my elbow again. These days, I practically had a shadow, he came over so often, to see if I could help him figure things out. The word Methusella did not understand was "hulking." I asked him if he had ever heard of the Hulk. Big green guy, superhero? He had no idea what I was talking about.

Simplify, I told myself.

"It means really big," I said.

Methusella drifted away, satisfied. Then, over came Plamedi. He had been watching Methusella seek all the right answers from me and decided he could do the same. Plamedi pointed to a word he did not understand in his book. The word was "hummingbird." I covered up the word "humming," showed him "bird."

"Do you know what that is?" I asked.

"This?" he responded, pointing to a drawing of a bird.

"Yes," I said. Then I put out my arms and flapped really, really quickly, so that he could see why this particular bird might be described as humming.

"Aha!" said Plamedi. He'd seen those fast little creatures before.

By March, Miss Pauline was making greater headway in getting the kids to open up emotionally. One day that month, the therapist from Jewish Family Service took half the class away for a group therapy session, as Mr. Williams worked with the remaining students. When the missing students came back, they carried dusty chalk drawings of their colorful inner selves. Miss Pauline announced that the students had made drawings to represent the feelings they had experienced upon coming to America—now that they knew some English words for what was going on inside themselves and had grown used to discussing such things out loud.

Students who wanted to share their work lined up at the front of the room. Nadia had drawn horizontal bars of light blue, rose, green, cream, and gold. She had labeled each of those bars with an emotion: "Anxious," "Scared," "Confused," "Sad," and "Happy." She had also drawn unlabeled green star shapes in her light-blue anxiety. Lisbeth had written nothing on her drawing, but it was a dramatic purple gloaming sky, with an enormous black bird swooping through the air. Solomon had sketched a large green circle against a deep blue background, and inside the circle he had written just one word, "Happy." Mariam had drawn a furious diagonal rainbow, with no words. Jakleen had refused to participate at all.

Then a stunning, shy girl from Africa glided across the room, her face all cheekbones and dignity. She held up a chalk drawing with two words: "Sad" and "Ashamed."

"Really?" cried Mr. DeRose incredulously.

The girl was so beautiful, and her face looked so fine—it was hard for him to believe her written declaration.

Her face fell. She had disappointed him. Inadvertently, dreadfully. "No, no, no, no!" Mr. DeRose rushed to say. "It's okay!"

The girl stared at him, turned around, and walked steadily away, heading off in the other direction.

What exactly had taken place was impossible to record, but I felt a current of feeling move through the room. Maybe something had happened in Africa to make the girl feel those heavy emotions and she had carried them all the way here, or maybe she had arrived light and free and it was her experience of America that had generated her distress. She had elected not to speak with me, so the riddle of what those words meant was hers; I could only watch from a safe distance, while rooting for her to succeed in resolving her unnamed dilemma. I saw that Mr. DeRose felt the same way. That was what he had managed to convey with his blunder: He cared about her well-being. That was what he had conveyed to me, anyway. Communication with the newcomers was so fraught that I could not begin to say what he had conveyed to the girl.

In the middle of March, while the students were reading their chosen folktales, I drove over to East High School to talk to Jen Hanson, the incoming principal of South. She was going to take over from the interim principal at the start of summer break. I described all of the students in Room 142, and she responded that it was unusual there was nobody who was entirely nonliterate. Typically, the newcomer classroom included at least one or two kids who had never learned to read in any language. But that year, Mr. Williams had gotten a roomful of kids who knew how to read and write in at least one language, if not several. Hanson talked about how Mr. Williams's multilingual students had what linguists call a "literacy road map" in their minds, a concept of how languages worked and how one language varied from another.

Hanson mentioned that her husband was Thai, and her children were bilingual. She had both a professional and a personal understanding of language acquisition. She knew from learning Thai herself that some languages do not make plurals by adding an *s*, and do not use verbs to show the passage of time. We discussed the main issues that affected the pace of learning for the newcomers: language proximity, interruption of schooling, education of parents, trauma, and motivation. Then Hanson listed an additional factor. I thought it was related to motivation, but she articulated it separately as the "push-pull factor," or volition. Had a given student showed up in Mr. Williams's classroom of his or her own choice? Or had the student walked into the room thanks to someone else's decision making?

Kaee Reh had advocated that his family relocate. He had been walking through the Ban Mai Nai Soi refugee settlement in Thailand, where his family had been living, when he saw a flyer about the possibility of resettlement posted on a bulletin board. Kaee Reh had gone to his parents and suggested that the family resettle in the United States. His parents had been reluctant. They had wanted to stay where they were, in the hope that someday the Karenni people might regain their former place in their homeland of Burma. Later, however, Kaee Reh's parents had changed their minds. They had come around to their son's way of thinking. In essence, Kaee Reh himself had instigated the family's decision to move to the United States.

Hanson was making the point that for a student like Kaee Reh, who had chosen to be in Room 142, language acquisition would happen more easily. Another student who had come to the classroom of her own volition was Abigail, whose mother had left Mexico when she was a small child, leaving Abigail in the custody of her grandmother. Her mother had worked to support them by cleaning apartment buildings in the United States and sending money back to Mexico. It was Abigail who had decided that she wanted to move to Denver, to live with her mother. Abigail told me, "I wanted to meet her, I wanted to know her. And my mother said, 'Yes.'"

Saúl and Lisbeth had also chosen to be in Room 142. I thought that Methusella and Solomon were pleased to have arrived there, and that Plamedi, Grace, Nadia, Dilli, and Hsar Htoo all wanted to be at South. Jakleen and Mariam, not so much. Once they had hoped that living in America would be a positive experience, but after they arrived, at a time when the subject of Muslim refugees figured so largely in the national discourse, they found that leading figures in American culture were overtly hostile to their presence, and they longed to return to Turkey. Amaniel, the boy from Eritrea with a star cut into his hair, also appeared to have reservations about being in Mr. Williams's class; he seemed to feel it was beneath him. And Bachan still looked as though he would prefer to be anywhere in the universe except a place as alien as the United States. As soon as I grasped the importance of volition, I could see how it affected the motivation of every student in the room.

Before transferring to East, Hanson had been the staff person at South who oversaw the school's ELA team. The main thing she had tried to convey to the other ELA teachers in her care, including Eddie Williams, had been the importance of using "comprehensible input." This was a fancy term for making sure the kids knew what you were talking about. The biggest mistake ELA instructors typically made was assuming they could explain things in English to kids who did not understand English. "You can't just stand up there and lecture at them," Hanson told me. "You need to make the input comprehensible."

Eddie Williams remembered being coached by Hanson. When he said, "Open your books," he folded his hands into a prayer shape and then opened them outward into a book-holding shape, to show the room what he meant. Hanson had taught him the importance of making those gestures. Later that same month, I watched her charm a roomful of Burmese and Bhutanese refugee parents at the aptly named Mercy Housing apartment complex, where she deftly shared stories about her own family, using many hand gestures to make things more comprehensible, as well as a variety of interpreters sprinkled around the room, in a way that communicated to the foreign-born parents her essential respect for their struggle. I left the meeting feeling the same elation as members of the high school's ELA team—Jen Hanson was inspiring.

At the end of March, Mr. Williams introduced a unit on U.S. currency, and then he spent many days on the subject of food. After speaking with Hanson, I paid closer attention to those moments when Mr. Williams rendered the incomprehensible comprehensible. For example, he thought it would be a great thing, while introducing the concept of food, to talk about tamales, because the room held so many Spanish speakers. Someone like Abigail might not understand English words for food, but she would know all about tamales. Mr. Williams's Spanish was imperfect, however, because he had learned the language as an adult. When he wrote the singular for "tamales" as "*tamale*," Saúl spoke up to correct him.

"It's *tamal*," the student said. "*No con e.*"

Lisbeth, meanwhile, was babbling to me about what kinds of tamales she liked ("*de pollo, de frijoles . . .*"). For inexplicable reasons, the subject of tamales reminded Lisbeth of something else, and she got terribly excited and began giddily showing everybody around her images of something apparently unappetizing on her cell phone. Ksanet waved her away with an expression of disgust, and Methusella tried to adopt Mr. Williams's stern demeanor to shoo her off. "*Cangrejo!*" Lisbeth sang to me. I had no idea what she meant until she showed me her phone, and then I saw a picture of a crawfish (comprehensible input). Ksanet spoke to Mr. DeRose of a thing known as teff, and I asked what that was, thinking they were discussing something in Tigrinya, but Mr. DeRose said, unhelpfully, "Teff is teff" (no comprehensible input). I kept determinedly thinking "teff" might be a foreign word, but Mr. DeRose eventually convinced me that teff was just this thing called teff, even in English. Then I looked it up on Google and learned it is a grain from a species of love grass that grows in the highlands of Eritrea and Ethiopia (comprehensible input). It's what is used to make *injera*, the spongy sourdough bread on which Ethiopian and Eritrean food is served.

A few days later, Mr. Williams captured the unwavering attention of every student in the room with an electrifying handout about the practice of eating bugs. We talked about this at length. A Japanese-American woman named Yumino, perhaps the most faithful of all the Goodwill volunteers, stunned the students by admitting happily that she had eaten insects as a child. In rural Japan, where she had grown up, it was common to harvest a certain type of cricket and to consume it as food. The handout said that in many parts of the world, bugs represented the most viable source of protein. Ksanet did not understand the meaning of the lesson until Mr. Williams crouched down beside her and said, "Insects, insects," and then he pointed to an illustration to show her what that meant (comprehensible input). Ksanet conferred with Yonatan in Tigrinya to confirm that Mr. Williams meant people were actually eating bugs, and then Ksanet taught her teacher the word for insect in Tigrinya.

"Pashara?" said Mr. Williams in confusion.

"*Hasharat!*" Ksanet and Yonatan said in unison, Ksanet laughing.

Shani heard this word and perked up instantly.

"*Hasharat!*" she cried, recognizing a word she knew.

Then Mariam nodded, saying, "*Hasharat.*"

That was how we all discovered that many languages in the Middle East and Africa all shared the same word for insect. While this was happening in one corner of Room 142, over on the other side of the classroom Lisbeth was trying to pantomime the actions of a scorpion, which involved her biting her own wrist. Nobody found this comprehensible, although many were entertained. Then she tried to shock Yonatan by showing him an image on a laptop computer of a green garden snake, as she hissed "*culebra!*" But Yonatan just announced "snake" in a matter-of-fact tone and walked away nonchalantly. Later, Shani found a picture of an innocent-looking freckle-faced girl with pigtails who had a large, hairy tarantula halfway in and halfway out of her mouth.

"Oh no!" said Mr. Williams, when Shani succeeded in surprising him with this picture.

Lisbeth scampered over to see what the teacher was reacting to so strongly.

"*Cómo se dice* Photoshop?" Mr. Williams asked Lisbeth, after he had recovered his equilibrium.

"*Foto falsa,*" she told him.

Then Saúl crossed the room going in one direction as Jakleen crossed the room going the other direction, and Saúl reached over to cup Jakleen's cheek lovingly in his hand and she boxed him happily in the chest, and they went their separate ways.

Jakleen picked up the English-Arabic dictionary that Mr. Williams kept on the bookshelf and looked up a word she wanted to explain to Lisbeth. The word was *musabbib*. I wasn't sure what this had to do with the subject of food (nothing, as it turned out), but Lisbeth was fascinated simply by the backward-flowing script that Jakleen wrote down. Seeking my help to convey her meaning to Lisbeth, Jakleen showed me the meaning of *musabbib* in the dictionary. Could I translate this word into Spanish? One of its definitions was "traumatic." To check if this was what she meant, I said, "Jakleen, Syria, Jaramana, car bombing—*musabbib*?"

Jakleen flashed me a big smile and gave me a thumb's-up. *Yes, that's right*, she was saying. I had given input she could comprehend. Then I tried explaining the concept of *musabbib* to Lisbeth in Spanish. In our own ways, all over the room, each of us was trying to bridge some sort of difference, even if we had gotten a little off subject. Not long afterward, Jakleen started wandering around the room with a baggie of cookies like the ones she and her family had given to me when I first visited, the ones filled with dates. Noticing he had lost some of them, Mr. Williams said in a sharp tone, "Shani, Jakleen, I am looking for participation here." Jakleen saucily offered a cookie to Mr. Williams, but he declined to participate, saying, "No thanks, I am great." Lisbeth, on the other hand, accepted a cookie gratefully. Then they all got back to the lesson, which involved writing down an English term for food and drawing a picture of that item.

Shani announced that her favorite food was soup, then drew a beautiful fried egg. Methusella wanted to talk only about cheese. If you said the word "cheese" to him, he would reply in a singsong voice, "Very, very nice!" All the other kids thought this phrase was funny, and over the next several days they began saying a whole lot of things were "very, very nice." Mr. Williams spent several more class periods grilling the kids on English vocabulary words for food ("pepper," "radish," "garlic," "lemon," "strawberries," "grapefruit"—"Mister! *What?*" "Grapefruit, grapefruit") using flash cards. We all learned that Shani could not say either "banana" or "potato" without dissolving into laughter, while Yonatan went around the room for a long time holding up the flash card for "celery" and listening to everybody say that word over and over, because for some reason this made him grin happily.

On the back of Yonatan's flash card, I saw that celery was the same in English, French (*céleri*), and German (*Sellerie*), but not in Spanish (*apio*). Oh, right, I thought—*der Sellerie!* I knew a lot of Spanish, and in the past I had known a fair amount of French, much of which was coming back to me as I tried to converse with Plamedi. But I had entirely forgotten that once upon a time, I also had known a little German. When I was seven years old, our family had moved to Austria, and we had lived in Vienna for one year. I had taken some German lessons. I remembered getting grilled by the adult, a rigid teacher with no sense of humor, on the basic rules of German. That language had some strictures that struck me as fanciful; for example, Germans capitalize all their nouns. (In a Rush, it came back, being grilled by the Adult, a rigid Teacher with no Sense of Humor.) Also, Germans make stupendous compound words, an activity known as *Wortbildung* (word formation). Some common compound words are *Jugendsünde* (youthful folly) and *Friedensabkommen* (peace agreement). Germans are also famous for making insanely long compound words, such as *Rechtsschutzversicherungsgesellschaften* (insurance companies providing legal protection).

More German came back to me over spring break, when I traveled with my son to Europe. I had forgotten how many cognates German and English shared. As we flew on Lufthansa, I saw that there was a *Schwimmweste unter meinem Sitz.* We were going to Spain to visit my sister and her husband (a Spaniard), who were living with their English-and-Spanish-speaking children in a sleepy little beach town about one hour south of Barcelona. An Irish cousin and her German husband joined us, along with their English-and-German-speaking boys. For one week, we played board games in German, ordered food in Spanish, and spoke over meals in English and Spanish and German.

I learned all kinds of new terms in the process, such as—because my son is a picky eater—the Spanish phrase *tikis-mikis*, also spelled *tiquis-*

miquis, which . . . well, there is no literal translation. Basically, *tikis-mikis* connotes "discerning," as opposed to "picky." It means someone who can be a little kvetchy but you admire him because he is impressively meticulous. It is one of those untranslatable terms, like the Japanese word *komorebi*, which means the dappled kind of light found on the floor of a forest when sun has been shining through tree leaves. Or the Swedish *gökotta*, to wake early wanting to hear birdsong. Or the German idea of *Fernweh*, a feeling of homesickness for a place to which you have never been.

While we were there, I remembered that when you change countries, *everything* is different. The language is different, of course, but so are the trees, the birds, and the insects. Cars look odd and so do trains and buses. Money is different and the television shows are not the same and the supermarkets are organized in completely novel ways. We visited over Easter. There was no Easter Bunny; our children were visited by Ratoncito Pérez (an Easter *Mouse*!).

The newspapers in Spain were filled with stories about refugees flocking in huge numbers to Europe. In response to the epic migration, nationalist movements were building in various European countries. The changing climate could be summed up by the evolution in significance of the phrase "*wir schaffen das*," which literally means "we make it" or "we create it" but connotes the idea "we can do this." It's what parents say to children when things are scary—it's a lullaby. Chancellor Angela Merkel had begun using the phrase the previous fall, speaking about the incoming Syrian refugees. "Germany is a strong country," she had said. "The motive with which we approach these things must be: We have done so much—we can do it!" By now, however, the phrase was taking on the opposite meaning—Merkel's opponents had changed it into the negative: *das schaffen wir nicht*—we cannot do this.

During our trilingual family gathering, we achieved a high level of *gezelligheid*, a Dutch word (often used as the prime example of untranslatability) that means "a convivial, warm atmosphere achieved in the company of loved ones, or a special feeling of togetherness." Our sense of *gezelligheid* was so memorable, in fact, that in the months that followed, as the United States began to turn away from the concept of openness, toward the idea of closing its borders more tightly, dismaying everybody I knew in Europe, my cousin's German husband would reach out to me and my sister by email. He asked us: Did we want to send our children to him? And he would send his boys to us. That way, all of our children could become more open to the world; they could learn that other cultures were not to be feared. Maybe they could even learn some things there were no words for in English.

Silly One

Because Hsar Htoo had expressed a desire for privacy around what had befallen his father, when I sought a way to learn more about the Burmese community (or, I should say, the community of ethnic minorities who had fled Burma), I chose to ask Kaee Reh if I could visit his home. Kaee Reh politely supplied a phone number for his father. With the help of a Karenni-speaking interpreter, I made an appointment to visit the family. Kaee Reh and his three siblings and their parents lived in a blond brick building on the other side of Colfax Avenue, not far from where I lived. Inside the building, I walked along a hallway with a chipped linoleum floor, punctuated by battered-looking doors. From behind the door to Kaee Reh's apartment, I could hear what sounded like rhythmic blows. When we stepped inside, I saw Kaee Reh's father, Peh Reh, using a large knife to chop a hunk of red meat into fine pieces. He worked at Cargill, a meatpacking plant in Fort Morgan, an hour-and-a-half drive north of Denver, and I imagined that he might have brought the meat home from work. His shift ended at midnight, and he typically got home close to 2 A.M. We were visiting on a weekend, which was the only time he was free to talk. "It's hard to find a job when you don't speak English," he said through the interpreter. "I applied many places, but they didn't hire me. The last place I applied was Cargill."

Peh Reh wore a long-sleeved green sweater and charcoal-gray trousers. He was kneeling on the living room floor, on top of a large straw mat, helping prepare the family's evening meal. There was no table, nor any other furniture anywhere in the room—except, in one corner, a narrow

233

twin bed and a wooden dresser. Kaee Reh's mother, Taw Meh—thin, hauntingly pretty—wore a T-shirt and a piece of patterned green fabric tied at her waist to make a skirt. She stood in the kitchen, grinding chili peppers with a mortar and pestle. Her face was startlingly similar to Kaee Reh's, with dramatic cheekbones and a wide crooked mouth, and when I saw her, I thought, She has Kaee Reh's mouth! (though really it was the other way around). So pungent was the chili oil that both the interpreter and I began to cough. Soon my throat started to burn from the fumes and my eyes began to water. Kaee Reh's parents appeared oblivious to the effects of the oil.

The couple's four children were not at home, although I could see evidence of their presence in the pile of shoes clumped by the front door. I believe the children may have shared the apartment's one bedroom, while their parents slept on the twin bed in the main room. I figured that Kaee Reh was probably playing soccer in a park somewhere nearby, as I knew him to be an avid soccer player. Solomon and Methusella lived only a few blocks away, and they sometimes battled with or against Kaee Reh in the neighborhood's impromptu street-style soccer matches.

Peh Reh told us that he was grateful to have any kind of job, because it was hard to find work in a country like the United States if you had no formal work history, did not speak English, and could not read or write. The only kind of work he had done previously was farming, and he had been unable to work at all while living as a refugee in Thailand. His job at the meatpacking plant was to trim fat off meat. I could see that his right hand was visibly swollen. Working second shift meant that he was asleep in the mornings when his children left for school, and they were asleep when he returned. "I see them on the weekends," he said.

Kaee Reh's parents had met in a refugee camp on the western side of Thailand called Ban Mai Nai Soi in 1996. They spent nineteen years living in the camp, and all their children were born there. Like Hsar Htoo, Kaee Reh had never lived outside the confines of a refugee enclosure before. I knew Mr. Williams thought Kaee Reh possessed great intelligence and was learning quickly, even though correct pronunciation of

English words remained a struggle. I had also seen the quality of Kaee Reh's drawings, and heard how well he could sing. I thought of him as an artistic soul. When I asked his father what kind of future he envisioned for his children, now that he had brought them to America, he said that he hoped they could stay in school. After he had started working at the meatpacking plant, and began earning enough money ($500 a week) that he no longer qualified for benefits such as TANF, however, money had gotten very tight. The one-bedroom apartment cost $900 a month, and he was spending half his earnings on housing. "We want them to continue their education for as long as they can," Peh Reh said. "But if we can't afford it, then they will probably have to work." He thought he might have to ask the children to leave school sooner rather than later. I found it dismaying to imagine what kind of work Kaee Reh would end up doing if he did not finish high school.

Peh Reh shared that he had a brother living in Denver, who also worked in the meatpacking industry, and many friends in the city as well. "There is a Karenni family upstairs," he told us. "We lived close to each other in the refugee camp, and now we live in the same apartment building here." Because of the comfort these social ties brought to Kaee Reh's parents, they preferred living in Denver, despite the high rent. The loneliness that Kaee Reh experienced in the classroom, where nobody spoke his home language (and even Google Translate could not help him communicate, as it did not include either Karen or Karenni), was mitigated, because the family had a few key friendships. And it appeared obvious—as Peh Reh handed his wife the chopped meat and she proffered some red and yellow peppers to cut up next—that Kaee Reh had the good fortune to be growing up inside a stable, loving household, with two parents who cared deeply for one another.

That was not necessarily true for all of the newcomers.

I genuinely did not understand (because I had led too easy a middle-class American life) what some of the students at South were grappling with on the home front until I spent time with Christina, the young woman who had acted as an informal interpreter during my conversations with

Hsar Htoo. Both Kaee Reh's and Hsar Htoo's families were originally from Burma, but in the end I did not establish a strong connection with either of those students. I liked both boys a lot, but they were brand-new to the English-speaking world, they had previously lived only inside of camps, and, with me, they were quite reluctant to say much about themselves. Christina, on the other hand, was voluble about her background. As I sought to understand what the thousands of refugees who had escaped from Burma had experienced, she helped me the most.

Christina lived with her adoptive parents in a large, comfortable two-story house in the southern part of Denver. South had been her neighborhood high school, back when she had entered the ninth grade. After we had gotten to know each other a little, Christina invited me over for lunch so that I could meet her parents. She had already given me a brief outline of her past. I knew that she was twenty-one years old, that she had been born in Burma but had spent most of her childhood living in a refugee camp in Thailand, and that after resettling in the United States her grandmother had tried unsuc-cessfully to marry her off to a much older man when she was only thirteen. Subsequently, she and her two siblings had been adopted by a white American family. "I love my family!" Christina gushed when speaking of her adoptive parents. "I have the best parents in the whole world!"

When I knocked, Christina answered the door. She introduced me to Martha, her adoptive mother—a woman with cropped iron-gray hair, a hefty bosom, and a worldwise manner, who was wearing a magenta T-shirt, black shorts, and a clunky leg brace.

"You hurt your leg," I said to Martha.

"Well, I have MS," she replied, in the tone of voice someone else might use to say, *Oh, I have a little cold.*

Christina's adoptive father, Steve, was a slim, bespectacled, kind-faced man in a brown collared shirt and worn-looking jeans. He kept ducking in and out of the house because he was transplanting things out in the garden. I followed Christina into the kitchen, where she was cooking for everyone. She loved cooking passionately and it had become a form of self-expression. She had even gotten to the point where she was creating her own concoctions, such as the one she was busy making at the moment, a mustard-colored curry into which she was putting a lot of hard-boiled eggs. The peeled white eggs floated like boats in a thick yellow sludge of potatoes, turmeric, garlic, ginger, onion, and lime leaves.

"What do you call that?" I asked Christina, expecting to hear an exotic name in Thai or in Karen.

"Egg curry!" she said.

Christina was simultaneously supervising her two younger sisters as they ground chili peppers—just as Kaee Reh's mother had been doing—to make chili paste. At Christina's house, however, the act of grinding chili peppers had to take place outside, because nobody else could tolerate chili oil in the air. Martha and Steve had learned to be careful around the potent oil. "When you wash dishes, the vapor will come up out of the sink!" Martha exclaimed.

In her "Autobiography," as she titled a paper that she wrote in high school, Christina memorialized some of the family members who had taught her how to prepare food.

> When I learned how to cook, my mom was the first one who taught me, but she wasn't a nice teacher. She always taught with anger and she always got mad at me without a reason. Whenever I cooked, my mom always yelled at me because she said I didn't cook really well.
>
> My uncle Sha Moe Ko was the one who later taught me how to cook and he was really nice to me. He was always patient with me when I learned how to cook. He taught me his favorite recipes and I really like his recipe for Kaw Now. Sometimes I cook his favorite recipe to remember him as my uncle. And I remember the day I lost him because of a land mine that blew up in front of my face; it was really a surprise. I myself cannot believe why it didn't happen to me in place of my uncle. Many people were surprised that happened to him, not me, because I walked along that road every day. He was my favorite uncle and a kind uncle. I am glad he taught me how to cook

before he died. I will always miss him. To remember him I cook his favorite food that he taught me.

Christina said her uncle's favorite meal was chicken curry. The egg curry we were going to have for lunch was a variation on that theme. Christina had also prepared white rice and spiced green beans. When the meal was ready, eight of us sat down at a long wooden table in a room painted the color of butter, with sun streaming in the windows. At the table were Martha, Steve, five of their seven children, and me. The couple had three biological children, a daughter they had adopted from China, and the three Karen girls. Christina and her blood siblings served Martha and Steve first. "That's our culture," one of the Karen girls explained. "We always serve our parents before we eat anything ourselves." Steve warned me about the chili paste, advising that I take a minute amount. Martha echoed his sentiment, saying, "Just maybe hover your fork over it. Two or three molecules and you're set." I put a tiny dab on my plate; Christina stirred three or four spoonfuls into hers. The family explained the term "Thai hot." When they went out to eat at their favorite Thai restaurant, Martha and Steve used the restaurant's regular scale of one to four to indicate how hot they wanted their food to be. Christina and her sisters instead told the waitress they wanted their food in the twenties or thirties.

The three Karen girls took turns getting up from the table and draping themselves over Martha, half lying along her shoulders, or went to the other end of the table and huddled against Steve. The amount of physical affection the adopted children showed their parents exceeded what I was used to seeing. Martha explained that she had used physical affection as a tool to reassure the girls during the difficult transition when they had changed homes. When they had first joined the family, they hadn't been able to tolerate much affection. Hugs used to make them flinch. What I was seeing was the product of many years of mothering.

After lunch, Steve wandered back outside, the other kids disappeared upstairs, and Christina, Martha, and I stayed at the table.

Martha listed the various traumas that she had gradually discovered, over many years of parenting Christina. I could see that she wanted me to understand how badly her daughter had been wounded. "You know, they're going to school and they don't know the language and there are all these cultural issues, but then underneath there's also trauma at the same time, and nobody at the school knows about it, and they're navigating all of that," Martha said. "It's so hard to tease that out from just 'doesn't speak the language,' which is also true, of course."

Martha went upstairs to gather some books she thought I needed to read, which she spread across the dining room table. Christina's favorite was *Undaunted*, a memoir by Zoya Phan, a young woman whose father was a leader in the Karen resistance movement in Burma. Phan's life bears notable parallels to Christina's—both were born in the Karen state, both fled their original home villages as small children, both went to school in refugee camps in Thailand, both almost died of cerebral malaria. Christina fan-worshipped Zoya and was communicating with her via email.

From the material Martha shared, I learned that the military regime that had controlled Burma for my entire lifetime had created more child soldiers than any other country in the world. The Burmese military also encouraged its soldiers to employ rape as a tool of war against women from ethnic minority groups, and used land mines rampantly across its own territory to suppress the various ethnic groups that had taken up arms against the regime. As a result, Burma was the most heavily mined country in the world. The Burmese military was also accused of beheadings, the butchering of infants, deliberate starvation of entire villages, and various additional atrocities that Karen activists based in Thailand worked hard to document by stealing across the border on fact-finding missions, because the repressive regime had shut down objective journalism inside Burma. Of all the countries in the world, it was Burma that sent the largest numbers of refugees to the United States during the fiscal year 2015, when both Kaee Reh and Hsar Htoo arrived in Room 142.

At lunch, Martha said it was Steve who had met Christina first. Steve belonged to the First Universalist Church of Denver, and he had volunteered to mentor a newly arrived refugee family—Christina, her two siblings, and their grandmother. When he came home bearing a photograph of the three Karen-speaking girls, Martha took one look at the faces of the children she had yet to meet, and asked, "Where are the parents?"

Christina was born in a small village in Kaw Thoo Lei state, which literally means "a land where the Thoo Lei flower can grow," or "a land without evil." It is what the Karen people call their home state in Burma. The Burmese considered the Karen armed rebels who needed to be suppressed, and the two forces had been battling ferociously since 1949. The fighting in Kaw Thoo Lei reached an especially fierce pitch in 1997, when Christina was only three years old. This is how Christina wrote about what happened in her Autobiography:

I lived in Burma for 3 years before I moved to Thailand. I moved to Thailand because the Burmese government treated us like animals and tried to kill us. Burma is a beautiful place but the government is dangerous. When I lived there I had to hide by the bush most of the time. When the Burmese government came to our village we had to hide because we knew that they are coming to kills us. On February 14, 1997 my family, my friends and other people we had to run and move to another country.

Prior to her arrival in the United States, all of Christina's schooling had taken place in Tham Hin Camp. She showed me photographs of hillsides crowded with makeshift huts made out of bamboo and tarpaulins, photographs of the Christian church she attended, and photographs of Basic Education Tham Hin High School. ("Karen people don't know how to name things!" she joked.) The school's walls were made of cinder block, and the roof of corrugated tin, and big green tarps served as awnings. In the refugee camp, Christina had learned to read and write in Karen, Thai, Burmese, and English. Karen and Burmese use distinct but related alphabets with letters that largely overlap, but

Thai uses a different script altogether, and none of those alphabets corresponds in any way with the Latin script used to produce English. So Christina's education involved learning to read and write while employing four different alphabets simultaneously.

Christina had excelled at schoolwork. One teacher who grew fond of her nicknamed her "Silly One," because although she showed up in her mandatory navy blue plaid skirt and short-sleeved white blouse, she invented her own idiosyncratic way of writing Burmese, which he alone spotted and teased her about. She would only write Burmese sentences using the Karen alphabet and Karen spellings, instead of employing the slightly different Burmese lettering. If called upon, however, she would pronounce the words as Burmese. "He thought it was silly," she said. "And he thought it was smart, too." Writing Burmese the wrong way had been, for her, an act of resistance.

Meanwhile, Christina's biological parents were not getting along. "They were always, always arguing," she said. Christina and her younger sisters were devastated when their parents divorced. The split resulted in the three girls being raised by their maternal grandmother, who had journeyed with them to the refugee camp. Malaria and other highly contagious diseases plague the residents of refugee camps all over the world, and one of Christina's most vivid memories concerns her bout with cerebral malaria. Malarial parasites affect the body in various ways, but in the case of cerebral malaria, parasite-filled blood cells block the small blood vessels to the brain, causing swelling that can result in brain damage, coma, or death. Christina was actually mistaken for dead by medical staff after she entered a coma. Of this, she wrote:

> I had to go to a Thai hospital and stayed about one month. When I was in the Thai hospital the doctor told my mom that there was no hope for me and then they put me in the place where dead people were put. My mom was very upset that the doctor had told her that I was no longer alive. After about 12 hours of being asleep, I woke up and I thought, "Where am I in the earth?" I saw a humans lying down with cloth covering their faces and then I started crying.

It was Christina's grandmother who applied for the family to resettle in the United States. Christina's mother was listed on the initial application, but when the family was chosen, Christina's mother decided not to accompany her daughters to the United States, because she would have had to leave behind her second husband and their children. Forced to pick between two sets of children, Christina's mother chose to prioritize the younger ones, trusting that the older ones would survive without her.

On the eve of their departure, camp officials briefed Christina and her siblings and their grandmother about what to expect once they left the camp. Posters pinned to a bulletin board covered the basics. One poster named the four seasons they would experience in the United States. The whole idea of winter boggled Christina's mind. A second poster named what they would encounter during the airplane ride: airplane seat, seat belt, bathroom door lock, tray table. About her transition to the United States, Christina wrote:

> When I heard that I would come to Colorado I was scared and nervous. I was scared because people told me that in Colorado there were a lot of cowboys and no Karen peoples. On November 7th my grandma, sisters and I left the camps. I was very upset because I didn't want to come at all but my sisters were looking forward to seeing a new place. I was sad to leave my mom.
>
> I arrived in Denver the evening of November 7, 2007. Between that day and December 1, 2008, many, many things happened in my life. It was a very hard time.

One day, I met Christina for coffee at Kaladi, a popular coffee shop near the neighborhood where she lived with Martha and Steve. Christina mentioned that the apartment building where she had formerly lived back when she first arrived in the United States was close by and asked if she could show it to me. We drove over there and parked by the side of the road and sat looking at the building for a while, just chatting about whatever came into our minds. Christina said that at one point she had gone up to the roof and thought about jumping off but had decided not to because her two younger sisters needed her to stay alive. She had to protect them from the wrath of their grandmother, who was abusive to all of the girls, according to Christina. I asked Christina if the level of domestic violence she had experienced at the hands of her grandmother was representative of Karen culture in general, or unique to her own family. Christina answered, without hesitation, "Unique." Later her adoptive mother, Martha, said she believed that the extremity of life inside a refugee camp affected families by amplifying their basic dynamics. Strong families grew stronger, dysfunctional families slipped into worse dysfunction.

Christina's grandmother was close friends with the mother of the man whom her grandmother said she should "marry." Her grandmother and her grandmother's friend had hatched the plan for the "marriage" together, according to Christina. She said that one day, the young man chased her all over the apartment building. The structure had rectangular balconies, one per apartment, and to escape, Christina jumped from a third-floor balcony down to a second-floor balcony, and then to the ground. She landed wrong when she hit the parking lot and hurt her arm. I could see why Christina's favorite book in the world was *Undaunted*— I thought she was pretty undaunted herself, to risk injury rather than endure the advances of a young man she did not want to sleep with.

Her grandmother used to let him into their apartment late at night when he came home from work or from socializing with friends, and he would wake Christina up and demand that she cook him dinner. Once, he came into the bedroom and instructed her little sisters to go sleep in the living room, but instead of staying in the bedroom with him, Christina went to sleep in the living room, too. She had no desire to be intimate with the man, who stank of beer and cigarettes. Christina never wanted to press charges against her "fiancé," but she wanted to say publicly that even though she had been raised never to contradict a man, she knew that what he was trying to do with her was wrong. And in her opinion, he should have known it was wrong, too.

We puzzled for a while over the mystery of what Christina's grandmother might have been thinking. We had no idea. Christina described various incidents between them, and it sounded to me as though they had been locked in a battle for supremacy over who would control the course of Christina's life. Her grandmother seemed to feel that Christina was noncompliant, both in terms of obeying her grandmother and in terms of kowtowing to her "fiancé." Often, when Christina made herself scarce to avoid spending time with her suitor, her grandmother went knocking on doors around the apartment building to hunt her down. Christina hid in various locations, including under the bed of her best friend.

At one point, however, her grandmother tracked her down and administered an especially severe beating during which she cut Christina's right hand with a knife. The cut was deep and the blow broke bones. Her grandmother packed the wound with tobacco, a homemade remedy to stop the bleeding. Almost exactly one year after her arrival in the United States, Christina showed up at Merrill Middle School with a swollen right hand, unable to hold a pen. One of her teachers, a Bulgarian-born woman named Miss Petrova, asked why she could not take a math test. Christina's ability to comprehend English had grown dramatically, but her ability to speak remained limited; she enlisted the help of a Karen-speaking friend to reply that she had hurt her hand. The teacher insisted on knowing how she had gotten the injury.

"What happened, Christina?" Miss Petrova asked.

"It was an accident," Christina replied.

"Christina, what really happened?"

"I hurt myself."

"How did you do that?"

"I cut myself with a knife."

"Christina, how could you cut yourself on your right hand, if you are right-handed? You have to tell me what really happened."

That's when Christina made the enormous leap of trusting a Bulgarian-born, English-speaking woman whom she hardly knew. Her grandmother had cut her with a knife, she confessed. At that point, everything in Christina's world turned upside down. It took her a long time to sort it out, but looking back on that moment from the vantage point of sitting in my car, parked beside her old apartment building, after a total of eight years had elapsed, she said that she believed Miss Petrova had saved her life. When I reached out to the teacher to confirm the details of what had happened, Miss Petrova wrote back in an email to say that she kept a picture of Christina on her refrigerator to this day. "Not having any other relatives in the U.S., my students become my family," she wrote. "Being an immigrant, just like them, I have a lot of empathy for them." She had recently seen Christina. "We talked about the book you are writing, our time together at Merrill, the unfortunate event with the injury, but above all, we remembered caring and supporting each other. We think of this time with a lot of gratitude."

Although the teacher had promised not to call the police, when they went to see the school's social worker, a uniformed police officer was there. School officials retrieved Christina's two younger sisters, both of whom became hysterical at the idea of being separated from their grandmother. The social worker explained that all three girls were being taken to the city's child welfare division. The social worker did not know what would happen next. When a family-worth of kids entered the foster care system, they usually did not remain together.

The social worker asked Christina if there was anybody she trusted, anybody she wanted to call. Christina answered, "Martha and Steve." The couple had been visiting their apartment all year, bringing over used toys and hand-me-down clothing. They had also invited the three Karen-speaking girls to their home on many occasions, to play with their own children. After the social worker called Martha (who was listed on the roster of people permitted to pick up Christina and her sisters), Martha appeared within minutes, in Christina's recollection—to this day, she marvels at how quickly Martha got to the school. Martha accompanied the three girls to the child welfare division of Denver Human Services, where an employee told the frightened girls they were about to go into foster care.

Martha said immediately, "They are not going anywhere but home with me."

The city official looked appraisingly at Martha, and said, "I can make that happen."

Growing accustomed to living with her adoptive parents was as momentous as a second resettlement for Christina. She wrote in her Autobiography: "Learning to live in an American family was very hard especially because I didn't speak much English." Martha and Steve went to extraordinary lengths to care for the Karen girls; Steve moved out of the master bedroom for a while, and the couple put up a set of bunk beds there, so that Christina's sisters would have a place to sleep. Christina was offered a bed, too, but insisted on sleeping on the living room couch. She had gotten used to sleeping on couches while she had been trying to duck her grandmother's wishes, and somehow the couch was more comforting than an actual bed. Eventually Martha and Steve built an addition onto the house so that there would be enough bedrooms for all seven of their children. Then Christina surrendered the couch and moved into her own room.

Still, she found it peculiar that Martha and Steve wanted to do strange things like hug and ask how she was doing. In Christina's experience, Karen people did not embrace routinely and did not talk about their emotional states. "They are starting to creep me out," Christina told her sisters. About that period in her life, which coincided with the second half of her eighth-grade school year and her start as a ninth grader attending South, she wrote:

> When I started my first year in high school I had lived with my new family for about eight months. It was a really confusing and hard time for me at home. Whenever I came back from school I would stay in my room the whole time. I did whatever I wanted to do on the weekends . . . . I wasn't used to parents that expected to know where I was going and what I was doing. Being with two different cultures was really confusing, especially at first. Sometimes I needed help with my schoolwork and I was scared to tell my parents because I thought they would start yelling at me. But they don't yell, they just always tell me if I need help tell them. Still, I was scared.

At the same time, Christina grappled with being ostracized by the Karen community. Her former neighbors in the old apartment building spread rumors that Martha and Steve had turned the children against their grandmother, which led many in the tight-knit refugee community to shun Christina. "People think that my American family stole me, and it's not true," Christina said. "I want people to know that. I was about to die if I ended up with a man I didn't want to be with. I probably would have gotten raped, and I probably would have ended up having children with him. I'm very thankful to my parents."

Learning English had proved as problematic for Christina as it was proving to be for Kaee Reh and Hsar Htoo. At first Christina stubbornly persisted in indicating changes in time by adding on other words—she would state something in the present tense and then throw in the word "yesterday." The whole concept of a language that was not tonal perplexed her, and she struggled especially with words that ended in consonants. The sound of spoken Karen is blunt consonants at the outset of a given word, followed by musical vowels; generally, there are no hard consonants at the end of words. For a while, Christina could not distinguish between two words like "scarf" and "scar"—to her, they both sounded like "skah." At South, however, Christina found teachers who helped her academically and socially.

My teachers Ms. Todd, Ms. Lingler, and Ms. Aldrich were the best teachers I had my first year at South. They always helped me when I needed help . . . I was always happy when I saw their faces. I can tell you that they are the best teachers ever and I love them so much.

At the same time, Martha and Steve provided Christina and her sisters with an alternative model of how to be parented. Steve took the girls hiking and taught them how to talk through disagreements. Martha offered unconditional love and physical affirmation and emotional sanctuary. She let Christina tell her story, little by little, and slowly, as all that Christina had survived was revealed, Martha showed Christina how to grieve. "My mom, she cries and cries!" Christina said, delighted to have found such a mother. Shortly after Christina turned eighteen, Steve and Martha formally adopted all three Karen girls. It cost $180 to adopt Christina, because she was an adult; her sisters cost even more.

"Mom, we are so expensive!" Christina said to Martha.

Martha told her, "Money is nothing. We have the money. Life is more important."

Martha and Steve had a tradition in their family, which they generously extended to the three new children they had suddenly acquired (which in reality had cost them much more than just the adoption fee, both in actual dollars and in terms of the emotional toll it took to parent three traumatized children who spoke little to no English). The tradition was this: When their children turned sixteen, they could take a trip anywhere they wanted to go in the world. It might not happen exactly when they were sixteen, because when the trip occurred would depend upon the family finances, but it would happen. Christina asked to go back to Thailand. She wanted to see the refugee camp where she had grown up, she wanted to see her mother, and she wanted to see her old friends.

Steve took Christina to Thailand shortly after she turned twenty-one. They traveled there in December 2015 (halfway through the school year I spent at South). Whenever she spoke of the journey, Christina kept saying that everything had gotten smaller. Roads seemed narrower and a river that meandered through the refugee camp appeared to have shrunk. "That river—I used to think it was so huge," she said. "And it's a trickle!" When she walked into her former school, her old teacher had taken one look at her face and cried, "Silly One!" He remembered: She was the girl who would not write the right way in Burmese.

It had taken Christina eight years to get to the point where she could talk about all this. She could not possibly have recounted her story back when she had only just arrived and was still trying to figure out how to stick a consonant on the end of a word, how to make nouns plural, and how to indicate that an event had happened in the past. She had fled her home village during warfare, watched an uncle die in a land mine explosion, moved into a refugee settlement, almost died of malaria, been separated from both of her parents, resettled in the United States, experienced domestic abuse, and almost been given away as a child bride. Those were the kinds of extreme experiences some of the newcomers had endured. I had sensed that some of the kids in Mr. Williams's room needed to stay well taped, just like the boxes they had made with Miss Pauline, but I hadn't fully appreciated exactly what some of the newcomers might have survived until Christina enlightened me. Getting to know her gave me a new level of respect for everyone in Room 142.

5

Qalb

At one point, when he was about to head back downstairs to his students after enjoying a momentary respite, Mr. Williams said to a colleague who was sitting at a table in the copy room, "All right, I think I'm ready for this. I've gone to the bathroom, I've put cold water on my face, I've played the *Rocky* theme music on my cell phone—here we go." It was early April, and the city's flowering trees had sprung into color, all the crab apple trees in Washington Park topped with clouds of pale pink. The students were in full bloom, too—socially and academically. Managing all of them at once was consuming a fair amount of the teacher's energy. The kids had been competing for several weeks in what Mr. Williams called the Newcomer Olympics, a heated contest that had begun at the end of March and resumed at the start of April, right after spring break. There were a series of events. First, the kids vied to compose grammatical sentences using parts of speech supplied by Mr. Williams. For example, he asked them to use the words "we," "and," and "big" in a sentence. They could earn up to four points.

Lisbeth's team wrote, "We visited to big city and village." Mr. Williams gave her group two points.

Plamedi's team wrote, "We see my mother every Sunday and my brother big car." That earned two points also.

Solomon's team wrote, "We like to go to South High School because it is so fun and so big." That one got three points. Solomon's team had exhibited better "language control," as Mr. Williams called it—not only had they gotten their meaning across, but they had also used each word appropriately.

249

And Grace's team wrote, "We have a big book and pencils." That was worth three points also.

Bachan's team wrote, "We and so big." One point for effort.

Meanwhile, Methusella's team lagged behind; he had been elsewhere in the building and had returned to find his teammates mired in last place.

"Methusella, help your team out!" Mr. Williams urged.

"I was not here," Methusella objected haughtily.

The entire room had gotten caught up in the competition. Even Jakleen was wearing a broad smile. When Mr. Williams asked the students to use the words "she," "great," and "South High School" in a sentence, Jakleen wrote, "Is the great school she is a student and she likes South High School." I noticed that she had written the sentence using the Arabic construction: verb first. This was deemed a two-point sentence, but Mr. Williams thought the most important thing was that she was present and participating. Meanwhile Saúl was balancing an oblong pink eraser on his right shoulder while working on constructing another sentence, and then he forgot that the eraser was there and turned abruptly to ask for some help from Mr. DeRose. The eraser tumbled to the carpet, which set Hsar Htoo laughing. The room was livelier than I'd ever seen it.

The next activity was a listening exercise. Saúl and Yonatan went head-to-head to see who could be the first to come up with the right answer to the following question: "I have one quarter, one dime, and one nickel," said Mr. Williams. "How much money do I have?"

"Thirty-five cents!" Saúl shouted swiftly. "Oh, forty! Forty cents!"

Saúl won, which meant that he advanced to the next round. His new opponent was Jakleen. Mr. Williams asked if I would like to pose a question.

"This is a kind of food," I said. "The ingredients are bread, lettuce, and meat. What is it called?"

"Sandwich!" Jakleen announced immediately.

"Oh!" cried Mr. Williams. "Jakleen! Jakleen wins!"

That particular victory pushed her team into the lead. When she went home from school, Jakleen bragged to her mother that she had helped her team win the day's competition. Excited that her daughter was enjoying school at last, Ebtisam gave Jakleen money to buy a new cell phone cover. Pink leather with sequins. Right in the middle of the Newcomer Olympics—which Mr. Williams introduced each day by playing the instantly recognizable "Olympic Fanfare and Theme" by John Williams—Jakleen arrived at school one day without a hijab. Her hair was dyed auburn and she had spent time blow-drying it and ironing it perfectly straight. I was not sure how to interpret this statement, and she never cared to enlighten me, but she never wore the hijab again. When I asked her directly about her transformation, all she said was, "Everybody changes their mind about things." I imagined that taking off the hijab was a reflection of her comfort with the idea of residing in the United States, which appeared to have grown significantly. To take off the head scarf, I believed, she must have felt more at home.

The most entertaining event in the Olympics, which stretched over several weeks, was an elaborate scavenger hunt. Mr. Williams handed out a sheet detailing the degrees of angles involved in each turn, the cardinal directions to head toward (he had taped the points of the compass on the walls), and other highly specific instructions for how to find ten unnamed objects. The students were told to turn left or right, to make a 90-degree turn or a 180-degree turn, to head north or south, and to go around or under or behind certain pieces of furniture. If the students followed all of the directions correctly, they would find the object of their quest.

Mr. Williams, Mr. DeRose, and I fanned out across the room to advise students who looked bewildered. Methusella led his group confidently to one destination after another, and needed little guidance. I was still helping other groups with early clues when I noticed Methusella's group tackling the challenge question at the end of the exercise. (Methusella was sailing into near fluency in English faster than any other student, and during that month Mr. Williams gave him more and more advanced reading assignments. Among the words that Methusella would ask me to explain to him in that time frame were "racism," "compromise," "exploit," and "prodigious"—which I thought his learning was.) Shani appeared mystified by what was happening, but she obediently tagged along with her group anyway, and they bumbled their way around the room with minimal error, albeit not as swiftly. Bachan got separated from his group and wandered around aimlessly, wearing a confused look. At one point, Jakleen's group reached a large round table, and one student after another bent down to crawl under it, as the instructions demanded, but Jakleen was too proud to crawl. She circled the table instead. They were all stumped by one word in the directions: "cabinet." I stationed myself beside the tall gray filing cabinet that stood in a corner of the room, so that I could wave at confused parties as they approached. When Yonatan got as far as that part of the room, he leapt up to hit an object on the wall.

"What is this?" he cried.

"That is a bulletin board," I told him.

"Bulletin?" he asked, unfamiliar with the concept.

"I'll write it down for you," I told him.

Then I showed him what a cabinet was.

At another point, Mr. Williams's directions were a little vague, and each team wound up in a slightly different location. They were supposed to find an object hidden inside a wooden cupboard, but the wall opposite the big windows was lined with cupboards, and each team opened a different door. A women's studies class that used the same room at a different hour had labeled one cabinet with the words "perpetuate," "acquiesce," "patriarchy," and "subordinate," and Nadia's team chose that door. Behind it they found a book. Solomon's team, on the other hand, chose a door that was labeled "subject—object—possessive," with a list of pronouns in their various forms, and inside that cupboard they found a box of chocolate. It was Lisbeth's team who won the scavenger hunt, but they did not score high enough to take the lead overall. Jakleen's team—which consisted of Ksanet, Grace, and herself—edged into the lead. "My team won," Grace said to me shyly as she left the room.

For the rest of that week, Methusella's team vied with Jakleen's for first place, and the competition between those two students grew intense. I had never seen Jakleen so involved with school before. Once Mr. Williams had captured her full attention, she could even go toe-to-toe with Methusella. Her sister Mariam did not get quite so caught up in the competition. At one stage, Mr. Williams caught Mariam and Shani (the two of them were now inseparable, while Jakleen was spending more and more time with Lisbeth) over by the pencil sharpener, whispering, giggling, and sharpening an inordinate number of pencils. "Ladies! Ladies! You don't need pencils now!" he admonished. After that, he caught Mariam talking surreptitiously to her boyfriend on the phone. "I'll have to take that cell phone, Mimi," he warned. Both of the Iraqi sisters had acquired new nicknames—Jakleen had become Gigi, a longtime family endearment that had crept into the classroom, and Mr. Williams had started calling her older sister Mimi, because it rhymed. In general, though, most of the students (with the intermittent exception of Lisbeth, Mariam, and Shani) remained pretty much on task throughout the multiweek competition. And Jakleen was like a different person: animated, confident, spectacularly fast.

Throughout April, each week brought more life to Room 142. The lessons grew more fun, the students worked harder, and the interactions between them grew more frequent and more complex. During the lunch hour, I hardly ever saw a single student sitting alone and isolated anymore; instead, happy clumps of kids would form, break up, and re-form, as they wandered from table to table, interacting across regions and languages. The degree of affection bestowed around the room increased palpably, and the students even started showering me and Mr. Williams with demonstrations of fondness. Lisbeth would cry, "Hi, Miss!" and then slam herself against me with both of her arms locked so tightly around my neck that she could grasp her own elbows, thus immobilizing me in a very friendly sort of headlock, until I could extricate myself. Shani lit up when she saw me and gave me little waves or quick hugs. Saúl sang to me almost every day, and Jakleen began happily bossing me around, which was her main form of expressing affection. "Miss, you sit here!" she commanded one day, pointing at the seat next to hers.

Meanwhile, during one stretch when I did not visit the Congolese family often enough, Solomon sent me a message on Facebook, saying, "I miss you." The following weekend, the city was blanketed with yet more snow, even though the lilac bush in my yard had slid into a fragrant lavender haze and my two redbuds had reached full purple-red glory. I was busy doing laundry when my phone dinged. At this stage, the students sometimes felt lonely for us on Saturdays and Sundays, and I saw that Methusella had messaged me to say hello. It was a sweet, inconsequential Facebook type of conversation, but I found it noteworthy in terms of how well he could communicate:

Hi Mrs

Hi Methusella! Have you been playing in the snow or are you staying inside to keep warm?

Am inside because outside is too much cold and am doing my homework

That's nice. My son is playing video games with our next-door neighbors. I wish he was doing his homework!

Oh that's great is this your son here in your profile picture

Yes that's him. But he was only about eight years old when we took that picture. Now he is 13. He plays soccer and baseball and likes sports a lot. He is also a good student, like you and Solomon. He is a great kid, I am a lucky mom.

Oh me too i like sports do you have only one child Mrs

Yes I have only one child. I wish I had many more! We Irish people like big families. Many of my cousins have four or five children. But in some ways having only one child does make life easier . . . I am going to go and check on my son and his friends—I hope you have a good rest of the weekend.

In journalism, traditionally, becoming close to your subjects is discouraged. The reasoning behind this is that the journalist might cross over a line—might lose his or her objectivity. And teachers generally do not talk about how much, emotionally, students offer them. But when the girls walked over with their arms open for an embrace or the boys were giving soul handshakes or Saúl was saying *Tia!* or Lisbeth was taking selfies with her cheek pressed tightly to my face, the warmth of the students' affection filled my life with a sunny kind of joy. The thought of the end of the school year, which would happen in just one month, induced in me an anticipatory sadness; I did not want the year to end. I confessed this to Eddie Williams one day, upstairs in the copy room, and he admitted that the jubilance emanating from the students was lifting him up as well.

"I just feel like there's so much more life in your room," I told him. "The kids are so much more exuberant and more talkative and they're interacting more with one another, and you can feel their personalities so much more. It's like a totally different classroom than it was back at the start of the year. I enjoy the time I spend in the classroom for so many reasons—watching the way you teach and watching all the kids evolve. But I also just enjoy interacting with them these days."

"They want to show their appreciation and their affection," Mr. Williams replied. "Yeah. I feel lucky, too, to be in the classroom with them."

As they grew more communicative, the students attracted more visitors. Eritreans flocked to Room 142 at lunchtime to chat with Yonatan and Ksanet, while Shani made friends with anybody from countries that bordered Tajikistan, and Jakleen pulled in a bevy of suitors. Her most frequent visitor was Ghasem, along with his perpetual shadow, Rahim (the two young men from Afghanistan who had moved upstairs at the start of the year). Ghasem's face took on a fiery, possessive look whenever he gazed at the object of his adoration, cat-eyed, stylish Jakleen. The main impediment in their just-about-flowering romance was the fact that they could not actually speak to one another—not much, anyway. Ghasem spoke Dari, Pashtu, and Farsi, but not Arabic; Jakleen spoke several varieties of Arabic, as well as Turkish, but not any of the languages Ghasem knew. They managed to conduct a full-blown flirtation nonetheless using Google Translate and pidgin English.

One day, over lunch, Jakleen held out her hand and said, in a curt voice, "Give me your phone!" Ghasem wore a dubious look on his face but handed over his device as bid. She played with it happily for a few minutes and then looked over at me to make sure I registered her command over the boy. Ghasem looked at Jakleen with a slightly haunted expression, as though he wished he could have either his phone or the girl holding it. She cocked one eyebrow at me jauntily, as if to say, *See what I can do?* It was indeed impressive. Jakleen kept all her suitors at a slight distance, which only enhanced her hold on them, but sometimes her methods were cruel. She would shun, ignore, and tease in a fashion that bordered on mean. At this point in the year, however, I began seeing Jakleen walk the hallways in Ghasem's company more and more often, as he assiduously showed up at the doors of her various classrooms. If I had to guess which boy she liked the most, I would have said it was this stocky, dark-haired young man from Afghanistan in a leather bomber jacket and designer jeans. He had a handsome face, steadily-gazing-at-you brown eyes, and sideburns that were slightly long, rock-and-roll style. Shani saw matters the same way and confided to me that Ghasem was Jakleen's first official boyfriend. "No!" objected Jakleen, when I checked to see if this was true. "No boyfriend! Friend."

Meanwhile, Jakleen continued to see what power she could exert over other boys. For the moment, Saúl remained the boy she interacted with most in Room 142. One day, Jakleen walked over to exchange pleasantries with him, then she drifted away and began studiously ignoring him. After a while, Saúl began yelling urgently, from across the classroom, "J-a-a-a-k-l-e-e-en, J-a-a-a-k-l-e-e-en!" She kept pretending she could not hear him, even though he sounded exactly like Marlon Brando crying, "S-t-e-e-l-l-a-a-a!" Lovelorn. The other newcomers were charmed by this half-genuine, half-farcical playacting; the classroom had turned into a stage, and Jakleen and Saúl had assumed the roles of the romantic leads. They all knew their appointed posts in the daily drama: Methusella commandeered leading man in the academic realm, Saúl played the incorrigible flirt, Jakleen served as the unattainable object of his affection, and Lisbeth provided comic relief. Everybody else served as extras, taking turns at little cameos.

Even as the newcomers' individual natures came into view more distinctly, they simultaneously started to braid themselves together more completely into one interwoven whole. With the advent of spring, as more and more interactions took place, I found myself able to appreciate in an entirely new fashion how all the different languages represented in the room converged in ways I had not previously recognized. I glimpsed this convergence one afternoon in the middle of April, while sitting with Shani, Jakleen, and Mariam. They were talking about a book that Mr. Williams had started reading out loud with the class. The book was called *Cesar Chavez: Fighting for Farmworkers*, and it was a nonfiction graphic novel.

For Mr. Williams, the story of Cesar Chavez held tremendous power. He got a little emotional, trying to explain the significance of this guy his students had never heard of before—trying to put into words why Cesar Chavez mattered. At one point, as I was listening to Shani, Jakleen, and Mariam discuss a poster they were making to illustrate the book's contents, I found myself wondering how the three girls were managing to communicate. Shani spoke Tajik, Russian, and a little Farsi, while Jakleen and Mariam were Arabic speakers—in other words, they did not share a common language. Yet they seemed to understand one another perfectly, and they were not using Google Translate, nor English. How were they interacting? I could hear all three of them saying the word *kitab*. What was that? "Book!" Shani told me. "My language, their language, same."

The word for "book" was virtually identical in each of their home languages. In Arabic, it was *kitab*; in Tajik, *kitob*. In Turkish, it was *kitap*, Jakleen pointed out, and in Farsi, Shani hastened to add, the word was *kitab*, just like Arabic. Initially, I thought this kind of convergence existed only in the Middle East, but as I spent more time with students from Africa, I came to realize I was wrong. Dilli told me that in Kunama, the word for "book" was *kitaba*, and Methusella said in Swahili it was *kitabu*. That was the moment when I finally grasped my own arrogance as an English speaker. I mean, the arrogance harbored by someone who knew only European languages, which rendered the well-laced interconnectedness of the rest of the world invisible. I was starting to see it, though—the centuries-old ties that bound Africa and the Middle East, born of hundreds of years of trade and travel and conquest and marriage. Once the students grasped that I would exclaim with delight if they found a word that had moved through many of their countries, they started flocking to me to share loanwords and cognates. More than one-third of Swahili comes from Arabic, meaning the links between those two languages are as powerful as those between English and Spanish. But it was also possible to chart the reach of Arabic across the entire African continent, into Kunama and Tigrinya as well.

Earlier, when Mr. Williams had been discussing the consumption of insects, Ksanet and Yonatan had discovered that Tigrinya shared the same word for "insect" as Arabic—*hasharat*. This turned out to be a fairly common term across much of Africa and the Middle East. Words for food were often shared as well. We discovered that "spinach" was nearly identical in many languages: Turkish (*ispanak*), Tajik (*isfanoç*), Amharic (*sipinati*), and Spanish (*espinaca*). Students from the Middle East and from Africa also shared many words for the passage of time: minute (*dakika*), hour (*saa*), morning (*asubuhi*), afternoon (*alasri*), century (*karne*), and the word for time itself (*wakati*).

As the kids discovered these commonalities, I began to feel as though I were watching something like the living embodiment of a linguistic tree. The classroom and the relationships forming inside of it were an almost a perfect map of language proximity around the globe. Generally, students chose to communicate most with others whose home languages shared large numbers of cognates with their own, which meant their first friendships often developed along the same lines as language groupings. As this took place around me, I grew to see my own position on the world's tree of languages more clearly. English speakers can easily grasp the vast coterminology of all the Indo-European languages—our own limb of the global tree—but we are generally deaf and dumb to the equally large influence of Arabic, Chinese, or Hindi across parts of the globe where English does not dominate. We cannot hear or see the tremendous coterminology that has resulted among various other language families, such as between Arabic and the African languages. It was to our detriment, not understanding how tightly interconnected other parts of the world are. When we make enemies in the Middle

East, for example, we alienate whole swaths of Africa, too—often without knowing.

Qalb was the word that the students wanted to teach me about most. One day over lunch, Shani got very puppylike about this concept, bouncing around in her chair as we were sitting with Rahim, Jakleen, and Mariam. "*Qalb!* My language, *qalb!* Arabic, *qalb!* Farsi, *qalb!*" Shani proclaimed. Okay, I thought, I get it; they've found another cognate. But what was *qalb*? "*Qalb* means 'heart,'" Rahim explained in more advanced English. "This word, it is the same in all our languages." I tried to get a better sense of the concept, which the students and I discussed over a series of days. Could you say that Mr. Williams had a *qalb* that pumped blood through his body? Yes, Ghasem confirmed. Could you ask, "How much *qalb* did it take for Mr. Williams to do this, year after year, with such infinite patience, for room after room of newcomers?" Yes, the students agreed. When two people fell in love—was that *qalb*? Yes.

I left South thinking that *qalb* and heart were one and the same. I used one word to refer to a muscle in my body and the concept of falling in love and the idea of what it takes to raise a family or to teach an entire classroom full of teenagers from around the world, and the students from the Middle East would use one single word for all of that, too. *Qalb* and heart seemed identical. Then I looked up *qalb* on Google Translate one weekend, while the kids were missing me and I was missing the kids. When I asked Google to change "heart" into Arabic, it gave *qalb*, as expected. But when I asked Google to switch *qalb* into English, I got heart, center, middle, transformation, conscience, core, marrow, pith, pulp, gist, essence, quintessence, topple, alter, flip, tip, overturn, reversal, overthrow, capsize, whimsical, capricious, convert, change, counterfeit. In addition, the word meant: substance, being, pluck.

I am in love with this word, I thought. What is all this movement about? My own concept of heart did not include flip, capsize, or reverse. Our two cultures did not have the same idea of what was happening at the core of our beings. There was something reified and stolid about my sense of heart, whereas the idea of heart that these kids possessed appeared to have a lighter, more nimble quality. Whatever it was, *qalb* seemed more fluid and less constrained than anything I had imagined happening inside of me.

While the kids were falling in love with each other, and I was falling in love with the room, and marveling at all this place had to teach me about the world that I did not know, Miss Pauline kept trying to supply the students with more words for saying what was going on inside their own hearts. Ever since our conversation about the well-taped boxes, I had been thinking of the therapist's ongoing work as an effort to get these students to untape themselves. I wondered if watching them do so would deepen our knowledge of one another, if the students would reveal more about their pasts, enlightening me as to their burdens. But I think Miss Pauline was probably aiming for something else—I think she was trying to facilitate growth, healing, the kind of change that springs from self-knowledge. For several months, she had been trying to instruct the newcomers on how to read their insides. This was a surprisingly difficult skill to master, especially for those who had experienced harsh events. They might not want to know, they might not want to look at their own awful *qalb*.

Miss Pauline wanted the students to experience any terrifying emotions (helplessness, despair, shame, anger, guilt, suffering) they might be harboring in a safe way so that they could be freed up, could find renewal. She had been asking the students to draw images of the emotions they contained for a while, because she thought art might surprise them into discovering what they didn't want to feel, while they were using a different part of their brains than they used for speaking or writing. One day in April, she distributed pages from an adult coloring book with complex line drawings of mandalas. She was giving them templates. She told the students to choose a pattern, decide which parts to color, and fill those in with whatever hues they desired. Then they were to write some feeling words to go along with the shapes and colors. She handed out a list of fifty-eight positive emotions and sixty-six negative emotions, in case the kids did not know the right English terms for what they were feeling.

After the first set of students returned with their emblazoned mandalas, Lisbeth beckoned me over, so that I could see all the emotions nameable in the English language according to Miss Pauline. Lisbeth pointed to one word in particular that had caught her attention: "Miss! Look: *Sexy.*" Then she made her can-you-believe-it-I'm-totally-outraged face.

Lisbeth had chosen a large circle, filled with little beaded spheres in paisley-like patterns. She had colored parts of her mandala leaf green, dark blue, hot pink, and deep purple. Beside that, in watery orange, she had written "beautiful." She had decided to be *bonita* on the inside. When I looked more closely at her copy of "The Feeling List," I saw that Lisbeth had actually circled five positive words: beautiful, good, happy, loving, sexy. And just one word on the negative side: angry.

It appeared next to impossible for Miss Pauline to get the other kids to look at the negative emotions they might contain. I wondered if she had discussed in group that day the meaning of the negative word "bitter," because a few students did return with that word written on their mandalas, instead of any of the other sixty-five negative terms they might have chosen. I saw "great, happy, bitter, good" written on one mandala and "great, happy, good, bitter" on another. I also saw a "happy, joyful, bitter" mandala. Otherwise, most of the students eschewed any expression of unpleasant feelings. Bachan had chosen a waves-of-fire mandala pattern and had colored his center orange, followed by a large ring of deep blue, and then a whole lot of yellow. I did not know what his ring of blue guarded, girdling his orange core. He had written, in a big loose scrawl, just "happy." It was either what most of the kids felt, or the only thing they felt safe naming.

Dilli was all stars and moons, in magenta, orange, blue, green, and brown, with a freely scrawled magenta h-a-p-p-y across the bottom of her page. Shani had written HAPPY in all caps and had made a girly-looking web of pale blue stars and deep red hearts. Nadia was waves of navy blue and pumpkin-orange fire, with a penciled happy, although in deep green marker she also wrote in Portuguese, *Ao nome a beleza.* To name the beauty.

Solomon had chosen a pattern with a sunlike center and four rings of fire encircling that orb. He had made the rings leaf green, bright orange, magenta, and forest green. His "happy" was orange. Methusella had been more expansive about his positive feelings. He had chosen a simple mandala, populated with triangles and diamonds and squares, all very right-angled, which he had colored in electric blue, fiery orange, and golden yellow. He wrote "HAPPY, joyful, excited, friendly, forgiving." One of the few students who named a bigger range of emotions was Kaee Reh. He had chosen the same template as Shani, but had colored his in shades of dark green, periwinkle blue, and lemon yellow—an entirely different palette. I liked the emotions he wrote because they were contradictory, and because he named them in three colors: a green happy, a red sad, and a blue confuse[d].

Even Jakleen warmed to group that day. She had picked an especially ornate starburst pattern, with strings of little spheres and strings of small hearts emanating from an asterisk-like center. She had colored the center cool green and navy blue. Her spheres were aqua, and she had made the hearts deep maroon. In between the cool spheres and the warm hearts she had drawn columns of lavender. It was a wheel of alternating cool spokes and hot spokes. In terms of her emotions, however, she had written only, somewhat impudently, "Not bad." As Jakleen had been refusing to participate in group for a while, it was progress for her to write anything. I also found it amusing that she remained so obstinate about not revealing her inner state. "Not bad" seemed like a deliberate attempt to thwart Miss Pauline, yet said so much. Jakleen's word choice was also more idiosyncratic and playful than anybody else's. She was the only person who had ignored Miss Pauline's extensive but relatively orthodox list of what one could feel.

Later that month, I went to South by accident on a day when the students had no school, and bumped into Miss Pauline in the hallway. We talked a little about her work. Her struggles turned out to parallel mine: Without disclosing anything in particular that a given student had shared in therapy, Miss Pauline admitted how difficult it was for her to get some of the newcomers to discuss the past. She often had meaningful conversations with the sisters from Iraq, but she was not as successful with the boys from the Congo. I told her that I had also found the Congolese brothers to be guarded. On the few occasions when I had tried asking about prior events, Solomon had been willing to give some sort of answer, albeit fairly abbreviated, but Methusella had a tendency to just laugh at my questions, as if they struck him as ridiculous—which I'm sure, from his perspective, they must have been. Miss Pauline had similar experiences. I did not know whether to consider this a problem. There was that whole Congolese reticence about digging up the past. How did that mesh with American ideas about therapy and "letting it all out"? Other issues might have been at play, too. My own son is highly reluctant to reveal his emotions, and he would have clammed up in such a scenario as well—in other words, I thought gender played a role. In terms of connecting with the students in Room 142, Miss Pauline was as adept as I could imagine any therapist being, but in certain cases other approaches seemed to work better. Such as sports, especially with the boys.

After Mr. Williams passed along the news that Yonatan was earning medals for the South track team, I started attending his track meets. It was unusual for newcomers to join a sports team during their first year in America, because they were typically too busy trying to learn the language and understand the bus system to figure out after-school activities. (The only other student in Room 142 who was playing a sport was Abigail, who had joined the school's tennis team.) Several other students from Eritrea were running track, however, and they had recruited Yonatan to join the team.

The school's long-distance coach—passionate, intense, freckle-faced, redheaded John Walsh, a math teacher at South—did not mind that he could not communicate directly with the newcomer. Usually he asked one of Yonatan's friends to serve as their interpreter. Despite their inability to speak one-on-one, by mid-April Mr. Walsh was referring to his new long-distance star as Yoni. Yoni proved to be a devoted team member who never missed a practice or a competition, earning his coach's respect.

At one track meet, I found John Walsh sitting in sweatpants on a bitingly cold aluminum bench, in the part of the stands where the South runners had congregated. It was spitting rain and windy—a day stuck halfway between winter and spring. Everybody was huddling into their rain gear, trying to stay warm. Mr. Walsh was surrounded by an island of kids in bright purple, several of whom were spreading mayonnaise onto slabs of white bread and heaping on cold cuts, as they badgered the coach for information about when their given races would be held.

Meanwhile, Mr. Walsh was conferring with a sports psychologist in training, a young woman in the middle of getting a graduate degree from the University of Denver. I asked her what she had been working on with Mr. Walsh's long-distance runners. She said she had been teaching them the art of reframing: thinking their way toward victory instead of toward defeat. She had been teaching them about the effect that anxiety had on their performance. Diaphragmatic breathing and positive self-talk were two tools the sports psychologist had given the runners to control their anxiety. "If they are saying to themselves, 'I won't get a good time,' I try to teach them to say, 'Oh, those are just thoughts, it doesn't mean it will happen,'" she explained. "Or if it's windy, like today, and they are worried about that, they should remind themselves that the wind will help on one side of the track, even as it will hurt on the other side, so the net effect might be inconsequential."

I could see how those tools might help Yonatan in all kinds of settings. Physical exercise itself was immensely healing, because of all the endorphins that the body releases. Also critical for children who have lived through trauma is the ability to form a safe, close relationship with an adult who causes them no harm. I thought of both Mr. Williams and Mr. Walsh as serving in that capacity. Mr. Williams was a gifted teacher, and Mr. Walsh meant the world to his runners, but these relationships were simultaneously augmenting the overall psychological health of their charges, beyond what they were accomplishing in the classroom or out on the track, by teaching the students that it was possible to trust an authority figure.

Midway through the track meet came the first call for the one-mile. Mr. Walsh mentioned this would be only the fourth time Yonatan had run the one-mile in a formal setting. I spotted the newcomer down in the center of the track, stretching his legs with two Eritrean friends I recognized from their visits to Room 142. Yonatan was wearing a gray sweatshirt with the hood pulled up over his head and a pair of scanty purple shorts. On his feet were fluorescent orange-and-aqua running shoes that he saved for races, carefully removing the expensive shoes and putting them into his backpack as soon as he finished a competition. Around his neck was the large crucifix that he wore in the classroom every day. He tucked it inside his shirt as he joined the mass of young men gathered at the starting line. A female official fired a bright orange starter pistol, and the young men surged forward.

Yonatan was blockaded in the middle of the pack. By the end of the first lap, however, he slipped into fourth place. He edged into third place, and then into second. In the final lap of the race, he clung to his second-place position, but then one of the other runners, who had saved more reserves for the close, drew near. At one point, Yonatan glanced back to confirm what he must have been able to hear: footsteps coming from behind. The other runner passed Yonatan about twenty yards from the finish. Once he could see that he was going to place third, Yonatan slowed down significantly. He was barely jogging when he crossed the line. Still, his time was 4:43—a personal best.

I joined John Walsh on the spectator side of the silver chain-link fence surrounding the track. When Yonatan and an Eritrean friend named Henok drew near, the coach asked Henok to repeat everything he said in Tigrinya. First the coach congratulated Yonatan on running a personal best. Then he told his runner how he could improve. "You looked back," said Mr. Walsh. "Never look back. Only look ahead. You can hear someone coming from behind, but you need to always be focused on where you're going." Yonatan listened to Henok, as his friend repeated what the coach had said, with his hand tucked inside his track shirt, feeling his heart pound from the race he had just run. He nodded at the coach. "Second, you have to finish at your fastest speed," Mr. Walsh added. "You've got to run all the way through the finish line. You can't slow down right before you get to the end, and you did that." Yonatan nodded again, as soon as Henok finished speaking.

Later that day, Yonatan placed second in the two-mile, running the race in 10:46. He took a picture of himself wearing the medal he received and posted it on Facebook and Snapchat, enhancing his fame at South. These days Yonatan's name was mentioned frequently in the school's email blasts, and other Eritreans were boasting about his prowess on social media. In the cafeteria, a bevy of followers surrounded him anytime he grabbed a booth. Yonatan was already outperforming most other runners in his age group, and he kept shaving time off his performances. At another meet later that month, Yonatan wore a long-sleeved white T-shirt that said on the back, THE WILLINGNESS AND CAPACITY TO SUFFER. It was a quote from the memoir of long-distance czar Alberto Salazar, a Cuban-American phenomenon, who believed that the key ingredient behind stellar distance running was mental capacity, or sheer guts. Yonatan had that quality, Mr. Walsh believed. He grew visibly excited whenever he spoke about Yoni's potential. Who knew how fast he would run next year, if he ran cross-country in the fall, and then track in the spring?

I could see the salutary effect running had on Yonatan here and now. There was a general loosening of his features, a friendlier attitude toward his peers. Once I began attending his meets, his relationship with me shifted, too, and I started to get shoulder bumps when we passed in the hallways. He had never reached out like that before. Running had filled him with confidence.

For a long time, I had been wondering what emotions Jakleen carried within. She had adopted the hijab without saying why, and then she had taken it off without much of an explanation. "Not bad" was about as explicit as she'd been in terms of naming her inner state. All year long, she kept herself veiled emotionally. That spring, however, as the park burst into color and the classroom came to life, Jakleen also began to reveal herself. One day toward the end of April, she watched Lisbeth engage me in yet another full-on headlock of an embrace. This time, Lisbeth was hugging me because I had inadvertently made her feel embarrassed. I had asked, in English, "What is your favorite food?"

And Lisbeth had answered happily, "I'm doing fine! How are you?" I had laughed out loud. Then I had said, in Spanish, "Lisbeth, no, no, I'm asking, 'What's your favorite food?'" She had said, "Oh! *Pupusas!*" And then she gave me the big, slamming hug, to accommodate her chagrin.

Jakleen took in all of this. Then she walked over with her composition notebook and opened it up to a page of black, flowing Arabic script. She knew that I loved the way Arabic handwriting looked. Previously, Mariam and Jakleen had spent an entire lunch hour amusing me by writing derogatory things about one another in beautiful yet indecipherable letters heading right to left across Mr. Williams's whiteboard. When I asked Mariam what she had written, she said gleefully, "Jakleen is a donkey!" And when I asked Jakleen to translate her response, she replied, "Mariam is a fish!"

But what was in her composition notebook? Jakleen stared expectantly at me. I knew she had been watching me interact with her new best friend, the compulsively gregarious girl from El Salvador. I figured she wanted to give me some sort of hug, too, but she possessed a more restrained personality; she had opened her notebook instead of her arms. And her face was saying, *Look at this.* She was sharing something important, I could see, but the page she offered was covered in that gorgeously drawn but to me unreadable script. All I knew was she was saying something from her *qalb.* I told her I wished that I could read Arabic.

"Yes, yes!" Jakleen said impatiently.

She grabbed her cell phone. She typed speedily into Google Translate, and I could see various English phrases pop up as Google tried to ascertain her meaning. Her cell phone said, alternately, "Do you like poetry?" Then it asked, "Do you like Allah?" And then, "Do you like amchi?" That satisfied her; she held up that question.

What was *amchi*? I had no idea, but I gathered it might be something untranslatable. Which probably meant that it was critical. What was she trying to convey?

"Jakleen, I don't understand, I'm so sorry," I told her.

She tapped her notebook and said, "My father."

"This is a letter to your father?"

"Yes."

I asked if I could photograph the pages, maybe someone could translate them for me. She nodded. When I ran my fingers over the paper, it was like reading Braille inversely. She had pressed down so hard the script was palpable. Although I couldn't read the letter, I liked being handed this undeciphered declaration. I was glad it was in Arabic. It made me wonder, What did she sound like in her own tongue? And, of course, I also longed to know, What did the letter say?

6

Busy, Busy, Busy

Ebtisam opened her door, hair tangled, wearing a camisole and pajama bottoms. It was 7:30 in the morning. We lived close to the mountains, in a place where winter stretched late, and even though it was April, outside the snow was coming down thick and heavy.

"Holiday!" Ebtisam announced sleepily.

It was not an official holiday. At South, Mr. Williams was busy teaching the students who had braved the lousy weather. Jakleen and Mariam were sound asleep in their beds, however, as their mother had looked outside and concluded that nobody was going anywhere. Her decision demonstrated a certain wisdom, for I had driven past three car accidents on my way to her apartment, including one crash that had left a city bus jackknifed across the road. I felt bad about rousing Ebtisam (we had planned to spend the day together), but the visit also illuminated for me the mind-set that existed in her household: Clearly she endorsed the idea of her daughters staying at home whenever the weather was foul. I told her to go back to sleep.

Several weeks later, it happened to be snowing again on a day when I had made plans to meet Jakleen and Mariam during their lunch hour. Knowing we would find the two girls at home, I telephoned Nabiha and she telephoned Ebtisam to ask if we could meet her daughters at the apartment. Ebtisam said that would be fine. She was not at home herself, because she had just found a job. She was working on an assembly line at a small family-owned manufacturing company, and her shift started at 6 A.M. When Nabiha and I arrived at Pine Creek, close to ten, we found Jakleen and Mariam still in their pajamas (another word that had moved from Arabic into English through Spanish), sitting at the breakfast table, eating flatbread and drinking black tea. Watching over them was a family friend named Sara, a Christian woman from Saudi Arabia. She was an old friend of Ebtisam's husband's family; at this point, she had become Ebtisam's closest friend in the United States. Sara was spending the week with the family, so that she could help with the girls as Ebtisam was transitioning into her new routine. That morning, Sara had been in charge of getting the girls out the door, but she had failed to do so because Jakleen had woken up saying that her arm hurt, due to another round of vaccinations, and then Mariam had said that if Jakleen got to stay home, she didn't want to go to school, either. They greeted us with guilty, pleased smiles about being caught at home, where they were patently enjoying themselves.

We all hung out for a while in the living room. Then Sara started watching a Saudi Arabian soap opera in Arabic, and Jakleen and Mariam showed us their bedroom. It was small and all the floor space was taken up by their two beds. Mariam slept in an attractive antique bedframe with tall legs that resulted in her double bed being perched very high off the ground. In contrast, Jakleen's single bed was very low. Her bedframe was white-painted wood, but the frame was broken, and one of the corners lurched to the ground at an angle. Jakleen had piled three pillows there, to keep herself level.

The only other furniture in the room were two dressers, which stood side by side. One was cheap, modern, and black, with a sadly hanging broken door, and the other was a nice old piece with a big round mirror. The girls kept their room orderly, and even the objects on their dressers were lined up in rows. On top of the antique dresser with the mirror they had grouped five bottles of perfume, three bottles of dark brown hair dye, one bottle of foundation, one tube of mascara, one tube of lip gloss, one box of eye shadow, and two hairbrushes. A perfume called Sweet Sensation came in a round pale pink glass bottle, and it had been placed in the very middle of the arrangement, like a centerpiece. Only two things hung on the walls: a Revlon hair dryer, attached by a thumbtack, and a black-and-white paper bag from Sephora, also affixed by a thumbtack.

In their closet, there were eighteen hangers, and many inches of empty space. Between the two of them, the girls had three jackets, two sweaters, six pairs of trousers, and half a dozen tops. Some folded-up sweaters lay on the floor in neat piles. High up on a shelf above the items of clothing stood a row of stupendously high heels. All eight pairs belonged to Mariam, who was much shorter than Jakleen, and who often said she wished for greater height ("I want tall!" she told me one day at school). When she had worked as a waitress in Turkey, she had devoted her earnings to amass this teetering shoe collection. One pair had scary-looking six-inch heels, while the rest were all at least four inches high—they were the type of shoes in which you could get hurt. Jakleen said her older sister was shoe-crazy. Catching sight of the vampy collection of heels was unexpected, because Mariam came to school every day looking like a librarian, with her hair in a long braid, wearing glasses and big cardigans. She seemed too straitlaced to possess such a daring shoe collection. After I saw what they had to work with, which was pretty meager, I was triply impressed by the way the girls always looked so pulled together.

While we were sitting on their beds, Mariam mentioned that she had been given a ring by her fiancé, Abdullah, who was twelve years her senior. He had known her when she was a small girl in Syria. He had moved to Turkey after they did, and Mariam reminisced about how he used to take the whole family to amusement parks in Istanbul and Ankara. Jakleen teased her older sister about her so-called dates consisting of activities that were suitable for small children. One month before they had left for the United States, Abdullah had asked Ebtisam if he could marry her daughter. Mariam showed us the engagement ring—a half-inch-wide gold band with tiny diamond chips circling the top and the bottom edges—which she kept hidden in a secret location. She explained that she did not want to wear the ring, in case it got damaged while she was washing the dishes. I wondered if not wearing the ring might also reflect the idea that engagement was not really happening, even though the idea of the relationship remained of central importance. How would they be able to live together? Mariam said maybe someday Abdullah might move to the United States. Meanwhile, Abdullah had been helping her with her math homework, which he was very good at, because he was an engineer. Then we talked about Ghasem, Jakleen's most assiduous suitor. Recently, the young man from Afghanistan had hopped onto their bus after school—even though doing so took him in the wrong direction—so that he could present Jakleen with a pair of dangling paste earrings, which he had bought with his hard-earned restaurant money. She showed us the earrings. The large stones glittered almost like real gems.

"He said, 'I got these for you,'" she recounted. "He said, 'They will look really nice on you.'"

"What did you say?" I asked.

"I told him, 'Oh, they are beautiful!'"

"Jakleen, I think he likes you," I said, stating the obvious.

She fell over sideways, laughing. "Yes!" she admitted.

"Do you like him, too?" I asked.

"No, I'm not thinking about anything like that," she insisted.

I asked how Haifa and Noor were faring. Jakleen and Mariam reported that the other two girls had arrived safely in Germany. They were being housed in an encampment, where their major complaint was that they were not permitted to light fires to cook their own food, but instead had to eat whatever their German hosts prepared. Haifa and Noor had also been struggling with learning German. Then Mariam and Jakleen confessed that they and their friends had had a falling-out. The problem was that one of the girls living in Germany had spread gossip about one of the girls living in America, and now both sisters in America were mad at both sisters in Germany. As a result, there had been a temporary interruption in their discourse.

Before the sisters had broken off contact, Haifa had sent Mariam a picture of the baby she had just delivered. Mariam showed us the photograph: I saw a thin little boy, reddish yellow in color, a little waxy-looking. He had been born prematurely, right after the girls had arrived in Germany. Then he had died, Mariam added. It was shocking to behold the photograph of the baby and then to be told he was not alive. Stories of pilgrimage are supposed to end with people finding sanctuary; I could barely accept that Haifa had made the long, wintry trek from the Middle East to Europe, only to reach such an unhappy outcome.

We lapsed into silence, all thinking about Haifa's grief. I saw that there was a small pile of books on the floor, in between the two beds.

"Oh, do you like to read?" I asked, mustering some enthusiasm for their tiny library.

"Not really," said Jakleen, eyeing the books with distaste.

I picked up a few of the books and discovered they were tedious-looking religious texts.

"Well, I wouldn't want to read *these* books, either," I conceded.

"Sara just gave us those books," said Mariam, obviously taken aback.

"Oh, I'm so sorry! I didn't mean what I said!" I backpedaled. "They look like wonderful books!"

The girls burst out laughing. They laughed so hard that Nabiha and I joined in, too. Then the fact that we were laughing so loudly while Sara was in the next room became comical, and we laughed even more while trying unsuccessfully to curb the hilarity. Nabiha broke Jakleen's bed further, when she shifted her weight and the frame suddenly lurched down at an even steeper angle, and that set us off again. We shushed each other and tried to laugh more quietly, which only made us laugh harder instead. All four of us might as well have been teenagers, hiding from the grown-up in the living room.

I told the two sisters that I was planning to drive to South High School. Culture Fest, a riotous celebration of ethnic dance, song, and music, showcasing the seventy different countries represented in the building, was taking place that afternoon. Jakleen wanted to go with me, though Mariam wanted to stay at home and clean the kitchen. The exterminator had failed to get rid of the bugs in their cabinets, and Mariam thought if she cleaned the kitchen very thoroughly, the insects might go away. It was what was within her control, I supposed—Mariam seemed to find domestic tasks soothing. Before I left, I asked if I could use the bathroom. Earlier that morning, someone must have done laundry, for in the bathroom I stumbled across many pairs of brightly colored cotton underpants draped all over the fixtures and towel rods, drying. Also, one pair of athletic socks. Mariam again, I suspected. I could see why the girls skipped school a lot; they liked to hunker down inside this snug nest, which they had created out of cast-off donations and a lot of domesticity. Whether or not there was an actual storm raging outside, as there was today, it was the bigger storm from which they sought shelter. The storm of war—the storm of life. I wished the girls would go to school more regularly, but I found their nest comforting, too. Here they could seclude themselves away from anything that felt threatening, dire, or just plain cold.

At Culture Fest, Jakleen and I watched West African girls dance in ways I had not previously envisioned possible. Then a Mexican girl belted out a Serena-style ballad. ("Un-be-lie-va-ble, right? Just boom, knock-down amazing," Steve Bonansinga, the math teacher who organized the event, said afterward.) Karen-speaking students including Hsar Htoo crooned a traditional song that sounded vaguely Hawaiian. When it came time for the parade of flags, Shani carried the flag of Tajikistan. And I recognized Uyen in a floor-length gown, in the center of a row of Vietnamese girls, performing a traditional dance that involved a lot of gracious swaying. Later Uyen would tell me that the other Vietnamese girls had sought her out when they were looking for additional performers, and after she began attending practices with them, the other Vietnamese girls had become her primary social circle.

Then Jakleen wanted to go to the gym to look for Lisbeth. We found Shani, but she told us that the El Salvadoran girl had left school, distraught, because she had gotten into some sort of dispute with the boy she liked so much. Supposedly they had kissed, a deed accomplished one afternoon in the nearby park, but then Lisbeth had learned that the boy actually liked somebody else. "I think he no a good boy for Lisbeth," Jakleen pronounced.

In the gym, hordes of students were milling around and visiting booths where they could learn more about the various cultures represented at South. Groups of students from all over had made posters and prepared ethnic food and dressed up in traditional clothing. At a booth about Mexico, we got free candy, but when we popped the hard sweets in our mouths, we were perturbed to discover they tasted of red chili pepper, when we had anticipated only sugar. Shani and Jakleen ran around clutching their mouths and looking for a trash can. That was when we crossed paths with Ms. Aldrich.

"Jakleen! Where were you today?" she demanded. "You weren't in science class!"

Jakleen shrugged and smiled at the science teacher, eyes laughing.

Ms. Aldrich looked over at me and made an exasperated face. "These girls are worried about their grades, but . . . *their attendance!*"

Coincidentally, I had just spent an afternoon visiting the science class for ELA students taught by Rachel Aldrich. Jakleen and Mariam had told me that Ms. Aldrich was one of their favorite teachers, even though they found it hard to sit through her class, because it fell at the very end of their (too) long (in their minds) school day. When I had visited, Ms. Aldrich had been going over a lesson on extreme weather. Solomon and Methusella were huddled next to her, seeking advice. She had asked students to create a weather map of the United States, showing the various conditions typical of different regions. Jakleen stood nearby, waiting her turn for a consultation. Mariam sat at the back of the room next to Shani. Abigail sat nearby.

"You: very, very beautiful," Mariam told Abigail, looking appraisingly at the girl from Mexico.

"Me?" Abi said in surprise.

"Yes," Mariam declared emphatically.

Abigail was indeed "very, very beautiful," but she did not seem at all aware of her own appeal, perhaps because of her extreme shyness.

Ms. Aldrich taught science to the newcomers using visual cues to make the subject more comprehensible. She also had a paraprofessional in the room named Miss Ali, who spoke Amharic, Tigrinya, and Arabic. After a while, Mariam started chatting with Miss Ali, who was wearing a hijab that consisted of a black scarf with a tie-dyed white pattern, as well as a black cardigan and a floor-length black skirt. She also had a set of jangling keys on a purple corkscrew spring bracelet pushed up to her elbow. Miss Ali explained key vocabulary words in Arabic to Mariam:

thunderstorm	tornado
updraft	wall cloud
water vapor	funnel cloud
downdraft	waterspout
flood	hurricane
lightning	

Meanwhile, Shani began coloring Mariam's fingernails with the colored pencils that she was supposed to be using on her weather map. Then Shani and Mariam held hands, as Mariam colored her map with her free hand, and Shani burrowed her face in Mariam's neck and ceased working altogether.

"I hate school," Mariam observed happily, with Shani snuggled against her. "No like science. Miss Aldrich and Miss Ali, both like, work, work, work!"

Mariam appeared quite content as she said this—the complaining seemed to be more of a joke or a longtime habit.

"Oh, my phone!" said Shani, suddenly sitting upright. "Mr. Williams!"

Mr. Williams had seized her phone while they had been downstairs, and she had forgotten to retrieve it when she left Room 142.

"Go get it," Mariam ordered her.

"Tomorrow," said Shani.

"No, now, please," replied Mariam. "Emergency!"

Shani asked Ms. Aldrich if she could leave the room and was told no. She needed to work on her weather map. I liked hearing the patter between the girls and noticed how far they had come—they were conversing almost entirely in English. They still mixed in occasional Arabic or Farsi words, and sometimes resorted to body language, but they were using English much more readily. Jakleen came over and asked where Shani wanted to go, and Shani pantomimed sliding a phone into her pocket and said, "Mr. Williams!" While she did this, I saw that Shani was now wearing a gold beaded bracelet I had seen earlier on Mariam's wrist. It had migrated from one girl to the other.

With encouragement from Miss Ali, the girls made steady progress on the assigned task. As they did, the sisters from Iraq and their new friend from Tajikistan began chatting about something called a *buhayra*. I asked what a *buhayra* was. Jakleen said "spark." I repeated what I had heard, and they laughed uproariously. Mariam took out her phone and showed me a picture of a lake. *Buhayra* was the Arabic word for "lake"; they were discussing whether to spend some time in the park across the street, walking around the lake, before they boarded the buses that would take them home.

"Tomorrow," Jakleen said authoritatively.

"No, today!" pleaded Shani.

Methusella finished the science assignment before anybody else and went to show his work to Ms. Aldrich. She nodded in approval. "Don't forget your percent sign," she told him. "You know how to make a percent sign?"

"Yes," Methusella said assuredly.

Shani turned to me. "Okay, Mariam is crazy. Write, your book."

"You want me to write in my book that Mariam is crazy?"

"Yes! And very, very small!"

"You want me to write that Mariam is short?"

"Yes! And very, very, play the phone—no working! And very, very sleepy—no go the school!"

Mariam was almost finished coloring her map. She did not even look up as she gave a lazy rejoinder: "Miss! Shani very, very crazy."

The bell was due to ring in one minute. Mr. Williams appeared at the door of the science classroom, held a cell phone in the air, and waggled the device. Shani ran happily in his direction, and then the bell rang, releasing them for the day. Later, when I spoke to Mr. Williams, he said it was in these informal conversations, as much as in the formal work he gave them, that the kids found a true comfort with spoken English. "I probably help them gain about one-quarter of the English they learn in their first year," he said. "The rest they get from being immersed in this environment."

*   *   *

Later that month, I accompanied Jakleen, Mariam, and Shani out of South, after science class ended. We walked across the big parking lot filled with haphazardly arranged students' cars and drifted over to the bus stop on the far side of the lot. We all boarded the number 73 bus, which filled up with other kids from the high school. The atmosphere on the bus was clamorous and cheerful, and virtually everybody on the vehicle was a teenager. I sat down next to Jakleen, while Mariam and Shani sat in front of us. Rahim sat down behind me and Jakleen. For a while, Shani and Rahim spoke over our heads in Farsi, while Jakleen and Mariam chattered in Arabic, a clutch of girls standing in the aisle spoke in Nepali, and two boys farther away spoke in Tigrinya. Then Rahim put in earbuds and pulled his hoodie over his head to muffle the noise of the bus, while Shani lapsed into silence as she studied the city views out the smudged window. Mariam began texting with friends in Iraq, and Jakleen started texting with boys from South.

The bus stopped near Shani's apartment complex, and she waved goodbye. Soon after, Jakleen and Mariam disembarked abruptly, and I scrambled to jump off after them. We walked to another bus stop and waited for a number 3 bus. We handed the driver our transfer slips and strolled to the back of that vehicle. To my surprise, I spotted Ebtisam there, wearing dark sunglasses, a black tracksuit jacket, black leggings, and bright pink sneakers. "Hey, your mother is on this bus!" I exclaimed. Jakleen and Mariam cast me amused glances, like, *of course she is.* The girls sat down near Ebtisam. Her shift at the factory went from 6 A.M. to 2 P.M., and I gathered that most days she managed to be on the same bus the girls caught on their way home. Apparently the family regularly intersected like this on public transit. I had not known that was possible—that a person could manage the bus schedule well enough to find another family member midcommute.

"How is your new job?" I asked Ebtisam.

"Good," she said.

"What kind of work are you doing?"

We were without an interpreter, but Ebtisam was inventive. She tapped her gums, put her fingers in her mouth, and pretended to take something out. Then she tapped one of her teeth, and pretended to put that into the object. She was making dental implants.

"My pay, one hour, $9.25," she added. "In three months, $10.25."

We watched the city scenery slide by as we rocked with the movement of the vehicle. The second bus had a more subdued atmosphere; most of its passengers were adults, and many looked tired. We got off right beside Pine Creek Apartments, and Ebtisam insisted I come inside for coffee. As we entered the apartment, I smelled stale cigarette smoke; on the coffee table, I saw a pack of Marlboro Lights. I had never seen evidence of smoking before and assumed this signaled an escalation in Ebtisam's stress. It must not have been easy, the transition from staying at home with her daughters to doing factory work.

Ebtisam bustled around in the kitchen and returned with a dish of flaky pastries filled with figs, as well as Turkish coffee in the same small red cups. Ebtisam, Jakleen, and I drank coffee, while Mariam went into her bedroom and got under the covers and called Abdullah on the phone even though it was after midnight in Iraq.

Ebtisam picked up a piece of paper that was sitting on the coffee table and handed it to me. It was her first paycheck. I saw that she was earning about $75 per day. She still had the temporary housing voucher, which meant that she was okay for the time being, but when it expired that December, she would be spending more than half her salary on housing. She would still qualify for food stamps, but it would be hard to cover the other bills with what she was earning. She was hoping to get a second job, Ebtisam said gamely.

"Go to work, come home," she said. "Make dinner. Go to work somewhere else."

Her mood shifted, and she said in a worried tone of voice, "America difficult, very expensive. My girls, no shoes, no clothes. Rent very high."

After coffee, I explained that I had to get home to see my own son. Jakleen checked the bus schedule and announced I could catch a bus on Mississippi Avenue in five minutes. The next bus would be forty-five minutes later. I decided to go for the bus that left in five minutes, and there was a furious scramble to get me out the door. Ebtisam insisted on driving me to the bus stop. We jumped into the old clunker she had bought recently for a couple hundred dollars. One week earlier, Nabiha had called to say that Ebtisam had reached out for advice; the car did not run reliably and she kept getting stranded in various parts of town. The problematic car turned out to be an ancient green Plymouth wagon with patches of exposed metal on the hood.

"I hate this car," announced Jakleen as she slid into the backseat.

Ebtisam sat down in the driver's seat on a plump brown cushion. She said a brief prayer to Jesus in Arabic (I heard her murmur "*Christos*") and then tried the ignition. No sound. She tried again. Nothing. Then she pumped the gas pedal twice and turned the key and at last the engine turned over.

"Did you drive in Turkey?" I asked, as she eased incrementally out of her spot.

"No," said Ebtisam.

"Did you drive in Syria?"

"No."

"Did you drive in Iraq?"

"No." Ebtisam smiled at me abashedly. "No driving!"

She had never driven a car before, apparently. Ebtisam was still figuring out basic moves, and she drove out of the lot at what felt like two miles per hour. We hovered at the side of the busy main road in front of their apartment building for many minutes, as she tried to gauge when to proceed. I asked how she had learned to drive. Ebtisam smiled broadly. She said, "Mariam, YouTube!"

After many false starts and hesitations, Ebtisam inched out onto the road during a pronounced gap in traffic.

"Good job, Mom!" cried Jakleen in English.

I thought that Ebtisam wanted to drive partly because she wished to regain the kind of middle-class standing she had once enjoyed in Iraq. A car was a marker of status in the United States. And Middle Eastern refugees often felt they had lost a lot of status. Refugee families from rural parts of Africa or from Southeast Asia generally felt that their living conditions had improved when they resettled in a country like the United States, even if they wound up in a low-rent neighborhood, whereas for Ebtisam the opposite was true—here her situation was much worse than the life she had enjoyed in prewar Iraq. She had formerly lived in a nicer home, and owned more material things. At one point, she would describe the home that she and her siblings had built for their parents in Karbala, and she would hold up three fingers, as she announced "three bathrooms." Ever since the Iraq War, however, she had been on a downward economic slide.

Ebtisam wanted very much to give her daughters a middle-class life in America, and it was painful to her that this was not possible right away. Hence, the Plymouth—it was a step in the right direction. I found myself wondering whether Jakleen and Mariam would feel obliged to find jobs themselves, once the housing voucher expired. If Jakleen and Mariam started working, it was hard for me to envision the two sisters staying in school. But if they did not finish their degree, they would be stuck in low-paying jobs for the rest of their lives. I was rooting for them to remain at South.

Two weeks later, we decided to celebrate the fact that Ebtisam had gotten a job and a semifunctional car and her driver's license by having dinner together. I brought takeout food from a Middle Eastern restaurant. Nabiha and I found Mariam sitting cross-legged on the floor in front of a mirror that was leaning against the living room wall. Her mother was out running errands, she said. Jakleen helped us unpack the food, while Mariam applied black eyeliner, then put her hair into a ponytail on the top of her head so that it cascaded down either side of her face. She had changed into a red minidress.

"Are you getting dressed up for us, or do you have plans later?" I asked.

Mariam said through Nabiha that she was going out.

"Where are you going?" I asked.

"I am going to check the mailboxes," Nabiha-as-Mariam announced.

"Oh, you're getting dressed up to check the mail?"

"Yes!"

"Do you meet exciting people when you check the mail?"

"I hope so!"

Mariam was waiting for a package because her face had broken out, and a friend had mailed acne medication from Iraq. Nabiha began to Google acne remedies on her cell phone, to show Mariam she could buy ointment for pimples here in the United States. But Mariam was keyed up about leaving the apartment and departed on her much-anticipated walk because—who knew?—she might meet someone interesting along the way.

Jakleen entertained me and Nabiha by announcing that she had just found an enormous earthworm. She took us outside to see it, ushering us onto a tiny concrete patio off the living room. Old furniture—a fabric love seat and a wooden coffee table whose finish was peeling—stood exposed to the elements. The family had strung up a piece of blue twine across the patio as a makeshift clothesline; socks, dresses, and dish towels hung up to dry. Against the building, an oversized dresser covered with a plastic tarp served as an outdoor storage area, holding extra pots and pans. They were making the best of what they had, using even outdoor space thriftily.

Jakleen decided that we should sit on the living room floor for dinner, because that was the traditional way. Nabiha and I helped pull the coffee table to one side, and then Mariam returned, and the sisters spread out a green plastic tablecloth. We transported the food there and the girls arranged a festive spread on the floor. Ebtisam arrived home, feeling triumphant because she had had a good day at work. Looking delighted to see that somebody else had provided dinner, she took off her jacket to reveal a gray tank top, which she wore with black leggings. It was springlike outside and Ebtisam asked one of the girls to open the sliding doors to let in some evening air.

We sat down cross-legged. I copied the girls and used pieces of Iraqi flatbread to scoop up hummus and baba ghanoush. We passed around plates of beef kebabs, lamb chops, and chicken shawarma. Ebtisam hopped up to get cans of Coca-Cola and Sprite, then told us about her recent adventures at the DMV. She confessed that she had made a few mistakes, but had passed her driving test anyway.

"Oh, did you get somebody who was nice?" I asked.

"Nice? No!" Ebtisam said, making a face. "Turn left! Turn right!" she barked, imitating the gruff manner of the person who had given her the test. The girls enjoyed her show.

I told Ebtisam she was doing incredibly well, if she had managed to get both a job and a driver's license. She was a real American! We asked if she had secured insurance and registration, and Ebtisam said yes, she had taken care of those things. Then she bent her right arm and showed us her large biceps. *I am very strong*, she meant.

Because she had started working, Ebtisam's benefits had just been cut. She had been getting $600 a month in food stamps, but the amount had dropped to $435. She had not yet received a second paycheck, and she was worried about money. She did not get stuck worrying, though. Nabiha assured Ebtisam that she would get raises in the future, and that she would find other jobs—work that she would like better. Nabiha said that had been her own trajectory: She had done unskilled work, and then she had built a better life. Ebtisam seemed reassured.

After we ate, Mariam handed her mother an envelope. The family-run business where she worked had mailed Ebtisam a greeting card, because the day before had been her birthday. She was so preoccupied with her new job, she had not even noticed. Getting up early and figuring out the routine at the factory and learning to drive seemed to have expelled any other thoughts from her mind. We marked Ebtisam's forgotten birthday by lighting a large white candle and holding it over the baklava that I had brought for dessert, wax dripping onto the pastry. We all sang "Happy Birthday" in English, and Ebtisam muttered a prayer in Arabic before she blew out the candle.

Ebtisam's daughters were in a playful mood. We reclined on the big green sofas feeling replete, as Ebtisam washed the dishes. Then Lulu took over because it was her mother's birthday. Somehow Nabiha and I wound up talking about sounds that exist in Arabic but not in English. Nabiha made a series of throaty noises, which I failed to emulate, to the great delight of Jakleen and Mariam. The sisters invented a new game, which they found sidesplitting: They would say the name of someone famous in Iraq—a movie star or a musician, well known to everybody else in the room—and demand that I pronounce the name, too. I would do a splendid job, by my own estimation, yet when they heard my version, the girls toppled over.

"Kadhim Al-Sahir!" Jakleen cried.

"Kadhim Al-Sahir," I repeated—perfectly, to my ears.

The girls shrieked. Mariam laughed until she started crying and then began pounding the green leather sofa with both hands.

"What's so funny?" I wanted to know.

"It just sounds a little strange when you try to say it," Nabiha said in a comforting tone of voice. "It's hard for you, you don't know these sounds."

"Fairuz!" cried Mariam.

"Fairuz," I said carefully.

Nobody laughed.

"Okay, that one was easy," said Nabiha.

"Nazem Al-Ghazali!" cried Jakleen.

"Nazem Al-Ghazali," I said, in absolute imitation.

The girls howled again; Mariam clutched her stomach, then doubled over with her head between her knees. Jakleen fell over sideways.

Nabiha looked up the Middle Eastern celebrities on her phone and showed me their biographies. It was an education; I learned a new repertoire of heartthrobs. During this exchange, Jakleen and Mariam were sitting with their knees tucked under their bodies and their feet sticking out to one side, positioned so that their feet were touching. The girls had pressed their soles together, and they were pushing back and forth on each other's toes. I had never seen anybody do this before. It was such a sisterly gesture, the kind of thing you don't see anymore, once people leave childhood. I was still having a hard time imagining Mariam getting married. I hoped Abdullah would be kind, if the marriage proceeded.

Ebtisam turned on the television and we caught the tail end of a news report in Spanish. The family didn't pay much attention to what language they got the news in—they just tried to make sense of the images. After winning enough primaries to seem like a shoo-in as the Republican nominee, Donald Trump was attempting to forge alliances with Republican Party leaders. Ebtisam wanted to know when the election would be decided; she was baffled by the incessant stories of results. I tried to explain about primaries and said the final decision would happen in six months.

The constant media coverage of Donald Trump unnerved Ebtisam. She had been living in the United States for only a short time when he had made his famous campaign promise to ban Muslims. "How do you think things will change if Trump is elected?" Ebtisam asked, via Nabiha. She was rooting for Hillary Clinton. Like most journalists, I voted Democratic most of the time (although I occasionally voted Republican), and I was just as out of touch with the state of the American electorate as everybody else in my profession. Trump had gotten further than I had imagined possible, but I still felt confident that this country would not elect someone who was making what I considered to be false statements about important matters such as refugee resettlement. I told Ebtisam that she did not have to worry about Trump becoming president—it would never happen. If he became the Republican nominee, then Hillary Clinton would win in a landslide.

The family had been paying much closer attention to the news from the Middle East, which they consumed via Arabic-language news shows. The big news from that region was that in Aleppo, Syria, bomb strikes had just demolished a hospital, killing perhaps the last pediatrician in that city. Politics and war proved subjects too heavy for us that evening; the girls were still in a celebratory mood. They asked if I would like to see their favorite YouTube videos. Jakleen connected her cell phone to the TV and we watched a series of belly-dancing clips, which proved far more entertaining than the news. The first video featured a veiled woman in a green bikini top and a long green skirt, who thrust her hips from side to side with astonishing rapidity and then did a serpentine move that involved slithering back to front for a while and then abruptly making her chest jut out. This routine had attracted 4.3 million views.

Next we watched a very young girl dancing alone in her bedroom, wearing a modest black skirt and white blouse. Despite her tiny stature and demure attire, the girl had mastered some mature-looking hip movements. A third video featured an older woman wearing a gold-studded bra, harem pants, and a belt of gold medallions that flew back and forth with her sashays. Jakleen and Mariam confided that they secretly practiced these moves in the privacy of their bedroom. I found the videos unintentionally hilarious. One buxom woman wearing another zany outfit—a red bikini top and a red skirt split up the side to reveal a fair amount of leg—enacted a routine that mostly involved standing still and jiggling everything that would jiggle. Ebtisam said in all seriousness as she watched this woman dance, "Very, very beautiful."

During a lull in the conversation, I told Jakleen that I was grateful she had shared with me the letter she had written to her father. It was a beautiful piece of writing, I said. The translation read like this:

My father,

After your departure, my heart went into a terrible silence that created fears and sadness inside me forever. I am overwhelmed by missing you. The longing to hear your voice is my only desire in life.

I feel that the whole world has compressed into a speck and all its colors have been drained. All my days are mixed with sorrow and sadness. I wish so much that I could see you again. I never imagined that I would lose you one day. Oh, Allah, it is too hard that I lost you.

I miss you, and life is loneliness, sadness, and sorrow when you are not here anymore. I have lost my smile and my dreams have disappeared and my future has evaporated. It burns me that I will never be able to return home and see you again, that I will never wake up and find you back, that I will never hear your voice echoing around our house.

I always pretend to smile, to keep busy so I can live like all those who have also lost loved ones, but this has all been in vain because my heart is too sad and always longs to meet you, my ears long to hear my name from your lips, my eyes long to see you, smiling or angry. I wish that you could see me in my wedding dress, and I wish you could see the outcome of all the effort and help that you offered me, the results of your care and your interest in my future. I wish you could celebrate what I have become. My tears have not stopped since your leaving. I feel like I am sick, but it is just sadness. The world is very empty. Yearning is all that I feel inside.

We didn't talk a lot about the letter. I just told Jakleen that her writing was eloquent and I had loved hearing her voice in Arabic. In response, she showed me a video she had put up on YouTube—it was another version of the same testament, adapted for social media. But mostly that evening, we watched silly things, because that was easier than getting lost in tragedy. After a slew of belly-dancing videos, the girls put on the Turkish version of *American Idol*, and then we watched a startling Russian talent show featuring gymnasts who did a lot of risqué moves that required extraordinary strength. It was nice to feel part of the family, with everybody snuggled down on the sofas, commenting on the various TV shows from far-flung parts of the world.

Later, as I was driving home, I thought about how cozy the evening had been. Our initial visit had been formal, but over time the family had incorporated me and Nabiha into their daily routines. It struck me that certain aspects of life were universal (the whole world over, teenagers longed to find the right acne medication), even while other aspects of life seemed more culturally mediated (Mariam dreamt of getting married halfway through high school). And I was moved by the fact that Ebtisam had forgotten her own birthday. The oversight constituted an apt measure of what the first year in the United States was like for a full-fledged refugee: an experience so overwhelming, she had forgotten to mark even the most basic milestones of time's passage.

Nabiha called later to say that Ebtisam wanted to thank us for our kindness. All we had done was show up with some food, ask about her new job, commiserate with her challenges, and light one candle, but it had meant the world to her. From the outside, the constant domestic activity taking place inside their all-female apartment made it seem as though Ebtisam were part of a convivial household, but in fact she was the only adult. Her girls were wrapped up in teenage dramas; she was the only person who worried about the rent. Nabiha and I seemed heaven-sent, because as adults ourselves we could see the full weight of all she carried. She was trying to gain a foothold in a new country, a new language, and a new economy, all at once, and it was hard and frightening. Simply being seen made a huge difference. Someone had witnessed her struggle.

The next time we got together, Ebtisam cooked an enormous meal, and a few weeks after that, I took the family out to Jerusalem. I had been working too many hours and had neglected to clean my car; on our way to the restaurant, Ebtisam looked around my untidy vehicle and said, in a half-scolding tone, "Busy, busy, busy!" I liked that we had reached the point where she felt comfortable teasing me. Recently, I had gone to the gold-domed statehouse, where a group of nonprofit organizations that worked with refugees had held a symposium. The state official in charge of resettlement in Colorado said the most important thing the rest of us had to offer refugees was our time. Companionship—spending meals with these families, getting to know them personally—meant more than anything else. It meant more than money and more than material aid and more than donations of furniture. They were far from home and achingly lonely, and they wanted to feel recognized. When I spoke with a member of the clergy who attended the same gathering, the word he used for this was "accompaniment."

Without consciously intending for this to happen, accompaniment was exactly what Nabiha and I had been providing for Ebtisam. We sensed her isolation, and we wanted to make her feel less alone. Because it was hard, what she was trying to do, and we both empathized, even as I was jotting down notes in my ubiquitous notebook. The relationship between us amounted to more than just reporter and subject, at least in my mind. I admired Ebtisam and cared about her well-being and suspected that if our roles had been reversed, I would have been besieged by waves of anxiety also. Nabiha felt at least as much compassion for Ebtisam as I did, and I liked Nabiha for being so big-hearted. The three of us had established bonds that mattered in just the way the state official had described. It mattered more than anything else—to be known.

Both Nabiha and I were pained, therefore, when we heard from Ebtisam that her life was starting to unravel. With her next paycheck, she bought a better car, a red Ford focus. Then it was stolen. Confusingly, one of the Iraqi men in the apartment complex—the security guard whose comments had bothered Ebtisam—seemed to know where to find the stolen car. The man told Ebtisam she should call a certain towing company, and that towing company proved to have her car. How had her neighbor known where to find the missing vehicle? Had he participated in its theft? When Nabiha and I visited, we found Ebtisam half frozen with paranoia. The apartment complex wasn't safe, her neighbor was persecuting her, the United States hadn't been a good choice, her factory job started too early, she earned too little money.

I'd brought her yet another pineapple, thinking maybe some fruit might help. As a journalist, I was always trying to make sure I did not give too much—I was always trying to keep my gifts proportional to what I was being given. Nabiha, who did not feel the same constraints, had shown up with her SUV stuffed with items she had been planning to sell in a garage sale. Nabiha brought seven black trash bags filled with clothing her daughters no longer wore, a clock, a lamp, a desk, an unused paper towel dispenser, and half-filled cans of air freshener. Basically, if it had been sitting in Nabiha's garage for a while, now it was here. Nabiha had also prepared an elaborate meal of dolmas—tomatoes, onions, zucchini, and eggplant stuffed with rice and lamb. I felt put to shame by her generosity. The girls had a field day going through the bags of clothes, and even Ebtisam cheered up a little, distracted by all the bounty. But the theft of the second car was just a precursor. Ultimately, that crime would set in motion a whole series of events, and after several more months passed, when I would look back on all that befell Ebtisam, I would think of the red Ford being stolen as the moment when things started to get really rough.

7

Miss, I Have Nerves

It was 7:30 A.M. and students were eating breakfast in the sunny, vast fourth-floor cafeteria. The room was only about one-quarter full, and far more peaceful than at lunchtime. I was sitting at a large round table with Shani and Lisbeth, both of whom had arrived at school early.

Lisbeth said brightly, holding up a nectarine, "*Qué es esto?*"

"That's a nectarine," I told her. She did not know that word. I tried another.

"Peach," I said.

Shani chimed in. "Miss, you like peach? My father—very, very, he likes it."

We discussed all the items on their plates, naming everything in English. Then it was time for ELA math. On our way to that class—it was held in a funny, tucked-away room, up another flight of stairs that could be found at the back of the cafeteria—we were joined by Saúl. I saw that he had gotten a haircut, quite severe.

"You look nice," I told him.

He smiled wanly. "It is very small," he said.

He meant the haircut was too short. It was May, and we had reached the delightful point in the year when the newcomers could get across almost anything, yet still spoke in peculiar ways (almost all of them had progressed to early speech emergence, the third phase of language acquisition). I found their imperfect English far more entertaining to listen to than English spoken perfectly. For example, Jakleen had recently told me that she was "very girl sad," when she was trying to say that she was a "very sad girl," but I have to say I found "very girl sad" kind of enchanting.

Mr. Speicher's math class was held in a room with floor-to-ceiling windows that opened onto a balcony with a stunning fifth-floor view of the soft, rolling foothills, then the craggy mountains. The blossoms on the crab apple trees in the park had faded, while all kinds of trees had leafed out. The hillsides were awash in that pale hue I thought of as the color of late spring. "Green, green, green," observed Lisbeth.

"Who is not here?" asked Mr. Speicher.

He glanced around the room, which contained most of the students from newcomer class. "Jakleen and Mariam," he said, answering his own question. "They'll probably get here soon—they usually arrive a little late. Okay, what did we learn yesterday?" he asked.

I sat down next to Lisbeth, who was preoccupied instead with tomorrow. She whispered to me, "*Cómo se dice 'juez'?*"

Confused, I thought I had heard her say "*nariz*," so I told her "nose."

Lisbeth started sniggering and waving her hands, then took out her phone and typed into Google Translate and held the device up for me to see: *Juez*. It meant "judge." Both Saúl and Lisbeth had court appearances the following morning at 8:30. She could think of nothing else.

Jakleen and Ghasem strolled into the room together, looking very much like a couple. "There they are," Mr. Speicher said. "Is Mariam here, too?"

"Yes," Jakleen told him, though Mariam was nowhere to be seen.

Jakleen had pulled her hair into a braid and was wearing a black sweater with gray sweatpants. Ghasem had on a plaid dress shirt, blue jeans, and running shoes; around his neck he wore a set of oversized red headphones. Mr. Speicher had taken a liking to the young man from Afghanistan because he worked sixty hours a week while also going to school full-time. "Ghasem, do you still work at that restaurant on Colorado Boulevard?" Mr. Speicher asked. He kept meaning to stop by for a meal. Ghasem never complained about his grueling schedule, yet the effect of it was palpable; the fervent way he shadowed Jakleen seemed partly a response to her well-maintained beauty and partly a response to his own self-sacrifice, as if he felt he deserved something nice in return. Meanwhile, she expertly held him at bay. The other newcomers covertly studied Jakleen and Ghasem, to see exactly how this was done.

Mr. Speicher got back to business. Yesterday, they had been talking about slope, he reminded the class.

"Show me x-axis," he commanded.

Everybody placed their right arm horizontally across their belly, level with their waist. This was another example of total physical response, or the concept that second-language learners may benefit from coordinating intellectual instruction with physical movement.

"Show me y-axis."

Everybody extended their right arm upward.

"Good! Okay. Today we're going to start plotting points."

Mariam strolled into the room, wearing a magenta sweater that I thought of as Jakleen's. I guessed she had been on the phone with Abdullah; it was 4 P.M. in Iraq.

"Rate of change," said Mr. Speicher. "The amount something changes—another name for that is slope."

Mr. Speicher showed the students a picture of a skier. "We can think about this in terms of the mountains," he explained. "Downhill—that's a slope."

He asked if anyone could name other examples of slope. Nadia said the flag, and Mr. Speicher confirmed that was a good example—the pole was standing out diagonally from the wall. Shani was still thinking about the downhill skier.

"Miss, you like?" she asked me.

"Yes, I like to ski," I said.

"My mom is, 'No,' very very—" and Shani made a scared face.

Mr. Speicher displayed an image of Elitch Gardens, a local amusement park. He showed a picture of a roller coaster climbing laboriously to the top of its ascent—an example, as he said, of "Slope! Slope, slope, *slope!*"

"Where is this?" Yonatan demanded.

Any American-born resident of Denver would have known exactly where the amusement park was located, but the kids in this room had no idea.

"It's downtown," Mr. Speicher said. "If you go on the light rail, it goes right to Elitch Gardens. So in the summer, if you want to go, it's a good way to have fun or to get a job. Lots of South students work there."

It was early in the morning, and Lisbeth's hair was still wet; the fruity smell of her shampoo wafted over to me. She was bouncing both of her legs rapidly up and down under her desk. Mr. Speicher digressed from the math lesson to coach the newcomers on riding a roller coaster.

"You have to put your hands up, and you have to scream loudly," he instructed.

Nadia was mystified. "Why?"

None of them had ever been on a roller coaster, I realized.

"That's just what people do," Mr. Speicher said. "So, the best roller coasters have slope—steep slope. The boring roller coasters have less slope, they are more flat."

Mr. Speicher quizzed the kids, calling on them to make sure everyone understood what he had been saying. He drew a line that went up from a low point to a high point and asked Nadia if this was a positive or negative slope.

"Positive," Nadia answered.

"Okay, good. And decreasing slope, what direction does that go?"

"Down," said Plamedi.

"What do you think, Jakleen?"

"Down," she agreed.

"And what kind of slope is that, positive or negative?"

"Positive," she said.

"Oooh, no, *negative*, negative," he corrected.

The most vocal students in math proved to be Methusella, Nadia, and Yonatan—the same kids who spoke up downstairs, with the addition of Yonatan, who had a knack for math. Kaee Reh did not say much but was equally proficient in this subject. Jakleen showed skill at solving math problems, while Mariam only half grasped this thing called slope. Shani appeared totally lost and Lisbeth completely distracted. The rest of the class seemed to understand the material, more or less.

Mr. Speicher glanced at the clock and then looked around the room. Who could help him stay on track? Bells were not audible in his room. Ghasem could help, Mr. Speicher decided. He asked the young Afghan student to let him know when the period ended. Ghasem nodded agreeably and set a timer on his phone. Mr. Speicher got the class busy plotting points. As the students bent over their notebooks, he went around the room helping those who required aid, starting with Lisbeth. Mr. Speicher looked a bit fringy that morning. When the wrestling team had advanced to the state finals, all of the wrestlers had used peroxide to dye their hair an unnatural shade of blond. As their coach, Mr. Speicher had adopted the new look, too. By this point, it wasn't so new, however, giving him black roots and whitish-orange ends to his hair.

Ghasem took out a ruler to draw very straight lines. Meanwhile, after Mr. Speicher moved along, Lisbeth tried on Shani's black leather jacket. "*Es de rusia*," Lisbeth told me in Spanish. Shani had bought the jacket in Russia, which Lisbeth seemed to find romantic. After she finished her problems, Jakleen sauntered over to Ghasem and attempted to steal his phone. He splayed one hand flat on her belly and held her off as he slid his phone securely into his back pocket. She tried reaching around to grab it, but he swiveled his hips away.

"Who's done?" Mr. Speicher asked, noticing that he was starting to lose control of parts of the room. "Stand up if you're done."

He had lost one soul entirely.

"Bachan, wake up!" the teacher said, giving the boy a gentle shake. "Wake up, wake up!" *It is way too early for slope*, Bachan's sleepy, confounded expression seemed to say.

Lisbeth was moving a heart charm violently back and forth along the chain around her neck. The charm had been a gift from her mother at Christmas, marking their first *Navidad* together in many years. A moment earlier, Lisbeth had been jiggling her heels rapidly from side to side, and later she began rocking herself backward and forward in her chair. All day long, her body was in constant motion.

Her hearing in federal immigration court took place the following morning in downtown Denver in a tall stone building that housed eleven federal agencies. When I had asked Lisbeth if it would be all right if I accompanied her, she had thrown her arms around me in a headlock hug and said yes. I found the right courtroom on the third floor and sat down in a large waiting area. A young woman showed up with a toddler, very active. The uniformed guard said, in heavily accented Spanish, "*Los libros, por el niño . . .*" and he pointed to the back of the room. The young mother got up and retrieved a picture book. Near the books, I saw a wall of pamphlets. A sign said SELF HELP LEGAL CENTER or CENTRO LEGAL DE AUTO AYUDA. I was not sure how effective *auto ayuda* would be, but I imagined not very. I wondered if Lisbeth had found a good attorney.

Lisbeth arrived wearing a salmon-colored blouse and black leggings. Her younger brother followed in her wake. He was reserved—the opposite of Lisbeth. We entered the windowless courtroom and sat together on a wooden bench. The room had stark white walls, fluorescent lights, a dark blue carpet, cherry-colored furniture, and an American flag. Carts overflowing with blue manila folders waited in the center of the room, a sign of how many lives were at stake. Lisbeth picked at the chipped red polish on her fingernails and jounced her legs incessantly.

"Miss, I have nerves," she said miserably. "*So much*, I have nerves!"

She had spoken in English—it was the first time she had communicated something essential to me in her new language.

Saúl walked into the courtroom, wearing his typical uniform, black track pants and a maroon T-shirt. The two cases would be heard by the same judge, on the same day. I was witnessing the bureaucratic aftermath of the surge in unaccompanied minors entering the United States. As El Salvador, Honduras, and Guatemala fell into violent disarray, with mafia-style gangs taking over swaths of countryside and whole city neighborhoods—targeting vulnerable young people who were coming of age—hundreds of thousands of children began crossing illegally into the United States by themselves. During fall 2015, when both Saúl and Lisbeth had enrolled at South, more than ten thousand unaccompanied minors had been apprehended by immigration authorities in the months of October and November alone.

The swell of traffic had caused a massive legal pileup in the federal system, leading to delays of up to five years in other types of cases. In Colorado, lower-priority cases that would normally have come before this court relatively quickly were being assigned dates three or four years into the future. Meanwhile, Judge Eileen Trujillo, the black-robed woman seated at the front of the room, was working furiously to fly through the higher-priority cases involving unaccompanied minors as fast as possible. Trujillo did this by squeezing as many cases as she could into a given day, and according perhaps five minutes to each matter.

When Lisbeth's case was called, she and her brother pushed through a swinging wooden gate and sat at the table for the defense, along with their attorney, Alejandra Acevedo, a tall woman in a gold sweater, black dress pants, and high heels. Acevedo worked for the nonprofit Rocky Mountain Immigration Advocacy Network, and she had a great familiarity with the laws concerning unaccompanied minors. She told the judge that they were not prepared to speak because the Department of Homeland Security had failed to respond to a Freedom of Information request she had submitted. This led to a flurry of tense exchanges with the prosecutor. Eventually, the judge ruled that the hearing for Lisbeth would be postponed until October 26, 2016—a date that was six months away. Trujillo seemed more concerned with getting on to the next case, as opposed to allowing the attorneys to squabble.

Lisbeth longed for resolution, but instead received a stay. That was better than deportation, though—at least she could finish her freshman year at South while living with her mother. When she reappeared before the court during the following school year, her attorney planned to submit either an application for asylum or an application for something called special immigrant juvenile status. Individuals seeking asylum had to prove they were being persecuted because of their religious beliefs, political beliefs, or their membership in a "special group." Lisbeth's legal argument for asylum would involve asserting that she belonged to a special group because of the danger presented by her mother's work as a police officer who had attracted the ire of a violent gang—but the question of whether a family could constitute a "special group" was being adjudicated in the courts. Acevedo wanted to wait and see how those cases turned out before she decided which option to pursue.

When it was Saúl's turn, his attorney announced that they were seeking special immigrant juvenile status, an alternative strategy to seeking asylum. Because Saúl's body was riddled with scars, some of which

Saúl attributed to his father's violent temper, Saúl's attorney thought he might win a special visa provided to those unaccompanied minors who had been abused, abandoned, or neglected by a parent in their home country. The idea was that such children could not be safely reunited with their families without the risk of further abuse or neglect.

That day, a score of other lawyers spoke for a series of scared but desperately optimistic-looking young people, each of whom took a turn at the defense table. The parade of children on the day's docket presented a poignant visual reminder of the numbers of unaccompanied minors who had entered the United States—a slew of young women who appeared just as conscientious as Lisbeth, and young men who seemed just as hardworking as Saúl. It was a social catastrophe unfolding mostly invisibly inside this government building, the particulars documented in all those blue manila folders. On each teenager's face I thought I could read the strain of having to participate in legal proceedings inside this tall building, even as they were trying to learn English and master American culture, while simultaneously getting used to living with parents they had not seen in years or living without parents they had left behind. At one point, I commiserated with Lisbeth about her circumstances, but she did not require pity. Instead she said, with complete acceptance of where she found herself, "*Es mi historia.*" It is my story.

By the time Lisbeth and Saúl reported for their hearing, the press had accepted that Donald Trump was going to win the Republican nomination at the convention that would take place over the summer, but still treated him as unelectable. The likelihood of a Trump ticket was described as a boon for Hillary Clinton, whom the media began to cover almost as if she had already won the general election. At South, the students who paid attention to politics continued to view Trump's bid as a form of comedy, making it feel like the election had turned into an especially weird reality TV show.

With Trump's ascendance, I found myself managing an increasingly divergent set of experiences. On the one hand, I spent most of my days in Mr. Williams's classroom, where the students had been opening up more and more, in a way that allowed me to appreciate their intelligence, their potential, their playfulness, and their capacity to learn. On the other hand, when I read the newspapers, it was becoming harder to reconcile what was unfolding on the national stage with what I was witnessing in Room 142. In particular, Trump kept making derogatory statements about exactly the sorts of families to whom I had devoted this period of my life. Because of the amount of time I was spending at South, the election had become for me a barometer of this country's appetite to help refugees.

In the news media, the question of how many refugees to admit into the United States was discussed as if the country had a noblesse oblige–type relationship to the rest of the world. I no longer viewed the matter in those terms. For a while, I had been trying to weigh Room 142 to take an accounting of the refugee crisis; I had been trying to use the students' stories as a means of assessing to what extent the United States was implicated in the Middle Eastern crisis, versus the African crisis, for example. I thought perhaps we bore some responsibility for the state of the world, and wondered if we owed a particular debt to this or that group of refugees. As time passed, however, such efforts at math keeping started to seem beside the point. Instead, I found myself surrendering to the joy I was experiencing in Room 142, which began to feel like an end in itself. I wasn't as interested in determining our collective guilt or innocence in causing one or another part of the global crisis; the refugees I had gotten to know simply felt like a gift.

As the noisy, rancorous election was unfolding, President Barack Obama announced that he believed the United States needed to play a bigger role in mitigating the circumstances of displaced people. The federal government had admitted 70,000 refugees in 2015, but Obama declared it would take in 85,000 in 2016; later, he would call for the United States to admit 110,000 refugees in 2017 (although he would no longer be in office when it came time to realize that goal). By the spring of 2016, as the students were finishing their first school year at South, the United Nations announced that the numbers of refugees around the world had grown—there were now sixty-five million displaced people on the globe, an increase of six million from the year before. Obama thought the rise in the global displacement meant that all developed countries should expand their resettlement numbers, and he wanted the United States to lead in that direction.

The goals Obama set for the U.S. resettlement program represented a steady uptick in the numbers resettled over the previous decade, but not the largest numbers this country had ever welcomed. Only after World War II did developed nations begin to categorize people legally as refugees. The greatest number admitted to the United States in a single year arrived in 1980, when huge numbers of people were fleeing Vietnam by boat; that year, the United States admitted 207,000 refugees, mostly from Southeast Asia. During the 1990s, the United States frequently admitted more than 110,000 refugees annually, prompted by the dissolution of the former Soviet Union, when large numbers of people sought to escape upheaval in that region. The number dropped precipitously after 9/11, however, due to fears about security. The targets set by the Obama administration represented a gradual return to what had been considered normal levels of resettlement pre-9/11.

Donald Trump made clear that he did not agree with the trend being set by the Obama administration. "I'm putting people on notice that are coming here from Syria as part of this mass migration, that if I win, they're going back," he told a crowd at a rally in New Hampshire. "They could be ISIS . . . I don't know that it is, but it could be possible so they're going back—they're going back." He seemed to believe that because ISIS had taken root in Syria, refugees from that country must be aligned with the terrorist organization. Those who worked in resettlement believed the opposite to be true: Aid workers understood the refugees streaming out of Syria to be running away from ISIS and its confrontation with Bashar al-Assad. Later, Trump said, "We have to stop the tremendous flow of Syrian refugees into the United States— we don't know who they are, they have no documentation, and we don't know what they're planning." These comments also perplexed those who worked in refugee resettlement, for while Europe was awash in asylum seekers, there was no comparable influx of undocumented Syrians to the United States, and federal authorities had already implemented a twenty-one-step vetting process for refugees coming from the Middle East. Those refugees were going through especially lengthy background searches and multiple security interviews. Trump's remarks did not reflect reality. Yet his audiences believed him, because he perfectly articulated their fears.

At the same time, as I continued to visit Ebtisam, I kept bumping into Mark, the evangelical Christian from New Life. It struck me as notable that my liberal friends who planned to vote for Hillary Clinton and thought they were pro-refugee were not logging many volunteer hours with families like Ebtisam's—but Mark was, every single week. Mark and I probably would not have agreed on a variety of matters, but we did agree on one central thing: that to live in comfort in the developed world and ignore the suffering of strangers who had survived catastrophes on other parts of the globe was to turn away from one's own humanity. In spending time with refugees, Mark found a kind of salvation, and I experienced something similar while mingling with the kids in Room 142. They affected all of us this way. Eddie Williams found his humanity in teaching the students, Miss Pauline found her humanity in providing therapy to them, and I found mine by documenting what was happening in their classroom and their homes. The students and their families saved each of us from becoming jaded or calloused or closed-hearted. They opened us up emotionally to the joy of our interconnectedness with the rest of the world.

That was what was at stake in the election unfolding in the United States, and in the similar-sounding political battles resounding across Europe, as far as I was concerned: the humanity of the developed world. Did the United States, did Europe—we who had inherited such spectacular privileges (hot showers, appliances, electricity, motorized vehicles)—want to turn away from, or turn toward, the rest of the globe? The world was offering us its refugees, due to wars we started ourselves, conflicts we helped to fund, violence we had tacitly condoned, or fights in which we had played no part. Did we want to say a casual no thanks? Was that how we wanted to live, while we had our spate of time on this earth? And if we did choose to live that way, closed-minded and hard-hearted, then what was going on with our *qalb*?

* * *

There were only three weeks left in the school year. Mr. Williams spent a lot of time evaluating his students to determine what classes they should be placed in next year. Now that most of them had entered the speech emergence phase, language control was the main thing he was looking for, as well as expanded vocabulary and increased linguistic complexity. With summer fast approaching, Mr. Williams also had to work harder and harder to corral the unruly energy that was coursing through his classroom. In the days before Lisbeth's court appearance, he had constantly redirected the nervous dynamism she had brought into the room. The main way Mr. Williams had grappled with the El Salvadoran girl's even more extreme than usual effervescence had been to place her next to the room's latest arrival, a tall shy boy from Africa named Mohamed.

At fourteen years old, Mohamed was the youngest student in Room 142. He had been living in his home country of Mauritania without his mother, in the care of other relatives. His mother had immigrated to the United States seven years prior, and had left Mohamed behind until she could get established, but it had taken her far longer to save the money needed to bring him here than she had estimated. She was ecstatic to have her son with her again. Mohamed showed up with all of his hard-won coping mechanisms fully in place. By and large, this meant that he behaved as if he were still motherless, adopting any available female figure. I became a frequent emotional touchstone—he approached me for advice about how to join a soccer team, how to get a bus pass, and how to register for school the following year (all of which I enabled him to figure out by pointing him toward the right authority figure at South). After Mohamed began sharing a table with Lisbeth, I got used to the sight of her tucking his head into her armpit so that she could play with his short curly hair, or attempting to dress him in articles of her own clothing, usually her hoodie. Mohamed was also drawn to Jakleen and Mariam because they spoke Arabic, one of several languages he knew. He spoke French as well, though his home language was Fulani. Amazingly, Mr. Williams found a student mentor who spoke Fulani, and that settled the boy tremendously.

301

When I interviewed Mohamed one day over lunch, he proved to be as sweet and vulnerable as it was possible for any semi-orphaned child to be. The matter of why his mother had decided to leave him for seven years appeared so sensitive that I refrained from asking him about that at all, even though it constituted the central incident of his young life. Instead, I asked him what he would like to talk about. What he wanted to talk about was his love of the Qur'an: Would I like to hear him sing his favorite verse? I would indeed, I told him. The boy's face lit up as he sang. Jakleen came over to join us, and I turned my notebook over to her, so that she could write down the words he was singing in that backward-flowing script.

Then, with my pen in her hand, Jakleen pivoted to stare at me. "Miss, what you feel?" she asked.

She had become the journalist, and I her subject. The only problem was that I found Mohamed's singing incomprehensible. I could appreciate why Jakleen wanted to ask me such a question, for she had spent the better part of a year being called derogatory names at bus stops and at grocery stores, because of her former habit of wearing the hijab. This was galling, because she had lost the person she loved most on this earth after he had cooperated with the U.S. military in a fight against terrorism. She had been mistaken for the exact opposite of what she was, in other words. Being misread had led her to fear that all Americans might be irrevocably biased against those who were Muslim. It made her wonder: Could an American like me hear the beauty of the Qur'an?

"The verse sounds important," I told her. "I can't understand what he is saying, but I can see on Mohamed's face that the verse has a lot of meaning." Later, I shared Jakleen's notes with a friend who spoke Arabic, and he told me that Mohamed had chosen a famous verse known as Al-Fatiha, or The Opening. It read: "Guide us on the straight path, the path of those who have received your grace; not the path of those who have brought down wrath, nor of those who wander astray."

In the days that followed, Shani, too, befriended Mohamed. The two of them began a running commentary on all they deemed *sheitan* (devilish) or *haram* (forbidden), such as the dark red nail polish that Mariam wore to school one day. This was how I discovered that Shani lived in a strict household and was not permitted to wear either nail polish or lipstick, which were considered *haram* by her devout Muslim father. She also was not allowed to use Facebook or to go on sleepovers. Shani listened enviously as Lisbeth planned a sleepover with Jakleen and Mariam, wishing she could participate. After the sleepover, Lisbeth showed up at South looking transformed, because Jakleen had spent a lot of time ironing straight each of her corkscrew curls. The sisters from Iraq liked to call them "pasta," because Lisbeth's ringlets reminded them of fusilli. We dubbed the new look "no pasta."

For a while, Methusella sat at the same table as Mohamed, Jakleen, and Lisbeth, but there he could not concentrate. Soon he broke away to sit at a table by himself, where he could focus on his work. He still walked across the room to visit me anytime he had a question. One day, for example, Mr. Williams asked the class to rewrite their homework, using more advanced vocabulary. Methusella came over to check and see if the synonyms he had found in a thesaurus made sense. The new words he had picked were "baffled," "tumbled," "rambling," and "guardedly." He had used each of them perfectly. Most of the room remained in the early speech emergence stage, but Methusella had progressed all the way to intermediate fluency, an incredible feat.

That month, Miss Pauline finally achieved what she considered a breakthrough with the boys from the Congo. She had been having a lot of trouble working with Methusella, as well as with Lisbeth. During the week when Lisbeth's court hearing was taking place, Miss Pauline confided that every time she tried to conduct soothing meditation exercises to ground the students, Lisbeth simply fell asleep, which I then thought of as the flip side of her extroversion. The therapist added that Methusella had been avoiding group altogether. I had witnessed an exchange to that effect. One day, Miss Pauline asked half of the class to accompany her to the room where they did artwork.

"Second group!" she called.

"No, no, no!" cried Methusella, who was engrossed in finishing an assignment.

"What are you trying to tell me, Methusella?" asked Miss Pauline.

"I will do it tomorrow," he replied.

"Can you tell me how you feel about group?"

"Somehow good." (I think he meant somewhat good.)

"What I'm hearing is you would like not to go."

"I'm in the middle."

"Do you want to stay here? Or do you want to go?"

"I will go," he relented.

The exchange left me with the impression that Methusella wanted to forge ahead with his academic work and felt as though time spent in group therapy was time squandered. Later that day, however, the students returned bearing tissue paper collages, and I watched recently motherless Mohamed rest his creation briefly on top of the frame of the bulletin board where Mr. Williams hung artwork, as if he was looking for a safe place to represent himself. He considered his collage there momentarily, then took it down and put it away. When they lined up at the front of the room, Hsar Htoo happily held his creation high up in the air, as Bachan clutched his over his chest, and Abigail held hers over the bottom half of her face so that only her eyes showed. Lisbeth held hers over her belly.

Methusella wasn't holding his collage at all; he just propped it up against the wall, on top of a radiator. Miss Pauline urged me to take a look at what he had produced, and I saw a small square of pink at the center, ringed by a lot of yellow, with many darker colors massed on the periphery. Methusella had explained to the therapist that the pink part represented his mother, because she liked that color, and it stood for what he wanted to protect. He added that the yellow part was "in charge," which in my mind meant it was associated with his father. The dark colors on the edges of his collage seemed to represent the threats his family had faced. The small pink square peeking out from amid all the other colors clearly constituted the center of the collage, though, which said to me that he considered his mother to be the mainstay of his universe. It was one of the few times that Methusella had revealed himself all year. Both Solomon and Methusella exhibited an extreme level of caution socially, but I could see them starting, at the very end of the school year, to open outward a bit.

* * *

While many of the girls in Room 142 had welcomed me into their circles, and some were even sharing important confidences (such as Jakleen's letter), I got to know the boys best by attending their sports events. That month I watched Yonatan tackle the two-mile again at another track meet. The race took place at South, where Yonatan faced a student from East who was his archrival in a blisteringly fast long-distance duel. As soon as the gun sounded, Yonatan blasted forward and set a furious pace, far out in front of the pack. The only runner who remained anywhere near him was a tall white guy with a mop of curly red hair pulled into a ponytail. This was Harrison Scudamore, a legend in the local track scene. His father had run in the Olympics, and he himself had earned an impressive string of victories. Yonatan ran the first seven laps at top speed, but halfway through the eighth and final lap, Harrison stole the lead right before they both bolted across the finish line.

John Walsh smiled broadly at Yonatan as he congratulated the runner on the race. Then the coach explained that he had made a classic rookie's mistake, saving next to nothing for the end. Nonetheless, he had completed the race in 10:36—a full ten seconds faster than his previous personal best. That was what Walsh loved about Yonatan: Many of the team's other runners had hit a plateau, but Yonatan kept improving by dramatic increments. Walsh felt sure the Eritrean runner had yet to show him his best. "He has not hit his limit yet," Walsh said after the race. "His mental capacity is extraordinary. For his first year in the United States, that was not bad at all."

Later that same weekend, I visited the church that Yonatan and his sister Ksanet attended. A close friend of theirs named Shambel had invited me. Shambel was an older student at South who had lost his mother and been separated from his father while living in Eritrea, making him effectively an orphan, and he had been taken in by an American foster family. He was a deacon at the church, even though he was only seventeen. He had approached Ksanet on her first day at South, to make her feel more comfortable. "That's my job, to bring the community together," Shambel told me. "That's my passion. It makes me happy. I don't want to see anybody eliminated."

"Excluded?" I checked.

"Right," he said.

The church was located in a redbrick building with a modest exterior. Inside I found a pile of shoes by the door and took mine off, too, and entered barefoot. All of the women had covered their hair with white cotton scarves; I was the only woman whose head was uncovered. At the start of the school year, I had thought that covering one's hair was a Muslim custom, but now I understood that Christian women from many parts of the world also cover their heads as a sign of respect for God. Even though I was bareheaded, I was greeted warmly by the other women and welcomed into the building.

Men sat in pews on the left, women on the right. The entire room smelled strongly of incense. There were three glass chandeliers, and the walls were lined with brightly colored paintings of scenes from the Bible. The service had started at 8:00, and it would continue until noon. People came and went throughout those four hours, though many sat through the entire service. I spied Ksanet in a white scarf on the women's side. Some of the congregants held tall wooden sticks, and I saw a collection of the sticks in one corner. Most of the service consisted of singing and chanting in Tigrinya; I could understand nothing of what was said, although occasionally I heard a familiar word such as *Jesu* or *Christos*. Children played and squabbled on the floor throughout, and the adults did not reprimand them.

From time to time, Shambel stood to bring a large, ancient-looking book over to one of the robed priests, which he held while the priest read out loud. Later in the service, women with small children filed forward, so that the priests could bless the children. I could feel the sense of community in the room, and also the particular kindness being shown to children. After the service, I got the traditional greeting of three kisses on my cheeks from Ksanet, who told me that she and Yonatan had arrived at 7:30—they were among the stalwart worshippers who remained for all four hours. Shambel asked how I liked their church. I told him that while I could not understand much of the sermon, nonetheless I could feel how unifying the experience had been for everyone. I asked Shambel to explain the meaning of various things that had eluded me, such as the long sticks. He said those were to help people stand, if they needed support. "They represent the idea of Mary," Shambel said. "She is our strength."

As I spoke with Yonatan, Ksanet, and Shambel, I noticed that their faces were softer than they were at school. It was visible how at home they felt in this place. Of course I had known there was suffering involved in navigating a foreign environment like South, but I had not known it was so deep as to be written into their features. Here, where they felt entirely accepted, they had relaxed to the extent that the habitual defensiveness was gone, and their faces were kinder-looking.

After I visited their church, Ksanet and Yonatan greeted me more enthusiastically when I saw them at South. When I got up to leave Room 142, Yonatan called out, "Miss!"

He dug around in the pocket of his blue jeans and handed me a large crucifix made out of silver and white enamel.

I knew that Yonatan sold crosses to earn money, so I asked if I could pay him.

"No," he insisted.

"It is a gift?"

"Yes."

Then he looked perturbed. "Miss, you know Israel?" he asked.

"Yes," I said. "I know Israel. It is the country where he is from." And I pointed at the figure of Christ nailed to the cross.

"Yes!" Yonatan affirmed, smiling in relief.

I believe he was checking to make sure that I understood the meaning of the crucifix. As a newcomer, one could never tell what Americans were going to understand and what they would not understand—sometimes they did not know anything at all about matters one considered fundamental.

I got to know other boys from Room 142—Solomon, Methusella, Hsar Htoo, Kaee Reh, Plamedi, and Mohamed—by watching them play soccer. The first annual South High School 4 x 4 World Cup Soccer Tournament took place at the very end of the school year. Mr. Speicher recruited them all to play. He drew a map of the school to show them where to sign up for the tournament but then realized they would probably get lost, so he kindly escorted them to the right room up on the third floor. Abigail came with us. Mr. Speicher said the students should pick a name for their team.

"Do you want to be the Congo?" he asked. "Do you want to be Mexico? Do you want to be Iraq?"

"Brazil," said Solomon.

Solomon saw that the teacher had signed up Abigail to play on the same team as the boys. He and Methusella conferred in Swahili about this, then staged a protest.

"Mister! We play with girls?" asked Methusella.

"Yes," said Mr. Speicher.

"No!" cried Methusella.

"We can't play with a girl, Mister," confirmed Solomon.

"Yeah you can," Mr. Speicher rejoined.

"Oh!" said Solomon. Pause. "We change, we go to another team."

The boys were implacable. Mr. Speicher relented and found a separate team for Abigail.

I was eager to see the boys compete, because I knew they were mad for soccer. The appointed afternoon was blazingly hot, not a cloud in the sky, and the air was parch-your-throat dry. They had roped in an additional player I did not know, a Karenni-speaking friend of Kaee Reh's.

Yonatan came over to watch. Then he gave me a hand-slap and a soul-shake, and said, "Miss, you hold my phone?" He left to run around the track for a while.

Brazil (Solomon, Methusella, Plamedi, Mohamed, Kaee Reh, and Kaee Reh's friend) was playing Luxembourg, a group of mostly white boys, several of whom I recognized from the Student Senate. The game did not go well for the newcomers. The other team had better gear—they were wearing soccer cleats, while Mohamed was scrambling around in gray plastic clogs—and also displayed greater cohesion. Brazil was riven by conflict, in part because of communication issues, and in part because of Mohamed. The younger boy had badgered the others into letting him start but then refused to come off the field. Methusella, who had stayed on the sidelines so that Mohamed could play, was fuming. Finally, Mohamed surrendered his yellow mesh jersey to Methusella, who ran onto the AstroTurf and tried to salvage the game. But Luxembourg was up, four to zero.

Mr. Speicher swung by to check on the newcomers.

He pointed to Mohamed's slip-on plastic clogs. "You are playing in those?" he asked incredulously.

Mohamed shrugged.

"Can you run in those?"

"Yeah!" Mohamed said enthusiastically.

The rules dictated that each team put four players on the field, with no goalie. Solomon, Methusella, Plamedi, and Kaee Reh began to look formidable; Methusella was all lightning action, no pauses. He played a hard, street-style version of soccer. I watched him slide right in front of an opposing player, taking him down, and then saw Kaee Reh do the same. For a while, they toppled anybody who approached their goal, committing many blatant fouls. Yonatan came back to cheer for his friends, who looked like they might turn things around. Meanwhile, Mohamed was objecting to being taken out. "Miss! I only play a little bit!" he complained. Yonatan started laughing, because the young boy felt so sure he was a soccer star. Then Kaee Reh sent a slicing drive into the other team's net. However, the newcomers had hit their stride too late. The whistle blew and Luxembourg won, five to one.

During the lull between games, Brazil paused to regroup. They needed to win the next two games to remain in the tournament. Solomon announced, "Me and Mohamed will stay out. The rest will play."

Methusella looked at his older brother gratefully, and Plamedi and Kaee Reh nodded, understanding that Solomon was sacrificing himself to keep the younger boy off the field.

Kaee Reh's friend was oblivious of the strategy, however. He said, "Oh, okay, if you're tired, I'll go in."

"I don't think he's tired," I told the Karenni-speaking boy.

"I want the best team," Solomon confirmed.

"I'm good! I'm the best team!" cried Mohamed.

But Solomon held firm, keeping both himself and the younger boy on the sidelines. Then the newcomers began to perform. Methusella scored right away, with a short punch from the center; Plamedi scored next; then Kaee Reh with a diagonal cross-shot from an almost impossible vantage. After they had established a clear lead, Kaee Reh stepped out so that Solomon could go in. Yonatan helped Mohamed get a turn, yelling to Kaee Reh's friend to give his yellow jersey to the younger boy, and pushing the new boy onto the field, saying, "Go, Mohamed!" Surprisingly, Mohamed proceeded to score a goal, despite the plastic clogs. He threw us a big smile as Yonatan got so enthused he started doing push-ups. Then Plamedi plowed down the field to score, and Solomon and Methusella did the same. Brazil won the second game, eight to two.

The sun had been beating down on the players for an hour and a half, and they had been in almost constant motion. I looked at their sweating bodies and flushed faces. They were dehydrating, fast. I jogged over to the far side of the AstroTurf, where a man was selling plastic bottles of water out of an ice-filled cooler, and jogged back carrying six bottles. When he saw what I was bearing, Kaee Reh bent over at the waist with both of his hands in prayer position, bowing deeply. The boys gulped down the cold water and studied the next team they were slated to play. It was a daunting-looking group of tall, well-muscled Eritreans. One of them came over to talk to me.

"Are you Yonatan's friend?" he asked.

"Yes," I said.

"Are you their coach?" he wanted to know.

"I am their cheerleader," I said.

"You won't be cheering for them after this!" he announced and strutted away.

I asked Yonatan if he was rooting for the newcomers or the Eritreans.

"The Eritreans!" he admitted.

They proved to be brutal foes. The Eritreans were bigger, older, faster, and stronger. Taking this in, Solomon and Methusella both went quiet and eagle-eyed. All of the action took place right in front of their goal. I thought Methusella had been playing rough before, but I was mistaken—that had been him being polite. He let loose during this game and it got extra-dirty, right away. The newcomers' strategy appeared to be to commit any kind of foul to block as many goals as possible. The Eritreans complained vociferously. Methusella slid horizontally right across the path of the biggest Eritrean, with no concern for his own physical well-being, toppling the bigger player. Another Eritrean yelled, "*See!* That's what I'm saying!"

The same Eritrean called out to Mr. Speicher, "Hey, Mister! You gotta watch this game!"

The teacher intervened and started calling the newcomers on their fouls. Mohamed was hopping up and down in his clogs on the sidelines, but nobody would turn over his jersey. "Wait, and you will play soon," Methusella called out. He did let Mohamed play for a moment but took him out again swiftly. After Methusella blocked another goal with one of his spectacular slides, Mr. Speicher told him to stay off the ground. Then he admonished Kaee Reh for guarding his own net as a goalie would do, a violation of the rules. Despite Brazil's efforts, the Eritreans kept scoring, and at the end of the game, Yonatan did a series of chest bumps with his victorious countrymen.

It was a hard loss for the newcomers because they had just come together as a team, and it meant they were eliminated from the tournament. Methusella questioned Mr. Speicher about this: "But do goals count, too? Because we scored eight goals in the last game." Mr. Speicher confirmed that they were definitely eliminated, and they trooped dejectedly over to watch the Eritreans advance into the semifinals. That team would now face Hsar Htoo and a group of Karen-speaking boys. The Karen-speaking team played hard and fast, but the Eritreans dispatched them just as handily as they had Brazil.

In the finals, the Eritreans faced England, a team dominated by a junior named Enoch, a bowlegged superstar with a shaved head and the physique of a grown man, wearing a green Barcelona jersey. He danced across the AstroTurf like he was performing ballet. The ball rolled anywhere he wanted, and he circumvented other players with stunning ease. I was sitting beside a group of male teachers who coached various sports. Solomon sat beside me, close enough that I could smell his deodorant as he perspired, quietly studying every move that Enoch made.

"I could coach this team—give the ball to Enoch," joked Ben Speicher, the math teacher who oversaw the school's wrestling team.

"It's Eritrea versus Enoch," added John Walsh, the long-distance coach.

The teachers explained that Enoch had signed up to play for a developmental team under the auspices of the Colorado Rapids soccer franchise. I passed this along to Solomon.

"Oh!" said Solomon. "He is the best."

After a moment, Solomon added, "Miss, you know where he is from?"

I turned to the teachers and asked them this question. They conferred for a while.

"Is Enoch from Ghana?" one of the coaches asked another.

They weren't sure, maybe Ghana. I told this to Solomon. The foreign-born paraprofessionals who worked at South generally knew exactly what countries students came from, but the American-born teachers had a harder time remembering this information, especially if students were from Africa. There were fifty-four countries on that continent, and they tended to blur together in the minds of the Anglo staff. Later, I looked up Enoch's background and learned that I had given Solomon incorrect information. I wrote to him on Facebook:

Hi Solomon, it was fun to see you play soccer yesterday, and I thought you did a very good job helping your team put the right players on the field. I want to let you know that I told you the wrong information about Enoch. The teacher who told me he was from Ghana was incorrect. On the Colorado Rapids website, I saw that his nationality was listed as "Congo, DR." So he is Congolese, actually. Have a good weekend and I will see you tomorrow.

Solomon wrote back:

Oh Thanks me too I was thinking that he is from Congo DRC because he looks like congolese, thanks for your information see you tomorrow.

In other words, Solomon had been able to study the player's features from a distance of many yards and know which country he came from. I noted that Solomon had been too polite to tell me I did not know what I was talking about when I had said maybe Ghana. Later, I would recount the story of the tournament to Mr. Williams. I told him about Solomon's maturity and how surprising it had been to watch Hsar Htoo and Kaee Reh play soccer. I had gotten to know the boys from the Congo well enough to recognize that their behavior on the soccer field confirmed what I had sensed already—Methusella's ferocious drive, Solomon's basic grace. I had not spent nearly as much time with the two boys whose families were originally from Burma, however, and their personalities had remained obscured. On the AstroTurf, I had seen an entirely new side to each of them. Hsar Htoo had been gregarious and communicative while playing with other Karen speakers, and Kaee Reh had come across as fiercely energized. To see him stand with his head thrown back, his body loose and confident, his demeanor pride-filled—he never looked like that in the classroom.

Mr. Williams nodded knowingly. He had played soccer in college and had coached a high school team. In fact, it was the unexpected pleasure he got from watching players improve under his tutelage that had led him to become a teacher. That's why he taught, still: He loved watching kids evolve as a result of being in his care. Mr. Williams was not surprised that Hsar Htoo and Kaee Reh appeared like entirely different people out on the soccer field. "It is something they are fluent in," the teacher observed. He knew the newcomers had hidden capacity, untapped reserves. He understood that his students might be able to say only a few hundred words today, but that did not reflect how many thousands of words they would know tomorrow.

* * *

Throughout the month of May Mr. Williams was working with the students on a unit about printed materials, called "I Need Some Information." It was the final topic they would tackle that year. They covered stamps, letters, envelopes, books, newspapers, magazines, advertisements, and reference books. When he wrote a list of those items on the whiteboard, somebody asked him how to say one particular word.

"This one here?" said Mr. Williams. "En-cy-clo-pe-di-a. En-cy-clo-pe-di-a."

The whole class began murmuring that word, trying it out, one syllable at a time. Then Mr. Williams asked them to write sentences about various kinds of printed materials, and went around the room checking their work. Noticing that Lisbeth was petting Mohamed again and crooning, "Is my baby!" (in English), while Mohamed wore a dreamy, faraway expression, Mr. Williams deftly suggested that Mohamed change seats and work with Hsar Htoo. When he got to Saúl, he leaned over to read out loud: "I like to read the newspaper each day because I can find a new job." Mr. Williams nodded and said, "Yeah, that's good."

Later that week, Mr. Williams took the entire class outside to look for signs, another example of printed material. The students were supposed to find signs while working in pairs. Mariam chose to work with Shani, and the two of them got so engrossed in conversation—primarily in English, along with a little Farsi, a little Arabic, and a little Tajik—that they fell several hundred feet behind the rest of the group. Nadia and Ksanet went off in their own orbit, too, and so did Grace and Dilli. Meanwhile, Jakleen chose to work with Saúl, and soon I saw Saúl wearing Jakleen's glasses. Then Saúl drew a blue ink ring on Jakleen's ring finger, which matched the blue ink ring he had already drawn on his own left hand.

"We are married," Saúl told me.

"Oh, you'll have beautiful children," I replied. "When did you get married?"

"In math class."

Mr. Williams was fond of a young adult book by Gary Soto called *Novio Boy*, and lately "Novio Boy" (Lover Boy) had become his favorite nickname for Saúl.

One day that month, Mariam took advantage of a lull in a lesson to show other girls a photograph of her dark-haired, handsome fiancé, Abdullah. Mariam announced that their wedding was going to take place over the summer. The other girls discussed the question of whether Mariam was old enough to take such a step.

"In Iraq, thirteen, fourteen, fifteen—it's okay to get married," asserted Mariam.

Nadia looked surprised. "For me, that's too young," she declared.

"Miss! Look!" Mariam said to me another day. Then she held up her phone to show me a picture of an elaborate pink gown with a tight satin bodice and a full tulle skirt.

"Is that a wedding dress?" I asked.

"Yes!" she said excitedly. "Mine!"

Mariam said the wedding was going to happen in Turkey. When I mentioned the impending nuptials to Jakleen, however, she pulled an exasperated face and said, "No! Not true." It took a while to sort out whether the wedding was on or off, but with Nabiha's help, I ascertained that the wedding would have taken place that summer if Ebtisam could have afforded plane tickets to Turkey, but Ebtisam did not have the money. Therefore, the wedding was postponed. Mariam appeared morose about this but she accepted that the plane tickets were too costly. The idea of getting married at sixteen remained hard for me to endorse; I could see that the postponement of the marriage caused Mariam genuine pain, but I thought she would be better off if she dated a few boys and learned through trial and error what made her happy. Such a course was unimaginable to Mariam at the present time, for she viewed the idea of dating a series of men as unacceptable, but I thought she might adapt in this regard.

Meanwhile, Jakleen's relationship with Ghasem had been causing friction between the two sisters. While adults such as Mr. Speicher thought highly of Ghasem, Mariam considered the way her younger sister was carrying on to be inappropriate. In the middle of May, for reasons that remained unclear, Jakleen suddenly cut Ghasem out of her life. He no longer walked alongside her in the hallways and no longer came to Room 142 during lunch. Upstairs in math class, he spent an entire period holding a hand up to the side of his face, to shield his countenance from Jakleen's view. About a week or two later, I found Jakleen eating lunch with a strapping six-foot-tall, muscular athlete. The two of them rode the same city bus to and from school. "Ghasem, very jealous!" Jakleen told me. Her expression conveyed a mix of emotions. She looked proud, concerned, guilty, and pleased, in roughly equal measure. Jakleen said the athlete was calling her *habibi*, which means "sweetheart" in Arabic (a word she had taught him). When I asked if she liked him, she said, "No, I don't know, maybe, yes."

The flirtation lasted for about two or three weeks, and then Jakleen hastily broke off interactions with the athlete after he sent what she considered to be a series of lewd text messages. For the rest of the year, Jakleen dallied with a flurry of other suitors, most of whom she kept at arm's length. Ghasem tried to regain his former standing as her primary admirer, but never quite succeeded. Among the boys competing for her attention was the student from her music class who had once called Jakleen a "terrorist." Jakleen appeared to be both dismayed and emboldened by his visits. "This boy very, very, very crazy, and very, very love girls," she said. It occurred to me that perhaps the boy had been toying with her all along. I knew she had suffered through genuine insults on her long bus rides, when the hijab had attracted verbal abuse, but it struck me that the boy from music class might have intended something different. I asked Jakleen, did she think maybe he had been attempting to tease her, when he had called her a terrorist?

"Yes," she conceded.

The boy was from Southeast Asia and spoke Burmese, Malay, and English. His locker was not far away from Room 142. He never failed to address Jakleen, in some fashion or another, when she walked by. One day, I heard him say to her, as she strode past, assiduously ignoring him, "*Konichiwa!*" (Japanese for hello).

Jakleen announced, "I hate this boy."

Then the boy said to me, "Beautiful girl."

Throughout the month of May, Mr. Williams and his students continued to read the graphic nonfiction book about Cesar Chavez. As summer approached, however, and the students grew more comfortable with English and more inclined to flirt or fight or make friends, it grew increasingly hard for Mr. Williams to get his class to focus. At one point, when he asked them to take out their books, Abigail said, in a tone of oh-no-not-that-again, "*Cuando es vacaciones?*"

Mr. Williams said that summer vacation was in *dos semanas*, two weeks.

Shani was in the middle of making some sort of Tajik joke about how Mariam had "ten mothers" (this seemed to be an insult, although I could never figure out why).

Meanwhile, Jakleen announced, "I want to go home," and then laid her body prone on the table for dramatic effect.

Mariam echoed her sister, saying, "Yes! I want to go now!"

It was the middle of the afternoon, toward the end of a long day, after many months of hard work, and school had exhausted them all. Mr. Williams asked the students to organize themselves into pairs and then struggled unsuccessfully to engage them in reading the book. Jakleen strolled over to Saúl, who was lying draped over two chairs, and bumped him with her right hip to get him to sit up. Then Mariam got so droopy that she slid over sideways, and Mr. Williams had to rouse her, which he did by chanting her nickname, "Mi-*mi*! Mi-*mi*! Mi-*mi*!" A little later, Mariam put her head down on the table. "Mimi, Mimi, we're not sleeping," said Mr. Williams.

Asking the students to read in pairs was not working, so Mr. Williams decided that the whole class should read aloud. They chorally recited a key passage from the book: "Many farmworkers were paid very little money, lived in poor housing, and suffered from health problems." Chavez had tried organizing the farmworkers, but doing so had been hard because their work was "seasonal," the book said. What did that mean? Mr. Williams was trying to get across the idea of work that took place according to the seasons when he noticed that Luwam—who had been assigned to Mr. Williams last year—remained in the room. Ever since lunch, the lonely Eritrean girl had been huddling unobtrusively beside Ksanet.

"Luwam! Can you please go to your proper class?" said Mr. Williams.

One table away, Mr. Williams saw that Lisbeth had spread various parts of her cell phone—case, back plate, main body, SIM card—out in front of her. She was more occupied with trying to put those pieces back together than she was with her book, which lay forgotten beside her. Mr. Williams got a little impatient.

"Please put that away," he said to Lisbeth. "Right now. No using the cell phone."

She looked up and grinned but continued to reassemble the device, sliding the SIM card into place. Mr. Williams walked over, picked up the disparate parts of the phone, and stuffed them into his pants pocket, to Lisbeth's evident distress.

Then he tried to get the class to discuss Cesar Chavez's work. What was nonviolent protest?

Methusella, who had stuck a yellow number 2 pencil horizontally through the top of his hair, answered that Chavez had been holding demonstrations to bring attention to the plight of farmworkers.

"Methusella, I liked that," pronounced Mr. Williams.

He wrote that answer on the whiteboard, and after it he added, ". . . without fighting." Then he went over the concept of nonviolence. Mr. Williams wrote five key concepts on the board:

labor
migrant
nonviolence
protest
rights

He asked the students to choose one word and define it. They were supposed to write their key concept in a bubble and then list attributes of that concept in satellite bubbles. Methusella wrote "migrant" in the center of his page, and in satellite bubbles he added "moving often," "working," "immigrants," and "low wages." He speedily defined the concept of a migrant as "a person who leaves his home country and moves to a new country." Meanwhile, Mariam and Shani became so involved with one another that they wrote nothing. Mr. Williams said,

"Mariam, I think I'm going to change your seat. That's not going to work. You and Shani can't focus."

While he was thus preoccupied, Lisbeth and Mohamed began sparring in a sibling-like fashion.

Lisbeth pointed at Mohamed, and said, "*Abalah!*"

Jakleen and Mariam had taught her the Arabic word, meaning "crazy" or "goofy." They had often applied it to Lisbeth herself.

"*Abalah*, YOU!" Mohamed retorted, pointing back at Lisbeth.

She threw her hoodie at Mohamed.

At that point, Methusella joined the fray, saying in a commanding tone, from his remote location, "*Cállate!*"

That was Spanish for "shut up," a word Lisbeth had taught Methusella.

This swept Lisbeth into a gale of giggles, at which point Mr. Williams interrupted. "Lisbeth, can you please do something? *No es una vacaciones ahora.*"

Seeing that Mr. Williams had his hands full, I went over to work with Lisbeth. Her word was "rights." We consulted the text to figure out what that meant. Eventually, after referring to the book a lot, we added "drinking water," "toilets," "rest periods," and "use of short-handled hoe" in the satellite bubbles. Then we wrote down the terms "discrimination" and "sexual harassment" as well.

Mariam got up to retrieve her cell phone from where it had been charging in a far corner of the classroom. Mr. Williams interrupted her pilgrimage, saying, "Mariam, would you like to work on your word?" Mariam reversed course. Shani was not working, either. She had somehow attached the piece of paper to her forefinger, possibly with spit, and was holding her finger out with the paper floating below it. Elsewhere, Saúl reached around behind Jakleen to tap her on the far shoulder, causing her to look in that direction, and when she realized she had been tricked, she shoved him hard by way of reprimand.

Tired of all this end-of-year antsiness, Mr. Williams spoke sternly to the students. "Guys, you're going to make us pull our hair out," he said, in a fed-up tone of voice. "Have you ever heard that phrase? That means someone is frustrated."

Mr. Williams thought for a moment. He needed a different approach. They had worked for long enough on defining the key concepts, he told the class. They should stand up, holding their books. At the whiteboard, the teacher listed the book's characters. They were going to act out the book in parts. In effect, Mr. Williams turned his room into a stage and his students into actors.

Solomon and Hsar Htoo played the starring role of Cesar Chavez. They read his dialogue together, their two voices combined as one. Methusella played "the Bad Man in a Hat," as Mr. Williams labeled the book's villain. To look appropriately sinister, Methusella pulled the hood of his sweatshirt over his head and tightened it around his face so that only his nose remained visible. Shani, Lisbeth, Jakleen, Mariam, and Nadia played the beleaguered farmworkers. Shani, Lisbeth, and Mariam mumbled a bit, but Jakleen and Nadia delivered a strong joint performance, at one point hushing the entire room, as they announced: "We crawl through spiny rosebushes for them. We work at top speed. The growers promised us $9 per thousand plants, but they pay us only $6.50." Saúl played a Catholic priest who advised Chavez. When it was his turn to speak, he jumped onto the seat of a chair and proclaimed in a thunderous voice: "They are asking for a 40-cent raise to $1.40 an hour. They are living in poverty."

The whole class got caught up in the saga. At a point when I would have thought it impossible, Mr. Williams channeled the strange energy caroming around the room into a rousing show. For many of the students, the book had been at the outer limit of what they could comprehend, and the idea to turn the room into a stage enabled many to finally grasp that the narrative concerned human beings oppressed by an economic system that had been unresponsive to their demands for a long time (presumably something most of them could relate to after watching their parents find work in the lowliest sectors of the American economy). Enacting the story allowed them to experience the central drama—Cesar Chavez's struggle to give the farmworkers a voice. It was one of the most inspired things I saw Mr. Williams do all year, turning around the topsy-turvy mood in the classroom that day. And at that point he had to have been feeling pretty ready for a vacation himself.

*   *   *

Mr. Williams closed the year with a raucous party in Room 142, which Miss Ruthann from Goodwill helped to organize. The students took turns sitting at different tables, while the teacher and the Goodwill volunteers taught them how to play various board games. Mr. Williams also let the students use his laptop to play musical selections from their home countries, and kids clustered around the machine vying for control of the playlist. Jakleen wore a revealing pink camisole, which I recognized as one of the items Nabiha had donated to the family. She had also curled her hair into ringlets. Gone was the girl who had hidden beneath a hijab—here stood an American teenager.

"Nice hair," I told her. "Pasta!"

"Pasta," she confirmed, eyes laughing.

Jakleen strode across the room to play a game with Kaee Reh, who appeared to have replaced Saúl in her affections. When I stopped to watch them battle each other in Quick Cups, Jakleen told me, "Miss! Kaee Reh very nice boy, very good boy!" Both Jakleen and Kaee Reh had fast hands, and they competed with furious passion. Kaee Reh looked less like the diffident student he had sometimes seemed to be in Room 142 and more like the confident young man I had seen on the soccer field.

Lisbeth, her own hair curly again, was playing Jenga with Mariam and Mohamed. At another table, Saúl, Grace, and Abigail were playing the same game—carefully stacking wooden pieces into a tall tower, slowly removing one piece at a time, trying not to cause their stack to topple. Elsewhere, Mr. DeRose was teaching Nadia, Amaniel, Methusella, Solomon, Ksanet, and Dilli how to play the card game Spoons. Shani had taken control of Mr. Williams's laptop, and she grew excited when she found a song by the renowned Tajik singer Noziya Karomatullo on YouTube. Shani said to me, "She's father—" then she pantomimed holding a gun at her forehead, adding, "She no have father. And he very good people, Tajikistan." When I looked all this up later, I learned that Noziya was the daughter of a famous Tajik musician who had been murdered by a militia group during the Tajik civil war, along with a number of other leading cultural figures.

Next it was Lisbeth's turn as DJ. She put on Daddy Yankee, then came over to announce, "It's my music, Miss!" Lisbeth danced away, singing the lyrics loudly. Then Abigail jostled with her for control of the laptop, but they found a selection they both liked. Lisbeth said hopefully to the other girl, "*Más volumen?*"

Halfway through the party, Mr. Williams came over with a news update. "Methusella is going to be in the Student Senate next year," he told me. "He's texting some of the seniors in the Senate right now to make sure he gets onto the right email lists."

"That's great!" I said.

"Yeah, it is." Mr. Williams was smiling broadly, taking pride in his star student's latest success. "He told me he was interested in politics and government, and that he wanted to be a school principal someday, and that, combined with his astronomical language growth, makes him a very good candidate."

"A great candidate!"

Mr. Williams had recommended Methusella for the Senate. He had also suggested that when he returned in the fall, Methusella should skip one and a half years of ELA instruction (passing over 1A, 1B, and 2A) and be placed in ELA 2B. I had not foreseen that anybody in the newcomer room would travel so far in just one year. Methusella had grown at a rate I had not known to be possible. I went to congratulate him and found both boys from the Congo in a corner of the room, locked in a death match of a checkers game. The hypercompetitive duel culminated with Methusella getting a king and dominating the board.

"I am the best, bro!" Methusella crowed.

Solomon asked sheepishly, "Miss, you write about this?"

"Oh, yeah!" I told him. "Two brothers, locked in mortal combat? Of course!"

"I'm becoming stronger, bro!" Methusella taunted. "I'm the best! *Oga! Oga! Oga!*"

"What does *oga* mean?" I asked.

Methusella pantomimed crowds going wild. I said, "Oh, cheering." I wrote that down in my notebook as the English translation for *oga*, and jotted that it was a Swahili word. (Actually, *oga* turned out to be a Yoruba word, and it meant "man in charge" or "boss.") Solomon and Methusella staged a rematch and feuded intensely, their pieces flying across the red and black squares. Once again, Methusella got a king and seemed poised to win, but then Solomon got two kings in quick succession.

"Shit," Methusella said.

It was the first time I had heard him say anything that could be possibly construed as impolite all year long. I decided that Methusella's cultural adjustment was nearly complete. Solomon walloped his younger brother at checkers in the second contest. And that was how their school year ended—jostling, happy, rambunctious. The transformation of Room 142 was complete. The class that had been filled with frightened silence at the beginning of the year was now filled with joyous play. Mr. Williams had brought them all this way, from paralyzed terror to happy integration. He called out that it was time to switch tables—everybody had to learn a new board game. Most of the students quickly got involved in learning the rules of the next game, but Jakleen, Mariam, Lisbeth, and Shani instead scrounged around for fruit-scented markers and some spare paper and started writing affectionate goodbye notes to their teachers. "*La queremos!*" they wrote on the fruity-smelling paper they gave to me, signed by each of them. "We love you."

During the art-making session, Shani acquired two new tattoos (*haram*, surely)—Mariam's name in Arabic, scrawled across both of the Tajik girl's forearms. Meanwhile, Saúl serenaded me one last time, while staring deeply into my eyes, with perhaps a hint of amusement behind the faux passion. So fervent was the young man, he convinced me that I was being sung a beautiful love song. Actually, the song was called "Ya lo supere" by Ariel Camacho, and the lyrics were about the singer telling a former lover somewhat disdainfully that she has been replaced. For a while, Solomon and Plamedi sat side by side, playing a car-racing game on their phones—here, at the very end of the school year, Solomon had made a friend—and I saw Plamedi wind one of his legs around Solomon's, as they might have done back in the Congo.

Then they all switched games again. For reasons I could not fathom, Mr. Williams went around the room with Yonatan, chanting "*Huelga!*"

They were on strike about something, apparently. Suddenly, we all stopped what we were doing at the sound of an enormous, shuddering crash. Everybody turned around to see Plamedi, a look of total astonishment written across his face, holding one single, innocuous-looking wooden Jenga piece in his fingers. Hsar Htoo sat across from him, laughing and laughing, their once tall tower fallen all around. Then Mr. Williams asked everybody to clean up, and most of the students packed up the games, while Lisbeth primped for one more selfie, and Shani leaned out the enormous windows, reached down into the spirea bushes blooming in pillowy billows outside the school, and broke off a white-laced branch of flowers. She presented this tribute to me, and then she and all the other newcomers walked out the door forever and disappeared into summer.

PART IV

Summer

1

Heal Africa

In June 2016, shortly after the school year ended, I traveled to the Democratic Republic of Congo with two instructors from the United States Air Force Academy who were researching how best to disarm militia groups, which is the Congo's central puzzle. They were studying how entities like the United Nations persuaded militia members to put down their weapons and return to civil society, and they planned to spend several days in Goma interviewing former rebels and the people who had disarmed them. Goma was the closest big city to Solomon and Methusella's home village, and I asked the Air Force instructors if I could travel with them, in the hopes of understanding the region better and perhaps being able to meet some of Solomon and Methusella's relatives. Parts of the Congo feel secure, but in some areas kidnappings are rampant. One month before we traveled to the DRC, bandits had stopped a truck filled with Red Cross workers in the province where Solomon and Methusella had grown up, and held the aid workers for ransom. I would not have felt safe going to Goma by myself and was grateful to be included on their trip.

The Congo is a huge place, about the same size as Western Europe. The three-thousand-mile-long Congo River forms one of the DRC's borders. So large is the river's basin, it spans two different rainy seasons, which means it is almost always raining somewhere in the river's immense watershed. Many books about the Congo—Joseph Conrad's *Heart of Darkness*, which unfolds during the Belgian colonial era, for example, and V. S. Naipaul's *A Bend in the River*, which takes place during the thirty-year-long reign of Mobutu—rely upon the great, wide, muddy river for their primary setting. But the river does not touch Goma. The city we hoped to reach lay on the eastern side of the Congo, twelve hundred miles from the capital city of Kinshasa. Because Goma is not connected by the Congo River's tributaries to the rest of the DRC, the city is more strongly linked economically to the Great Lakes region of Africa, i.e., the country's neighbors to the east. Goma lies on the floor of the East African Rift Valley, where it hugs the shores of Lake Kivu, one in a long series of rift lakes. This part of the DRC has seen more violence than any other.

We chose to approach Goma from the Rwandan side because that was the easiest route to the city. We drove through mountainous terrain, steeply terraced with fields, the engine of our van reaching a high pitch on every climb. The relative scarcity of farmland was one of the primary reasons genocide erupted in Rwanda in 1994; when the mass killings took place, Rwanda was the most densely populated country in Africa, and one of the poorest. Our journey retraced the history of conflict in the area. This was the route by which Rwanda invaded the Congo (then Zaire), precipitating the First Congo War, which lasted from 1996 to 1997. After the genocide, Hutu militia groups had fled from Rwanda into the Congo. The Tutsi-led government of Rwanda believed that people in the eastern part of the Congo, many of whom were Hutu themselves, were harboring Rwandan Hutus. Some Hutu militia groups based in the Congo were conducting ongoing raids in Rwanda. Rwanda teamed up with its ally Uganda to launch a war to stop these incursions; the vast wealth of their neighbor must also have been appealing, for Zaire possessed huge deposits of copper, tin, gold, radium, uranium, cobalt, and diamonds. Both Rwanda and Uganda, by contrast, relied almost entirely on the production of tea and coffee. On our drive through Rwanda, we passed tea plantation after tea plantation, women bent over the bright green shrubs, picking leaves by hand.

The Rwandan and Ugandan armies joined opposition figures within Congolese society and pushed all the way across Zaire to Kinshasa. Aided by allied groups from Angola, they converged on the capital city and ousted Mobutu Sese Seko. Opposition leader Laurent Kabila took his place as president and renamed the country the Democratic Republic of Congo. Kabila quickly fell out with his former allies, however, and after only one year of peace, the Second Congo War began. Nine African countries became embroiled in the conflict, also called the Great War of Africa or the African World War, and five million people died, more than in any other modern conflict except World War II. The war officially ended in 2003, but dozens of armed groups remained active to the present, especially on the eastern side of the country.

Three and a half hours after leaving Kigali, Rwanda, we rounded a corner, plunged down another hill, and suddenly beheld a huge expanse of gray-blue water, covered in lines of ripples: Lake Kivu. Heat rose as the day waxed, but the extraordinary foot traffic swelled nonetheless as we approached the city. I saw many women wearing close-fitting dresses with frilly sleeves and flared skirts, made of exuberantly patterned fabric in intense shades of hot pink, electric blue, golden yellow, deep purple, and orange. The dresses, known as *pagnes*, gave the women a look of being ready for church, even though it was the middle of the week and they were running errands on foot. At first I wondered how women of such varying shapes all found perfectly form-hugging *pagnes*, until I spied the roadside *tailleurs* hunkered down over black manual sewing machines. The women were walking with their hips circling from left to right in a dance-like manner, so that they could carry goods on their heads. Balanced on the heads of various women, I saw: an enormous sack of potatoes, an entire case of orange Fanta, a box of dishes, a stack of sheets, a bundle of firewood, a bag of charcoal, bricks, a yellow jerrican, a vast bowl of bananas, a tray of mangoes, and dozens of ripe red tomatoes neatly arranged in a pyramid shape on a platter.

At the border itself, a large green sign with white writing proclaimed DEMOCRATIC REPUBLIC OF CONGO, with a big white arrow pointing onward. First we had to show our documents to officials on the Rwandan side, where soldiers in black uniforms with their pant legs tucked into black military boots carried AK-47s as they patrolled the area. A keen-eyed man wearing a uniform, sharply pointed black dress shoes, and no socks scrutinized my passport for several minutes, queried me about my profession, then waved me along disinterestedly. A small crowd of men hovered nearby, under the shade of an enormous magnolia tree, studying the goings-on for opportunities to make money. We were the only *mzungus* in sight (literally, aimless wanderers, a Bantu term for white people). Petroleum tanker after petroleum tanker stood waiting to cross into the DRC. Both the Congolese government and the United Nations were devouring gasoline, for the movement of their troops required massive amounts of fuel.

Our main worry was that we had been denied visas to enter the DRC. I was also breaking the law by entering the country through Goma; journalists were required to enter through Kinshasa, after seeking permission from the Congolese Ministry of Information, which I did not do. We assumed the denial of our visas had to do with the recent political unrest. Joseph Kabila had replaced his father as president, but he had grown unpopular and was facing serious opposition. The question of whether the country might hold an election had become a favorite topic of conversation in the Congo. Talk of an election coincided with an uptick in violence, and *Newsweek* had just run a story with the headline, "Can Democratic Republic of Congo Afford Another Civil War?"

We were hoping to buy tourist visas at the border. A local fixer named Emmanuel Bugingo had made our travel arrangements. This had included renting vehicles, hiring drivers, finding hotels, making contact with people we hoped to interview, and, euphemistically, "tipping." As Emmanuel had explained in a series of emails, many people in the Congo expected to be paid small bribes. I had decided not to bribe any family members I might be lucky enough to meet, so that I could pursue my main story without feeling compromised, but I had agreed to join in meetings arranged for the researchers, whether or not they involved bribes. The instructors from the Air Force Academy had asked Bugingo to minimize the number of "tips" he made, while giving him permission to pay small amounts (generally $20) as needed.

To make the idea of being tourists seem plausible, we had bought a minisafari to see some chimpanzees. We did not know if this gambit would work, but arriving with proof of a safari seemed our best hope of entering the DRC. As we waited in a line to pay $30 for our tourist visas, a white airplane with UN stenciled on it roared overhead—it was the first of hundreds of white UN vehicles (planes, pickups, SUVs, armored security vehicles) we would see. The UN at present had twenty-three thousand employees stationed in the Congo, most of whom were themselves armed soldiers. Because of the level of ongoing violence inside its borders, the DRC held the infamous honor of being the site of the UN's largest peacekeeping mission anywhere in the world.

Bugingo's plan worked—we passed for tourists. Elated, we walked to our hotel and met a driver who showed us around town. Goma turned out to be a despoiled but unforgettable place. My main impression was one of constant commerce: A group of men walked by us carrying red and gold armchairs over their heads; a man pushed a *chukudu*, a two-wheeled wooden scooter, loaded with rebar; another man used a *chukudu* to haul a greasy generator. Meanwhile, fantastically dressed women in eye-catching *pagnes* sat by neat piles of red tomatoes, brown potatoes, green cabbages, fresh brown eggs, reddish-orange mangoes, bags of shelled peanuts and sugarcane. Other women sold lumps of charcoal, the primary cooking fuel used by the city's residents. Every inch of roadside space had been commandeered for commercial activity. At a communal tap, children were bent over double carrying yellow jerricans filled with water; each jerrican held approximately five gallons, and a typical household consumed several cans per day. The sky was gray, the roads were gray, and most of the structures were gray, but the streets were crowded with bright red *boda bodas*, the local word for motorcycle taxis. In this violence-plagued nation, I had expected to find difficulty, but I had not anticipated witnessing exuberance in equal measure.

An active volcano loomed on the horizon, and its intermittent eruptions had covered major parts of the city with lava. Local people joked about how quickly the soles of their shoes wore out because of the sharp volcanic rocks embedded in the lava flow. The roads we drove down were alternately paved with tarmac, paved with lava, or unpaved, and were frequently riddled with enormous potholes. We saw several SUVs and pickups paralyzed by broken axles, and the air smelled acrid from a combination of vehicle exhaust, burning charcoal, and volcanic emissions. Yet Goma remained highly functional, despite the lava, the potholes, the danger, and the bad air. Young people flocked there to attend college, the United Nations stabilized the local economy, and enterprising business owners sold goods imported from East Africa to villagers who traveled to the big city for everything they could not find in the eastern Congo's small towns.

In one of the city's mazelike markets, I wandered from stall to stall. Near the front entrance, vendors hawked solar panels, radios, earbuds, and other electronic devices; then blue jeans, dresses, and beaded leather sandals; after that, dishes, glassware, thermoses, and cutlery. The market sold the old-fashioned type of irons, the kind that were heated in a fire. Beyond the household items was the food area, tables piled high with fresh fruit and vegetables. Then I saw fresh fish, fish that had been smoked, and fish that had been salted and dried. One table featured piles of sorghum flour and ground roots, and another smoked caterpillars (*hasharat*). White-aproned butchers sold raw meat, but I veered off toward stalls filled with wildly colorful Congolese fabric. I selected two bolts, one with a pattern of orange roses and another with red and yellow geometric shapes on a purple background, to give to Beya, Solomon and Methusella's mother. Despite threats to their safety on nearby roads, hundreds of people had traveled great distances to come to Goma to do exactly what I was doing: shop.

Everybody in Goma spoke of the extreme level of danger in the surrounding province of North Kivu. Originally, I had hoped to drive from Goma to the village of Buganza, so that I could visit Solomon and Methusella's relatives. However, I was told emphatically that I could not make the trip without risking my own life and the lives of anybody who traveled with me. The road to the village ran through the Virunga National Park, one of the planet's most biologically diverse areas and a UNESCO World Heritage Site, which had also become a base for various armed militia groups. I felt cowardly about not attempting the trip until I spoke with a white woman from Colorado who had just survived a journey in which her vehicle had been stopped by armed marauders. She had been seated in the far back of a van otherwise filled with local residents, and the African passengers had hastily buried her under chickens and packages, for fear that if the bandits noticed a white passenger, they would all be taken hostage. Then a man on a motorcycle had paused to pelt the bandits with stones, rescuing them all. I abandoned the idea of attempting a trip to the village.

The United Nations official responsible for Disarmament, Demobilization and Reintegration—a fancy term for taking guns away from rebels and persuading them to return to farming—gave us a lucid summary of the armed groups in North Kivu that occupied most of his attention. Two of the groups had foreign origins. One was the Democratic Forces for the Liberation of Rwanda, the main Hutu rebel group that continued to oppose the Tutsi-led government of that country. It had been hiding out in the unpopulated parts of North Kivu for decades, though recently the group's sway had waned due to internal squabbles and issues of leadership. The second foreign group, and the one that worried the UN official the most, was the Allied Democratic Forces (ADF), a rebel militia that had recently acquired the status of a terrorist organization. Originally, the ADF had formed to oppose the government in Uganda, but it had evolved over time into a radical Islamic group whose main activities were now "robbing locals and being scumbags," the official told us. It was a tricky organization to combat, because of its diffuse nature. There was "pure ADF," "splinter ADF," and "what the locals call ADF but isn't really," he said. Also, this organization had a strong grip on the imaginations of its adherents. "They are much more ideological, and they are much nastier," he added. "We are getting very few surrenders from this group."

Besides the armed groups of foreign origin, people living in the villages of North Kivu were besieged by local militias known as *mai mai*. Initially, the *mai mai* had formed to defend villagers against outside threats, but over time the *mai mai* also began raiding villages. All of the armed groups relied on pillaging for sustenance, preying in a parasitic manner upon the residents of rural areas. For food, the armed groups would swoop down and steal people's harvests. For sex, the armed groups relied on kidnapping young girls and forcing them into unwanted marriages or raping village women. Basically, whatever men in civil society worked to acquire by peaceable means (food, family, physical contact), both the rebels and the *mai mai* took by force. For them, the gun had become a way of life.

Researchers were calling the situation in the eastern part of the DRC "the world's deadliest humanitarian crisis." One peer-reviewed study, published in *The Lancet* in 2006 (when Solomon and Methusella were still living in North Kivu), reported that the mortality rate in the DRC was 40 percent higher than in Central Africa as a whole. Many of the deaths occurred due to violence, but an even greater number resulted from illnesses that would have been treatable if aid workers could have accessed imperiled communities; because of the insecurity, however, huge numbers of people in the Congo had been going without health care.

The United Nations official explained that he could not offer the rebels what they wanted most, which was money; offering cash payments in exchange for guns would only create a market for weapons and provide a stream of revenue to support the very groups he hoped to disable. Instead, the UN was offering enticements such as one motorbike for a bundle of five AK-47s, or an entire cooking set for an individual AK-47. Sometimes UN troops gave child soldiers soccer balls in exchange for their weapons. Those who defected also earned the chance to acquire job skills at rehabilitation camps run by the UN, where they could learn activities such as driving, farming, and hairdressing. The only problem was that the former militia members terrified the very villagers who had to welcome them back if they were to return to civil society. At the moment, due to the precarious political situation, the rate of repatriation had slowed significantly, as elders were refusing to accept violence-prone young men back into their communities at a time when everything felt combustible. "The situation in North Kivu and South Kivu is very volatile, and therefore to pour in former combatants now would be unwise," the UN official said. Word of the bottleneck in the rehabilitation camps had leaked out, and after hearing about the prolonged stays in the compounds, fewer rebels were turning over their weapons.

Fear of another full-blown conflict hung over Goma much as the active volcano dominated the skyline. We had dinner one evening with an attorney who was overseeing the attempt to create a viable judicial system in the eastern Congo for the United Nations. Previously, the attorney had been stationed in Afghanistan, and before that, in Bosnia. She believed passionately in the UN's efforts at peacekeeping, and her work involved an initiative to take court officials out to villages where mass killings had occurred. "It's easier to take twenty people from Goma out to the bush than it is to take one hundred people from the bush here to Goma," she explained. Her hope was that if the Congolese people could experience justice, the habit of committing atrocities might be interrupted. At the present moment, however, she appeared to fear it might be a losing battle. About the future of the Congo, she asked rhetorically at one point, "Will it be burning?"

We also met several local journalists for drinks or for a meal. All acknowledged that they were employed directly by the federal government, and explained that if they tried to report a story that made government officials appear inept or corrupt, they would be jailed. The journalists were obliged to report that there were no more rebel groups operating anywhere in the Congo, for example, even though that was not true. When I asked one of them what he had talked about on the radio that day, he said he had done a feel-good story about a government-sponsored holiday. Bugingo gave each of them $20 for talking to us.

At one point, our driver vanished, and we found a new chauffeur sitting in his place, a taciturn man with acne-pitted skin. Later, we learned that he was a captain in the Congolese army; Bugingo wrote in an email that the man "volunteered to ensure your comfort." The Congolese government exerts almost total control over the dissemination of information inside the DRC and tries to keep tabs on foreign journalists; I assumed the army captain had various motives for accompanying us, and that guaranteeing our comfort was only one of them. I believed he probably also apprised local military commanders of our whereabouts. We watched what we said in the car.

While visiting an orphanage (armed conflict leads to fatalities and poor health care, both of which produce orphans), we stumbled across a young father who had come to surrender his child, swaddled in a white blanket. The mother had died in childbirth, the father said. He was turning the baby over to officials in the laundry room, of all places—nearby industrial-sized washing machines churned dirty clothing in soapy water. The father spoke in a matter-of-fact tone, as if the abandonment of his child were one more domestic routine, akin to housekeeping.

Outside, children in rags were kicking a ball made out of old plastic bags wound into a sphere. The head of the orphanage brought over a former child soldier. The onetime rebel was now in his twenties, and he worked as a laborer at the orphanage. He wore dark blue coveralls tucked into boots splattered with manure and he carried a switch, as if at any moment he expected to herd cows.

The young man said his parents had been killed during the Second Congo War, and he had been kidnapped by a militia group that reported to Bosco Ntaganda, known as "the Terminator." Ntaganda was a notorious commander in the National Congress for the Defense of the People (CNDP). He was later accused by the International Criminal Court in The Hague of rape, murder, sexual slavery of civilians, and kidnapping hundreds of boys, plying them with drugs and alcohol to numb their fear, and using them to cook, clean, or fight alongside his adult soldiers. "I was not happy to fight," the former child soldier told us. "I was forced to do this." He added casually that he had killed many people. "Sometimes I dream that now they are coming back to attack me," he said, in the same flat voice.

Before leaving Goma, we visited Heal Africa, one of the city's largest hospitals. It specializes in treating victims of sexual violence, and its doctors have become experts in surgery required by rape victims, such as fistula repair. Women travel to Goma from many neighboring provinces to seek treatment. The Democratic Republic of Congo is not unique in experiencing epidemic levels of sexual violence, as rape has been used for some time as a weapon to terrorize populations elsewhere in Africa and in other parts of the world, but the prevalence of rape in the Congo has been especially severe and long-lasting. Women in North Kivu report significantly more sexual violence than women in other parts of the Congo. As a result, Goma has earned the sad distinction of being named the rape capital of the world. Another study, published in the journal *Conflict and Health*, about the experiences of 193 survivors of rape in the eastern part of the DRC, found that 83 percent said their attacker wore some kind of military uniform, 69 percent were gang-raped, and 46 percent had been abducted in the process of the assault.

At Heal Africa, we spoke with staff about their efforts to lead a regional campaign for more open conversations about the extent of sexual violence, so that victims would feel comfortable seeking help. The study published in *Conflict and Health* reported that almost half the women surveyed had waited more than a year before obtaining medical treatment. The study also reported that 29 percent of the women who had been raped were subsequently rejected by their families. The hospital was conducting the outreach effort in partnership with local pastors throughout the nearby provinces of North Kivu, Rutshuru, and Oriental. The goal was to explain that rape was widespread, that women who experienced it were not alone, and that rape victims should feel no shame about coming forward to ask for medical attention.

After speaking with staff at Heal Africa, we stepped back outside into the powerful glare of the sun at the equator. Off in the distance, I heard singing. It occurred to me vaguely that I had heard the same sound earlier, when we had arrived at Heal Africa. Who was singing? I wandered off in the direction of the voices, which were harmonizing in a compelling way. On the far side of a pickup truck, gathered in the shelter of a generous shade tree, I found a dozen women standing in a circle along with a man who was holding a Bible. Many of the women were dressed as nurses; I saw one in rose-colored scrubs, with her hair curled into ringlets, wearing gold hoop earrings, clapping her hands over her head. Next to her was a woman wearing a form-fitting *pagne* in a majestic shade of purple, and beside her, a nurse in aqua scrubs, then a woman in a lemon *pagne*. The group was swaying in unison, making the flared skirts of the form-hugging dresses flounce as the singers moved back and forth. We asked why they had assembled in the courtyard of the hospital. One of the singers said they belonged to a local church, and they thought the women seeking treatment might find it comforting to hear the sound of gospel music. In this way, I kept being reminded that the Congo is full of people who choose to meet the challenges of life in a sometimes harsh place with courage, faith, and generosity. Such uncelebrated gentleness, alongside the publicized atrocities. Here, in the middle of the week, people gathered to sing hymns. It was the kind of truth that does not make headlines, giving Goma a lopsided reputation. From afar, it seemed like a terrible place, but up close I saw evil and extraordinary goodness manifested side by side.

As we drove away from Heal Africa, I thought back to the day when Miss Pauline from Jewish Family Service had told me about her break-through with Methusella: his tissue paper collage with a pale pink square at the center. Both Miss Pauline and I had known it meant something—even if we couldn't say what, exactly. Visiting Heal Africa, I felt as though I understood better what Methusella had been saying. In fact, he had been speaking quite plainly; I simply had not known enough about the place he was from to understand. Of course he would have worried every day about his mother's well-being, and about the sanctity of women in general. He would have thought it was his job to save his female relatives if the rebels had found their hiding spot. How terrifying it must have been for him to think of what might have ensued had he failed.

That evening, I was standing outside our hotel in Goma, admiring the blue-gray expanse of the vast lake, when I turned around to see a tall, handsome young man in a pale pink dress shirt and black trousers walking toward me. He looked like Solomon. This was Imani, the boys' first cousin. He was twenty-eight years old, and he lived in Goma, where he worked as a uniformed security guard for the United Nations. Imani wore a cautious expression, but I smiled broadly at the sight of his familiar-yet-unfamiliar face and tried to put him at ease. I described how well his cousins had done during their first year in America, bragging about Solomon and Methusella's prowess in the classroom, and mentioning that Methusella had been invited to serve in student government. Imani remembered the two boys fondly from the era when they had lived in Buganza. "They were always playing football," he said. "They were always calling their friends to play with them. They would have constant football games. They were so active."

Because I could not make it safely to Buganza, Imani returned to his home village, picked up one of his uncles, and traveled across the border into Uganda so that we could meet in a location that was safer for me. This was Nehemie, Tchiza's younger brother. The only brother to remain in the DRC, Nehemie had become the de facto leader of the family members who remained there. I met with Imani and Nehemie at Lake Bunyonyi, where we spent several days together. Nehemie was a tall, thoughtful man who reminded me a lot of my maternal uncles. They were the kind of men who could pull silver-sheathed calves out of recumbent cows, who could pick up runts from pigs' litters and guess their weight by holding them in one hand, who could eyeball a tree and know its age. Men who understood birth, death, dirt, and animals. One day, Nehemie and I took a walk along the shores of the lake, and he named all the plants we saw. It was what my uncles would have done.

The village of Buganza was secreted away in a remote location, and it had remained largely untouched during the early phases of the Congo's strife. At that time, it had been home to approximately nine thousand people. Most of the villagers made a livelihood by farming, although a few merchants sold salt, soap, and sugar. As the wars ground on, however, the village's population was cut by one-third. Many residents were killed by militia groups; others died of diseases that followed in the wake of the conflict; scores more fled, seeking safety. The violence escalated slowly over time, hitting a peak in 2008. After some local young men joined groups of *mai mai*, and the *mai mai* began pillaging to support themselves, the attacks grew more frequent, because the young men knew the location of all the nearby villages. "Things got worse because they got guns," Nehemie said. "Every day, attack; every day, attack. Maybe you are digging in the fields, and you hear guns and shouting, you hear the sounds of bullets. And you see *mai mai* moving through the area, going to another forest that is nearby. It is like a daily process. The other day, some people were carrying baskets of peas, and the rebels attacked those people, and took them into the forest."

Nehemie and Tchiza had a sister named Hinja, who was killed at the hands of rebels. Imani's father died during this period, too. They provided no details, and I was left to imagine what must have happened to family members who had perished. Nehemie conveyed the extent of the violence, however, saying: "In the morning, you might step over four dead bodies." Rebels were constantly wiping out the livelihoods of the villagers. I learned this after Nehemie explained why he had gotten married only recently, although he was in his forties. "The rebels stole everything I owned, four different times," he said. "Each time, I had to start over. Everything was stolen—sorghum, goats, it was all stolen. It was like starting a whole new life. So it took a long time for me to have enough money to be able to propose to a woman."

The violence had peaked during what became known as "the Kivu conflict." Local *mai mai* had feuded with Nandes from the nearby Rwenzori Mountains, a range of snow-capped peaks on the border between the DRC and Uganda. Widespread violence broke out again after the formation of the CNDP, a militia group friendly to Tutsis and Nandes but hostile to Hutus. This was the same militia group Tchiza had mentioned during one of our early conversations—"say, ehn, day, pay"—and also the same group that had abducted the child soldier we spoke with at the orphanage. For a period of several years, the CNDP clashed repeatedly with both the DRC's military and the main Hutu militia. The violence was especially marked from 2006 through 2008. Anybody who played a role in local politics became a target.

Wondering what impact these circumstances had upon Solomon and Methusella, I found a study of adolescent mental health in the eastern Democratic Republic of Congo, published in 2009 in *JAMA Pediatrics*. It described a survey conducted between November 2007 through February 2008 in the Ituri district, a neighboring province that also saw high conflict during the same time frame. A total of 1,046 teenagers participated, their average age between fifteen and sixteen years old. Of the total, 95 percent witnessed at least one traumatic event, and the average number of traumatic events a given teenager had witnessed was between four and five; about 10 percent had witnessed nine or more. The types of events the teenagers had lived through were the loss of a family member or a friend due to a violent event (72 percent), witnessing someone being killed (66 percent), experiencing attacks involving gunfire (66 percent), seeing dead or mutilated bodies (66 percent), experiencing the looting or the burning of their own homes (62 percent), witnessing the act of rape (33 percent), losing a parent (26 percent), and being kidnapped themselves (19 percent). Just over half the respondents reported symptoms that researchers identified as post-traumatic stress, including intrusive thoughts, hyperarousal, avoidance, or numbing.

In August 2008, after the violence had grown intolerable, Tchiza and his entire extended family had fled on foot from Buganza. All of Tchiza's siblings left, including Nehemie. So did Tchiza's mother, even though she was seventy-four years old and suffered from rheumatism, poor circulation, and an irregular heartbeat. They all made it across the border into Uganda, where they sought refuge in various transit centers (temporary structures set up to house refugees) or in the homes of good Samaritans. Then Tchiza and his siblings, along with their children, began the long walk to Kyangwali. However, Tchiza's mother kept falling behind. After UN peacekeeping forces clashed with the CNDP in a series of heated battles at the end of 2008, the rebel forces and the peacekeeping forces announced a cease-fire. During the ensuing calm, Nehemie turned back to Buganza, because his elderly mother could not manage the journey. Essentially, Nehemie, who was childless, sacrificed himself so that his siblings who had children could continue on to Kyangwali.

During the time we spent in Goma beside the blue-gray waters of Lake Kivu, I gradually became aware of the extensive economic links between the Democratic Republic of Congo and the place that I called home. These links primarily involved the manufacture of smartphones and laptops. Over its history, the Congo has served as a place from which other powers have extracted resources; as Adam Hochschild documents in *King Leopold's Ghost*, Belgium's plunder of the Congo began with the desire for rubber and later expanded to include gold, copper, and precious gems.

In the present moment, many miners were digging for coltan. After the black metallic ore is refined into tantalum, it can hold a high electrical charge and yet resists heat. Coltan has become essential for the miniaturization of electronic devices, and approximately 30 percent of the world's supply comes from the Congo. Warlords frequently capture mines in the DRC and use the proceeds to fund the operations of their militia groups. According to news reports, children make up

40 percent of the mining workforce, and miners work in highly unsafe conditions. The same issues apply to the trade in cobalt, a mineral used in the manufacture of lithium-ion batteries. Sixty percent of the world's cobalt comes from the Congo.

Although manufacturers such as IBM, Apple, and Samsung employ entire departments to ensure that minerals sold by Congolese warlords do not wind up in their products, this is difficult to enforce. Cobalt is bought by middlemen and sold as if it originated elsewhere, while coltan is smuggled out of the Congo and commingled with ore from other places. Everywhere we went, people referred to the coltan rush. They said things like, "Coltan is worth more than gold." The United Nations estimates that perhaps three-quarters of the coltan coming out of the DRC originates in illegal operations. In other words, the violence taking place in the Congo "feeds off of the global demand for electronics," as a video from Intel acknowledges. What is happening in the DRC sounds barbaric and far-off, and we want to believe that we are not complicit, yet we carry small parts of the Congo everywhere we go, in the very devices we use to define ourselves as belonging to the developed world.

The two instructors from the Air Force Academy planned to remain in Goma for several more days to interview former rebels. I separated from my traveling companions in the hopes of gaining admittance to Kyangwali, the refugee settlement where Solomon and Methusella had lived before moving to the United States. It was located in an especially remote part of Uganda. Getting there would take fifteen hours, and I was told to expect a bumpy ride. It was a relief to leave the gray cityscape of Goma behind. We drove through the countryside's reassuring refrain of red dirt, emerald-green crops, and turquoise sky for what felt like an eternity. I saw many fields of sorghum and many fields of tea. In Rwanda, we drove on the right side of the road, and in Uganda, we drove on the left, because that country had been colonized by the British. We reached our hotel close to midnight and got on the road again the next morning by 6:00. The settlement did not appear on many maps, and we wanted to allow for the possibility of getting lost. On our second day of driving, most of the roads we took were unpaved, and in our wake billowed a long train of seething red dust. We drove past scores of children walking to school in their uniforms—light blue in one village, maroon in the next—and the children covered their mouths, so as not to eat the dust.

As we drew nearer, we began asking for directions of anyone we saw on the road. We stopped to consult with an especially well-dressed woman wearing a gold *pagne*. She had a lavender boa draped around her neck and wore black pumps, even though she had been walking along a dirt road. The woman asked for a lift—she was headed to Kyangwali as well. She climbed into our vehicle and said her name was Tamari. Her family had moved to the refugee settlement from North Kivu when she was a small child, and she had lived there until the age of eighteen. Recently, Tamari had moved to Kampala, where she had been putting herself through college. She traveled to the Congo to buy its brilliant fabrics, then returned to Uganda to sell the cloth. When she amassed enough proceeds, she paid for a year of tuition. She was studying to become a social worker.

At Tamari's instruction, we turned down an unmarked dirt road. Almost two miles later, we came to a sign that said KYANGWALI REFU-GEE SETTLEMENT, with a gatehouse. A sign there asked, WHAT IS YOUR CONTRIBUTION IN PREVENTING GBV? (gender-based violence). Tamari guided us toward a cluster of administrative buildings, near an enormous magenta bougainvillea. She pointed out the field office, a yellow building with a blue metal roof. Inside, an officious man sat behind a desk, stubbornly thwarting all who sought entrance. We grappled with him ineffectively until Tamari scolded the man. Then he ushered us into a conference room, a harried secretary materialized, and I met with the settlement's efficient commandant.

The commandant accepted a used laptop computer that I had offered to donate to the refugee settlement. Then she provided a thorough overview of the settlement's population. One-quarter of the world's refugees housed in formal camp settings live somewhere on the continent of Africa; Uganda's refugee population had swelled to half a million, and Kyangwali was one of five major settlements located in that country. The refugee population at Kyangwali had grown to forty-three thousand people as of May 2016; the vast majority were Congolese. The settlement was more than fifty years old and consisted of sixteen villages spread over ninety-two square miles. It had been receiving a continual stream of new arrivals, over one thousand individuals in the preceding three months, primarily from North Kivu. The most recent spasm of violence there had caused another sizable influx.

Uganda has a friendlier attitude toward refugees than most countries, and it employs the word "settlement" to indicate that refugees are free to come and go. Uganda's settlements have also been praised for fostering a culture of self-sufficiency. At Kyangwali, refugees were expected to grow their own food. "On arrival, everyone qualifies for land," the commandant explained. "We also provide plastic sheeting, so that you can build a makeshift house as you prepare to build something more solid. Over time, we expect you to be able to put up a semipermanent structure to live in, and to start earning a bit of livelihood." Refugees get full rations during their first three years, but after four years they receive only half rations, and after eight years they no longer qualify for rations at all. In that way, settlement officials tried to promote self-reliance.

The commandant assigned a subordinate to show us around. From the field office, we drove through the main commercial area, a collection of adobe buildings with tin roofs that included a restaurant, a pool hall, and shops that sold sugar, salt, cooking oil, beer, and locally manufactured gin. After the shops, we drove past a series of mud houses with roofs of thatch or tin. To build a home, residents placed posts of saplings vertically around the perimeter, then bound more saplings horizontally to the vertical posts. After making a second grid, homebuilders packed mud between the two sets of saplings. The technical term for this is wattle and daub. A good roof was essential, or the mud walls would wash away when it rained.

Many homes featured open doorways, though some had doors. On top of perhaps one-third of the structures, I spied a single solar panel, sufficient to generate enough power to charge a few cell phones and provide some lighting. Every house was surrounded by crops: leafy banana trees, tasseled rows of corn, beans growing on stakes, and cassava. Cassava was the starch of choice—basically, it is the potato of Central Africa. Every so often, a resident had beautified a particular home. One house featured two flowering trees in the yard, and another had been painted with the words GOD IS GOOD.

The first primary school we visited served 1,606 students and had eleven permanent classrooms, as well as several large canvas tents that served as temporary classrooms. Wooden benches stood before wooden desks, but the rooms sat empty. It was the start of a new term, and most of the students had not yet reported back from their holidays. The canvas tents provided evidence that the school would be crowded when the children materialized, yet there was not a lot of education happening on the day we visited. Handwritten posters taped to the walls suggested a didactic teaching style. In one room, I saw a drawing of a fish with all its external parts labeled, and in another a drawing that described the formation of a rift valley—when two tectonic plates pulled apart, the floor of the valley dropped down in between. The posters had yellowed and their edges were curling.

Kyangwali had eight primary schools and one secondary school. In the government-run primary schools, tuition was free, although parents had to pay for shoes, uniforms, and school materials. Uniforms cost about $20 apiece, and it was hard for families with no access to employment to come up with that much money. For children to continue at the secondary level, parents had to pay substantial tuition. The vast majority of children growing up in the settlement did not attend school beyond the primary level. Younger students received instruction in their home language, but older students received instruction in English. The English used by school administrators seemed a bit whimsical. Posted beside the door to the principal's office was a hand-lettered list of strictures:

1. Coming early at school is a must.
2. We should always be smart.

3. The class must be kept clean always.
4. Teachers must be respected.
5. No fighting in class.
6. Eating in class is highly prohibited.
7. No escapism from school.
8. Going out of class is not allowed.
9. Absentism [*sic*] is not allowed.
10. Extra lesson is to all pupils.

Of the 1,606 students served by this school, all but nine were Congolese. The principal looked blank when I described Solomon and Methusella; if the boys had ever gone to this school, she did not remember them.

The second primary school we visited was privately run. It received funding from outside donors and appeared to be a model of public-private partnerships. Later I would be fortunate enough to meet one of the cofounders of this school, a well-known leader in the Kyangwali refugee community named Bahati Kanyamanza, after he accepted a resettlement offer and moved to Elizabeth, New Jersey. Coincidentally, Bahati knew Tamari, the woman who had helped us find the refugee settlement. She had been one of the lucky children who received a scholarship from Bahati's organization to fund her secondary education. I knew that Solomon and Methusella had not attended a private school, but I told the principal about the boys anyway; again, there was no recognition.

Before we left the premises, I was accosted by a woman who appeared befogged. Beside her mouth, she had a crust of drool, as if she had vomited recently. She thrust a set of registration papers at me. Perhaps she thought I held the power to choose which refugees got to resettle.

"Is your name Espérance?" I asked, looking at one of the forms.

The woman nodded. The word was French—it meant "hope."

Espérance had been born in 1967, the papers said. She was originally from the DRC, and she had three children. I wondered what had put a mother of three into an incapacitated state at eleven in the morning. Before I could ask more, however, the settlement official shooed Espérance away.

"This one is drunk already," said the commandant's number two.

He worried that she had been a nuisance. Actually, I had heard that substance abuse was rampant in refugee camps, and in her disheveled condition, Espérance had provided me with a glimpse of the issue first-hand. I did not know what had caused her to drink till she was weaving before lunch, but it seemed likely she had lived through trauma.

We set off toward a health clinic. Along the way, we passed a group of boys in blue jeans walking down the road with a herd of skinny cows. Then four girls walked by carrying large bundles of firewood on their heads. The girls were maybe eleven or twelve years old, and the boys perhaps fourteen, but none of them were in school—they were busy helping their families survive.

In the courtyard of the health clinic, seventy or eighty people stood in the shade of a big tree, waiting to see one of the clinic's two doctors. The doctor who paused to speak to us wore navy trousers, a light blue dress shirt, and a white smock. He showed us the clinic's most recent monthly report. In April 2016, the two doctors had seen a total of 2,183 patients. By far the largest complaint was malaria; that month, they had seen 449 patients with symptoms. "May will be worse," the doctor told us. "Malaria is seasonal. When maize grows, it harbors water in the leaves that are close to the stalk, and the mosquitoes hatch there." Other patients had shown up with diarrhea, sexually transmitted diseases, urinary tract infections, skin diseases, ordinary colds, and pneumonia. "We have twenty-nine pregnant women with malaria," the doctor added. "We need to treat them, but it's tricky because quinine can induce premature labor."

The doctor turned to a different stack of paper, a series of assault reports stamped CONFIDENTIAL. He estimated that he performed about two rape examinations per day, although when I studied the April report more closely, I saw there were twenty-seven cases of injuries due to gender-based violence at the clinic that month, which suggested the correct average might be more like one rape case per day. Clearly, the constant parade of women with injuries from sexual assault had worn on the doctor, for while he spoke of this subject his mood turned fuguelike. Noting that the Congo was known for its high incidence of rape, the

Ugandan-born doctor said he believed the trend had increased with the arrival of more refugees from the DRC. Many of the cases required the doctor to make a court appearance, meaning a long, bumpy drive on bad roads to the courthouse in Hoima, the closest big city. Wearily, he told us, "I'm supposed to go to court later today."

We let the doctor return to his patients. Our official tour was over, but I called Tamari, to see if she might be able to help us find the rest of Tchiza's family. The more time we spent at the settlement, the more I felt the desire to trace their trajectory through this place. Which village had been theirs? What had their house looked like? I wished I could meet Stivin—Methusella's closest friend. Finding one individual among the forty-two thousand residents of the sprawling camp seemed impossible, but I felt I had to at least make an attempt.

Tamari said she would be glad to help. We picked her up and she made a few phone calls to various members of the refugee community. Using the settlement's grapevine, she narrowed down our search to one village, where many former residents of North Kivu were concentrated. After a twenty-minute drive across the settlement, along red dirt roads, past a lot of banana trees and a lot of corn, we arrived in the center of that village. A small crowd formed—we were a novelty. Villagers invited us to sit down on blue plastic chairs, which they placed in the shade of a small tree. After the villagers conferred, Tamari reported they knew a couple who were related to Tchiza, but neither the husband nor the wife was at home. The husband was working in the fields, and the wife had taken a sick child to a health clinic.

After some more group discussion, a villager ran off to retrieve the husband. Perhaps ten minutes later, the man appeared, wearing worn black trousers and an old gray polo shirt, darkened by sweat. Tamari called out a warm greeting; the man turned out to be a well-known pastor. I was still explaining myself to him when his wife materialized. She had a beautiful face with high cheekbones and wide-set eyes. This was Maman Roger (the honorific meant she had a son named Roger); she wore a lime-green polo shirt with a red-and-white cotton skirt, and she had a child tied to her back with a piece of red cloth. When I showed Maman Roger pictures of Solomon and Methusella, her face broke into a huge grin. They were her first cousins. But she reached out to take my phone into her own hands when I showed her a picture of Imani taken in Goma. Maman Roger beamed at my phone, transfixed by the sight of his face.

"That is her brother," Tamari explained. "The same mother, the same father."

Once upon a time, all of Solomon and Methusella's relatives had lived together in Buganza, but the Congo's violence had divided the family into four factions. Some remained in Buganza, others had moved to Goma, many more resided at Kyangwali, and a lucky few had resettled in the United States. In this case, war had put miles and miles of bumpy roads between a sister and brother. Four years had passed since Maman Roger had seen Imani. Her brother had traveled from Goma to the settlement by bus to attend her wedding, and it had taken him more than fifty hours.

Maman Roger got into our car, along with the baby she was carrying, to show us the way to an uncle's home. We drove past dozens of homes, and Maman Roger pointed to one—it was where Solomon and Methusella had lived. I saw a wattle-and-daub structure perhaps ten feet wide by twenty feet in length. Tan adobe had once covered its walls, but much had crumbled off, revealing dark-brown mud beneath. The house had one small window, two wooden doors, and a roof made of silver corrugated tin. I could see at a glance how far the two boys had traveled: Before moving to the United States, they had lived in a home with no electricity, no appliances, no running water, no heating, no light switches, no glass windowpanes, and no doorknobs.

We turned down one side road after another, and every time we made a turn, the road got smaller. Eventually we parked near a house of dark brown mud riddled with cracks. On a blue tarpaulin spread by the front door, the family was drying cassava in the sun. Corn grew nearby. Maman Roger picked up a wooden bench and moved it into the shade, as her uncle stepped outside. He was a tall, stately man, wearing black trousers and an olive-green dress shirt. His hair was lightly threaded with gray. This was Samuel—the oldest of Tchiza's brothers and the leader of the family that remained in Kyangwali.

Samuel greeted us with weary grace and listened intently as we spoke. His manner softened when I showed him a picture of his younger brother. As I held up my iPhone, Samuel leaned forward to stare at the glowing photograph, which showed Tchiza standing inside the gold-domed statehouse in Denver, which we had visited together one day. My intention was to forge a connection with this man as best as I could, given the limited time we had together, and I thought it would be reassuring for him to see that I knew Tchiza. The chance to glimpse his long-lost brother had such a palpable effect on Samuel, however, that I forgot my questions and simply began sharing my pictures. As we went through my extensive catalog of images, additional family members gathered—Samuel's wife, a daughter-in-law, a son, and several grandchildren. I wound up showing the crowd every picture of the boys that I had.

"This is Methusella in his classroom," I said at one point.

"Metu!" the small children cried, crowding in for a closer look.

Then I pulled up a picture of Solomon.

"Gideon!" exclaimed Samuel's wife.

Solomon had grown since she had seen him last, and she had mistaken him for his older brother. This was discussed for a while—they could see the passage of time written on the boys' faces. I remembered having conversations like this one when I was a child. My parents had brought us back to Ireland every other summer, where our freckled faces would be inspected closely by aunts and uncles, the smallest changes eliciting lengthy commentary. We were told that we resembled certain dead people we had never met, and then we would be released to play outside with our Irish cousins. Solomon and Methusella had not returned in person, but at least I had brought these high-resolution images. They were the first visual depictions this part of the family had seen of all that had transpired since the boys had left Kyangwali, and it was like a virtual homecoming.

I described the litany of successes the two boys had won at school in the United States: They had earned top marks, they were skipping forward one full grade, Methusella was joining student government. Tamari, who spoke fluent English, served as our interpreter. Samuel put one arm over his head to lean against the side of his house, and stilled himself to listen with his whole being. On his face I saw warmth, caution, intelligence, and curiosity. I could sense why everyone turned to him for leadership. If we had experienced an emergency while we were together, I would have done whatever he suggested.

Samuel asked if I could do him a favor. When camp officials had delivered the surprising news that Tchiza and his family had been granted permission to resettle in the United States, they had been told they would depart that same day. They had no time to walk around the sprawling settlement to say goodbye to the rest of the family, and Samuel had learned about what was happening in a rushed call on his mobile phone from Tchiza. At the time, Samuel had just borrowed a much-loved book from his younger brother. Would I return the book to Tchiza in America? Samuel ducked down to enter the mud hut and returned carrying a handmade book. Over the years, its leather cover had melted away at the edges, suggesting the book had been consulted frequently. It was a book of Christian hymns, written in Swahili.

I promised to deliver the book. I asked if I could bring news of the family as well. How had everybody at Kyangwali been faring?

"Tell them we send our greetings," Samuel said, with tired elegance. "Tell them we are all doing fine. But tell them that we are still leading the refugee's life—so they should stay in that place, where they are now."

He wanted to assure his younger brother that he had done the right thing by leaving—even though he had gone without saying a proper goodbye. As we drove off, I asked Tamari if she could help me understand what Samuel had meant. What was "the refugee's life"? Tamari sighed audibly, and then explained that the plots of land assigned to each family measured only fifty by one hundred yards. This was a tiny amount of land, compared to the acreage the families had farmed previously. It was not possible to earn a real livelihood on such a small tract; families could barely grow enough to feed themselves. Even if a family amassed a surplus, they could not readily sell the food, as few people in the settlement boasted spare cash. Also, while each family was permitted to cultivate land, they did not legally own property; all of the land belonged to the government of Uganda. Life was structured in a way that it was possible (barely) to subsist, but impossible to better your circumstances.

Tamari's comments were confirmed by the scholarship on Africa's "protracted refugee situations." In a far-reaching report about African camps, published by the UNHCR, analyst Jeff Crisp cited lack of economic opportunity coupled with material deprivation as among the top factors affecting well-being. Insufficient food was generally the number-one complaint. There was also a general psychosocial malaise; despair and low self-worth were prevalent. Many basic human rights were curtailed, among them freedom of movement (in most camps, residents are not permitted to leave), civil and political rights (they cannot vote in their host countries), and most legal rights (they are not official residents of their host countries). "The right to life has been bought at the cost of almost every other right," wrote Crisp.

Before leaving Kyangwali, we drove over to a primary school that Samuel had identified. I had told Methusella that I would try to find his friend Stivin. As it turned out, Stivin was Samuel's grandson, and Samuel gave us directions to the right school. The principal asked us to sit down in his office and I described how I knew Solomon and Methusella. Then he informed us that he had no such boy named Stivin. We had made a mistake, apparently; I got ready to depart. Before we could go, Tamari spoke up in a gentle tone, to say perhaps the principal was mistaken, for the boy's relatives had given us the name of the school very precisely. Also, she had been chatting with one of the teachers outside, and he had confirmed that the boy was present.

Thus confronted, the principal reversed himself and dispatched a teacher to find Stivin. Within minutes, the teacher returned, bringing a boy dressed in navy shorts and a red, short-sleeved, collared shirt. The boy's face wore an expression of puzzled apprehension. He feared he'd been summoned to the principal's office because of a transgression.

"Are you Stivin?" I asked.

"Eh," he said, which I recognized as the colloquial way of saying yes.

"Do you know Methusella?" I asked.

Stivin looked at me blankly. Tamari translated my question into Swahili, but we still got no response.

"Metu?" I ventured, trying the family nickname.

"*Eh!*" cried Stivin.

I took out my iPhone to show him the same pictures that had delighted his grandfather. The photographs had a curious effect on Stivin. At first, the sight of his cousins' images caused his body to relax and his face to break into a sunny smile. Stivin's expressive countenance was alight with the same playful intelligence as Methusella's, and he was clearly pleased to see pictures of his cousin. But his face clouded as I described how well his relatives were doing in the United States. Noticing his obvious intellect, I felt sure that Stivin would have been capable of the same achievements, if given the chance to prove himself. But he had not been given that chance. The American classrooms in my photographs had wall-to-wall carpeting, glass windows, colorful chairs, shelves of books, and carts filled with laptop computers. The classrooms at his school had concrete floors, no lights, and no windows. There were no books and no computers. I was showing Stivin a glimpse of a paradise to which he had not been invited.

I told him that his cousin Methusella said hello.

But Stivin's face hardened, because looking at these images of his cousin's flush new life was hurtful.

"Tell him to work hard and send me money for a school uniform!" Stivin replied, in a slightly bitter tone.

Carelessly, I had thought the pictures would have the same heartwarming effect on him that they had on his grandfather, but he was a child and he felt the difference between Methusella's circumstances and his own too keenly. My sense that Stivin's ability to pursue higher education would be highly compromised was confirmed when I found an academic case study of education at Kyangwali conducted by Meital Kupfer while she was a graduate student at the School for International Training Graduate Institute in Kampala, Uganda. According to Kupfer, only 68 percent of children between the ages of six and thirteen at Kyangwali were enrolled in school, compared to 94 percent enrollment for children of the same ages elsewhere in Uganda. Enrollment in primary schools at the settlement dropped significantly after third grade, when older children started staying home to help with chores. Of the students attending school, 26 percent reported they could not focus on their education because they were hungry. Only 16 percent of adolescents were enrolled in secondary education, which involved bigger fees. Also, the secondary school at Kyangwali did not continue to the point of a degree. To qualify for college, a student had to leave the settlement and complete two final years of high school in Hoima, many miles away, at schools that charged even higher fees.

In other words, Stivin was almost certain to become one of those children the world was going to leave behind. I believe I caused him real heartbreak, showing him pictures of all that he was missing. Stivin came to stand in my mind for all those who had not been chosen, all the children who would spend their days collecting firewood and filling yellow jerricans with water. That night, I wrote an email to the friend who had loaned me books about the DRC. "Isn't the Congo the saddest, most beautiful, magical, friendliest place in the world that's also tortured in one thousand ways?" he wrote back. Yes. But that place and the one I called home were also more closely interrelated than I had imagined. Our histories were one shared story. Europe's wealth had been gained at the expense of its colonies, and the electronic device that I had used to show Stivin those photographs—the fancy phone for which I had paid such a hefty sum—had subsidized the very wars that had put Stivin into his dusty, hopeless predicament, where he found himself stuck without a viable future, unable to get the attention of the developed world.

PART V

Fall

1

Careless Driving

On August 22, 2016, the first day of the following school year, I walked into South High School and unintentionally crossed paths with Mr. DeRose and Mr. Speicher, who were busy shepherding a clump of bewildered-looking students around the vast building. The two teachers were giving a tour to the latest batch of newcomers the world had sent to South.

"Miss!" someone cried excitedly.

It was Shani. She had not placed into one of the more advanced classes upstairs, so she was returning to the newcomer room for one semester. She had big news, though: "From Tajikistan, more people, here! Here, my brother! My friend, boy, here, and girl, here. More, my country, my apartment, here. Very fun!"

Mr. Speicher and Mr. DeRose and the new newcomers were on their way to the gym. The students were clutching paper printouts of their schedules and trying to follow along as Mr. Speicher pointed out critical aspects of high school.

"Locker room!" he announced.

"*A la derecha, hombres,*" Mr. DeRose translated. "*Damas, a la izquierda.*"

A couple of boys from El Salvador pretended to assail the girls' locker room, sniggered about this, and then froze as the bell rang.

"How long do you have to get to Mr. Williams's class?" asked Mr. Speicher. He answered his own question, bellowing, "*Five minutes!*"

Then he showed them the way. This year, Mr. Williams had moved to a new room, one closer to the front office. After the latest newcomers settled into their chairs, he began all over. He went around the room, introducing himself to the mostly silent arrivals, saying, "Nice to meet you." Then he asked where they were from and pointed out artwork he had displayed by students from their home countries. On the first day of school, Mr. Williams had thirteen students, twice as many as the year before. Among the brand-new arrivals was a young man who possessed so little English that he could not answer the question: What language do you speak? Shani looked around at this collection of strangers and said wistfully, "Maybe, tomorrow, come Lisbeth, all the girls."

As Shani soon discovered to her dismay, Lisbeth and all the girls had moved upstairs. The only student from the prior year who also remained in Mr. Williams's room was Mohamed, the once motherless boy who had sung from the Qur'an. I found him wandering the hallways, bewildered as to where he belonged, and escorted him to Mr. Williams's new location. All the other students Shani knew from the previous school year were spread across ELA levels 1B, 2A, and 2B.

I found Jakleen and Mariam in Noelia Hopkin's sunny, colorful, second-floor classroom, a place mysteriously accessed by a door located inside a stairwell. The sisters had performed well enough on the end-of-year evaluations to test into 1B, along with Grace, Hsar Htoo, Abigail, Bachan, and Plamedi (still huddled into his gray ski parka even though it was balmy). Bachan appeared far more engaged and alert, possibly because he was sitting beside a nearly identical-looking boy who turned out to be his cousin—at last, he had someone with whom he could speak. Meanwhile, Jakleen had dyed her hair blue black and was wearing bright red suspenders. Sporty Abigail had discovered makeup, and Grace had gotten red extensions that fell to her shoulders. Grace looked unsure about finding herself in a room without her sister Nadia, who had moved to 2A, but she quickly befriended several other girls from Africa placed in the same class.

The move upstairs had a galvanizing effect on Jakleen and Mariam. Pictures of pink flamingos brightened the walls of the classroom and

Ms. Hopkin kept her instruction as lively as the décor. She had grown up in Puerto Rico, was bilingual in English and Spanish, and also had an Arabic-speaking paraprofessional working in her room. Ms. Hopkin was not shy about expressing anger if the students got out of control, and if they were slow to perform she was as likely to hector as cajole. She was highly entertaining, and Jakleen and Mariam immediately began saying they adored their new ELA teacher. Ms. Hopkin began the school year by asking the students to write about themselves. She suggested they could tell her what they liked to have for a snack or about the best moment of their summer vacation.

"Miss! What is snack?" Mariam asked.

"What do you like to eat?" replied Ms. Hopkin. "Do you like pizza? Hot Cheetos?"

Mariam nodded happily—she knew about Hot Cheetos—and began wiggling her heels back and forth rapidly under her chair as she wrote. Jakleen sat beside her chewing gum vigorously and wearing red lipstick in a shade that exactly matched her red suspenders.

"How do you spell 'cafeteria'?" Jakleen asked.

Ms. Hopkin leaned over to see what Jakleen had been writing.

"When you're on vacation, do you go to the cafeteria?" the teacher asked.

Ms. Hopkin turned to the rest of the class and asked the room, "If you are not here, where do you go to eat?"

"Home," whispered Grace.

The teacher laughed—that's right, these kids did not go out to eat very often.

"Ideally, home, yes," she acknowledged. "But if I have to go out, I would eat in a restaurant."

She turned back to Jakleen. "Restaurant? Is that what you mean?"

Jakleen nodded. She wrote: "The best vacation I had was go to a garden and then go with friends to a restaurant."

Ms. Hopkin showed the class a picture of a white beach bordered by curved palm trees and an aquamarine ocean. "Colorado is home, but my heart belongs somewhere else," she admitted. "What language is spoken in Puerto Rico?"

"Spanish," Grace replied, in her near whisper.

"Correct," said Ms. Hopkin. "And what number of countries speak Spanish?"

The students made a few wild guesses and then Ms. Hopkin said actually there were twenty countries in the world that spoke Spanish, plus Puerto Rico.

"Jakleen, what do you do to relax?" asked Ms. Hopkin.

"Sleep!" Jakleen said immediately.

"What do you do?" the teacher asked Mariam.

"I sleep!"

"You sleep, too? Okay. Here's what I do to relax," said Ms. Hopkin. "I get in my car, I put on my sunglasses, I turn on the radio, and I sing. The only problem is when I do that I tend to drive too fast."

Ms. Hopkin quickly reviewed how to conjugate the verb "to be." In the PowerPoint she had prepared, she showed a slide that said, "Today I will be able to utilize the verb to be in sentences to communicate information about myself and others."

"In Spanish, *utilisar*, right?" she said to Abigail.

Abigail dimpled, smiled, and nodded.

Noticing that her students had gotten a little sleepy, Ms. Hopkin said, "Tired? *Cansado?* Been a long day? All right, party people! We are going to practice using the verb 'to be.'"

She asked for a volunteer. Jakleen raised her hand.

"All right, I appreciate that," Ms. Hopkin told her. "You get a purple mechanical pencil."

She waved the pencil at Jakleen, and Jakleen sauntered over to receive the gift.

"Okay, I need you to tell the class who you are."

"I am Jakleen," said Jakleen. She added, "I am really happy."

"Nice job," said Ms. Hopkin.

In the days that followed, Jakleen and Mariam quickly befriended several Arabic-speaking girls from Somalia and Sudan. I often saw them conversing with their new friends in the hallways, seeming far more joyous than they had the previous fall, when they had spent so many days wrapped in sadness. I thought their difficult transition was complete.

As the former newcomers adjusted to their new rooms, the change also caused a reconfiguration of their social lives.

One day, Jakleen told me, "Lisbeth, she has new friends. She forgot about me!"

"Do you miss Lisbeth?" I asked.

"No! She always talking," Jakleen said, laughing. "This is better."

Lisbeth had been placed into a class that met on the opposite side of the same stairwell, with a firecracker of a teacher named Jenan Hijazi. She taught ELA levels 2A and 2B. Ms. Hijazi had been born in Kuwait but had grown up in the United States, and at the start of the year she told her students that her first name meant "beautiful gardens" in Arabic. She was a runner with an athletic body who favored skinny jeans, and she kept a pair of tortoiseshell reading glasses perched on top of her head. Ms. Hijazi had a big heart but could be acerbic. Her voice hopscotched from sounding warm like a caress to sharp like cut glass, or brassy like a trumpet. She darted around constantly, clutching a travel mug filled with coffee, and from time to time even jumped on top of furniture because she was not tall and that was the only way she could reach the upper part of the whiteboard. Moving directly from Mr. Williams's room into Ms. Hijazi's room involved a certain adjustment. Everything happened at a higher velocity.

Ms. Hijazi taught level 2A in the afternoons, and that was where I found Lisbeth, Nadia, Saúl, Kaee Reh, and Yonatan. The 2A cohort was big—thirty-three students. Because she felt lonely without Jakleen and Mariam, Lisbeth gravitated toward Nadia, who felt similarly bereft without her sister Grace. Nadia and Lisbeth sat together every day. After a while, Nadia began translating everything the teacher said into Spanish, because Lisbeth could not follow Ms. Hijazi's rapid-fire English. Translating was perfectly acceptable in Mr. Williams's room, but not Ms. Hijazi's. "Nadia! *Stop!*" the teacher snapped one day. She wanted Lisbeth to comprehend English on her own.

Yonatan lolled in his chair on the far side of the room, surrounded by other students from Eritrea. Ms. Hijazi heard that he was a star runner and attended one of his cross-country meets. When she returned, she told the whole class that Yonatan ran so fast, he almost zoomed by without her noticing. Yonatan wore a new T-shirt that said ALL IN on the front and DENVER SOUTH DISTANCE on the back. My son also ran cross-country, as it happened. One day, when they both had a meet in Colorado Springs, my son ran the 5K in twenty minutes, and placed 103rd overall (not bad for a freshman). Yonatan ran the same race in sixteen minutes and placed 3rd. I told Yonatan this, and he joshed about the fact that he had placed exactly 100 runners ahead of my son. "Miss, you tell him, 'Good job,'" Yonatan instructed me. "'Next time: Run faster!'"

Floating around the 2A classroom was Christina, the young woman from Burma who had served as my interpreter with Hsar Htoo. I had stumbled across Christina on the first day of school, looking professional in a sheath dress and a blazer. She had brandished a plastic ID badge that she wore around her neck daily and declared proudly, "I'm working here now!" Back when Christina had entered the high school as a freshman, she had been placed into the classroom of an energetic young ELA teacher named Jen Hanson. One of Ms. Hanson's first acts as principal had been to hire additional paraprofessionals who spoke a variety of languages commonly used in the building, including her former student Christina, who spoke Karen, Thai, and Burmese. Whenever Kaee Reh had a question about what Ms. Hijazi was saying, he consulted with Christina in Burmese. It was the first time in Kaee Reh's career at South that he had a staff person with whom he could communicate easily in his ELA classroom.

Christina also spent a fair amount of time teasing Lisbeth.

One day, when Nadia began translating for Lisbeth again, Christina walked over and said, "Lisbeth! Speak English!"

"I have nerves when I speak English," Lisbeth told her, in nearly perfect English.

"That's because you don't speak English enough!" Christina chastised affectionately.

Because her class was so large, Ms. Hijazi had a second paraprofessional, a woman from Somalia named Fatuma. She wore floor-length dresses and a hijab every day, even when the classrooms were sweltering.

After fleeing from war in Somalia, Fatuma had grown up primarily in Dadaab, Kenya, the largest refugee camp in the world. An older sister was still living there, although Fatuma was hoping that her sister might join her in the United States soon. While Christina helped various students from Southeast Asia, Fatuma went around the room helping students from all over Africa and the Middle East.

A few weeks after the start of school, Ms. Hijazi asked her thirty-three students in 2A to take out their journals and write in response to the question, "What would you do if you could fly?" A boy from the Congo wrote that he would fly back to the Congo, and a boy from Iraq wrote that he would fly back to Iraq. Lisbeth surreptitiously took out her phone and tucked it into an outer pocket of her backpack, so that she could consult Google Translate clandestinely. In Ms. Hijazi's room, the use of cell phones was strictly forbidden, even for translation, so Lisbeth searched secretly for the English words she needed to say that she wanted to fly back to El Salvador to see her beloved *abuela*.

Yonatan was also struggling to come up with the right word for wherever it was that he wanted to fly, but it was not home. He wanted to go to *allyrium*.

"Is it a place in Eritrea?" I asked.

"No!" said Yonatan, looking slightly scandalized.

"Is it in Africa?"

"No! It's in the sky."

"Is it a real place?"

"It is God place."

"Oh, *heaven*," I told him. "We say, heaven. H-e-a-v-e-n."

The one other student who chose an alternative destination was a girl wearing jeans, an orange hijab, and a T-shirt with a Superman emblem. "I would fly to Germany, because my best friend is there," she told Ms. Hijazi.

Over the ensuing weeks, the students in 2A read a series of short stories, and Ms. Hijazi went over basic academic terms she thought they should know, such as "Literature. Say it! Lit-er-a-ture!" Soon Lisbeth and Nadia and all the students could answer Ms. Hijazi's questions about words such as conflict, protagonist, antagonist, synonym, antonym, characterization, plot, and setting. Many of the words were easy for Lisbeth to grasp, because in Spanish they had near perfect cognates, such as *narrador*, *protagonista*, and *sinónimo*, but she got stuck sometimes with the words that did not have a close twin. One day, while I was sitting behind Lisbeth, she arched over backward to put the top of her head onto my desk so that I was looking at her face upside down, then she stuck out her tongue. After that, she conceded she had no idea what "plot" signified. I told her it was a series of dramatic events. "For example, your mom was a police officer who arrested some gang members, and they threatened to kill her, so she had to move to the United States," I said to her in Spanish. "Then you were threatened and you had to move here, too. That's the plot of your story."

"Okay!" said Lisbeth, nodding happily—now she understood plot.

In the mornings, Ms. Hijazi taught ELA 2B to a smaller group. That was where I found Methusella, who had skipped over 1A, 1B, and 2A. In January, when he would finish 2B (each upper-level ELA section lasted for one semester), Methusella would exit the school's English Language Acquisition program and enter a mainstream English class, where he would tackle assignments on a par with his native-born peers. Ksanet and Amaniel had also tested into Ms. Hijazi's 2B class. During the first week of school, Ms. Hijazi showed her students a photograph of a polar bear in a comical stance and asked them to write a paragraph about the animal. Methusella, wearing blue jeans and a gray T-shirt that said on it MAYBE YOU SHOULD PRACTICE, bent over his paper. He finished before anybody else and handed the sheet to his new teacher.

"Wow," she said in a surprised tone. "This is perfect English."

A few days later, Ms. Hijazi asked her students to write about a happy memory. Methusella wrote that he was overjoyed to be "living in a peaceful country." When he raced through another writing assignment ahead of everybody else, Ms. Hijazi told him to look in the closet where she kept books and pick something to read. Methusella selected a classic, *My Side of the Mountain*, by Jean Craighead George (a book I had bought for my own son), and then got lost in its pages. Ms. Hijazi told me after class that everything Methusella showed her was written in full sentences, and he spelled every word correctly—a level of competence she almost never saw.

Initially, Methusella, Ksanet, and Amaniel were the only students from Mr. Williams's room who had been placed into Ms. Hijazi's level 2B class, but Solomon soon joined them. He had been placed in level 2A, but Ms. Hijazi thought the work was too easy for him. On Solomon's first day in the higher-level class, he wrote down seven new vocabulary words (ambitious, prodigy, discordant, accusation, expectation, inevitable, reproach) and looked up their meanings. Later that week, Ms. Hijazi remarked on the temperamental differences she saw between the two brothers. She pointed to Solomon and said to me, "Like, the gentlest human being, ever." Of Methusella, she said, "He has an edge! He gets angry!" She spoke with fondness—she liked Methusella's imperious side.

A few days later, Ms. Hijazi described the ideal structure of a basic paragraph (topic sentence, supporting details, closing sentence), then asked everybody to practice what she had described. As she walked around the room, Ms. Hijazi noticed that Solomon had placed a sheet of lined paper on his desk with the three holes on the right, his pen hovering over the back of the page. She turned it over, saying, "Always have the holes on the left side." The teacher made a grimace, as if to say, *The things these kids don't know!*

After they worked on writing paragraphs, Ms. Hijazi told her students to take out their textbooks and open them to a story called "The Moustache," by Robert Cormier.

A talkative kid announced, "I have a mustache!"

"We're really happy for you," Ms. Hijazi said sarcastically.

She showed the students how to take Cornell notes. In the left column, they should list the main idea, the setting, new words. In the right column, they should transcribe an assiduous summary of the story, citing specific evidence for their assertions, along with page numbers. As they went along, Ms. Hijazi grilled the students on the meaning of certain words, such as "obscure." She drew their attention to an abstract illustration.

"Is that a clear picture or an obscure picture?" she demanded.

"Obscure!" chorused the students.

"Oh, I *love* you guys," Ms. Hijazi sang out.

About one month into the school year, the students in 2B began reading *The Absolutely True Diary of a Part-Time Indian*, by Sherman Alexie. *The Absolutely True Diary* resonated for many of the students, because of how closely a reservation resembled a refugee camp. In both situations, large groups of people who were considered foreign by a dominant society were detained inside an enclosure, ostensibly for their own benefit, but in a way that actually seemed to be more about protecting everybody else from those deemed "other." Alexie's sidesplitting yet painful autobiography begins with a description of life on the rez in which the narrator jokes about belonging to the "Black-Eye-of-the-Month Club." Later he describes how good a chicken leg tastes when he has not eaten for eighteen and a half hours. "That's true!" one of Ms. Hijazi's students affirmed, in a tone of recognition.

The narrator recounts what happens after he leaves the reservation to attend a white school—a move analogous to the act of resettling in the developed world. As a result of changing schools, the author loses his original friends, who consider him a traitor; at the white school, he is greeted by a solid wall of racism. Negotiating the two disparate worlds is not easy, and survivor's guilt is a major theme. As serene, blue-skied days gave way to windy, yellow-leaved days, Ms. Hijazi read all of *The Absolutely True Diary* out loud with her 2B class. Most days, she gave the students a writing exercise, then settled her rear end on top of a desk, put her feet on the seat of a chair, slid her reading glasses down to her nose, and asked Methusella where they had left off. He always knew the exact page number. Then they resumed the story of Junior and his battle to feel accepted.

Ms. Hijazi wrote lists of challenging words from the book on poster-sized pieces of paper, which she taped up all around the classroom. Slowly the walls accrued words, until the students were surrounded by multisyllabic vocabulary. At random moments, Ms. Hijazi would quiz them on the significance of a given word. ("What does 'pathetic' mean?" she barked. "Sad!" responded the room.) She also asked them to make a cartoon strip about the book's major events, complete with evidence for every assertion. The students thought the assignment was fun, but she was actually teaching them skills they would need to write an academic paper. Methusella drew a picture of Junior leaving the rez and quoted one of the characters telling Junior: "You're going to find more and more hope the farther and farther you walk away from this sad, sad, sad reservation" (p. 43). As the months flew by, and Methusella sailed into full-fledged intermediate fluency, I found it incredible to see the speed at which he absorbed a more complex English vocabulary.

Across the stairwell in 1B, Noelia Hopkin was handing out envelopes filled with small pieces of colored paper. Each piece of paper displayed a word, which she asked the students to assemble into color-coded sentences. The students in 1B were still in early speech emergence, and Ms. Hopkin was working with them on language control—right where Mr. Williams had left off. The students puzzled happily over the colored words. They became so quiet that I could hear singing coming through the air ducts; somewhere in the building, a choir was performing. At one point, I noticed that Mariam had arranged several pieces of orange paper in the following order: "Was hungry I." That would have been correct sentence structure in Arabic, I pointed out, but in English we say, "I was hungry." Mariam nodded. Her sentence, when she got all of the orange words in the right order, read, "Dad asked me if I was hungry and I said yes."

For the first six weeks of their second school year, Jakleen and Mariam remained present, engaged, and happy. Anytime I saw them—in Ms. Hopkin's room or in the crowded hallways, surrounded by new friends—they appeared lighthearted. Their lives had taken a turn for the better, I thought. During the second half of September, however, Ebtisam simultaneously experienced another spate of trouble. After her car had been stolen the previous spring, Ebtisam had grown fearful about the possible involvement of the part-time security guard. In the middle of the summer, some kind of altercation had taken place between Ebtisam and the man's eleven-year-old son. Ebtisam said she yelled at the boy—nothing else. But the father claimed she had pushed his son off a bicycle, causing the boy to scrape his elbow. Although the boy's injuries were slight, the father pressed charges. As a result, Ebtisam faced allegations of assault and "wrongs to minors." Then Ebtisam received an eviction notice, because the manager of the apartment complex heard that she had assaulted a child. "Every day brings a new problem," Ebtisam said dejectedly. "I don't know what happened to me in this country."

Whitney Haruf from Lutheran intervened with the manager of the apartment complex, arguing that Ebtisam had not been convicted of a crime and pointing out that the child in question showed no sign of serious injury. The manager relented, allowing her to remain in the apartment. After that, Ebtisam had to take a day off work to appear at her arraignment at the plush new downtown courthouse. I found her sitting on a blond wood bench near a picture window, just outside the courtroom, chewing the inside of her cheek. She was dressed like a teenager, in jeans and a purple jacket; Mark from New Life Community Church sat nearby. As it turned out, Ebtisam could not enter a plea, because the court had neglected to provide an interpreter. The judge reacted with impatience, as though Ebtisam had failed to mention this would be necessary (in fact Whitney Haruf had made two phone calls to the clerk's office to try to ensure that an interpreter would be provided, to no avail). The judge rescheduled the proceedings, meaning that Ebtisam would have to miss a second day of work.

We rode downstairs in an elevator with a young African-American man wearing a backward baseball hat and a stony expression. Mark tried to offer him a postcard about New Life, but the young man refused to meet his gaze. "Jesus came for everyone," Mark told him. I felt uncomfortable about his proselytizing, as the atmosphere in the elevator grew tense. Yet I admired how Mark kept showing up for Ebtisam, whenever she had a problem, time and time again.

Ebtisam returned to the courtroom a few weeks later to enter a plea of not guilty. As she walked out dispiritedly, I tried to lift her mood by pointing out that none of the cases heard by the judge appeared serious. Another person had been accused of shoplifting a vape pen from a tobacco store, while someone else had been charged with playing a stereo too loudly. Ebtisam could not keep the matter in perspective, however, and as soon as we exited the courtroom, her face crumpled and her shoulders started shaking. It was frightening, having to appear in a formal legal setting. She said unhappily that nothing like this had ever happened to her before.

A few days later, I went over to Lutheran Family Services to speak with Whitney Haruf and found her conferring with her colleague Eh Klo, the woman who had secured the housing voucher for Ebtisam. Eh Klo was wearing a cotton tunic that I recognized as a traditional Karen-style shirt, a marker of her status as a former refugee. Eh Klo asked if I had heard the terrible news: Ebtisam and one or two of her daughters had been in a serious car accident. Eh Klo and Whitney worked with that subsection of refugees who struggled more than others, and every once in a while, they saw this—an awful series of predicaments, piling on top of one another. "Add, add, add, add," said Eh Klo, demonstrating how the problems accrued.

I drove to Denver Health, the city hospital, the following morning. In the pediatric Intensive Care Unit, I found Jakleen wearing a white hospital gown and thick red socks with white rubber zigzags on the soles. She sat in a glider, rocking forward and backward, forward and back. She looked unscathed, but did not greet me. Ebtisam had slept on a chair that pulled out into a bed, and from her shattered expression, I gathered it had been a bad night. Two nurses bustled around, and one of them started feeding Jakleen some yogurt, one spoonful at a time. The nurses were adamantly cheerful. One of them said, "She's taken four bites of yogurt—that's something."

I asked Jakleen how she was feeling. Her eyes slid over me incuriously. Very slowly, she pointed to her collarbone. I told myself maybe she wasn't doing *that* badly, for I could not see a single cut or bruise. Then the two nurses hoisted Jakleen up by her armpits, saying it was time for a shower. She swayed between them and her knees buckled and her head lolled to one side. Both nurses rushed to step closer, so they could sustain more of her weight. Jakleen had a broken clavicle, broken ribs, a broken pelvis, several skull fractures, and a traumatic brain injury.

The primary thing that concerned the medical staff was the bleeding in her brain. They were taking daily CAT scans until her condition stabilized. Due to the broken pelvis, she could not walk properly, and a bad fall could be catastrophic. She would not be safe anywhere but in the ICU for the foreseeable future.

The nurses wrote down essential tasks that Jakleen had to accomplish on a whiteboard ("pee" and "walk a lot"). They strapped a large black belt around her waist and held the belt tightly so that she could not fall and made her walk around the ICU. Jakleen exhibited a strange lurching gait, and I did not know if that was due to the broken bones or the brain injury. Ebtisam never left her side, as Sara, her friend from Saudi Arabia, moved into the apartment at Pine Creek to care for Lulu and Mariam. Meanwhile, Ebtisam fielded a constant stream of phone calls about her rapidly deteriorating finances. At one point, Yasir called; the county had mistakenly terminated her food stamps benefits, and he was trying to get her back onto the roster. Ebtisam wasn't reporting to work, so her income had ceased. And her car was stuck in a lot where it was accruing daily fees, even though it was totaled. She also faced criminal charges of careless driving.

"I want smoke," Ebtisam said at one point.

She wanted to light up as soon as we stepped outdoors, but a sign written in English said there was a $300 fine for smoking on Denver Health property.

"Not here!" I warned.

We walked over to a little park, where several hospital employees stood in a circle, smoking.

"I want go back, Iraq," Ebtisam announced.

What a statement, I thought—that returning to a country blown apart by war might be easier than this. Then I realized maybe she meant go back to prewar Iraq, go back to a time before all the disasters. Ebtisam wore the same kind of red socks as Jakleen, the ones with white zigzags on the bottom, which I read as a gesture of solidarity with her daughter. She wore her sneakers with the heels pushed down, to accommodate the thick socks. On her wrist were two paper hospital bracelets, one neon yellow and the other neon orange. We sat on the grass under some catalpa trees. Ebtisam seemed blasted apart, emotionally.

Two weary-looking veterans arrived, one in a wheelchair, the other pushing a bicycle. The vets carried a large American flag and all their personal belongings. Homeless, probably—probably Vietnam, judging by their age. In one park, the representatives of two wars hunkered down, seeking comfort in nicotine. In each theater, we had been hampered by our inability to comprehend other cultures, especially those involving people of non-European descent. We went to war in places where people spoke languages that were not close to English. We went to war in places where people ordered their sentences differently, generated meaning through tones we could not hear, wrote their letters one after another in the opposite direction from us. I did not believe this was a coincidence. Our inability to comprehend one another lay at the heart of conflict.

Away from the gloom of the ICU, I could see that someone had sewn neat black stitches around one of Ebtisam's eyes. She listed all her problems, one after another, going over the whole litany. She asked if I thought that her apartment might be haunted. Was that why so many bad things had happened? Jakleen had said the accident was her fault. Ebtisam looked at me with a question on her face. I thought she was asking whether I thought she was guilty of causing all those fractures, all that internal bleeding. I told her that I had not witnessed the accident, I did not know if it was her fault. But I had caused a car accident once myself, three decades earlier, and I still felt guilty. I wanted to let her know she was not the only person who had taken a wrong turn and bashed into something hard.

We drove over to her workplace, so that Ebtisam could explain her absence.

"Smiles!" the manager said, when he saw her.

That was her nickname. We described Jakleen's injuries and Ebtisam said she did not know when she might return.

"Get better, help your daughter get better," he told her. "We miss you."

When I asked a representative of the company if I could identify her place of employment, the owners asked that I refrain from doing so. They feared reprisal for giving an American job to a person who spoke Arabic.

For the next month, as I drove to and from the ICU, I tried to absorb the news I was hearing on my car radio. Bunker-busting bombs were being hurled at Aleppo, and the presidential election had tightened, as a series of scandals burst forth like fireworks in the media. Donald Trump might not have paid any income tax for the past twenty years. He had bragged of groping women. Hillary Clinton had misused a private email server for official communications, jeopardizing national security, and FBI director James Comey announced a renewed investigation into the matter. I could not stand what was happening in the ICU, and the news of what was happening in the world at large felt almost as destabilizing.

Nabiha visited Jakleen; afterward, she called me, devastated.

"I forgot my job, I forgot my own family, I feel like she is my daughter," Nabiha said, her voice breaking. "I am so sad, I am just crying. You know—same time interpreter, same time like family."

Yes, I did know. Same time journalist, same time like family. Many days elapsed in which Ebtisam kept watch over Jakleen, and I kept watch over Ebtisam, showing up with coffee or magazines. One day in the ICU, I found Jakleen in bed, rocking her knees from side to side, surrounded by flowers. Ghasem had visited the evening before and brought her a bouquet of daisies, roses, and lilies. She looked the same and yet not the same, because her eyes were empty. I did not know whether this was from her brain injury or the eight different drugs she was taking. Also, Jakleen's memory had holes in odd places.

"Who is Shani?" Jakleen asked. "Yesterday, Ghasem tell me, 'She is your friend.'"

I took out my phone and showed her pictures of Room 142 and said we had spent the last school year together in that space. Jakleen reacted with disbelief. She did not remember that classroom. Nor did she remember most of the students in my photographs—though she did recognize Lisbeth.

"That is Shani," I told her. "She is Mariam's friend, and she is your friend, too."

"I forget Shani," admitted Jakleen ruefully.

I said I liked the way Ghasem's flowers smelled.

"I can't smell," she said.

"Maybe tomorrow," I assured her.

But in truth, I didn't know what would happen tomorrow. Would the holes in her memory fill? Would the dancing intelligence return to her eyes? I could handle the fractures and the funny walk, but I missed the silver-bright knowingness that once animated Jakleen's face. She was suddenly slow and placid, and she had never been either of those things. Strangely, I suspected her of acting. I knew she wasn't, but I had a stubborn feeling of this-isn't-her. I kept hoping that Jakleen's real self would return from hiding. Her prognosis was unclear, the doctors said. Everything depended upon how diligently she worked at her rehabilitation. Jakleen was going to have to work very hard—harder even than she had in Room 142—just to return to the person she had formerly been.

2

What Is Resolution?

What is resolution?" Ms. Hijazi asked her students in 2A.

It was the very last day of October, it was Halloween—that peculiar holiday recent arrivals found so baffling. The newcomers I befriended had spent twelve months living in the United States. Last year, nobody in Room 142 had worn a costume, but this year, both Nadia and Lisbeth dressed up. They were acclimatizing.

During the ten weeks they had spent together in 2A, Nadia and Lisbeth had grown close, and they planned their costumes together. Both looked like Japanese schoolgirls. Nadia wore a white blouse with a short black pleated skirt and black-and-white-striped kneesocks, while Lisbeth displayed florid magenta hair extensions, magenta nail polish, and magenta lipstick, as well as an alarmingly short black minidress with black kneesocks and black tennis shoes. "Anime is, like—*sexy*," Lisbeth boasted in a stage whisper, so Ms. Hijazi wouldn't hear. Ever since Miss Pauline had included that word among the fifty-eight positive emotions one might feel, "sexy" had become one of Lisbeth's favorite terms in English.

I called Lisbeth's costume a *costumbre*, but the Spanish-speaking kids corrected me. No, the correct word was *disfraz*, which means "disguise." *Costumbre* actually means "custom" or "habit." ("*Costumbre*" and "costume" are examples of what linguists call "false cognates" or "false friends," i.e., when words sound like cognates but are not genuinely so.)

Ms. Hijazi did not want the class to be thinking about *disfraces*; she wanted the class to be thinking about resolution.

"How do you think this book will end?" she asked.

The students were reading *Hatchet*, an award-winning young adult novel by Gary Paulsen. *Hatchet* tells the story of a thirteen-year-old boy who finds himself alone in the wilderness after an airplane crash and has to figure out how to get by with only a hatchet. One of the book's themes is the power of positive thinking; the boy learns that the greatest danger he faces is his own despondency. The class talked about how the main character learned from his mistakes. He had made a poor shelter and then he built a better one. He had buried turtle eggs in a shallow grave and a skunk had stolen them, and then he moved his food stores into a crevice in a sheer rock face accessible only by a ladder he fashioned out of dead tree limbs.

Once again, we had reached the time of year when teachers at South caught the brunt of the annual rush, those weeks in late September and early October when refugee resettlement agencies hurried to place large numbers of new arrivals. That year, the Democratic Republic of Congo sent the largest number of refugees to the United States, followed by Syria, Burma, Iraq, and Somalia. As usual, the new arrivals at South reflected national trends. When students from Syria began arriving in greater numbers, they were situated all around the building, depending on their level of English. At the beginning of October, a seventeen-year-old named Marwan had appeared in Ms. Hijazi's 2A room and chosen a seat at the front of the class. Tall and rangy, with movie-star good looks and a fetching black leather jacket, he had an engaging the-world-is-my-friend personality. One day, I caught him asking Mariam for her phone number in a bustling second-floor hallway, much to Mariam's embarrassed delight.

At the end of his first week at South, Ms. Hijazi told the class that they were going to read a short story called "The Necklace" the following week. On Monday, when Ms. Hijazi asked the students to open their textbooks to that story, Marwan announced, "I went to the library this weekend and I read the story already."

Ms. Hijazi stared at him in astonishment. "Well, what the heck are you going to do now?" she said, her tone conveying, underneath the sarcasm, both awe and praise.

"I am prepared!" Marwan responded.

After escaping the wreckage of Damascus, Marwan had spent several years living in Turkey, where he had worked to help support his family and had not been able to attend school. The joy he felt at finding himself back inside a classroom was obvious. A few weeks later, I overheard Marwan ask Ms. Hijazi, "How do I get into AP classes?" Marwan was a superstar—he was the Methusella of 2A. On the day when Nadia and Lisbeth wore their *disfraces*, when the kids were several chapters into *Hatchet*, and the question that Ms. Hijazi wanted them to think about was how this book was going to end, the class paused to go over the meaning of the word "poverty." Ms. Hijazi asked the students to use that word in a sentence. Marwan said astutely, "War leads to poverty."

Indeed, the U.S. invasion of Iraq had impoverished millions, in both that country and in Syria. That day, Marwan happened to be wearing a white dress shirt, navy chinos, and a red-and-white kaffiyeh, and his clothing seemed like a red-white-and-blue statement about dual identity. Because the clangorous presidential election was thundering into its final weeks, I could not help but think, as I sat in the back of the classroom, Oh, America, land of the brave, here is the Syrian refugee of whom you've been so afraid, and he is nothing more than a kid who goes to the library on the weekend so that he can prepare for class.

Ms. Hijazi brought the subject back to resolution, back to how the story might end. Marwan wanted to address this matter, but he had been speaking a lot. Ms. Hijazi growled at him—literally, made a *grrrrr* sound. Marwan flashed an I-can't-believe-my-teacher-is-growling-at-me face at his teacher. Ms. Hijazi flicked a hand in his direction. "Somebody *else* talk, *please!*"

Another student said the resolution of *Hatchet* would probably have something to do with the main character feeling safe. The class concurred; they decided *Hatchet* would end when the reader knew for sure that the protagonist was going to make it out of the wilderness alive. Then Ms. Hijazi said something about handing in an assignment on Friday. Kids chorused, "Miss! No school! Miss, no school on Friday!"

"Really?" said Ms. Hijazi, puzzled. "Why not?"

"You have the day off from teaching," Marwan told her, "because you have parent-teacher conferences from three to seven P.M. that day."

Ms. Hijazi swung around to stare, rather imperiously, at the brand-new, terribly good-looking Syrian.

"How do you know *everything?*" she marveled. "I mean, seriously! *How?* Didn't you just get here, like, *last week?*"

Across the stairwell, in Ms. Hopkin's 1B class, everybody was missing Jakleen. Students were asking when she might return, and teachers wanted updates, too. One day, while I was giving Ms. Hopkin the latest news from the hospital, I noticed Grace standing stock-still two feet away, wearing a peach-colored minidress, holding open the door to the room where 1B met. She was pretending to be a peach-colored statue. Realizing that Grace was eavesdropping, the teacher said, "Sugar, *please*, would you get inside the classroom?"

Jakleen had moved recently to Children's Hospital, where she was in acute rehab. Physical therapists were helping her regain the ability to walk and to write. All her injuries were on the right side of her body, and she was right-handed; at first she had not been able to hold a pen, but within a short time she progressed to the point where she could write three sentences. She still listed when she walked, but no longer needed the big black belt or the two nurses. Her fifteen-year-old body was healing at an astonishing pace, but the big question remained what effect the traumatic brain injury might have on her mind. In speech therapy, hospital staff activated her brain with various tasks and then insisted that she put down her phone and turn off the TV and do nothing but let her mind rest. Alternating periods of mental activity with periods of total rest was the latest technique for healing the brain.

I visited again and found Ebtisam depleted. It had been twenty-one days since the car accident, and she had not slept in her own bed once. That evening, I drove Ebtisam home, so that she could spend the night at Pine Creek. She found it hard to separate from Jakleen, and we did not make it past the nurses' station without Ebtisam pausing to ask a nurse if she would sleep on the pull-out bed in Jakleen's room. The nurse explained there were many patients on the ward, and she could not devote herself entirely to Jakleen. But her daughter would be well cared for, she assured Ebtisam.

The following weekend, Mariam stayed at the hospital in her mother's place, and the sisters acted like kids having a sleepover party. The next week, Lisbeth visited, then Ghasem and Shani. Afterward, Jakleen announced to me, with great feeling, "I love Ghasem." The young man from Afghanistan had been courting Jakleen with ardor for months, and in all that time he had been unwavering. I admired him for working two jobs so that he could help support his mother even as he went to school full-time. Ghasem was compelling. Before the accident, Jakleen had kept Ghasem at a distance, but now, in her impaired state, she wanted to pull the boy close. I worried whether her feelings would endure, or wane as she healed. Clearly the idea of being in love was an enjoyable distraction, however, for we talked about Ghasem for quite a while. Then we leafed through some magazines that I had brought, looking at pictures of clothes, makeup, recipes.

"I want go home," Jakleen said.

"I bet you do," I said.

The following week, Ebtisam called: Jakleen had been released from the hospital. Despite the severity of her injuries, the doctors wanted her to return to school, because it was critical she activate her brain. Ebtisam had no car, no money, and no job (she had quit the factory job so that she could care for Jakleen). She also faced two pending jury trials, one about the alleged assault on her neighbor's child and one about the car accident. Ebtisam could not drive Jakleen herself and did not want to put her daughter on a city bus, which would have involved walking three-quarters of a mile to the bus stop, with all those still-healing bone fractures. I heard myself say, "Well, I'm headed to South now. If you want, I could come and pick her up."

It was a leaf-spinning, windy day with no clouds and the trees ablaze with color. Jakleen applied her cat-eyed makeup and ironed her hair straight. She put on skinny jeans, a black sweater with a large gold zipper down the front, and black suede moccasins, and when she finished she looked more like her old self than she had for weeks. At South, we were told to see the school nurse. The nurse's office was located on the same hallway as Mr. Williams's old classroom, just a few doors away. The nurse, José Espinosa-Santiago, was a chatty ex-Marine in camo scrubs. He knew all about head injuries. He had been expecting Jakleen—he had already spoken with her doctors. The nurse got up from behind his desk and walked around to sit down next to Jakleen. He went over all the negative symptoms she might experience and said if she felt any of those things, she should see him right away. "We are going to take care of you like you are a baby," he crooned.

Upstairs, Ms. Hopkin was conducting a writing assessment. When Jakleen walked tentatively into the room, she cried, "You're back!" in a tone of clear delight. The windows were open and the wind made a shushing sound like the ocean as it moved through the trees outside. Jakleen set to work immediately, writing sentence after sentence. Mariam, who sat beside her, could not think of anything to write in English. Then I saw Mariam lean over, peek at her sister's work, and copy down every word that Jakleen had written. I had been afraid it would be the other way around—that Jakleen would have to rely on Mariam—but the familiar setting of the classroom had brought back half-forgotten habits. I understood then why the doctors wanted to get Jakleen back to school so quickly, for as soon as she returned to South, the high school setting called up dormant aspects of her old self. Being back at school transformed her into a student again.

Abruptly, Jakleen was exhausted. All the sparkle left her face, she closed her eyes, and she laid her head down on the desk. The 1B class met for two full periods, and she had intended to stay for both, but when the bell rang marking the midway point, Jakleen asked groggily if I would take her back home.

The following day, however, Jakleen successfully spent two full periods in Ms. Hopkin's room. The nurse conferred with her doctors, and the following week they upped her schedule from two periods a day to four. The medical personnel marveled at the speed of Jakleen's recuperation. At one point, the nurse said, "She is healing very, very fast. I've seen people take a full year to get where she is right now."

At the same time, Jakleen remained fragile, and it was hard for her friends to comprehend this. She had no casts, no scars, and no stitches, and she always arranged her beauty with care, so there was no outward sign of the collision.

One day, Jakleen and Mariam were walking down the hall on their way to see the nurse when they passed by Shani, standing in front of her locker. When the girl from Tajikistan saw Jakleen, her face fell.

"No remember," Shani said in a sad voice.

"You are Shani!" Jakleen told her, with that knowing, amused look.

Shani threw herself at Jakleen and began rocking her back and forth exuberantly. Mariam exclaimed, "Shani! Be careful!"

Even Ghasem had no idea how badly Jakleen had been hurt. One day, I tried to enumerate her injuries by pointing to corresponding parts of my body as I spoke, in case his English wasn't good enough to follow along. "She has a fractured skull," I said while pointing to my head, "and broken bones here" (pointing to my clavicle), "and here" (my ribs), "and here" (my pelvis). "Also, bleeding in the brain" (pointing to my head again).

"Bleeding in the brain?" he said, to double-check.

"Yes."

"I didn't know," Ghasem said in an unsteady voice. "Nobody told me. Jakleen, her English isn't good enough to explain. She just point to here" (he gestured to his collarbone) "and here" (his rib cage), "but I didn't know about the rest."

One afternoon that week, Mariam and Jakleen and I visited the nurse again. Ghasem, Rahim, and Shani converged on us in the hallway beside the nurse's office. Rahim bent over a water fountain, as Ghasem glued himself to Jakleen's side. I glanced over at the door to Room 142, where we had spent so much time talking about *qalb*. The nurse emerged from his office and surveyed the boisterous group animating the hallway. Clearly, they'd been friends for a while.

"You all speak the same language?" he asked curiously.

"Well, these two are sisters." I pointed to Mariam and Jakleen.

"Yeah, you speak the same language," teased the nurse.

"And these two are in love," I added, pointing to Ghasem and Jakleen. "*Aha!*" the nurse exclaimed.

Ghasem wore a possessive look, while Jakleen appeared more vulnerable. Maybe she was wondering exactly how far to take this experiment. Ghasem approached to negotiate which of us would get to take Jakleen home.

"I can give her a ride," Ghasem announced, full of fiery pride at having both a girlfriend and a car.

"Her mom said you drive too fast," I countered.

"I don't drive fast!" he objected.

Ghasem glowered at me. Then he phoned Ebtisam and reported that she had given permission for him to drive her daughter home. Jakleen wanted to go with him, that much was clear. I thought it might do her some good, after so much adult supervision. The nurse seemed to feel the same way, but before he let Jakleen get into Ghasem's car, he got a little parental.

"You have a license?" José asked Ghasem.

Ghasem withdrew his license and thrust it at the nurse.

"Car insurance?" asked the nurse.

"Yes!"

"It's not expired?"

"No!"

"Drive *slowly*," instructed the nurse. "Don't stop like this"—he jerked his body forward and then back. "Because she can't sustain any impact, okay?"

"Okay," said Ghasem.

And then we let them go. They had seen so much already, between the pair of them—the war in Afghanistan, the war in Iraq, and the Syrian civil war. Making a new home in the United States had proved exceedingly difficult for Jakleen, which seemed terribly unfair after everything she and her family had endured already, but I hoped she had put the hardest part of the transition behind her. The two young lovers set off into the unsupervised afternoon, visibly more carefree, delighted with their liberty. They would make their own way forward from here on.

A few weeks later, Ebtisam stood trial on the charges of assault and endangering the well-being of a minor. Back in the plush courtroom, she huddled into an olive-green winter coat throughout the proceedings, as though seeking protection. Ebtisam had depleted herself while nursing Jakleen back to health, and she was too fragile to take the stand; she chose not to testify on her own behalf. The security guard with whom she had difficulties turned out to be a barrel-chested man with black hair and a receding hairline. He walked across the courtroom with a swagger, as though he owned the place. I felt put off by his manner. Perhaps members of the jury felt the same way; after deliberating for less than an hour, they returned with a verdict of not guilty on all counts. Ebtisam's worried face broke into sunny relief. She could not stop smiling. "America, very good country!" she told me, as we walked out of the courtroom.

Shortly after that, Eh Klo helped Ebtisam secure a new apartment through Section 8 housing. This allowed her to devote her time to chauferring Jakleen to her frequent medical appointments. After leaving her job, she also went back onto TANF. Because Jakleen qualified for Medicaid, her hospital bills were subsidized. Out of all the refugee families who had been represented in Room 142, Ebtisam was the only parent I knew of who was not working. As soon as Jakleen's medical situation resolved, however, Ebtisam hoped to move off TANF; the maximum amount of time she would be allowed to remain in that program would be five years. By then, one or more of her daughters would probably be working, and with multiple incomes it was easy to envision the family achieving self-sufficiency in the long run.

Mr. Williams had welcomed two dozen students during the prior year, and the bulk of them were sailing along in their second year of instruction. When I returned to Ms. Hijazi's morning class, to see how the students in 2B were faring, I found them discussing *The Absolutely True Diary of a Part-Time Indian.*

"What is hope?" Ms. Hijazi asked.

"Like, you hope your country gets better," said a student from Iraq.

"Yes," said Ms. Hijazi. "I hope you all go to college. Who's going to college?"

Only one boy raised his hand. I felt surprised to see that neither Solomon nor Methusella raised his. Apparently so did Ms. Hijazi, for she demanded, "You! Solomon! Are you going to college?"

"Yeah," he said very quietly, without much conviction.

I asked Methusella why he didn't raise his hand.

"I know that I am going," he replied in his imperious tone.

Ms. Hijazi asked the students to take out their journals and dictated the following assignment: "How do lowered expectations and feelings of hopelessness affect people? Explain." For several minutes the room was entirely soundless, as the students bent over their desks to write. Ms. Hijazi took attendance, noting that everyone was present except Ksanet. Level 2B had been challenging for the older-than-everybody-else Eritrean student, but she had never missed a class. Fatuma, the paraprofessional from Somalia, called out to report that Ksanet had just withdrawn from South. When I wrote to her on Facebook, she confirmed this was true. She had moved to Utah because a friend had told her that although she was now twenty, there was a high school there that would allow her to earn a degree before she turned twenty-one, and aged out of public education. Her younger brother Yonatan remained in Ms. Hijazi's 2A class, but Ksanet never returned to 2B, because at South she had felt demoralized.

She wrote to me on Facebook:

> Miss I miss you so so much guys especially miss hjazi class. Please say hiii for all my classmate and miss hjazi . . .
>
> I just decided to came hear becuse my age like if I stay there I can't graduate that's way I came hear miss thank you very much for everything
>
> I know my english is bad, but I hope it will be fine for you miss becuse you know me like my English is limited

In her admittedly imperfect sentences, I could hear both the loneliness of Utah and the despair she had felt at South after being told she couldn't move forward quickly enough to finish school. Ksanet had a habit of tilting her chin up as she spoke, which gave her a look of stubborn, angry determination. I thought her life would have been easier if she had remained in Colorado, where she had friends and family, but I also thought her implacable drive would take her far, wherever she lived.

After the students wrote in their journals for a while about hopelessness, Ms. Hijazi held a more extended conversation about college.

She said this question of harboring hope or despair did not apply only to Junior in *The Absolutely True Diary*. They should look at their own aspirations. She wanted her students to aim high; she wanted them to take full advantage of the opportunity they'd been given. It turned out the entire room believed college out of reach, because of the expense. Ms. Hijazi pointed out that higher education was virtually free for students from low-income families. This appeared to be news to every student in the room—in fact, some looked dubious. But Ms. Hijazi insisted they *could* go to college, and by the end of the class, she had half of them convinced. I had no trouble believing in a future that included college degrees for Solomon and Methusella. Other newcomers who had shown a similar capacity for growth had made the leap to higher education. That fall, Kimleng—the former newcomer who had once served in the Student Senate—had enrolled at the University of Colorado in Denver. I believed the two boys from the Congo would follow in his footsteps.

For the rest of the semester, Ms. Hijazi continued to berate, sweet-talk, and interrogate the teenagers in 2B into doing their utmost. Right after it snowed for the first time, when one of the students kept forgetting to employ the past tense, Ms. Hijazi exclaimed, "Agghhh! I'm going to start doing bad things to you, like throwing you out the window! And the snow is soft, so you won't die!"

She kept going over new words, too. One day, she asked her students to define the following list of new vocabulary: spontaneous, susceptible, decrepit, mutilated, translucent, eccentric, scintillating, souvenir, and ecstatic.

"What does 'eccentric' mean?" quizzed Ms. Hijazi.

"Weird!" chorused the class.

"What is 'scintillating'?"

"Exciting!"

And that's what it was, to see the words that Ms. Hijazi wanted her students to grasp. When I had first met the two brothers from the Congo, my own expectations for them had not included such spectacular progress; they had far surpassed what I imagined possible. As Ms. Hijazi told them to form sentences using their new words, I watched Solomon write careful, well-constructed phrases, while his younger brother effortlessly scrawled sentences that were more playful.

"My teacher is eccentric," wrote Methusella, to the amusement of Ms. Hijazi.

She squeezed him by the elbow, and then said fondly, "This one is amazing."

During the same time frame, I happened to meet a man from Africa named Francis Gatare, a charming, well-spoken, exuberant forty-nine-year-old who served as a cabinet member under Paul Kagame, the president of Rwanda. He was visiting Colorado and coincidentally we attended the same dinner party. We chatted a bit and then I mentioned having recently visited the Kyangwali refugee settlement.

"Oh, I grew up there," Gatare said.

During his high school years, he had won a scholarship to attend a boarding school in Hoima. He used to walk to that city from the settlement; the distance was forty-seven miles, and walking there took several days. Paul Kagame had grown up at Kyangwali, too. The settlement had been founded by refugees who had fled Rwanda in the 1960s, and now those former refugees were leading Rwanda. That two men so influential in the remaking of Rwanda had both started out as refugees in the very settlement I had visited made me revise yet again my already sky-high expectations of what Solomon and Methusella might achieve. Someday, a new generation would try to repair the damage that had been done to the Democratic Republic of Congo, and I would not be surprised if individuals who had grown up in Kyangwali turned out to lead that future renaissance. If, despite the odds, they managed to get an education.

On November 8, 2016, the day of the presidential election, I returned to South to visit the Student Senate, figuring that if anybody would be discussing politics that day, it would be those civic-minded students. When I visited the Senate, I saw Methusella wearing the same uncertain expression that I remembered from his early days in Room 142. The American-born students chatted effortlessly about matters that he found inexplicable—things they called hat day, twin day, pajama day. Or the allure of dodgeball and Pop-Tarts. Methusella remained mute, as if he had returned to the silent receptive phase of learning. Eventually, he would find his voice in this room, but it had not happened yet.

In honor of Election Day, the Senate held a mock debate. The student who played Donald Trump spoke passionately about creating jobs, while the student who impersonated Hillary Clinton argued woodenly that she had a nice résumé. It was an apt parody of the past year and a half. The majority of students at South were ardent Clinton supporters, however, and they could not stomach the idea of Trump winning the election, so they voted instead to have "no president." The atmosphere in the room was jolly, but that was before the actual election results were tallied. Several million people who had voted Democratic in the previous election cycle stayed home and did not cast ballots, and many were African American or Latino. Meanwhile, 80 percent of white evangelical voters cast votes for Trump—that bloc went for Trump by a higher margin than for any other candidate in a decade. Turnout spiked in rural counties and dropped in large cities. This combination of trends handed Trump a narrow upset victory, secured in the electoral college, stunning everyone at South High School.

I found it hard to absorb the outcome myself, so unlikely had it seemed. My first instinct was to give Trump a chance. I wanted to see if he could rejuvenate parts of the American economy that had been stagnating and bring jobs back to places where employment was sorely needed. Right after the election, however, a series of incidents took place on the city buses that South High students rode to and from school. Trump's election had created a distinctly unfriendly climate for the very kids I cared so much about. Some students were called "dirty," while others were told to "go home." A student wearing a hijab was denied admittance to a city vehicle by a bus driver who said she "looked like ISIS." Another girl was told by a fellow passenger, "We are going to kick your ass out of this country." There were many cases of mistaken identity. One girl was told by another commuter that she should "go back to Mexico." Someone else intervened to say the girl being addressed was actually Arab, and then she was called "a terrorist." In fact, the girl was Bangladeshi.

The faculty at South did everything they could to help their charges grapple with this unleashing of vitriol upon the foreign-born part of the student body. The number of kids who sought counseling reached levels that nobody had ever seen before, and two students attempted suicide. Jen Hanson hired nine temporary counselors to augment her existing staff. "That was probably the hardest week I've ever experienced in a school in seventeen years," she said afterward.

Hanson had grown up in a small town in Illinois. She believed that her own parents had voted for Donald Trump. She said her parents rarely traveled outside Illinois and had not been exposed much to other cultures. Once, when Hanson had been an ELA teacher herself, she had overheard her mother tell a friend, "Jenny teaches language-disabled kids." Hanson did not think the kids she taught were "disabled," but that's how they appeared to her mother. "They are never around people who are not just exactly like them," said Hanson. "Ever."

The new principal led an institution that depended upon the steady inflow of refugees for its collective identity. What impact was the election going to have on the future of South? On every front, in terms of the big questions facing the students I had gotten to know, Donald Trump represented the opposite of resolution. Lisbeth and Saúl, for example, longed to receive the blessing of a federal judge to remain in the United States. With Trump as president, however, the outcome of their cases suddenly seemed far less certain. Shortly before the election, both Lisbeth and Saúl had been granted a second reprieve by the same federal judge, and they were not due to appear before the court again until after the conclusion of their sophomore year. What would happen at that point was suddenly completely unclear to their lawyers, however, as laws pertaining to immigrants, refugees, and asylum seekers were now in flux. The lawyer who represented Lisbeth, Alejandra Acevedo, viewed the outgoing student as a younger version of herself, and she was encouraging Lisbeth to consider a career in law. Before the election, Acevedo had felt confident that Lisbeth had a good legal argument for remaining in the United States, but Trump instigated so many changes with a flurry of confusing executive orders, tweets, and off-the-cuff statements that the outcome of Lisbeth's case was now impossible to predict. "Here is somebody who has the potential to be an amazing leader," Acevedo said, "and we don't know what's going to happen to her."

In the school's refugee community, those who had already resettled had the security of knowing that their existing visas were not likely to be revoked. But families divided by the world's conflict who longed to be reunited suddenly faced much greater uncertainty. When I had first met Fatuma, the paraprofessional from Somalia who helped out in Ms. Hijazi's 2A class, it had been hard for me to see past her floor-length dresses and long-sleeved cardigans and the omnipresent head scarves, because her studiously modest attire struck me as alien. Over time, however, I grew used to her style of dress and stopped noticing it. Instead I became aware of how much Fatuma knew about what was going on with the students in her care.

In January 2017, Fatuma had been expecting to welcome her older sister to the United States. Her sister had been scheduled to board an airplane in Nairobi three days after Trump's initial executive order banning refugees and immigrants from Muslim-dominant nations went into effect. Fatuma's sister had been living in Dadaab for a quarter of a century, and after an extensive, multiyear vetting process, including interviews with representatives from both the United Nations and the U.S. Citizenship and Immigration Services, she had been cleared to leave the refugee camp and resettle alongside the rest of her family in the United States. Because she was originally from Somalia, however—one of the banned countries—she was not allowed to board her plane. Instead, she was rebuffed and sent back to Dadaab. Fatuma was stoic on the outside and heartbroken on the inside. "I'm still hoping for the best," she told me.

Staff members at resettlement agencies such as the African Community Center and Lutheran Family Services were flabbergasted by Trump's stance. The idea that terrorists would choose to camouflage themselves as refugees made little sense to aid workers, because there was no more onerous path into the United States. Refugees were subjected to a process that often lasted for as long as a decade, with slim odds of success—less than 1 percent of those with refugee status were chosen to resettle. Meanwhile, the refugees had to subsist on rations that barely constituted a livable diet. The idea that anybody would deem this an easy route by which to gain admittance to the United States was hard to fathom for someone like Ebtisam's case worker, Yasir Abdulah, who had gone through the arduous process himself. Trump's actions also struck people like Yasir as wildly ahistorical, for if there was any part of the global crisis that the United States owned, it was the chaos that was unfolding in the Middle East. The United States had not played a direct role in the ethnic cleansing that had taken place in Southeast Asia, or the wars that had broken out across Africa. But the United States was directly responsible for the chain of events that led to the destruction of Iraq and the related dissolution of Syria. If there were any refugees this country might have felt a moral obligation to accept, it would be people from some of the very countries listed in the ban.

Over at the African Community Center, frustrated staff members, including Troy Cox, confronted something they had almost never seen: an empty bulletin board—no more Arrivals Notifications. Trump had suspended the entire refugee resettlement program for 120 days and capped the number of refugees that would be admitted that year at 50,000, instead of the 110,000 goal set by the Obama administration. The emotional torque of the empty bulletin board was hard to bear, for the staff at the ACC had never felt a greater sense of urgency about their work, and at the same time had never been given so few people to resettle. The world was asking the United States to do more, and Trump wanted to do less, and Troy Cox could hardly stand it. The election created a lack of resolution for everybody working in refugee resettlement—people who felt their work to be a genuine calling and were grief-stricken by the actions of the newly elected president.

If there was any hope of boosting the number of refugees admitted into the United States in the future, it seemed likely that parishioners of churches such as New Life would play a role. Many evangelicals believed the Bible stated clearly that the task of a Christian was to welcome the stranger. Given that evangelicals had voted for Trump in such large numbers, I believed that if anybody could sway the new administration, it was going to be leaders of the evangelical movement.

When I dropped by Mr. Williams's new classroom one last time, I saw that he was having a tough year. He expressed nostalgia for the days when he had wondered at the progress of Methusella, and worried about the well-being of Jakleen. His current cadre included several boys who presented behavior problems. There had even been one actual fistfight. Mr. Williams had taped a new poster to the wall. It said:

BEHAVIOR CONSEQUENCES (CONSEQUENCIAS DEL MAL COMPARTIMIENTO)
1. First warning.
2. This is your final warning. If you continue to disrupt the class, then you will need to sit outside in the hallway.
3. Dean's Office (officina del director).

Mr. Williams remained philosophical, however, even about the obstreperous boys and the letdown of an election. He was disappointed the country had voted into office a leader who did not appreciate the value of his life's work, but he viewed every obstacle as an opportunity to improve, and that's what he was focused on—becoming a better teacher. He had nothing bad to say about Trump; he simply reported that the outcome of the contest had made him want to pour himself into the classroom with redoubled force. "It gives me solace, working with the kids," he said. I knew what he meant, for I felt buoyed up every time I returned to South. A few hours with students struggling to learn English served as a reliable tonic; as soon as I stepped inside an ELA classroom, I could imagine a completely different future ahead. What was happening around the globe, which was invariably reflected at South, called for us to redouble our efforts, called for us not to let ourselves be defined by the last election. At least while I was at the school, I could envision what it would be like for the United States to realize its true potential—for my country to become what the world needed it to be.

As Mr. Williams and I were speaking, we were interrupted by Lisbeth, who dropped by to visit her old teacher. She hung in his doorway, her hands on the doorjamb, her feet out in the hall, and her face peeking inside the room.

"Hi, Mister!" cried Lisbeth.

"Hi, Lisbeth," Mr. Williams said warmly.

She had become one of those former students who liked to visit, so that she could remember the sense of security she had felt in his presence.

"Do you miss Mr. Williams?" I asked Lisbeth.

"*So much!*" she said dramatically.

"Lisbeth! When are you coming back to newcomer class?" Mr. Williams teased.

"Right now!" sang Lisbeth.

And then she danced out of view. She had not used a single word of Spanish during the entire exchange, even though Mr. Williams and I both knew that language. Mr. Williams had done his job, despite everything—despite the traumas the kids had lived through, despite the tumultuous political backdrop, despite Lisbeth's incessant socializing and Methusella's tremendous need to be challenged and the days when Jakleen and Mariam had hunkered down at home with their cell phones instead of showing up at school. He had taught them all English.

There were several quotations near the school's front door, and as I walked out of the building, I noticed another one: BEFORE SCIENCE THE BARRIERS OF FEAR AND SUPERSTITION VANISH AND THE MYSTERIES OF THE UNIVERSE UNFOLD. That's what I took away from the year and a half that I spent at South High School. Meeting people whose life trajectories were so different from my own enlarged my way of thinking. Outside the school, arguments over refugees were raging, but the time I had spent inside this building showed me that those conversations were based on phantasms. People were debating their own fears. What I had witnessed taking place inside this school every day revealed the rhetoric for what it was: more propaganda than fact. Donald Trump appeared to believe his own assertions, but I hoped that in the years to come, more people would be able to recognize refugees for who they really were— simply the most vulnerable people on earth.

Inside this school, where the reality of refugee resettlement was enacted every day, it was plain to see that seeking a new home took tremendous courage, and receiving those who had been displaced involved tremendous generosity. That's what refugee resettlement was, I decided: acts of courage met by acts of generosity. Despite how fear-based the national conversation had turned, there was nothing scary about what was happening at South. Getting to know the newcomer students had deepened my own life, and watching Mr. Williams work with all twenty-two of them at once with so much grace, dexterity, sensitivity, and affection had provided me with daily inspiration. I would even say that spending a year in Room 142 had allowed me to witness something as close to holy as I've seen take place between human beings. I could only wish that in time, more people would be able to look past their fear of the stranger and experience the wonder of getting to know people from other parts of the globe. For as far as I could tell, the world was not going to stop producing refugees. The plain, irreducible fact of good people being made nomad by the millions through all the kinds of horror this world could produce seemed likely to prove the central moral challenge of our times. How did we want to meet that challenge? We could fill our hearts with fear or with hope. And the choice would affect more than just our own dispositions, for in choosing which seeds to sow, we would dictate the type of harvest. Surely the only harvest worth cultivating was the one Mr. Williams had been seeking: greater fluency, better understanding.

Afterword

In his first year in office, Donald Trump spewed a blizzard of executive orders, travel bans, pronouncements, rants, and tweets riddled with WORDS IN ALL CAPS on the subject of immigration. Even seasoned attorneys who had spent decades working in that field were knocked sideways by the proposed pace of change, inconsistent leadership style, and moody temperament of the White House's latest occupant. In quick succession, Trump pronounced he wanted to stem most kinds of immigration, stop asylum seekers, turn back unaccompanied minors, end deferred action for undocumented students, and cap refugee resettlement, though at times he also said totally contradictory things, such as that he wanted to continue deferred action for students. He accomplished little on the legislative front, but through executive orders he did upend the nation's refugee resettlement program almost completely.

At the same time, further upheavals took place in some of the hot spots that had been producing the largest numbers of refugees. In Burma (now more often called Myanmar), three-quarters of a million Rohingya streamed out of their home villages and stumbled into Thailand, weary, starving, and bloodstained, where they confided to aid workers devastating stories about what they had endured at the hands of the Burmese. In the Democratic Republic of Congo, rebel groups clashed with government troops on the eastern side of that country, and more than two million people fled their home villages, spilling by the thousands into neighboring safe havens such as Uganda. More than half of the newly uprooted Congolese came from North Kivu. "The growing insecurity and logistical challenges have made camps for the displaced largely inaccessible to aid organizations," wrote the *Guardian*, a British outlet that covered the crisis. "Médecins Sans Frontières, one of the few international NGOs working in the area, is struggling to respond to a wave of sexual violence that has accompanied the renewed fighting."

Syria continued to unravel, and Venezuela fell apart. Its citizens began starving, sending thousands of hungry asylum seekers across its borders into surrounding countries. Meanwhile, Trump seemed eager to charge into any available conflict. This left many people concerned that he might start a new war that would only create yet another stream of refugees. I thought we should be doing more, in terms of helping the existing refugees who had already been displaced, before instigating some additional catastrophe, but the appointees now running the United States program felt determined that we should do less. After capping the number of refugees that the United States would accept at 45,000 per year (less than half as many as planned under the Obama administration), the Trump team then slowed admissions down to such an extent that it accepted even fewer refugees than its goal. During all of 2017, the United States took in only 33,000 refugees, just one-third of the number it had resettled compared with one year prior, according to the United Nations. Once the US had welcomed more refugees than the rest of the world combined, but for the first time in many years, this was no longer true. American resettlement agencies began closing branch offices and laying off staff.

Meanwhile, Denver Public Schools opened two additional newcomer centers for high school students at the start of the 2016–17 school year, to serve the increasing numbers of teenagers with a need for beginner-level English. The two new centers were located closer to the city's remaining pockets of affordable housing, which made it easier for students to travel to and from school. By that point, the segment of the DPS student population classified as English-language learners had swelled to 42 percent. School districts around the nation had seen dramatic jumps in the proportion of English learners served. During the first decade of this century, the number of English-language learners enrolled in American schools increased by 51 percent, from 3.5 million to 5.3 million. This presented educators across the country with the challenge of communicating with students who did not yet know English—in other words, schools all over the United States were trying to hire teachers like Eddie Williams.

Eddie himself left South High at the end of the 2016–17 school year, in search of renewal. Tired after welcoming many years of newcomers, Eddie felt in need of a change. He put himself into night school, learned how to teach math, and found a new job working with the kids he loved best—he started teaching math to English-language learners at another school in Denver. The rapid shift in the political climate bewildered everyone in education who worked with students who came from other places. Teachers and principals struggled with the sense that the children entrusted to them were under siege. Many school leaders felt compelled to take a more public stand in celebration of students who had come to them after making difficult journeys. In Des Moines, for example, Thomas Ahart, the superintendent of the Des Moines Public Schools, learned about a student in his care named Jennifer Galdames. Aged seventeen, Jennifer was originally from Guatemala; her father had been killed in her home country and her stepfather was in jail when her mother was picked during an ICE raid. Jennifer had a year and a half left to go before she finished high school. Ahart and his wife decided that Jennifer could live with them until she finished her degree, and then spoke to the *Des Moines Register* about the decision. As a columnist for that paper wrote, "Occasionally in these nationally trying times, you run into a story of kindness and generosity to remind you that away from divisive politics, exploitation, and profiteering there is, in some people, a fundamental goodness."

The refugees I had met in Room 142 continued to thrive. With every passing year they put their troubles further behind them and figured out more about America. Solomon and Methusella sailed into mainstream classes, where they continued to excel, bringing home report cards filled with A's and B's. In the Student Senate, Methusella spoke up more and even started telling his story to the prospective eighth-grade "shadows" who visited to learn what going to school at South would be like. He also started playing for South's varsity soccer team; he asked if I would pay his soccer fees, and I gladly did so. Both boys perfected their English and began to wonder out loud where to go to college. One day, as we ate dinner at their house, Solomon asked whether I thought he should pursue his original dream of being a doctor, or whether he should become a dental hygienist. He fretted that becoming a doctor would require too much time; he couldn't wait to start earning a salary. Methusella still dreamt of becoming a pilot, although he worried that he was not good enough at math. At the same time, their father, Tchiza, had dreams of his own. He had started looking at houses to buy. He showed me a listing for one house that he was considering, a three-bedroom, two-bath home in Aurora, listed for $289,990. The monthly payments would be about $1,400, which was $200 less than he was paying in rent. It looked like a good deal—but the real estate agent whom he had found online was offering to help him buy the house without a down payment. I worried he was being taken advantage of by someone who was going to set him up with a predatory lender. I endorsed the idea of home ownership, but suggested he should not sign any loan documents without first consulting a financial expert at the African Community Center.

The Iraqi family had moved recently. After Jakleen's health stabilized, Ebtisam obtained a more permanent rent subsidy and then found a new apartment on the north side of Denver. The attractive building—new construction, fashionable gray exterior with bright orange accents—was located within walking distance of a popular shopping center, which delighted the girls. But it was even farther away from South. Jakleen and Mariam staged a rebellion and announced they would no longer take epic bus rides to that school. They would walk to the neighborhood school instead, even though it had no formal English Language Acquisition classes. Their ELA teachers were skeptical as to whether the girls were ready for full immersion in mainstream classes, but after they enrolled at the new school, their English exploded. When I dropped by one afternoon, Jakleen prattled away without once resorting to Google Translate or to sign language and translated for her mother as needed. "You are Nabiha now!" I told her. "Yes, Miss!" Jakleen said. "I am Nabiha."

Mariam was nowhere to be seen that day, and Jakleen seemed a little lost without her older sister. To Ebtisam's dismay, Mariam had begun spending a lot of time out of the house with friends and had dropped out of high school. They had argued about this, Ebtisam said, and then Mariam had grown ever more scarce. Ebtisam tried calling an imam at a local mosque for advice, but the imam just said wearily that in America, teenagers behaved like this; there was nothing he could do. It seemed as though he got a lot of similar calls. Nabiha and I told Ebtisam that maybe one of these days, Mariam would realize how important family was and start spending more time at home. None of us knew what would happen, however, and we all worried for her welfare.

Jakleen broke up with Ghasem and started dating another boy. ("Miss, you take Ghasem out of your book!" she ordered.) But she remained in school and earned solid grades. By the spring of 2018, Jakleen was chatting in fluent English to me about the difficulties of junior year, her fear of the SAT, and her excitement about graduating from high school in one year. I had not seen Mariam for many months.

In April, I announced that we would go to a Middle Eastern restaurant that featured belly dancing, an expedition the girls and I had discussed multiple times. I parked and knocked on the sliding glass door of their ground-floor apartment. Lulu shoved aside the blinds and gave me a thumbs-up, then came to admit me.

In the apartment, I was astonished to see Mariam.

"You are home!"

"Miss! I haven't seen you in so long!"

"You look pretty—you've lost a lot of weight. I'm glad you're home. Your mom said she was worried about you."

"Oh my God, Miss."

Mariam confirmed that she and her mother endured a period of disagreement, then changed the subject. She announced that she had just taken the GED and was about to enroll in classes at Emily Griffith Technical College, to become a medical assistant. She might earn $70,000 a year, she said. She was putting her life back together, and she looked proud; I was impressed.

Jakleen appeared, carrying a gray-and-white cat.

"This is Errol," Jakleen announced.

Then she buried her face in Errol's side, making the cat purr loudly. Mariam slid off her stool and went over and cuddled into her sister and the cat.

"There is so much love for Errol in this house!" Jakleen announced.

"I can see that."

And I could see that with Mariam's return, a missing equilibrium had been restored. The younger girls had grown quiet without her, which I noticed only now that they returned to their formerly vivacious selves.

Then Ebtisam emerged from the bathroom, wearing a tight black mini-dress and barroom makeup.

"You have all your girls again," I observed.

"Yes!" Ebtisam confirmed, beaming.

At Phoenician Kabob, the owner fell into conversation with Ebtisam in Arabic. He told us that he was sorry, but the belly dancer had not shown up. He promised he would dance for us instead. The girls lapsed into consternation. "A man? A man is going to dance?" wailed Mariam. "No!"

Jakleen left to use the restroom and after coming back she whispered, "He was only joking. I just saw the belly dancer! She is very pretty."

Music boomed through the restaurant, and the dancer slid between the tables, wearing a skimpy gold bikini as she encircled herself in scarves. She slapped metallic castanets together and sidled up to customers so that they could tuck money into elastic bands around her biceps. She made her belly distend and hollow in such a way that a string of beads around her waist traveled up and down her midriff. I found the moving waist necklace a bit hypnotic. The girls studied the woman appraisingly.

"She's good," Jakleen announced at last.

With that, the three sisters took out their cell phones and took videos of the belly dancer, which they immediately posted on Snapchat.

Ebtisam ordered a combo platter and ate so much meat that she fell quiet. She looked tired but thankful. It was spring break, and the girls had been at home all week. They had reverted to that cozy sisterhood I remembered from earlier days when snow had blanketed the city, barricading them inside with one another. Having the family reunited felt like cause for celebration, and I said so. Ebtisam agreed. "Our lives have been up-and-down," she said. "Sometimes it has been hard, but things are good now. We're glad to be here. Life is good right now."

The belly dancer looped around the restaurant tables bearing fire in her castanets and then later she cavorted with a sword balanced on top of her head. Afterward, I went home and thought about the fact that Jakleen had transformed from a scared refugee into an ordinary American teenager, worrying about the SATs and dreaming of college, while Mariam had gotten her GED and was hoping for a job in a doctor's office. Watching them become so like their American-born peers, it occurred to me that the label "refugee" was itself misleading. The predicament of the refugee was not something a person wore full-time, like an identity. Entry into the United States had been especially hard for this family, but even they had journeyed to the other side of the transition. And now that they had grown more secure in their new home and had gotten properly settled, they were no longer refugee-like. They had traveled through the experience of refugee-dom. Any of us could find ourselves unhoused; being robbed of a safe home was an experience a person passed through, rather than the summation of that person. If only more of us who lived in stable countries could understand this, perhaps we would not feel so afraid of the displaced. Over time, the foreign-born students kept acquiring new habits that allowed them to blend with native-born classmates. Meanwhile, they kept teaching their peers about the places from which they came, and how parts of the developed world had participated in their unsettlements. I was watching the kids from Eddie Williams's class adapt to American ways, and watching them shape Americans into more global-minded citizens. South's mix of refugee, immigrant, and nonimmigrant students produced individuals better equipped to understand the world as it actually was and better able to work with allies around the globe. All of the students evolved upon learning their home language was not the only way to communicate and their home culture was not the only way to find harmony.

I am partnering with Denver Scholarship Foundation to help the new-comer students written about in this book attend college. If you feel moved by these stories and would like to join our effort to help students with similar stories attain a college degree, please contact Lorii Rabinowitz at lrabinowitz@denverscholarship.org to learn more about how you can support newcomers in your community.

Acknowledgments

All thanks to my family for their support during this project. My parents, Marie and Larry; my sister, Lorna, and her husband, Marcos; and my brother, Brian, and his wife, Donna, have provided a lifetime of great company and constant inspiration. To my delightful nieces and nephews—Devin, Siobhan, Daniela, and Gael—thank you for being such a source of joy. My son, Teddy, occasionally had a forgetful mom during the creation of this book. Sometimes we didn't have milk in the fridge and sometimes I forgot to put money on his debit card and sometimes dinner wasn't ready on time. Teddy, about all of this, you were quite patient. Thank you for letting your mom work so hard and for being willing to share me with all these other kids. Thanks also for your sunny disposition and your amazing self-sufficiency and for making me laugh so much.

To my wonderful literary agent, Alia Hanna Habib, I'm blessed by your belief in narrative nonfiction and in me. You gave me great counsel and you made this entire journey a lot more fun. Being named a finalist for the J. Anthony Lukas Work-in-Progress Award provided welcome support and confirmation of the importance of this subject at a critical time, and I want to thank Linda Healey, the Nieman Foundation for Journalism, and the Columbia University School of Journalism for this honor.

Eddie Williams allowed me to observe his classroom for an entire year and that cannot have been entirely easy. I am deeply grateful. Alan Gottlieb, formerly of Chalkbeat, suggested that I visit South in the first place. Principal Kristin Waters granted me permission to spend time inside the high school, and her successor, Jen Hanson, enhanced my understanding of language acquisition. I'm also indebted to Denver Public Schools superintendent Tom Boasberg for his confidence in allowing me to report on DPS students. I want to express my gratitude to many additional teachers: Noelia Hopkin, Jenan Hijazi, Ed DeRose, Jason Brookes, Ben Speicher, Rachel Aldrich, John Walsh, Steve Bonansinga, and Wilson Vadakel. Thanks to the following staff: Beth Strickland, Karen Duell, Stephanie Onan, Lisa Kelly, Tony Acuna, and José Espinosa-Santiago. Ruthann Kallenberg, Pauline Ng, Carolyn Chafe Howard, Jaclyn Yelich, and Greg Thielen also shared keen observations. Finally, I want to thank the many paraprofessionals at South who broadened my understanding of the cultures represented in that building: Rebecca Aweit, Batoul Ali, Sushantika Bhandari, and Fatuma Yusuf.

Many people in the refugee resettlement world and immigrants' rights community shared their insights. I'm thankful to Steven Manning and Anna Greene at the International Rescue Committee, Jennifer Gueddiche at the Spring Institute, Robin Finegan and Tim Bothe at Red Cross, Alejandra Acevedo at Rocky Mountain Immigrant Advocacy Network, Camila Palmer and Phil Alterman at Elkind Alterman Harston, Joe Wismann-Horther at Colorado Refugee Services, and Meg Allen at Colorado Providers for Integration Network. I'm also indebted to everybody at the African Community Center (Melissa Theesen, Erin Efaw Frank, Troy Cox, Hussen Abdulahi, and Barbara Guglielminotti) and Lutheran Family Services (Jaime Koehler Blanchard, Yasir Abdulah, Whitney Haruf, Eh Klo, and Katherine Koch) who helped me understand resettlement in action.

Several families took me into their homes and I will always be thankful. Gratitude to Ebtisam, Tchiza, Beya, Peh Reh, Taw Meh, Christina, Martha, and Steve for their time and their confidences. I could not have written this book without the help of the many interpreters: Hugo Rivas (Spanish), Nabiha Hasan Hussain (Arabic), Julius Amicho (Swahili), Berhane Kassa (Swahili), Cacilda Nunes (Portuguese), Ephirem Tesfamichael (Tigrinya), Komi Camille Seshie (French), Shen Meh Elena (Karenni), Lydia Dumam (Kunama), Deven Chhetri (Nepali), Valeriy Stuban (Russian), Georgette Kapuku Mabi (Swahili, French). Heart-

Acknowledgments

felt thanks to everyone at Spring Institute and the Colorado African Organization for such amazing interpreters and for all the good you do in the world. Asaad Ibrahim has been a wonderful resource about Middle Eastern culture, especially in regard to the Qur'an. Bernadette Zars translated Jakleen's letter. Linguist Andrea Feldman explained language structure and annotated passages in this book. My copyeditor, Cynthia Merman, vastly improved this manuscript and augmented passages about language structure.

The following books helped me understand refugees and the parts of the world that they come from: *City of Thorns* by Ben Rawlence, *King Leopold's Ghost* by Adam Hochschild, *Dancing in the Glory of Monsters* by Jason Stearns, *The Democratic Republic of Congo: Between Hope and Despair* by Michael Deibert, *Back to the Congo* by Lieve Joris, *East Along the Equator: A Congo Journey* by Helen Winternitz, *Strength in What Remains* by Tracy Kidder, *What Is the What* by Dave Eggers, *Americanah* by Chimamanda Ngozi Adichie, *We Need New Names* by NoViolet Bulawayo, *For Us Surrender Is Out of the Question* by Mac McClelland, and *Undaunted: My Struggle for Freedom and Survival in Burma* by Zoya Phan. I'm also a big fan of *Immersion* by Ted Conover, an essential guide for how to do this sort of journalism.

My trip to the Democratic Republic of Congo was made possible thanks to Jamie Van Leeuwan, Ryan Grundy, and their staff at the Global Livingston Institute. All thanks to the Air Force instructors who allowed me to join their trip. Jason Niwamanya was a superb driver and noticed many things that I failed to see. Conversations with Yazan Fattaleh, Amy Grace Austin, and Bahati Kanyamanza enabled me to better understand North Kivu and Kyangwali.

To all the friends who buoyed me up, heartfelt thanks. Fellow writers Peter Heller and Lisa Jones provided accompaniment every step of the way. Peter, I can hardly imagine going through a long project without your kindhearted encouragement; Lisa, you told me to keep going when I thought I should give up, and then plowed through an extremely rough draft. Some of the best moments in this book are thanks to your suggestions. John Hockenberry wrote many letters of encouragement. Mary Caulkins provided refuge at her studio, as I wrestled with sometimes tough subject matter. Gillian Silverman, Ed Wood, and Betsy Hollins marked up early drafts with spectacular improvements. Ana Maria Hernando and Kat Jones played key roles in helping me be ready to write this book; Emily Mandelstam enabled me to write differently about material that is grim; and Belle Zars got me up into the mountains for many welcome respites. My neighbor Cindy Paulin had my son over on innumerable occasions when I was busy working and allowed me to talk with her about all aspects of this book. At a certain point, I started chauffeuring Jakleen to and from school, which threatened to impede my ability to finish this project; after I spoke about this at Mountain View Friends Meeting, Charlotte Miller, Susan Bailey, and Judy Danielson took over driving Jakleen. Jeff Hobbs and I discussed our respective reporting efforts during a yearlong series of phone calls that made me feel I had a comrade-in-arms. John and Robin Hickenlooper, I'm grateful for your friendship and support. To all at the Tattered Cover, you remain my favorite place to be outside my own home.

   I am indebted to everyone at Scribner for the chance to become the kind of writer I have always wanted to be. Nan Graham, Susan Moldow, and Roz Lippel—your stalwart support over many years means a great deal. Kate Lloyd, Jessica Yu, Sarah Goldberg, Emily Remes, and Elisa Rivlin, I'm thankful for your help. My editor, Colin Harrison, poured an extraordinary amount of energy into making sure this book came to fruition. He listened to me search for this idea, encouraged me to spend time in Room 142 when I felt doubtful about what it might yield, and expressed enthusiastic interest about all aspects of these kids' lives. He also lifted my spirits when I felt overwhelmed. Then, he edited this book, salvaging what was important and encouraging me to let go of the rest. I am tremendously grateful for the chance to have worked on three books together over the past decade. Colin, thank you for everything—*gracias, shukraan, asante sana.*

About the Author

Helen Thorpe's journalism has appeared in the *New York Times Magazine*, *The New Yorker*, *Texas Monthly*, and *Slate*. Her radio stories have aired on *This American Life* and *Soundprint*. She is the author of *Soldier Girls* and *Just Like Us*. Her work has won the Colorado Book Award twice and the J. Anthony Lukas Work-in-Progress Award. She lives in Denver, Colorado.

CPSIA information can be obtained
at www.ICGtesting.com
Printed in the USA
LVHW101227211121
704027LV00011B/1501

9 781501 159107